I0070111

# The Conversion of Rental Housing to Condominiums and Cooperatives

## A National Study of Scope, Causes and Impacts

Division of Policy Studies

**Books for Business**
**New York-Hong Kong**

The Conversion of Rental Housing to
Condominiums and Cooperatives:
A National Study of Scope, Causes and Impacts

by
U.S. Department of Housing and Urban
Development
Office of Policy Development and Research

ISBN: 0-89499-090-X

Copyright © 2001 by Books for Business

Reprinted from the 1980 edition

Books for Business
New York - Hong Kong
http://www.BusinessBooksInternational.com

All rights reserved, including the right to reproduce
this book, or portions thereof, in any form.

In order to make original editions of historical works
available to scholars at an economical price, this
facsimile of the original edition of 1980 is
reproduced from the best available copy and has
been digitally enhanced to improve legibility, but the
text remains unaltered to retain historical
authenticity.

**U.S. Department of Housing and Urban Development**

Moon Landrieu, Secretary

Donna E. Shalala, Assistant Secretary for Policy Development and Research

Michael A. Stegman, Deputy Assistant Secretary for Research

Martin D. Abravanel, Director, Division of Policy Studies

Kathleen A. Peroff, Project Director

| | | |
|---|---|---|
| Charles E. Connerly | Charlene Anderson | Venida Brown |
| Cloteal L. Davis | Mary Atkins | Paula Casson |
| Ndeye Jackson | Joseph E. Cater | Barbara M. Daly |
| Jean Larvo | Margaret Ensign | Ellen Elow |
| Becky A. Maguire | Rita Gantt | Kelly Flaherty |
| F. Stevens Redburn | Mark Hoffman | Rick Krechevsky |
| Michael E. Roanhouse | Ron E. Jones | Deborah Murray |
| Lester Rubin | Gregory S. Lipton | Douglas O'Leary |
| Howard Savage | Anna Lloyd | Amy Pecht |
| Elizabeth Twigg | Paul K. Mancini | Julie Stern |
| | Carole Robertus | |

Surveys conducted for this report were done in conjunction with Research Triangle Institute, Sam Leaman, Project Director, with: Jane Bergsten, Zelda Cohen, Mildred Hardy, Don Jackson, Barrett Joyner, Dave McFadden, and Jack Shirey.

Legal research for this report was done in conjunction with Patrick J. Rohan, St. John's University Law School, assisted by Claude Priolet.

Additional assistance was provided by: Fannie Anderson, Dee Arnold, Barbara Armstrong, Sandy Bicos, Gloria Bing, Laura Boyd, Jo Ann Brooks, Paul Burke, Phyllis Clarke, Rick Davis, Linda DeFilippo, Beatrice Dukes, Louise Fairfax, Jo Ann Garlic, Le Juane Green, James Greenfield, Frank Gregor, Kent Hiteshew, Phyllis Hedeman, Pamela Hicks, Melvin Howard, Doris Lesesne, Cynthia Lewis, Beth Marcus, Mike Molesky, Timothy O'Hara, Robert Van Order, Michael Owens, Barbara Pate, Carol Schaake, Bernard Seward, Sammie Sneed, Althea Tinson, Deborah Washington, Raymond Wedell, and Sharon White.

**THE SECRETARY OF HOUSING AND URBAN DEVELOPMENT**
WASHINGTON, D.C. 20410

TO THE CONGRESS OF THE UNITED STATES:

In accordance with the provision of Section 109(b) of the Housing and Community Development Amendments of 1979, I herewith forward to you a report entitled "The Conversion of Rental Housing to Condominiums and Cooperatives: A National Study of Scope, Causes and Impacts."

Moon Landrieu

June 1980

# FOREWORD

This landmark national study of the extent and impacts of condominium and cooperative conversions promises to be of major policy and program significance. It also vividly demonstrates the importance, to an agency such as HUD, of maintaining a substantial in-house research capacity that can be mobilized quickly to respond to a priority Congressional mandate. In this case, that mandate was to deliver, in a very short time period, a high quality research study requiring the collection and analysis of national data.

The readers of this report are undoubtedly aware that, up to now, most information on conversion activities has been largely anecdotal, highly localized or incomplete, not susceptible to place-to-place comparisons, or has been produced by organizations which represent specific client groups and their respective points of view. Recognizing this, we decided to make the most important objective of our study the development of a national picture of conversion activities. This type of policy study is intended to initiate, frame and inform the policy debate without drawing closure around it. Hence, we emphasize consistency in our place-to-place definitions, and stress the accuracy of our information. This allows us to assess, with a high degree of confidence, impacts of conversions across a wide range of housing markets, programs, and policy issues.

By emphasizing place-to-place consistency and accuracy in our national data collection effort, it is likely that some of our findings will vary from those produced in local studies or those anticipated by local observers. I expect, therefore, that the national benchmarks contained in our study will generate lively policy discussion and debate at all levels of government and in the private and community sectors. We welcome such discussion both with respect to our research approach and to the policy implications of our findings.

This study was designed and carried out by research staff in the Office of Policy Development and Research. Michael A. Stegman, Deputy Assistant Secretary for Research, was responsible for overseeing the project. It was prepared under the general supervision of Martin D. Abravanel, Director of the Division of Policy Studies. Kathleen A. Peroff directed the study. I am proud of their collective efforts and of the fruits of their labor.

Donna E. Shalala
Assistant Secretary for Policy
Development and Research

TABLE OF CONTENTS

SUMMARY


The recent growth of condominium and cooperative conversions is a
response to basic changes in the Nation's social and housing market
conditions which, in its course, helps some and hurts others.  For
this reason, conversion has sparked considerable controversy -- a
controversy exacerbated by the shortage of information about what is
taking place.  This report, prepared in response to a Congressional
directive, presents the results of a multi-faceted study designed
to provide this information.  It documents the present and probable
future extent and location of conversions, the factors contributing
to their increasing numbers, and their effects -- on people, neighborhoods, and communities.  As will be apparent, the scope, causes,
and consequences of the conversion phenomenon are, in many ways,
quite different than is generally understood.

                          * * *

Conversion changes the legal form of a multi-family rental property
from single ownership by a landlord to multiple ownership.  In most
condominium conversions, the landlord first sells the property to a
developer specializing in conversion who then sells the individual
units.  Most conversions are accompanied by some minor or cosmetic
improvements to the property's condition, equipment, or amenities;
however, a few conversions have involved the substantial rehabilitation
of older buildings.

Up to now, the number of conversions which have taken place in the
Nation has generally not been known because of the difficulty of
assembling information from local public records, because the
processes which govern conversions in various housing markets differ,
and because of differences in terminology regarding conversions across
these markets.  Having a common definition which applies across
jurisdictions is a prerequisite for arriving at a national count and
analyzing the significance of the volume of conversion activity.
For the purposes of this study, a rental building is considered to
be converted to condominium ownership when the first unit is sold as
a condominium.  In New York, where most of the Nation's cooperative
conversions occur, a rental building is considered to be converted
to a cooperative when the legally required number of tenants have
purchased shares.

Very few rental properties were converted to multiple ownership in
this country prior to 1970.  Since then, 366,000 rental housing
units have been converted.  Of these, only 18,000 are cooperative
conversions.  The rate of conversion has been accelerating:  in the
period 1977 through 1979, 260,000 units were converted, 71 percent
of the decade's total.  To date, conversion activity has been con-

centrated in larger metropolitan areas: 76 percent of all conversions have occurred in the 37 largest SMSAs, and 59 percent have taken place in just 12 of these areas. There is some evidence, however, that the conversion phenomenon may be expanding to or increasing in smaller metropolitan areas.

Within the largest metropolitan areas of the Nation, a surprisingly large amount of conversion (49%) has occurred in suburban jurisdictions; the remaining 51 percent has taken place within central cities.

By the end of 1979, 1.3 percent of the Nation's occupied rental housing stock had been converted. However, there is considerable variation from one metropolitan area to another, as well as within each area. For example, in the New York City and Los Angeles areas, 1 percent of all rental units were converted during the 1970s, compared to 6 percent or more in the Chicago, Denver and Washington, D.C. areas. There are some atypical suburban communities and smaller cities where as much as 20 to 30 percent of the rental stock has been converted, and a few sections of cities where more than 30 percent of the rental stock has been converted.

Nationally, the volume of condominium and cooperative conversion activity is expected to increase through 1985. The analysis suggests that the number of conversions will increase each year, but at successively decreasing rates. A trend-line projection of conversion volumes through the year 1985, based on past experience but modified to consider supply, demand, and current financial market factors, suggests that about 1.1 million rental units will be converted during this six year period. Of course, future conversion volumes may be influenced by many currently unknown factors, including long-term financial conditions, government regulation, or any changes which may be made to the Federal tax code.

There are a few metropolitan areas where the supply of rental properties most suited to conversion (using market-derived standards which have applied to date) will be nearly exhausted within five years.

Conversions have been more numerous in metropolitan areas characterized by strong and growing market demand for homeownership. Conversions are not, as some market specialists believe, associated with distressed rental markets. For example, there is no evidence that conversions are concentrated in metropolitan areas with higher than average rental vacancy rates or depressed rent levels. Furthermore, legislated rent controls are not necessary conditions for or leading causes of conversions, if for no other reason than that so few of the jurisdictions with conversions have enacted such measures.

In most parts of the country, however, average operating margins for rental properties do appear to be declining. This has contributed to apartment owners' willingness to sell their buildings to converters. For many rental property owners, no projected amount of rental income, allowable tax depreciation, property appreciation, or tax sheltering can equal the return received on the sale of their properties for conversion. Strong demand for the kinds of housing represented by condominiums and cooperatives, combined with potentially large profits, has made converters willing to pay prices for rental properties that are far in excess of what these buildings could command based on continued use as rentals. The ability of converters, then, to turn over individual units in these buildings for higher prices is, in great measure, a function of increasing demand for homeownership which is fueled by rising incomes and inflation. Recent inflation also tends to shift the homebuying demand of an increasing number of middle-income households from traditional single-family houses, that may be priced too high, to less expensive condominiums and cooperatives.

The number of conversions tends to be somewhat greater, in metro-politan areas which are characterized by growing household populations and larger proportions of households having one or two persons or headed by an individual 35 years old or less. Conversions are also somewhat more numerous in areas where more households have incomes above $25,000, where luxury buildings form a higher proportion of the rental stock, and where the rental housing stock is relatively new.

Conversions are products of a shift in housing demand, and a corre-sponding shift in the use of the existing housing supply away from rental toward ownership. The net effect of conversions on the balance of supply and demand can be estimated by considering the pre and postconversion tenure status of households affected by conversion. Those renters who buy contribute to a reduction of overall renter demand; many converted units remain available as rentals; and some tenants move out upon conversion and purchase a unit elsewhere. The cumulative effect of these factors contributes to a significant moderation of the actual supply impact on the rental market. This analysis indicates, nationally, that for every 100 rental units converted, there is a net increase of 5 units for sale to owners, and a net decrease of 5 available rental units. In other words, when changes in demand and supply resulting from conversion are juxtaposed, the effect on the rental market is considerably less than the total of all units converted.

Based on these figures and the volume of conversions nationally, the net effect of conversions on the rental market has been to reduce the Nation's supply of available rentals by 18,000 units in the 1970 to 1979 period.

The impact of conversions can also be assessed in relation to other components of change in the rental housing market. Considering total demand for rental housing, the amount of new rental housing being produced, and losses to the rental inventory through various means, there has been a shortfall of rental housing in the last several years. Conversions have contributed to this shortfall. For example, in 1977, they accounted for 17 percent of excess demand over supply. Unlike other losses of rental housing, however, conversion often results in a concomitant reduction in renter demand because previous renters become homeowners.

Conversion can produce either very substantial or minimal movement of households in and out of converting buildings, depending on the proportion of prior tenants who either buy converted units or remain in the buildings as renters. Of all households occupying units in buildings that were converted after January 1977, 58 percent had moved out as of January 1980. The remaining 42 percent continued to live in the buildings as either owners (22%) or renters (20%) along with new occupants who had moved in since the conversion; most of the new occupants (41% of all current residents) owned their units but the remainder (17%) rented. Consequently, the residents of these buildings after conversion were 63 percent owner occupants and 37 percent renters.

Of the 37 percent of postconversion residents who rent their units, about one-half currently lease from the converter/developer and one-half from investors or relatives. That there are households renting from converter/developers reflects the fact that some recently converted buildings are still in the transition process: a portion of these renters are finishing out current leases; and a portion are continuing to rent, as permitted by local law. Some of these units may also be held as long-term investments by the converter.

Thirty-nine percent of converted units are bought by households earning more than $30,000 annually; but, since converted rental units are often less expensive than newly constructed condominiums and cooperatives or single family homes, they also provide a new avenue of ownership for smaller, younger households who have incomes insufficient to buy other types of housing.

Nearly two-thirds of the owner occupant households in converted buildings are headed by an individual who holds a professional or managerial position; about one-half are 35 or younger, while only one-fifth are over 55, and only 9 percent are over 65. About 10 percent of the owner occupiers of converted units are black, whereas only 7 percent of all owner occupants in the Nation are black.

Fifty-seven percent of the owner-occupant households in converted buildings are single persons (36% single women and 21% single men) compared to merely 14 percent (10% women and 4% men) of all owner occupants in the Nation.

Compared to all owner occupants nationally, fewer owner occupants of converted buildings are elderly (9% versus 22%). When buyers who previously rented in the converted buildings are compared with buyers coming from outside, the former tend to be older and to have higher incomes

Two-thirds of all owner-occupants name economic factors as their primary reasons for buying: to gain a hedge against inflation; to stabilize housing costs; to provide a tax shelter or investment; to find an alternative to single family housing; or to obtain a buyer discount. Tenant buyers are more likely than outside buyers to say they bought because they liked the location and did not want to move.

Most of those who buy converted units increase their expenditure for housing. Total monthly outlays made by tenant buyers are typically 36 percent higher than what they paid in rent, while the median increase in monthly housing costs for buyers coming from other housing is 62 percent; however, these figures do not take into account tax benefits associated with owning a home or potential appreciation.

Those who do not buy but either move from converting buildings or remain there as renters come from all age and income categories. Renters in converted units tend to have lower incomes than owners in the same buildings; but incomes that are much higher than all renters nationally. While 39 percent of converted unit owners earn over $30,000 annually, only 22 percent of renters have this level of income.

Tenants of converting buildings typically are given about 70 days by the converter to decide whether or not to buy. Many tenants are distressed -- at least initially -- by the prospect of conversion. About one-fourth of tenants who bought or continued to rent their units after conversion report that they felt under pressure to buy; the pressure was not so much caused by harassment or high pressured sales tactics as it was by being faced with an unanticipated housing decision. However, nearly three-fourths of those who move from converting buildings (former residents) say that they felt under pressure, more than likely caused by the disruption and uncertainties associated with such a move. More elderly than non-elderly tenants (28% versus 18%) felt pressured by the conversion experience.

One-half of all former residents of converted buildings had some difficulty in finding new housing; elderly, non-white, and lower income former tenants are more likely to report such difficulty.

One of the major concerns relating to conversion is the extent to which it involuntarily displaces prior tenants. Including both those who had moved out as of January 1980 (58%) and those who continue to rent but may yet move (an estimated 8%), the average proportion of prior tenants who move out following conversion may be as high as two-thirds. However, not all of these moves will be involuntary; nationally, nearly 40 percent of all renters move at least once each year.

If displacement is defined as movement to rental housing that is of similar or lower quality at higher cost, or of lower quality at equivalent cost, then 18 percent of all households (27% of households with persons age 60 and over) who moved from converting buildings have experienced the adverse effects of displacement; this is equal to 10 percent of those who resided in converted buildings prior to conversion.  Another 6 percent of all former residents moved to lower quality housing renting for less than they had paid prior to conversion

Some conversions require people with low or moderate incomes to move because they cannot afford to buy their apartments.  About 42 percent of those who moved out of converted buildings had incomes which, according to generally accepted criteria, were too low to have permitted them to buy their converted units; 47 percent of all former residents say they did not purchase because they believed they could not afford to do so.

Seventy percent of all former residents continue to rent after conversion, and they typically experience rent increases of less than 10 percent; however, 28 percent pay at least 25 percent more for rent. Those former residents who decide to buy housing elsewhere typically pay 68 percent more per month for housing, without taking into account possible tax savings and appreciation.  Less than one-fifth of all former residents consider their new residence to be inferior to the one they lived in prior to conversion.

Ninety percent of all former residents indicate they are satisfied with their new housing; this is roughly the same degree of housing satisfaction reported for those replacing them in the converted buildings.  Nearly three-fourths of all former residents have moved to a new neighborhood as good as or better than their old one.  Eighty percent live as close or closer to friends and relatives as before the move.  Those with lower incomes, however, are more likely to report that their neighborhood is worse than the old one.

Forty-three percent of all former residents are under age 36 and one-fifth are over 65.

Those who move have incomes that are, on average, lower (20% under $12,500) than buyers of converted units (12% under $12,500) but higher than renters in converted buildings.  About 12 percent of all those who move from converted buildings are elderly households with incomes of less than $12,500.  Eleven percent are black; one percent are Hispanic.

Conversions, when sufficiently numerous and concentrated, can have significant impacts not only on individual households but also on entire communities or neighborhoods.  Reassessment of property following conversion leads to increased revenue from local property taxes.  The degree of impact is a function of the particular jurisdiction's tax rates for various classes of property, its assessment practices, and provisions providing tax relief for special classes

of property owners. When weighed against the total revenue from
property taxes, however, the total impact of conversions to date on
local property tax revenues has been very small. Less clear is the
impact that conversions may have, in neighborhoods where concentrated,
on demands for public services and, therefore, on the long term pattern of public expenditures. Available evidence, however, suggests
that the demand for public services in these neighborhoods is basically
unaffected by conversions.

It is useful to classify conversions as occurring in one of three
types of neighborhood: central city nonrevitalizing, central city
revitalizing, and suburban nonrevitalizing. In almost two-thirds
of the central cities located in the 37 largest metropolitan areas,
conversions are concentrated in nonrevitalizing neighborhoods
characterized by above average median incomes, rent levels, and housing
values, and by rental vacancy rates equal to or below the city average.
One-third of the central cities had conversion activity in at least
one revitalizing neighborhood. However, these same cities had a
majority of their conversion activity in nonrevitalizing neighborhoods. Conversion has tended to lag behind rather than serve as a
catalyst for other reinvestment in revitalizing areas. Conversion
activity has had little impact on housing conditions in either type
of central city neighborhood; however, as indicated earlier, some
converting buildings in revitalizing neighborhoods do undergo major
rehabilitation.

In neither type of central city neighborhood has conversion activity
produced very much change in the socioeconomic characteristics of
residents. In central city revitalizing neighborhoods, however,
socioeconomic changes appear to result from the overall revitalization
process, not necessarily from conversion; significant population
changes had occurred in these neighborhoods prior to the onset of
conversions. In central cities, pre and postconversion residents are
similar in most respects.

However, postconversion residents are slightly less likely to be
non-white (15% versus 21% before conversion), over age 65 (17% versus
23%), or retired (17% versus 23%), and more likely to be employed in
professional or managerial jobs (63% versus 59%). Just over one-fourth
(27%) of those moving to converted buildings in central cities lived
in the same neighborhood prior to the move, 34 percent lived in
another city neighborhood, 12 percent lived in one of the city's
suburbs, and the balance (27%) came from another city.

Conversion has occurred in nonrevitalizing suburban locations in 27
of the 37 largest metropolitan areas; 19 such areas have higher
proportions of their total conversion activity in suburbs than in
their central cities. These are nearly always close-in, economically
stable suburbs, whose residents are typically middle to upper-middle
income whites. More of the conversions here involve garden and

townhouse style rather than high-rise apartments. These conversions have had a negligible impact on housing quality, since most involve minor repairs to properties already in sound condition. Pre and postconversion residents of these buildings are similar, although postconversion households are slightly more likely to be non-white (17% versus 12% before conversion) and to hold professional or managerial positions (59% versus 52%) and less likely to earn incomes below $12,500 (16% versus 27%), to be retired (11% versus 21%), or to be over age 65 (13% versus 18%). Less than one-fourth of the postconversion residents of these buildings come from other housing in the same neighborhoods.

Federal government programs have so far played minor roles in relation to condominium and cooperative conversions. Programs of secondary mortgage market institutions (the Federal National Mortgage Association and the Federal Home Loan Mortgage Corporation) make it easier to finance and resell converted units which meet their criteria for purchase; thus, FNMA and FHLMC indirectly influence such practices as the proportion of presales, proportion of units occupied by owners, and condition of properties. A few state and local governments, many with financial support from the Federal government, have developed innovative programs intended to provide technical and financial assistance to groups seeking to convert their buildings, to subsidize low- and moderate-income households in converted buildings, or to assist households relocating after conversion.

State and local governments also have begun to respond to conversions with various types of regulatory legislation. Conversion-related regulations can be categorized as follows: those designed to protect tenants of converting buildings; those intended to protect buyers of converted units; those developed to preserve the supply of rental housing; and those aimed at preserving the supply of low- to moderate-income housing. To date, very few states and localities have passed the latter two types of legislation.

Just under one-half of the states have legislated protections for tenants of converting buildings; and, about one-half have laws protecting purchasers of both new and converted condominium units. States which have enacted tenant or buyer protection measures often contain metropolitan areas which are experiencing high levels of conversion.

At the local level, although just over one-third of all jurisdictions have had or still have conversion activity, fewer than one in five of those experiencing conversions has passed a regulatory ordinance. Larger jurisdictions and those with more conversions are more likely to adopt such legislation. About 6 percent of jurisdictions with past or present conversions have at one time or another adopted temporary moratoria halting all conversion activity.

Nearly all local regulatory ordinances provide some protections to tenants in converting buildings. Such ordinances typically require 90 to 180 days notice to tenants of a planned conversion. A few localities offer special protections to elderly and handicapped tenants, such as the right to extend their lease period.

Most ordinances protect condominium buyers by requiring code inspection, engineering reports and disclosure statements, or warranties on major structural features. A few ordinances seek to preserve the local rental stock, typically by restricting conversions when the rental vacancy rate drops below a certain percentage.

With regard to government action to affect the level of conversion activity, three of every four local chief executives prefer that neither the state nor Federal government act either to encourage or to discourage conversions. Over 60 percent also believe that local governments should avoid such actions. Of those who do see a role for government, a somewhat larger proportion prefers actions that would encourage rather than discourage conversions, such as programs to enable low- and moderate-income households to purchase their units or technical assistance programs for tenant-sponsored conversions.

Officials representing jurisdictions with heavy recent conversion activity are more likely than others to favor government regulatory intervention. About one-fifth of these would have any level of government act to discourage conversions. Similar proportions of this group would have local or state governments act to encourage conversions. Nevertheless, majorities of those local officials with the most conversion experience prefer that the state and Federal governments neither encourage nor discourage conversions.

Future changes in the volume, location, and character of conversions could, of course, alter the impacts that have been specified here -- both positive and negative -- on people, neighborhoods, and communities. For instance, if there is a homeownership market for units that are older or of lower quality than those currently being converted, a larger proportion of future conversions may involve rehabilitation and revitalization. This would result in more dramatic changes in the housing stock than has presently been observed. On the other hand, if such buildings contain higher proportions of elderly, minority, or low-income residents, the frequency with which conversion creates hardship for such households may also increase.

# 1

# The Dynamics
# of Conversion

# Chapter I
## Issues Surrounding Conversion

Among the elderly in the Tampa area, the fear is commonplace. Several retired couples have been give 180 days to either buy their apartments or move. Some -- after talking with sales people -- will decide to use all or part of their savings in order to buy; others will decide that, even with a large down payment, the montly cost of buying is just too much, or they will see no advantage to owning. They will begin to search the diminishing number of similar rental buildings in the area for a new apartment, hoping also to find a place that will not soon "go condo." The stress and anxiety associated with conversion is not something that these people bargained for when they settled in Florida's retirement communities.

*

Now that their last child has gone off to college, the big home on its one acre lot in suburban Philadelphia suddenly seems to echo with their every footstep. They are an active couple, and they spend their vacations travelling. Evenings they are often in the city for dinner and the theater. The yard work that used to be a pleasure has lost some of its appeal. In short, these are two "empty nesters" who are ready for a change. Last month they put their house on the market; with the proceeds from its sale, they can easily afford a condominium in one of the luxury buildings near downtown that has been recently converted. There, someone else can handle the maintenance, and there is no lawn to mow. The pool and built-in shopping facilities are other attractions. An apartment in the city seems to fit well with the new pattern of their lives.

*

For more than a year, the 30-year-old bank manager and his wife searched with growing frustration for a home they could afford. In California's rapidly inflating housing market, even the small ranch houses similar to those where they had grown up were completely beyond their financial reach. Finally, they bought instead a $70,000 two bedroom condominium apartment. It was, they felt, the only acceptable housing in their price range; and with inflation gaining on them, they felt they could not afford to wait. Like many others, they would prefer to have the kind of suburban home on a separate lot in which they were raised; but they have very reluctantly chosen a very different kind of housing -- and with it a different style of living. However grudgingly, they have traded the advantages and problems of the separate house for an amenity-rich, high-density environment that they may or may not, in time, find acceptable.

*

*When she took her first job as an associate in a Chicago law firm the young woman rented an apartment in a high-rise building overlooking Lake Michigan, just a short bus ride to her office in "the loop." A year later, to her surprise, the building went condo: unable to afford to buy and content as a renter, she moved to an older, smaller apartment building in adjacent Lincoln Park -- a neighborhood that has recently seen a new influx of such middle-income people. There, two years later, she faced conversion again; her landlord had sold to a developer, who than spent several months restoring the once fashionable building to its former elegance. Reluctant to move again, the woman consulted friends who had purchased condominiums; they were enthusiastic, especially about the tax advantages of ownership and the rate at which condo units were gaining value. She decided to buy. Thus, she joined the growing number of young professional households -- including many single women -- whose first home purchase is a converted condominium.*

\* \* \*

The conversion of rental housing to condominiums and cooperatives affects different kinds of people in different ways. These and other anecdotes suggest that conversion reflects certain changing social and market conditions and that it has certain social and market impacts. But, because it is a relatively new housing market phenomenon in the Nation, these conditions and impacts are not yet well understood.

## The Controversy Over Evidence

The absence of solid information about the extent, causes and consequences of conversion has been a source of considerable controversy. As with most controversies, some debate has stemmed from differences in values, points of view, and basic policy preferences. In this controversy, however, maybe even more so than in others, the debate over evidence has been particularly prominent.

Some of the controversy surrounding conversion is caused by uncertainty about its extent and future growth. Have large proportions of the rental stock been converted in most metropolitan areas, or not? Will so many buildings convert that, by 1985, it will be impossible to find a rental apartment? Or, will rental units continue to be available?

Some controversy is associated with the effect of conversions on various groups of tenants. To what extent are elderly, minority, or low-income renters affected by conversions? How many tenants, especially the elderly, are being forced from units they have occupied for years? How many tenants are able to remain in their units, either as renters or buyers? When tenants do move from converted units, how are they affected? Can tenants who move find comparable units in the same areas at similar prices?

Some controversy arises concerning the <u>concentration</u> of conversion activity in particular areas. Do conversions typically occur in stable or in revitalizing neighborhoods? In central cities or their suburbs? Are they concentrated in particular regions of the country?

Some controversy centers on the <u>reasons</u> for conversion. Are conversions on the rise mainly because landlords can make large profits from selling buildings for conversion, or because operating rental property is unprofitable relative to other investments? Have converters created a demand for converted units by making many tenants feel they have no alternative but to buy, or do people want to buy because of the attractions of this housing and the financial advantages of homeownership?

To date, available information has been insufficient to address these questions in a systematic way. Therefore, in December 1979, the U.S. Congress authorized a nationwide study of conversion activity. This report presents the results of that study.

## The Congressional Mandate

In the 1979 amendments to the Housing and Community Development Act of 1974, Congress directed the U.S. Department of Housing and Urban Development (HUD) to submit a report, within six months, addressing the conversion of rental housing to condominium and cooperative ownership. Congress asked for:

1. An estimate of the number of conversions which have occurred since 1970;

2. A projection of the number of conversions likely to occur from 1980 through 1985;

3. An assessment of the impact that conversions have had or are likely to have on the availability of housing for lower income persons;

4. An assessment of the extent to which conversions are concentrated in certain areas or types of areas of the country; and

5. An examination of the factors contributing to the increase in conversions.

In response to the Congressional directive, this report presents the results of a multi-faceted national study designed to address these points and other major issues regarding the nature, causes, and consequences of condominium and cooperative conversions.

The groundwork for presenting the study's findings is laid in this first chapter. Included are definitions of terms, a brief description of previous research in the area, and a delineation of the many issues associated with conversion.

## Definitions 1/

The condominium and the cooperative are legal forms that permit multiple ownership of a multi-family building or complex. In the United States, each form is defined by the states, so that details of laws governing condominium and cooperative formation and operation vary from place to place.

---

Condominium: A housing unit in a multi-family building or complex owned by an individual, who also owns a partial interest in the common areas of the building or complex.

---

Although this form of ownership has a long history, particularly in Europe, condominiums became popular in the United States only in the 1960s. In a condominium, individuals purchase and obtain title to specific units, in which they generally live, but may also rent to others.

The unit owners simultaneously acquire a fractional interest in the entire property's common elements -- including halls, roofs, main walls, stairways and entryways, land, parking areas, and recreational or social facilities. This partial interest in the common elements and facilities is usually proportional to the dollar value of the individual unit purchased.

Each unit bears its own deed and mortgage, and individual unit owners are liable for any taxes levied against the unit. In addition to any mortgage payment, each unit owner generally pays a monthly maintenance fee to an association of all unit owners.

---

1/ Additional information may be found in Keith B. Romney, Condominium Development Guide (Boston: Warren, Gorham and Lamont, 1974); "Condominiums and Cooperatives," Housing and Development Reporter, 25:0011-0021,0111-0114 (Washington, D.C.: Bureau of National Affairs, 3-28-77 and 4-24-78); Patrick J. Rohan and Melvin A. Reskin, Condominium Law and Practice (New York; Mathew Bender, 1979); Patrick J. Rohan and Melvin A. Reskin, Cooperative Housing Law and Practice (New York: Mathew Bender, 1978); and in chapter X of this report.

The association board then contracts for the maintenance and operation of the individual units and common elements. Basic requirements for the bylaws governing the form and operation of condominium owners associations are provided in state laws.

Whether a condominium is newly built or converted from rental, it is established first by the public filing of a master deed or declaration, accompanied by a property description. Usually, an interim mortgage loan is obtained on the whole property to finance either the cost of new construction or the purchase and renovation of a rental property. As individual units are sold, the interim mortgage is repaid and ownership is transferred to the unit purchasers. If the financial institution providing individual unit mortgages plans to sell the mortgages to either the Federal National Mortgage Association (FNMA) or the Federal Home Loan Mortgage Corporation (FHLMC), the regulations of these two organizations govern the sale of units. (A description of FHLMC and FNMA programs is contained in chapter X.)

> Cooperative: A nonprofit housing corporation in which individual households own shares entitling them to live in a particular unit in a multi-family building or complex and to use the common areas and facilities of the building or complex.

In a cooperative, individuals do not buy their units but instead purchase stock in a corporation which owns the entire property. The corporation generally obtains a blanket mortgage for the property, and cooperative members contribute toward its repayment, as well as paying a proportional share of operating and maintenance expenses. Cooperative members are actively involved in the management of their housing, but they give an elected board of directors certain discretionary responsibilities. These include deciding who may join and live in the cooperative and enforcing the obligations of membership.

The owner of a condominium may default on the unit mortgage without directly affecting the legal rights and solvency of other owners. This is not the case in a cooperative. If a cooperative member fails to make payments toward the blanket mortgage, other members are responsible for his or her contribution. If a number of cooperative members fail to make payments toward the blanket mortgage, there is significant risk of foreclosure on the property, possibly causing solvent members to lose their units. Partly for this reason, financial institutions, outside of New York, have been reluctant to finance cooperatives. However, the record in New York, where most cooperatives exist, indicates that foreclosures have been extremely rare over the last 50 years.

A variation of the cooperative, generally known as a "limited" or "low equity" cooperative has been used primarily to provide housing for people of moderate or low income. Often the initial down payment for membership is very modest. The mortgage interest is subsidized by a governmental body, which then sets rules for the cooperative's operation. In a limited equity cooperative the price at which shareholders may resell their interest is determined by a formula. The intended result is to keep the resale price of cooperative ownership below the market value and within the reach of low- or moderate-income households.

---

Conversion: A change in the legal form of a multi-family rental property from single ownership by a landlord to multiple ownership.

---

In some cases, a building is converted by whoever has operated it as a rental; however, more often, a property is sold to a developer specializing in conversion. The developer then manages the entire process from legal declaration through unit sales. 2/

In a condominium, the individual unit owner ordinarily has the right to lease the unit to someone else. This means an investor could purchase a unit and rent it to anyone he or she chooses, within guidelines established by the condominium owners association. But in a cooperative, the decision to permit leasing is at the discretion of the cooperative board, unless superseded by state or local law. For example, a number of recent cooperative conversions in New York City have taken place under a "noneviction" plan that gives prior tenants the option to continue renting indefinitely after their building becomes a cooperative.

In this report, a property is not considered converted until both a declaration, master deed, or equivalent document has been recorded, and the first unit has been sold. 3/ This definition offers a precise means of documenting the volume of conversion activity. However, the estimates of converted units produced by this definition

---

2/ In some places, non-residential buildings have been converted to condominiums or cooperatives. These are not considered conversions for the purpose of estimating numbers of units converted but are discussed, where relevant, in subsequent chapters.

3/ In some areas of the country, where it is difficult to determine when the first unit has been sold, or where regulations require a minimum number of sales to tenants, the operational definition of conversion is slightly different. Details are provided in chapter IV.

are somewhat larger than the number of units actually sold. As a hypothetical example, if only 100 units have sold in a building with 300 units on sale, 300 units are converted according to this study's definition. While these estimates are slightly larger than the actual number of units purchased, they are smaller than the number of units which have only been legally recorded as condominiums or cooperatives.

## Previous Research

In the course of this study, a detailed search of existing data bases, professional organizations, and libraries identified hundreds of bibliographic sources which bear some relevance to conversions. The most pertinent of these are presented as an annotated bibliography in Appendix 1. Included in this body of literature are various studies of the conversion phenomenon.

Most previous studies have focused on a single state -- such as New York, Florida, Connecticut, and Hawaii -- or locality -- such as Chicago and Evanston, Illinois, San Francisco, Washington, D.C., Seattle, Pittsburgh, Baltimore, Kansas City, and Cambridge, Massachusetts. 4/ There is now a sizeable body of literature on the subject of the conversion of rental housing to condominiums and cooperatives which contributes to an understanding of the phenomenon in different types of housing markets. However, these reports and the many investigative news stories which have been done on conversion are limited in terms of geographical coverage, sample size, and the issues addressed.

The first Federal study dealing with condominiums and cooperatives was done in 1975 when the emphasis was primarily on new condominium developments that were being built in Sunbelt locations. 5/ At that time, the number of condominium and cooperative conversions was small compared to the number of conversions which has occurred during the second half of the decade.

Other, more recent reports on the conversion phenomenon, have also taken a national perspective, but have generally relied on local studies and secondary data sources.

---

4/ For a complete list of these studies, see the Annotated Bibliography in Appendix 1.

5/ U.S. Department of Housing and Urban Development, Condominium/ Cooperative Study, 3 vols. (Washington: U.S. Government Printing Office, 1975).

The National Council of Senior Citizens, for
example, undertook an overview study of condominium conversion -- and its causes and
impacts -- with special focus on the elderly.
Its report also looks at the various legal
responses to conversion, primarily at the
local level, and discusses policy options
available to the Federal government. 6/

The Urban Consortium has completed a condominium conversion study which examines the
issues of consumer protection, tenants' rights,
and displacement.  It reviews the Uniform Condominium Act and various local controls which have
been initated in response to conversions.  Their
report concludes with recommendations for Federal
and local research and policy initiatives. 7/

Building upon this body of existing research, the present study
represents the first effort to collect primary data at the national
level with which to address the most significant and controversial
issues related to conversion.  The remainder of this chapter high-
lights these issues and chapter II describes the research approach
employed to study them.

## The Controversy Over Volume and Location

Two deceptively simple questions about conversions have been at
issue:  how many are there and where are they located?  The data to
answer these questions have generally been unavailable but, once
collected, these data tell a great deal about the character of the
conversion phenomenon.

The volume.  To estimate the number of multi-family housing units
converted from rental to multiple ownership is in some places quite
easy, and in other places very difficult.  In part, this is caused
by differing local definitions of conversion, and in part, by varying
and sometimes inadequate public recording practices.  The result is
that controversy often arises over the most basic of facts regarding
conversions -- the volume of activity.

---

6/ Condominium Conversions:  Options for Tenants and Rental Market
Protection (Washington, D.C.:  National Council of Senior Citizens,
1979).

7/ Jennifer Silver and Cathy Shreve, Public Technology Inc., Urban
Consortium, Condominium Conversion Controls (Washington, D.C.:  U.S.
Department of Housing and Urban Development, Office of Policy Development
and Research, 1979).

The most widely circulated national source for estimates of conversion activity in major metropolitan areas is the U.S. Housing Markets Report, published by Advance Mortgage Corporation & Citicorp Real Estate, Inc. Their figures are based on conversations with a small number of market experts in each metropolitan area. Other estimates, for these areas, based on a review of public records, are likely to differ. In states such as California, the problem of counting conversions is complicated by the multiple stage approval process. Another estimation problem is caused by developers who apply for conversion without intending to immediately offer the units for sale. Converters do this as a hedge against future restrictions on conversion activity, such as a local moratorium.

The result of such complexities is that conversion estimates published to date sometimes vary widely one from another. To remedy this, chapter IV presents national estimates of activity from 1970 through 1979 based on an extensive and systematic data collection effort.

The location. Aside from questions about volume, it is important to know exactly where conversions have been occurring. Location, of course, is closely related to the type and quality of building which is converted. Information on location, so far, has come from scattered studies and reports. They indicate that there are some metropolitan areas where conversions are taking place in prime neighborhoods within the corporate limits of large cities. Some are luxury or semi-luxury buildings.

> In Philadelphia, the Society Hill Towers, a high-rise building of 705 units, was converted. It is located on the site of the old Dock Street wholesale food markets and overlooks the Delaware River, an area considered to be very prestigious.

> In Cleveland's Shaker Square area, two older, luxury buildings that combine an aura of history and prestige with good location and architecture are being converted. Oriental carpeting in entrance halls, crystal sconces on the walls, hammered grillwork, copper mansard roofs, lofty gables, butlers' pantries, and the like, make such buildings attractive to buyers and profitable for converters.

In a few cities, some conversions have been of older, sometimes deteriorated rental buildings located in revitalizing neighborhoods.

> In Boston, for example, the majority of conversions have been in Beacon Hill and Back Bay, two areas with a substantial historical and architectural heritage. Sections of each neighborhood are revitalizing after a period during which they had become rather run-down,

but still attractive to young people and
students who sought less expensive rentals.
Boston targeted portions of these areas for
revitalization and invested in new public
facilities before major conversion activity
began. Most of the converted units are in
small buildings formerly owned by small-
scale landlords and converted by local developers
who preserve the distinctive exterior features,
yet modernize the interiors. Buyers are typically
white, middle-income professionals, mostly singles
or couples without children.

Not all conversions requiring major renovation are so successful,
however.

In a Midwestern city, for example, two developers
who successfully built and sold new townhouses in
an historic area near downtown, converted a vacant
two-unit building. The initial price for the
100-year-old building was $10,000. After three
years, many labor problems, two refinancings,
and $140,000 in rehabilitation costs, the
developers offered the units for sale -- at about
$100,000 each. Overpriced relative to the market
in that area, the units were unsold in late 1979.
Faced with a sizable loss, the developers disclaim
any further interest in converting old rental
buildings.

The suburbs of many large metropolitan areas have also experienced
conversions. As in cities, various reports suggest that some suburban conversions are luxury, high-rise buildings, while others
involve relatively modest structures once rented to people with
moderate incomes. Converted middle-income garden or townhouse style
complexes often differ little in appearance from nearby properties
of similar age that remain as rentals. If they differ, it is most
often in the degree of soundproofing, space between and size of
units, or presence of certain amenities. At the time of conversion,
additional special features and cosmetic improvements may be added
to increase market value and stimulate sales.

In the San Antonio suburbs, most of the conversions have been of fairly ordinary gardenstyle
apartments in nonprime locations. However, the
relatively low rate of return to apartment owners
in this overbuilt market gives owners an incentive
to sell to converters. Units have been offered for
sale at moderate prices, ranging from $20,000 to
$60,000.

Chapters IV and VIII indicate exactly where conversions are occurring, whether primarily in the cities or suburbs, revitalizing or stable neighborhoods, luxury or nonluxury buildings.

## The Controversy Over Causes

The conversion of rental housing units to condominiums and coopera-tives has accompanied other major changes taking place in the Nation and in local housing markets. How these changes relate to conver-sions, however, is not yet well understood.

For example, some communities have experienced increasing numbers of households and decreasing household sizes; revitalizing older, inner-city neighborhoods; declining profitability of rental properties; landlord abandonment of rental apartment buildings; rising energy prices; and local government regulation of rent levels. Conversion seems to fit well with some of these changes. For instance, a growing proportion of those people financially able to purchase housing live in smaller households; this may increase the proportion that will purchase a condominium or cooperative rather than a single-family home. Similarly, the increase in single-person and childless middle- to upper-income households may contribute to increased demand for city living. But, exactly what contribution, if any, these changes make to the increasing number of rental conversions, has been the subject of debate.

The rental housing market. The rapid growth of conversion activity has coincided with an apparent decline in the profitability of building and operating multi-family rental housing. Reasons for this decline include higher operating and maintenance costs, higher land and construction costs for new apartments, changes in the Federal tax law, and increased government regulation -- including rent control in a few areas. Many see these changes contributing to a long-term shortage of affordable rental housing. Some observers have asked whether they will lead eventually to the end of unsubsidized rental housing in this country. 8/

Current conditions in the Nation's rental housing market present a paradox. Several factors -- declining vacancy rates, rapidly rising operating costs, little new construction -- seem to indicate an existing or emerging shortgage of rental housing. Other evidence --

---

8/ See Roger Starr, "An End to Rental Housing," The Public Interest (Fall 1979), pp. 25-47; and Rental Housing: A National Problem that Needs Immediate Attention, Report to the Congress of the United States by the Comptroller General, U.S. General Accounting Office (November 8, 1979).

such as the tendency for rent levels to rise less rapidly than
operating costs and less rapidly than other components of the cost
of living -- seems to indicate that rentals may not be in short
supply. 9/

In some cases, it is clear that rental buildings of declining
profitability have been converted to condominiums or cooperatives.

> In Baltimore, the apparent unpopularity of
> living in high-rise buildings created above-
> average vacancy rates for some such proper-
> ties and a consequent poor return on invest-
> ment.  As an alternative to continued operation
> at lower profit, landlords sold these high-rises
> for conversion.

The rates at which rental units are being removed from the stock,
either by conversion to ownership (generally at the high end of the
market) or by abandonment (generally at the low end), are cited by
both those who see a rental housing shortage and those who deny it
as evidence for their positions.  The former group emphasizes that
both conversion and abandonment reduce the rental stock, contributing
to further tightening.

> In New York City, however, where there are an
> estimated 300,000 abandoned housing units, some
> observers argue that conversion may help to
> prevent future abandonment and to retain units
> in the housing stock.

Those who dispute the existence or extent of a rental housing shortage argue that current rates of conversion and abandonment are inconsistent with a genuine shortage.  They believe scarcity would allow
landlords to raise rents and thereby increase their investment
returns; this, in turn, would reduce rates of conversion and abandonment.  They claim that the failure of rent levels to keep pace with
operating costs indicates a surplus.  Finally, those who question the
existence of a rental shortage generally view the current lack of
new rental construction as a temporary market response to the continuing effects of overbuilding during the early 1970s and the relatively
increased attractiveness of other uses of capital.

---

9/ In fact, renters may actually have increased their housing
consumption during the middle 1970s.  If so, the trend is
inconsistent with the presence of a rental housing shortage.
John F. Kain; Herman B. Lenard; and Karl E. Case; Condominium
Conversion in Massachusetts:  An Evaluation of Its Benefits and
Costs (Unpublished paper, April 1980).

On the other side, those who see a serious shortage of rental housing emerging claim that the lack of new construction signals a secular shift in the economics of unsubsidized rental construction and operation due to the combined effects of inflation, the tax benefits of ownership for higher income households, and the emergence of the conversion option. They claim that demand is, in some cases, insufficient to sustain higher rents because renters' incomes are not, on the average, high enough to support rent increases needed to maintain costs. They believe also that interferences with the market in the form of government regulation, tax policies that favor ownership, and organized tenant resistance make it impossible for some landlords to raise rents fast enough to meet their costs.

Debate about whether or not there is a rental housing shortage may result, in part, because the two sides focus on the balance of rental supply and demand at different income levels or in different local housing submarkets. For instance, it may be that surpluses at higher rent levels and shortages of moderate-income rentals exist side by side in many markets.

One's view of condominium and cooperative conversion is likely to be partially a function of one's position in the debate concerning the present and future state of the Nation's rental market. These issues are discussed further in chapter V.

Inflation, Energy, and Ownership Demand. In the last decade, owner-occupied housing has attracted an increasing share of private investment. More and more people are purchasing housing not simply as shelter, but also for speculative purposes or for protection of capital from inflationary impacts. For these two reasons, housing prices have escalated significantly. 10/

An inflated housing market makes it more difficult for young people of modest income and limited savings to buy homes. Many will continue to rent but others may find that newly constructed or converted condominiums provide a desirable alternative to the traditional single-family home. Since converted rental units generally cost less to deliver than comparable new units, and are cheaper per square foot than single-family homes, they may offer the best opportunity for home-ownership to small households with moderate incomes.

---

10/ George Sternlieb and James W. Hughes, "Condominium Conversion Profiles: Governmental Policy", Journal of The American Real Estate and Urban Economics Association (Winter, 1975), pp. 61-80.

> In Houston, for example, many conversions are
> occurring in rental townhouse complexes close
> to downtown.  The units are very competitive
> with new townhouses and slightly lower priced
> than single-family houses located farther from
> the city's business districts.  Advertisements
> for the converted condominiums are aimed at
> young households just entering the market.

If converted condominiums and cooperatives replace the construction
of some single-family homes, it is possible that more efficient land
and energy use could result.  Some consider this a benefit of converted units, given the country's concern with energy conservation
and reducing wasteful land use patterns.

> In St. Petersburg, Florida, a strong selling
> point for converted condominiums is their
> energy efficiency relative to single-family
> houses.

The conversion of rental units must be understood as occurring within
the context of other major changes in the Nation's housing market.
Chapter V will examine the extent to which condominium and cooperative
conversions are a result of, or contribute to, these changes.

## The Controversy Over Impacts

Much of the controversy over condominium and cooperative conversions -- that is, whether they are beneficial or harmful -- hinges
on the following questions of fact:

1. Who buys and lives in converted units, and what
   are their experiences?

2. Who moves from properties being converted, and
   what are their experiences?

3. What are the housing market, neighborhood, and
   fiscal impacts of conversion?

Since virtually all previous studies of condominium and cooperative
conversions which were intended to address these factual questions
have been done in a single jurisdiction or neighborhood, realistic
answers on a national level have not been possible.  The following
illustrations are meant to prepare the way for a presentation of
national trends and findings, contained in part III of this report.

The Experiences of Those Who Buy and Live in Converted Units. The kinds of people who buy converted condominiums and cooperatives will vary somewhat from place to place.

In midtown luxury buildings, some buyers are probably young professionals and others are older "empty nesters" whose children have left home. Converted suburban units are more likely to attract young families with a few children, particularly if they are garden or townhouse complexes. In retirement and resort communities, such as Phoenix and St. Petersburg, the elderly and "snow birds" from colder climates are known to purchase many converted units.

The proportion of tenants who purchase units when their buildings are converted is likely to vary greatly and to depend on several factors.

> In Montgomery County, Maryland, a luxurious high-rise building was converted to condominiums but few tenants purchased. Many former residents claimed they were dissatisfied with the renovation job done by the developer and refused to buy.

Purchases by former tenants may also depend on the sales pitch used by developers. 11/

> In the Cleveland area, for example, one converter who specializes in luxury buildings and consistently sells about 80 percent of the units to current tenants emphasizes the importance of his low-key approach. He provides all tenants with a weekly newsletter containing details on each sale as well as other news related to the conversion process. The newsletter's objectives are to squelch rumors and to remind tenants of purchase options and approaching deadlines. No sales force is used, nor are direct approaches made to tenants. During the marketing period, the converter maintains an office in the building, and simply waits for tenants to make purchase inquiries. Outside prospects, most of whom are small investors, are solicited by telephone.

> In one Cleveland suburb, however, a firm which converted a luxury high-rise used pressure sales tactics that some tenants found offensive. A large contingent of sales personnel moved into the building's vacant units and saturated the remaining renters with sales pitches, written advertising, and offers of

---

11/ The following two examples are adapted from Frank Kuznik, "Condo-millionaires", Cleveland Magazine (V8, n6, June 1979), pp. 82-89.

discounts. One tenant was called out of a
business meeting to take an "emergency" phone
call that turned out to be from the converter's
salesman, whose opening line was "Bill, do you
realize that you only have until midnight to
purchase your condominium and save $750?" Such
techniques are designed to reduce the time, and
therefore the cost, of selling out the converting
building.

Even when a more aggressive sales pitch is used, sales may be very
slow if the demand for condominium ownership is weak.

In Milwaukee, Wisconsin, for example, an
intensive marketing approach used by an
out-of-town converter was relatively unsuccessful in stimulating sales of units in a
high-rise luxury building in the downtown area.
According to Milwaukee bankers involved in
financing the conversion, unit purchases would
have been slow in coming, no matter what type
of sales pitch, because people were neither
very open to this form of ownership nor
especially interested in living in the downtown area.

On the other hand, in areas where demand for condominium or cooperative
ownership is strong, prospective buyers hardly need a strong sales
pitch.

In Washington, D.C., a developer decided to
hold a lottery in order to cull prospective
buyers from the long list of nontenants who
wished to buy.

Converted condominiums are likely to be very attractive to some
investors, particularly to professionals, who are interested in a tax
shelter, and to small-scale investment syndicates. Absentee ownership in buildings with unit mortgages bought by FHLMC is initially
limited to 20 percent of units. But in buildings without such
restrictions, investor ownership can be higher.

In Dade County, Florida, for example, which
includes Miami, some buildings are 30 to 50
percent investor-owned. Among these investors
are owners from both South America and Canada
who shelter their income in Florida.

In Hawaii, investors own a large share of the
units converted to condominiums. The units are
rented for most of the year to tourists and other
visitors to the Islands.

Investor-owned units can be rented, but there are instances where children have bought a unit as a tax shelter and then allowed their parents to live there rent-free or at a nominal price. Some developers are known to set aside a certain number of investor-owned units for rental to elderly and handicapped households, and others have made efforts to match tenants who cannot or do not wish to buy with an investor who subsequently continues to rent the unit to the tenants.

Experiences of those purchasing converted units will obviously vary. Tenants who buy units when their buildings convert sometimes have to undergo a disruptive renovation process. At other times, the work done by a converter is handled rapidly and efficiently with few complaints from tenants who buy.

After purchase, problems sometimes arise when a developer will not relinquish control to the owners association or when conflicts arise between owners and those who rent from investors.

> In Denver, for example, a condominium association was illegally controlled by the developer for its initial three years. Control was finally given to the association, but the developer continued to withhold legal records and financial information from the association and failed to make promised repairs and improvements. In addition, arguments were frequent between owner-occupants and those renting from investors on issues such as individual utility conservation.

A complaint sometimes made against developers is that the reserve fund for major repairs is not sufficient.

> In New York City, for example, this is usually a significant issue. During the process of converting their buildings to cooperatives, tenants often make the size of the reserve fund a principal negotiating point with the landlord.

Converted buildings may also be susceptible to problems after they are turned over to the owners association.

> In San Francisco, for example, a firm which manages both new and converted condominiums reports more problems with conversions caused by lack of budget experience, inadequate cash reserves, and structural deficiencies in older buildings. In addition, many tenants who buy expect to receive free unit maintenance and other services.

Factionalism and personality conflicts may plague some associations, especially when debate arises on the need for special assessments. Problems can also occur between absentee investor-owners and owner-occupants or between owner-occupants and renters. Absentee owners may not always follow or inform their tenants of the covenants, conditions, and restrictions governing occupancy. Although not central to this report, these issues are examined in chapter IX.

The Experiences of Those Who move from Properties Being Converted. Some people who move from converted units do so because they cannot afford to buy. The monthly cost of buying a condominium or shares in a cooperative is likely to be, in many cases, equal to or higher than the rent being charged; when the expense is considerably more, tenants who cannot afford a higher expenditure for housing may leave

> In San Mateo, California, for example, a 229-unit building had deteriorated because low rent levels could not meet rising maintenance costs. In 1977, the building was converted to condominiums, and the one to three bedroom units were sold at prices ranging from $49,000 to $145,000. The wide gap between existing rents and the anticipated monthly payments meant few tenants could purchase.

Higher costs may not be the only reason for moving. Some elderly persons may not wish to be burdened with a mortgage, with membership in a condominium owners or cooperative association, or with the responsibilities of homeownership. Tenants may not buy because they are dissatisfied with the condition of the building and do not believe conversion will correct its shortcomings. Others may not buy because they want to be able to move easily.

> In Cambridge, Massachusetts, for example, over half of the movers from recently converted buildings were over age 62.

> In Boulder, Colorado, some cheaply constructed buildings once rented to students at the University of Colorado have been converted to condominiums. The student population either cannot afford to buy or does not wish to purchase units for the short time they will be in the city.

Those who move from converted buildings may encounter various problems. People who leave a converted building may discover, shortly after relocating, that their new residence is going to be converted. Elderly tenants who relocate may be affected by the inconvenience of moving, which is aggravated by age-related infirmities. The loss of social ties and access to familiar services is another problem some elderly persons may experience.

Some movers from converted buildings will pay higher rents for new units or will be unable to find comparable housing in the same neighborhoods.

> In Washington, D.C., for example, tenants who moved in 1979 typically paid higher rents, but their new units were slightly larger. Most were able to find units in the same general areas of the city; but locating the new unit took an average of two months. 12/

Other tenants moving from converted units may have more positive experiences. Some developers offer relocation payments to tenants who move or supplement payments required by local or state laws.

> In Hartford, for example, converters make considerable efforts to help relocate low-income tenants from converted buildings. It is estimated that the program costs $1,000 per relocated household.

> In Los Angeles, the city has designed a tenant relocation program which it encourages converters to use.

Housing Market Impacts. One argument made against condominium and cooperative conversions is that they reduce the supply of rental housing. This situation, it is claimed, is aggravated by the current lack of new multi-family construction and other market factors which make owning and operating rental property less profitable than other investments.

The proportion of converted rental stock varies from one metropolitan area to another. The proportion also varies within a single metropolitan area by type of building, neighborhood, or particular jurisdiction.

> In Boulder, Colorado, for example, over 20 percent of the rental stock has been converted. Conversions have been so extensive that, in late 1979, it was estimated that most of the units suitable for conversion had been removed from the rental supply through this process.

---

12/ Condominium and Cooperative Conversions in the District of Columbia (Washington, D.C.: Raymond, Parish and Pine, Inc., Development Economics Group, 1979).

In some areas of concentrated conversion activity, rental vacancy
rates may be very low.  Low vacancy rates may lead, in turn, to
higher rents.

> In Evanston, Illinois, for example, 14 percent
> of the rental stock has been converted and local
> officials estimated the 1979 rental vacancy rate at
> 1 percent.  Officials noted, too, that rents
> were rising rapidly.

Despite these examples, the impact of conversions on the rental
housing market is difficult to determine.  First, the reduction of
rental supply due to conversion is mitigated somewhat when converted
units are bought by investors who continue to rent them.  Second,
if converted units are purchased by those households who otherwise would have continued renting, there may be a reduction in
future demand for rental housing, because these tenants have
left the rental market.  In such circumstances, conversions
have little effect on vacancy rates or rent levels.  On the
other hand, if buyers of converted units are primarily those
households who previously owned, conversions will have more of
an effect on the rental market.

It is possible that, in a given locality, a 10 percent reduction in
multi-family rental stock caused by conversion might be offset by a
10 percent reduction in demand attributable to shifting preferences.
However, it is also possible that the demand for rental units in a
locality would remain steady or rise.  If few new rental units are
constructed during this period, the result could be a very tight
rental market, higher rents, and pressure on lower income households
to move elsewhere.  Careful analysis, as presented in chapter VII,
is required to determine the likelihood of each scenario.

Neighborhood Impacts.  There are examples of condominium and cooperative conversions occurring in both neighborhoods which are relatively
stable and those which are experiencing revitalization.

> In St. Paul, rehabilitation of single family
> houses in the Historic Hill area began in the
> late 1960s.  Rental housing began converting to
> condominiums in 1971, but did not intensify until
> the late 1970s.

> In Columbus and Cleveland, Ohio, conversion has
> been a late, very small feature of reinvestment
> that began in the 1960s and early 1970s, possibly
> because most housing in these neighborhoods is in
> one and two-unit structures.  The role of conver-
> sions in neighborhood revitalization is not clear
> and may vary from city to city.

Conversion of some buildings may lead to changes in the population composition of both buildings and neighborhoods.

> In an affluent northern Virginia suburb, a large moderate-income rental complex was converted after receiving substantial rehabilitation. Although the units were modestly priced, they were nevertheless beyond the reach of virtually all tenants. The middle-income families who purchased subsequently enjoyed substantial appreciation in the market values of their units as the area grew in attractiveness due to this and other investment.

In other instances, very high proportions of current tenants purchase units in the converting buildings, so virtually no change in population results. Chapter VIII contains an analysis of the types of neighborhoods in which conversions occur and the impacts that they have on those neighborhoods.

Fiscal Impacts. Another aspect of condominium and cooperative conversions is the effect they have on a local government's fiscal condition. Changing a multi-family building from single to multiple ownership may raise its assessed value. The local government can, in turn, realize added property tax revenues from such increases. It is possible, too, that differences in the demographic characteristics or behavior of new residents in converted units may affect the demand for public services and have some impact on local government spending patterns. However, the evidence on this is not clear.

> In Chicago and Brookline, for example, two recent studies showed assessment increases of about 30 percent. In the Brookline study, an attempt was made to determine if conversions had an effect on service demand and cost. No definite conclusions were reached.

While condominium conversions can yield higher local tax revenues, there is one interesting case in which conversion led ultimately to a significant decline in local tax receipts.

> Just outside the city of Pittsburgh lies a hilltop, white-collar community of 500 converted garden style and townhouse condominiums. Known as Pennsbury Village, this complex, which was converted in 1974, has approximately 1,000 residents. Units in the Village were priced at between $20,000 and $25,000 when offered for sale in 1974. In 1976, this 48 acre complex was granted permission to break away from its mother township to become a separate municipality.

It is believed to be the Nation's first borough
composed solely of condominiums. The incorporation removed about 10 percent of the tax revenues
of Robinson Township which unsuccessfully con-
tested the secession. The stimulus for the
secession effort was dissatisfaction with municipal services provided by the township, especially
an expensive tie-in to a township-wide sewer system.

The impacts that conversions have on local tax revenues are
systematically examined in chapter VIII.


## The Controversy Over Regulation

Local governments and tenant groups have responded to conversion
activity in various ways. These responses, in turn, affect the
incidence and character of conversion.

In some jurisdictions, organized opposition to conversion activity
has led to imposition of a temporary moratorium. Sometimes, local
government uses the moratorium period to study conversion in their
locality and determine a policy for dealing with the phenomenon.

> In Philadelphia, the city council passed an
> ordinance in 1979 which prohibited all conversion
> activity for 18 months. Passage of the measure
> was greatly influenced by a coalition of tenants,
> local developers, and others concerned with out-
> side involvement in the city's housing market.

> In Seattle, a 120-day moratorium on conversions
> was imposed in July 1978 partially at the urging
> of the Seattle Tenants Union and the Seattle
> Displacement Coalition. These same groups also
> were involved in subsequent passage of the city's
> ordinance regulating conversion activity.

Both local jurisdictions and states have passed regulatory legislation, some of which provides protection for purchasers of converted
units and some of which safeguards tenants living in buildings
being converted.

Chapters XI and XII discuss the various approaches used by governments to regulate conversion activity. Chapter X presents existing
Federal, state, and local programs that relate to conversion. The
perceptions and policy preferences of local officials across the
Nation regarding condominium and cooperative conversions are also
presented in chapter XII.

* * *

This chapter has highlighted some of the issues surrounding the conversion of multi-family rental housing to condominiums or cooperatives. These issues are numerous, complex, and controversial; to date, there has been insufficient reliable information to inform the debate which has surrounded the phenomenon. The examples cited in this chapter illustrate particular cases or sides of issues, but many of the basic facts regarding condominium and cooperative conversions have yet to be established. Chapters IV through XII present the findings of HUD's national study designed to establish the facts.

To recap. The key issues are as follows:

Volume. How large and widespread is the phenomenon of rental housing conversion? How large and widespread will conversion activity become between 1980 and 1985? (See chapters IV and VII.)

Process. How are most conversions accomplished and financed? What roles do various actors play in the conversion process and what market and other factors influence their behavior? How does the conversion process vary among different buildings and different cities? (See chapter III.)

Causes. How do housing market conditions, financial incentives, and other factors influence the volume of conversion activity? (See chapter V.)

Demand. Who wants to own and live in converted condominiums or cooperatives? Why do others decide not to buy? (See chapter VI.)

Impacts. What are the effects of conversion on renters and the rental market? What are the effects of conversion activity on the buildings, neighborhoods, and communities where it occurs? (See chapters VII, VIII, and IX.)

Responses. What have been the responses of tenants to conversion? (See chapter IX.) What have been the responses of Federal, state, and local governments to conversion activity? (See chapters X, XI, and XII.)

# Chapter II
# The Study Approach

The recency of the conversion phenomenon means that there is neither a body of research, nor any model, for studying its incidence, causes, or impacts at the national level. Specifically, there is no generally accepted definition of conversions and no national data base with which to estimate their numbers and geographic distribution. In addition, no previous efforts have been made at the national level to relate the occurrence of conversions to other housing market phenomena. Consequently, although some press reports have provided dramatic examples of conversions' impacts on individual households and local studies have provided some information on a limited number of municipalities, there has been little methodological guidance for a study of the scope undertaken here.

Given these circumstances, the research challenge has been to develop and execute an original methodology that provides answers to the many questions that are asked concerning conversion, and to do so within the six months allotted by Congress.

The research approach adopted to meet this challenge was to begin by collecting basic data on buildings converted, the number of units they contained, and their locations. In an effort to maximize both breadth and depth, data were collected on a national sample for issues that required such coverage and in larger metropolitan areas only for those questions requiring an indepth metropolitan-level focus. For instance, analyses of the conversion process and the causes of conversion rely on detailed information for the nation's 37 largest metropolitan areas. Analysis of conversion impacts is based primarily on intensive data collection in 12 SMSAs with high levels of conversion activity. Greatest attention has been paid to the questions raised by the Congress; however, other major issues have been addressed as time and resources have allowed. Thus, some questions are answered in considerable detail, whereas others are addressed only in an exploratory fashion.

The remainder of this chapter provides a non-technical overview of methods and sources, linking these with specific research issues and questions. Appendix 2 of this report provides a thorough technical explanation of each of the methods reviewed here. The data sources and methodologies can be divided into four categories:

  (1)  An in-person survey of current and former households in building units which have been or are in the process of being converted;

  (2)  Interviews with federal, state, and local officials;

(3) Field visits by HUD staff to 37 SMSAs during which about 400 personal interviews were held with local experts from both the private and public sectors; and

(4) Existing data sources, including the Annual Housing Survey, other Census data, legal documents, HUD and other Federal program-related data, and existing research on conversions.

Table II-1 is a matrix of major issues (and the chapters of this report in which they are addressed) by type and importance of information source. The remaining sections of this chapter describe in more detail each of these information sources and issues relating to their use.

In-Person Survey of Households

Several questions in this study could be adequately addressed only by conducting a survey of those households directly affected by conversion. Questions were posed to these households in order to ascertain: What kinds of people buy converted condominiums or cooperatives? Why do they buy? What is their overall level of satisfaction with their purchase? What proportion of rental tenants does not buy? And, why do they not buy? Do they have difficulty in finding alternative housing when they move? What costs are involved? How many people buy but do not live in the units?

As indicated in chapter I, several local surveys of households affected by conversion have been conducted, but no broader-based survey exists to date. 1/ Therefore, for this study, an in-person survey of households

---

1/ In various localities and states, formal studies have been conducted to determine the incidence and impacts of conversions. Most of these investigations have one or more of the following characteristics: (1) they generally focus on a limited geographic area, usually a single jurisdiction or neighborhood; (2) many studies rely on a small sample of those affected by conversion, or they contain limited amounts of data and hard evidence; and (3) they often examine questions which relate to the interests of the particular group sponsoring or conducting the study, leaving unanswered many other questions about conversion. The following are typical of such state and local studies:

In Evanston, Illinois, a 1978 study conducted for the city's Human Relations Commission surveyed 51 tenants in buildings being converted and 326 owners in new or converted condominiums. The study compared the characteristics of tenants renting in buildings with those purchasing units in such buildings. It also attempted to estimate the proportion of tenants likely to purchase, satisfaction levels of purchasers, and the reasons why some tenants did not purchase.

## TABLE II-1
## Information Sources

| Question/Issue | In-Person Survey of Households | Telephone Surveys of Local Officials | Field Visits to 37 SMSA's | Existing Data Research |
|---|---|---|---|---|
| Description of Conversion Process (Chapter 3) | | | **X** | X |
| Estimates of Past and Future Conversion Activity (Chapter 4) | | **X** | **X** | X |
| Causes of Conversions:<br>— Housing Supply and Financial Conditions (Chapter 5) | | | X | **X** |
| — Demand-Related Factors (Chapter 6) | **X** | | X | X |
| Impacts of Conversions on:<br>— Rental Supply (Chapter 5) | | | X | **X** |
| — Local Tax Revenues (Chapter 7) | | | **X** | X |
| — Housing Stock and Neighborhoods (Chapter 7) | | **X** | **X** | X |
| — Households in Converted Buildings (Chapter 7) | **X** | | X | X |
| Public Sector Response:<br>— Views of Local Officials (Chapter 8) | | **X** | | |
| — Federal, State, and Local Regulations (Chapter 9) | | | **X** | **X** |
| — HUD Programs (Appendix) | | | | **X** |

Note

**X** Primary Information Source

X Secondary Information Source

was undertaken during January 1980 in 12 SMSAs with high levels of
conversion activity between 1977 and 1979, the period in which most
of the decade's conversions occurred.  Comprehensive lists of all
properties converted in the 1977-79 period were obtained from the
following SMSAs in September 1979;

|                        |                        |
|------------------------|------------------------|
| Boston                 | Minneapolis-St. Paul   |
| Chicago                | New York               |
| Denver-Boulder         | San Francisco-Oakland  |
| Houston                | Seattle-Everett        |
| Los Angeles-Long Beach | Tampa-St. Petersburg   |
| Miami                  | Washington, D.C.       |

From those lists, a sampling frame was developed which yielded
an equal probability sample of 280 converted buildings in the 12
SMSAs. 2/

---

In San Francisco, a study on condominium conversions
was done jointly by the Department of City Planning
and members of the local real estate industry.  Postal
surveys were conducted of 266 condominium owners and
304 tenants in buildings being converted.  Like the
Evanston research, this study investigated the differences between renters and purchasers.

In New York State, the Temporary Commission on Rental Housing
issued, as part of its mandate, a volume on the conversion
of residential property to condominium or cooperative status
in light of current and proposed state statutes.  Included
as part of the volume are sections on:  the legal mechanics
of the conversion process; the authority and role of the
N.Y. State Attorney General's Office; statistical analysis
of residential conversion plans; and a detailed analysis
of tenants rights under various regulations within the state.

In Brookline, Massachusetts, a study of conversions focused
on households living in rent controlled apartments and
households who purchased converted units.  The report looks
at, among other things, the reasons why people purchase
condominiums, the nature and impacts of the conversion process
on existing tenants, and the potential impact of conversion on
tenants and on Brookline's tax revenues.

2/ Subsequently, more reliable conversion figures were obtained which
indicated that, while the original 12 SMSAs had very high levels of
activity, they did not constitute those with the highest amount of
activity.  The 12 highest-activity SMSAs include Cleveland and
Philadelphia but exclude Seattle-Everett and Tampa-St. Petersburg.
In number of conversions, the latter two are ranked 13th and 14th,
respectively.

The sample is representative of households affected by conversions
in the 12 SMSAs, which represent 60 percent of all conversion activity in the country.

Two groups of households were surveyed:  (1) those currently residing
in buildings which have been converted or are in the process of converting (at least one, but not all sales must have been completed
between January 1, 1977 and December 31, 1979); and (2) those households who moved from converted buildings as a result of conversion.

Current Residents.  A total of 861 households within the first group
(current residents) were interviewed.  These households comprise four
distinct groups:

    (1)  Tenant Buyers:  current residents who rented a
         unit prior to conversion and purchased a unit at
         the time of conversion;

    (2)  Continuing Renters:  current residents who rented
         a unit prior to conversion and have continued renting
         in the building after conversions;

    (3)  Outside Buyers:  current residents who purchased and
         moved into a unit after the building was converted,
         and

    (4)  New Renters:  current residents who moved into a unit
         after conversion but who rent rather than own.

A comprehensive description of sampling issues and the various steps
involved in the field survey operations is presented in Appendix 2.

Former Residents.  A representative sample of 301 former resident
households was also interviewed.  This includes households who had
resided in buildings converted during 1978 or 1979 but who had moved
out of the buildings before January 1980, when interviews were conducted. 3/  The purpose of this survey was to ask former residents
about their reasons for not purchasing converted units and their
experiences in finding other housing after they moved from the
converted building.

Locating and interviewing former residents is a costly and time con-
suming task.  The first step in the process, which proved to be
particularly difficult, was to obtain the names of former tenants
who had resided in a pre-selected sample of units.  These names were

---

3/ A sub-sample of units in buildings was taken from the 1977-79
sample in order to interview former residents whose experiences
in locating other housing reflected more current rental market
conditions.

obtained from previous landlords, various directories, neighbors, and real estate or management companies which had been involved in the conversion or which managed the building for the condominium owners association. Once the names were obtained, households were traced to their current addresses using numerous sources, including: building managers; current occupants of the converted building; standard and criss-cross telephone directories; city directories; and the Post Office. A detailed description of the sampling and tracking procedure is provided in Appendix 2.

## Interviews with Local, State and Federal Officials

Local, state, and Federal officials served as another source of information on a variety of issues. 4/ Two sets of interviews were conducted at the local level. The first was a national telephone survey of mayors, county executives, or their designees, conducted in December 1979 and January 1980, to elicit their views on the causes and impacts of conversions on their jurisdictions. A second set of telephone interviews was conducted with local planning and housing officials in February 1980 to assess their views about the impacts of conversions on individual neighborhoods in their jurisdctions. In addition, Federal and state departments and agencies were contacted at various times throughout the study for information on legislation, regulations and programs.

Interviews with Mayors and County Executives. Mayors, county executives, or their delegates were asked a variety of questions tapping their perceptions of the salience of the conversion issue in their jurisdictions, its causes, and both positive and negative impacts. They were also asked a series of questions on the current and antici pated local response, if any, to conversion activity as well as their positions on regulatory issues. Calls were made to 347 mayors and 106 county executives.

The types of communities covered in the survey include the following:

---

4/ As part of the planning for this research, a conference coordinated by the Urban Consortium, a national research organization for the Nation's largest cities and urban counties, was attended by HUD research staff and officials from Atlanta, Boston, Chicago, San Francisco, Seattle, and Washington, D.C. A second conference, coordinated by the Joint Center for Urban Studies of Harvard University and the Massachusetts Institute of Technology, was held to discuss research design issues and study approaches. Participants included HUD research staff and several scholars from universities and consulting firms.

(1) The central cities of the 37 largest SMSAs, those SMSAs in which most of the conversion activity had taken place. The 48 central cities associated with the SMSAs were included in the sample with certainty;

(2) The remaining jurisdictions, i.e., cities, counties, and New England towns, located within the 37 largest SMSAs;

(3) All other cities with a 1970 population of 25,000 or more; and

(4) The remaining jurisdictions, i.e., counties and New England towns, associated with these cities of 25,000 or more in stratum (3). 5/

These four groups comprise about 77 percent of the Nation's 1970 population. A more detailed description of sampling issues is provided in Appendix 2.

Local Planning Officials. A second round of telephone interviews was conducted in February, 1980 with local planning officials in the 18 central cities of the 12 SMSAs with high levels of conversion activity.

These interviews were to elicit information on neighborhood characteristics and the impact of conversions on these neighborhoods, since 1970 Census information was considered too dated to provide an accurate picture of current neighborhood characteristics. 6/

---

5/ The telephone survey was also used to estimate the volume of conversions outside the 37 largest SMSA, complementing data obtained on the 37 largest SMSAs through field visits. Therefore, for sample sites outside the 37 SMSAs, (that is, strata (3) and (4)) two interviews were conducted, one with the local chief executive and another with an official knowledgeable about the volume of activity, such as an assessor or planner. These latter interviews focused on more specific questions concerning current and projected (1980 to 1985) conversion activity.

6/ Prior to contacting these officials, census tract numbers were obtained for locations of all converted buildings in each of the central cities. These were used as a basis of discussions of neighborhood characteristics and impacts.

The officials were also asked to discuss any neighborhood changes which had occurred as a result of conversion activity. Based on these interviews and other available data, demographic and housing profiles were developed for those neighborhoods containing conversion activity. These profiles serve as a data source for the analysis of conversion-related neighborhood and housing issues presented in chapter VIII.

Federal and State Officials. State and Federal agencies were contacted to obtain information on conversion-related legislation, regulations, and programs. For example, officials from the Veterans Administration and the Farmers Home Administration were interviewed concerning their agencies' programs pertaining to condominiums and cooperatives, and from the Securities and Exchange Commission concerning their regulations regarding the two forms of homeownership. Issues related to the financing of condominiums were discussed with officials of the Federal Home Loan Mortgage Corporation, the Government National Mortgage Association, and the Federal National Mortgage Association. In addition, various representatives of state government, such as attorney general's offices, legislative research office, and real estate departments, were contacted to discuss recent developments concerning conversion. 7/

Staff Visits to 37 SMSAs

To obtain information not available through other means, HUD staff conducted a two-phased field study. The first phase took place in September 1979, when staff members visited the 12 high-activity SMSAs in which the household survey was eventually conducted. During these visits, comprehensive lists and addresses of buildings which had been, or were in the process of being converted between 1977 and 1979, were compiled. These lists comprised the universe from which the sample of converted buildings was drawn. In compiling these lists, a large number of sources were used. Because of the variation across SMSAs in the regulations affecting the conversion process, the types of sources differed considerably across jurisdictions. In New York, for example, the information is centralized in the New York State Attorney General's Office. Information on converted

---

7/ Many members of national organizations in the private sector were also interviewed. These groups included those backing real estate and banking concerns and those representing neighborhood and tenants' interests. During this first field trip, staff members also held preliminary interviews with selected individuals, both in the private and public sector, and obtained information on state laws and local ordinances which had been enacted or were being considered for passage

properties is also centrally located in Florida, but in the State
Division of Land Sales and Condominiums.  In most other areas, however, the information is not centrally maintained, and may not be
accessible at all from public sources.  In Chicago, where the greatest
number of conversions have occurred, a local title company is considered to have reliable figures but even it does not have an easily
accessible list of building names and addresses.  These were obtained
from a private real estate consulting firm and cross-checked with
other lists obtained from other sources.  For other SMSAs, lists of
properties were often obtained from more than one source, including
Offices of the Recorder of Deeds; county or city assessors; city,
county, or regional planning officials; developers; and various
housing market experts.  These procedures are discussed in Appendix 2.

The second stage of the field study took place in November, 1979,
during which staff members conducted intensive interviews in the
Nation's 37 largest metropolitan areas (each of which had an estimated population of one million or more persons as of 1977, the
latest date for which these population figures are available).
See figure II-1 for the names of those SMSAs which were visited.
Discussions were held with over 400 individuals either involved in
the conversion process or having specific knowledge about this phenomenon.  Interviewees included, among others, real estate brokers and
lawyers, tenant groups, bankers, developers, landlords, researchers,
local government officials, and housing market specialists.  These
semi-structured interviews tapped a variety of local opinions about
the factors driving conversions in their housing markets, the various
impacts of conversions, and local policy preferences related to the
issue of rental conversion.  Some quantitative and a great deal of
qualitative information were gleaned from these interviews, which are
used to illustrate or highlight particular findings.

Detailed notes on each SMSA were prepared following the field study.
Although they are not intended as comprehensive case studies of condominium and cooperative conversion activity in these metropolitan
areas areas, they provide a rich body of information about interarea variations in the conversion phenomenon.  These field notes are
included in Appendix 1, and the names of persons with whom discussions
were held can be found in Appendix 2.

## Existing Data Sources

The fourth category of information includes all existing or secondary
data sources.  This type of information is used in a variety of ways
throughout the report.  Studies of conversion activity conducted by
groups such as consulting firms, state and local governments, and
interest groups are used to suggest hypotheses and/or confirm findings derived from the primary data collected and analyzed for this
report.

Figure II-1

# The Nation's 37 Largest SMSAs* in Which Field Research Was Conducted

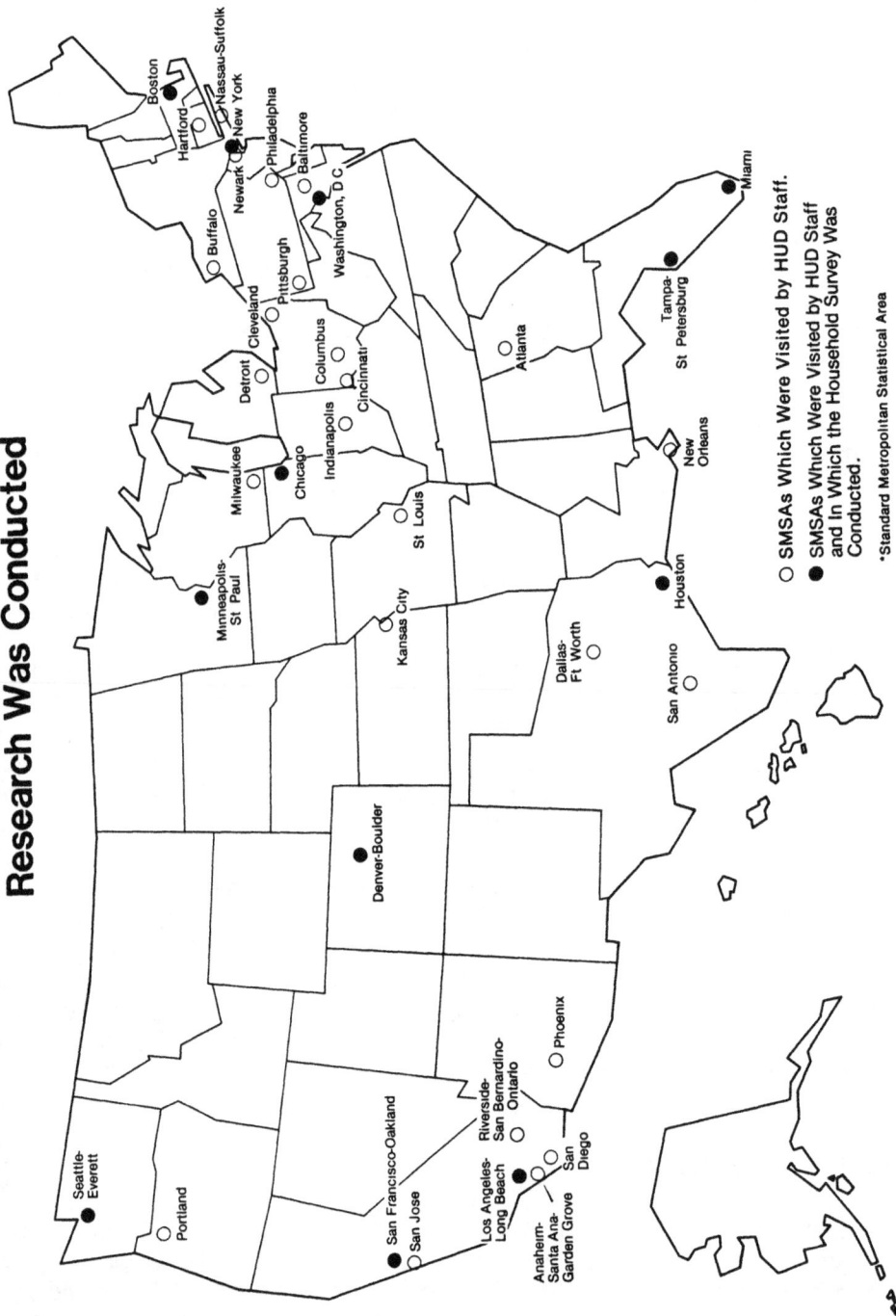

○ SMSAs Which Were Visited by HUD Staff.

● SMSAs Which Were Visited by HUD Staff and In Which the Household Survey Was Conducted.

*Standard Metropolitan Statistical Area

The Annual Housing Survey, 8/ conducted by the Bureau of the Census in conjunction with HUD, is a major source of information for the analysis presented in chapter V on the relationship between housing markets and conversions.  Secondary analysis of Annual Housing Survey data for 32 of the 37 largest SMSAs is used to describe the housing stock, and general housing market conditions such as the vacancy rate and the average rent level. 9/

In the analysis of Federal, state, and local responses to the conversion phenomenon, presented in Part 4 of this report, numerous Federal, state, and local legal documents were reviewed and categorized.  In addition, program documents from HUD, as well as those from other Federal agencies whose programs are related to condominiums and cooperatives, were examined.

* * *

This chapter has presented the various methods and data sources including personal and telephone interviews, legal and program documents, Census data and field visits, which are used to analyze the issues outlined in chapter I.  Chapter III describes the conversion process and comprises the remainder of Part I, "The Dynamics of Conversion."

---

8/ The Annual Housing Surveys of 1974, 1975 and 1976 were used for this report.

9/ The Annual Housing Survey did not include information for the following SMSAs:  Hartford, Nassau-Suffolk, San Antonio, San Jose, and Tampa-St. Petersburg.

# Chapter III
# The Conversion Process

Converting multi-family rental housing to condominium or cooperative ownership is an expensive, complicated, and time-consuming task involving many individuals and organizations. It is a difficult procedure to summarize, since no "typical" process applies to all conversions. As Exhibit III-1 indicates, 12 different types of conversions are possible, depending upon: whether the units are converted to condominiums or cooperatives; the extent of rehabilitation accompanying the conversion; and whether the conversion is done by the original landlord, a developer, or the tenants themselves. Data collected for this study indicate that each of the 12 types has occurred, but the most common type by far is a condominium conversion, done by a developer who performs minor rehabilitation to the building. 1/ The frequency with which the other types of conversion take place is discussed under "Conversion Managers," below.

## Exhibit III-1

| | | | |
|---|---|---|---|
| Units Converted to **Condominium** by **Landlord** With **Minor** Renovation | Units Converted to **Condominium** by **Landlord** With **Major** Renovation | Units Converted to **Cooperative** by **Landlord** With **Minor** Renovation | Units Converted to **Cooperative** by **Landlord** With **Major** Renovation |
| Units Converted to **Condominium** by **Developer** With **Minor** Renovation | Units Converted to **Condominium** by **Developer** With **Major** Renovation | Units Converted to **Cooperative** by **Developer** With **Minor** Renovation | Units Converted to **Cooperative** by **Developer** With **Major** Renovation |
| Units Converted to **Condominium** by **Tenants** With **Minor** Renovation | Units Converted to **Condominium** by **Tenants** With **Major** Renovation | Units Converted to **Cooperative** by **Tenants** With **Minor** Renovation | Units Converted to **Cooperative** by **Tenants** With **Major** Renovation |

---

1/ Unless otherwise noted, references to a "building" also include garden or townhouse style rental complexes.

Although the process associated with each type of conversion is somewhat different, four steps usually occur: (1) obtaining financing; (2) selecting and, usually, rehabilitating a building; (3) complying with government regulations; and (4) marketing the units and relinquishing control of the building to an owners association. 2/ The order in which these steps take place varies considerably from conversion to conversion. To some extent the variability depends on the type of conversion, but differences can also be attributed to the practices of financial institutions, the extent and nature of government regulation, and the market for converted units.

## Factors Which Affect the Type of Conversion

Three basic factors determine the type of conversion that is undertaken: the ownership arrangement -- either condominium or cooperative; the renovation which takes place -- either minor or major; and the conversion manager -- either landlord, developer, or tenant group.

Ownership Arrangement. Conversion to condominium ownership differs from a cooperative conversion in several respects. A person who buys a condominium owns the unit as well as a proportionate share of the common areas; therefore, the purchase is considered a real estate transaction. The condominium owner is responsible for paying the principal and interest on any mortgage loan made to buy the unit; the cost of maintaining the individual unit; a portion of the operating and maintenance expense for the common elements including any utilities not individually metered; any association fees or dues; and, in some cases, contributions to a reserve fund used to finance major repairs to the building. In addition, special assessments may be levied on condominium owners if the reserve fund cannot meet the cost of needed improvements.

Unlike condominium ownership, a person joining a cooperative housing corporation does not purchase a housing unit but, rather, a share in the corporation which owns the entire building; therefore, the transaction is considered a stock transfer. The share entitles the cooperative member to enter into a proprietary lease 3/ which permits the owner to live in a particular unit and use the building's common areas. The cooperative member is responsible

---

2/ The common features in the conversion process were discovered during interviews with developers and other participants in the conversion process.

3/ A proprietary lease (also called an occupancy agreement) gives a shareholder an exclusive right to occupy a particular unit and specifies the rules and regulations governing the occupancy. This document also obligates a cooperative member to pay a proportionate share of the principal and interest on the blanket mortgage and other expenses related to the operation of the cooperative.

for paying the principal and interest on any mortgage loan or
consumer loan made to purchase the share; 4/ a portion of the
operating and maintenance expense, including any utilities
not individually metered; any dues or fees owed the cooperative
corporation; and contributions to the reserve fund.  In addition,
the cooperative member must make a pro rata contribution (usually
each month) to the principal and interest for the blanket mortgage
covering the entire building.  Unlike a condominium, when major
repairs to the cooperative are needed, the blanket mortgage may be
refinanced to meet their cost.  A condominium property then has
individual unit mortgages (unless cash is paid for a unit).  A
cooperative has a blanket mortgage on the entire building and,
in many cases, mortgages for shares held by individual owners. 5/

| | |
|---|---|
| A Person Buying a *Condominium* Owns a Unit and a Proportionate Share of the Common Areas. | A Person Joining a *Cooperative* Owns a Share in the Cooperative Housing Corporation Which Owns the Entire Building. |

Further differences exist between the two forms of multiple
ownership.  Condominium conversions are regulated to a much greater
extent than cooperative conversions, except in New York (where the
cooperative form of multiple ownership predominates), the District
of Columbia and California (which have regulated cooperative conversions only since 1979 and 1980, respectively).  In the past,
one result of limited regulation was that the costs associated
with a cooperative conversion were somewhat less than those for

---

4/  Since cooperative shares are considered stock rather than real
estate, financial institutions, until recently, would not make long
term loans for their purchase.  Purchasers of cooperative shares
had to pay cash, finance the cost through a consumer loan or, when
permitted by the cooperative board of directors, make installment
payments to the cooperative corporation.  In 1971, the New York
State Legislature authorized lending institutions in that state to
make long-term mortgage loans for cooperative shares.  This is
probably one reason New York cooperatives became so popular in the
1970s and why most cooperatives are in this state.  In 1979, the
Federal Home Loan Bank Board authorized savings and loan associations
throughout the country to make cooperative mortgage loans.  Little
use has been made of this authority, because it was granted just
at the time interest rates began their rapid increase.

5/  For purposes of this chapter, the two types of mortgages will
be called a "blanket mortgage" and a "cooperative mortgage."

III-4

converting a building to a condominium.  A slight savings is still
realized by purchasers of a cooperative share, since the cost of
transferring stock is not as high as the closing costs for a real
estate transaction in most jurisdictions.

If the owner of a cooperative share is unable to sell the cooperative
stock when desired, the cooperative corporation sometimes buys the
share.  In fact, cooperative corporations often have a right of
first refusal for all shares, i.e., a cooperative member must give
the corporation an opportunity to buy the stock before it is offered
to others.  The owner of a condominium does not usually have this
option if the unit cannot be sold. 6/

When a conversion is completed, both the unit owners in a condominium
and the shareholders in a cooperative form organizations which are
governed by an elected board of directors.  In cooperatives, the
board of directors is given more discretion than the condominium
board, especially regarding who may join the cooperative.  Potential
share buyers may not be barred for any reason which violates civil
rights laws, but they may be rejected if the board decides, for
example, that their income is not sufficient to meet the costs of
living in the cooperative.  Cooperative corporations are particularly
concerned about a shareholder's ability to make payments toward the
blanket mortgage on the building, since a default on the cooperative's
blanket mortgage may occur if a large number of members are unable
to make payments. 7/  A condominium owner may usually sell a unit to
any qualified purchaser.  In addition, condominium boards generally
permit investors who own condominiums to rent the units to third
parties.  Few cooperative boards allowed investor ownership of
shares in the past; recently, however, a few cooperatives have
permitted investor ownership and rental of units.

Extent of Renovation.  Most buildings are renovated to some degree
during the conversion process.  It is estimated that minor renovations are made to about 75 percent of the buildings in central
cities and 85 percent of those in the suburbs.  The remaining
buildings undergo some form of major rehabilitation. 8/  For purposes
of this report, minor rehabilitation includes so-called "cosmetic"
or "as is" conversions.  Renovations are limited to painting,

---

6/  Although a right of first refusal may be included in the declaration of condominium or in a condominium's bylaws, condominium
associations seldom exercise this option.

7/  One New York City market expert interviewed for this study
commented that in New York only one cooperative had defaulted on its
mortgage in recent history.  However, the concern is prevalent and
cooperative corporations still fear this possibility of default.

8/  U.S. Department of Housing and Urban Development, Survey of Current
and Former Residents of Converted Buildings, December 1979 and January
1980.

carpeting, making minimal repairs to mechanical systems and structural features, improving landscaping, refurbishing recreational
facilities, and upgrading parking areas. Major rehabilitation
may involve all the "cosmetic" improvements as well as the substantial repair or replacement of one or more major mechanical systems,
significant structural alterations, or the complete gutting and
reconstruction of a building's interior. (See chapter VIII for
additional information regarding renovations.)

Conversion Managers. 9/ A high proportion of the rental buildings
that are converted are changed to condominium ownership, and most
conversions are carried out by developers. 10/ A developer is
more likely than a landlord to convert a building since, under
Federal tax laws, a landlord who converts and sells individual
units would be considered a dealer in real estate. Profits earned
would be treated as ordinary income and taxed at a relatively high
rate. If, however, a landlord's property is sold to a developer
who then converts and sells the units, the landlord's profits are
considered a capital gain and are taxed at a rate much lower than
that for ordinary income. (Chapter V discusses in more detail a
landlord's incentives to sell a building for conversion.)

Developers who handle condominium conversions operate on a national,
regional, or local level. National developers are few in number and
appear to handle only high-quality buildings which can be converted
and sold rapidly. Some national developers started their operations
in Chicago and, with the expertise gained in this high activity
area, expanded into other major metropolitan areas. Two Canadian-
based firms also operate on a national level in the U.S. Regional
developers are similar to national developers in that they began
their activity in one city and then moved into other markets. However, regional developers usually limit their expansion to nearby
cities or SMSAs. For example, some Los Angeles-based developers
have completed conversions in San Jose. The largest share of
condominium conversions are carried out by locally-based developers.
These developers are also responsible for most of the conversions
requiring major rehabilitation. 11/

---

9/ For purposes of this chapter, all individuals and groups --
whether developers, landlords, or tenants -- will be referred to as
"conversion managers."

10/ Developers who convert buildings to condominiums are becoming
an important segment of the real estate development industry, as
shown by the fact that a national trade association was formed in
1979 to represent the interests of these developers.

11/ U.S. Department of Housing and Urban Development, Field
Interviews in 37 SMSAs Conducted by HUD Staff. September and
November 1979.

Regardless of their geographic scope, many developers form separate, limited partnerships for each conversion project they undertake. Individual partnerships are established so that any liability arising from one venture will not extend to a developer's subsequent business activity. Under a limited partnership, the developer, as the general partner, has overall responsibility for completing the conversion and is legally liable for the full amount of any financial losses incurred. Financial institutions, investors, and sometimes employees of the developer join as limited partners. Except for the employees (who may be offered the limited partnership as a work incentive bonus), these participants do not play a major role in the conversion process and view their involvement as an investment.

Developers cite the typical advantages to the limited partnership as their reason for using this form of business: (1) limited partners are responsible for financial losses only up to the amount of their investment; and (2) profits earned by the partnership are not taxed until they are distributed to individual partners, and are then usually taxed as ordinary income. This is in contrast to the corporate form, under which earnings are first taxed as corporate profits and then again as income when distributed to the stockholders of the corporation. Some developers have also entered into joint venture partnerships with financial institutions, former owners of buildings being converted, construction contractors, and investors. Again, a primary intent is to avoid the double taxation associated with the corporate form of business.

Unlike condominium conversions, very few cooperative conversions are managed by developers. 12/ Those developer conversions which do occur are found in areas -- such as Washington, D.C. and the San Francisco suburbs -- where condominium conversion is heavily regulated. In 1980, California extended its state condominium law to cooperatives; and thus, developers in that state may find that cooperative conversions are no longer easier to perform. Washington, D.C. has a law regulating cooperative conversion, but it is not nearly as stringent as the city's condominium regulations. In other respects, including their use of limited partnerships, cooperative developers are very similar to condominium developers.

Despite the apparent tax disadvantages, some landlords have converted buildings to condominiums rather than sell to developers. This is an infrequent occurrence, but appears to be increasing as landlords become more familiar with condominium conversions. Landlords claim that the additional profit realized by eliminating the middleman offsets the higher tax liability. Real estate brokers often assist landlords with

---

12/ Most cooperative conversions take place in New York, where the landlord, as opposed to a developer, actually manages the process. A discussion of landlord-managed cooperative conversions appears later in this chapter.

conversions, but other than this business relationship, landlords usually operate as entrepreneurs or under the same form of business they used when the converted building was a rental.

As mentioned, most cooperative conversions occur in New York, and a large share of them are carried out by a building's landlord. Under these circumstances, the landlord -- whether an individual or a real estate partnership -- becomes the "sponsor" of the conversion. A real estate lawyer or other professional in the field (referred to as a "broker") actually handles most of the day-to-day work related to the conversion. To receive capital gains tax treatment of profits, the sponsor/landlord sells the converted building to the cooperative corporation which, in turn, sells shares representing individual units. Sponsors selling the shares directly would be considered securities dealers and possibly liable to the higher ordinary income tax rate. During the conversion process, the landlord/sponsor generally retains the same form of business organization under which the building was rented.

Tenants have successfully managed condominium conversions in Evanston, Illinois, where one small building was converted, and in Washington, D.C., where ten buildings have been converted by tenants. In fact, tenant managed condominium conversions are becoming so popular in Washington that local firms with conversion experience have been placing newspaper ads offering their services to tenants wishing to buy and convert their building. Future condominium conversions are being planned by tenants in Cleveland, Minneapolis, Washington, D.C. and Montgomery County, Maryland, a Washington suburb. Tenant conversions are particularly popular in Washington and Montgomery County because of local ordinances giving tenants the right to purchase a building before it is offered to other buyers. 13/

To carry out a conversion, tenants incorporate as a non-profit organization, legally capable of holding real estate. On completing the conversion, this organization dissolves, and tenants who buy units, along with other purchasers, form the condominium association. Tenant associations generally hire a condominium developer to actually carry out the conversion, but the tenant association, particularly the Board of Directors, has overall responsibility for the process.

---

13/ Field Interviews, op. cit. In Chicago, tenants in one building organized in response to rumors that their building was to be converted The group raised money, entered the highest bid to purchase the building, and pre-sold units to current occupants. Nevertheless, the bank receiving the bids claimed the group's offer was not in proper form and awarded the building to a developer who made a lower bid. The tenants immediately offered to buy out the developer, giving him a $200,000 to $300,000 profit. This offer was turned down. No other examples of unsuccessful attempts by tenants to buy and convert their buildings were found in field interviews.

Within the category of tenant-managed cooperative conversions, there are market rate and limited equity cooperatives. 14/ The first type of tenant formed cooperative is most prevalent and is found most often in New York and in Washington, D.C. Under this form, a tenant group incorporates as a nonprofit corporation for the duration of the conversion process and becomes the sponsor of the conversion. Lawyers, brokers, consultants and other real estate professionals assist tenants in the conversion. When conversion is nearly completed, the tenant association dissolves and all potential shareholders re-incorporate as a cooperative corporation.

Limited equity cooperatives are also established by tenants, but their incomes are usually at a much lower level than those of tenants who form market rate cooperatives. Low income tenants also incorporate as a nonprofit corporation to manage the conversion process, but the assistance they receive in supervising the conversion is more diverse than that obtained by higher income tenants. Most limited equity cooperatives have substantial governmental involvement. Federal assistance may be in the form of below-market interest rate mortgage loans, mortgage insurance, and rehabilitation loans. State and local governments provide similar help, as well as offer technical aid, front-end subsidies to share buyers, and partial down payments. Private sector participation, particularly by church groups and community organizations, may also be extensive. 15/

When conversion to a limited equity cooperative is completed, the tenant association reincorporates as a cooperative corporation and sells shares. The price at which the shares are initially sold is determined by the board of directors in accordance with a procedure outlined in the corporate bylaws. If government or private sector involvement in the future operation of the cooperative is extensive, the responsible entity may have a significant say in the sales prices. Similarly, when shares are resold, the board of directors and any other participants set the resale value. Usually, the sales price permits only a small increase over the original purchase price to account for inflation and any improvements made to the shareholder's

---

14/ A "limited equity" cooperative is one whose corporate bylaws regulate the resale value of membership shares. The resale price is determined by a formula which considers the original down payment for the share, plus increments to account for inflation, improvements to a unit, and that portion of the blanket mortgage paid by the shareholder.

15/ In 1978, the Federal Government established the National Consumer Cooperative Bank which, among other things, provides technical assistance and mortgage loans to low income housing cooperatives. As of May 1980, the Bank had not yet made loans to finance low-income cooperatives, but is expected to do so soon.

unit. Holding down the resale price is intended to discourage
members from selling shares (particularly when housing values in
the area escalate rapidly) and to give other low to moderate income
households an opportunity to purchase shares at an affordable
price. Limited equity cooperatives are found mainly in New York.
In the late 1970s, a few cooperatives were established in
Minneapolis, Berkely, California, Washington, D.C., and Montgomery
County, Maryland. More limited equity cooperatives are being planned
in these jurisdictions and in Baltimore and Arlington County, Virginia

**Four Steps in the
Conversion Process**

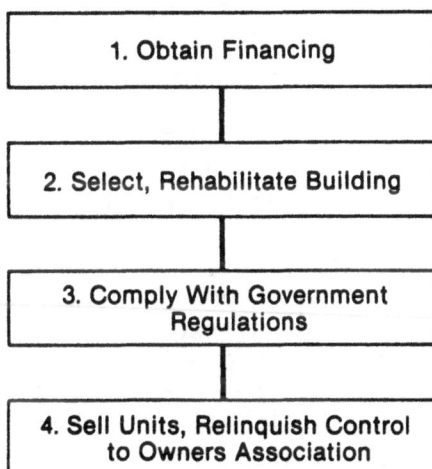

```
┌─────────────────────────────────┐
│     1. Obtain Financing         │
└─────────────────────────────────┘
                │
┌─────────────────────────────────┐
│  2. Select, Rehabilitate Building│
└─────────────────────────────────┘
                │
┌─────────────────────────────────┐
│   3. Comply With Government      │
│          Regulations             │
└─────────────────────────────────┘
                │
┌─────────────────────────────────┐
│ 4. Sell Units, Relinquish Control│
│     to Owners Association        │
└─────────────────────────────────┘
```

1. Obtaining Financing. As with most real estate development,
financing for condominium and cooperative conversions is provided
by a combination of equity and debt. Equity is supplied by the
conversion manager, any partners, and governmental entities; it
generally finances 20 to 25 percent of conversion costs. 16/ Two
forms of debt -- interim and long-term -- cover the balance.
Significant differences exist between the financing arrangements
made for condominium, as opposed to cooperative, conversions.
Therefore, the two financing forms are described separately.

In a condominium conversion an interim loan finances the "hard costs"
of conversion, such as building acquisition and rehabilitation.
"Soft costs" are also met by the interim loan and include fees paid
to attorneys, real estate firms, consultants, engineers, and government bodies. Long-term mortgage loans are made to individuals
buying units in the converted building. The conversion manager is
usually responsible for securing both types of loans.

---

16/ Field Interviews, op. cit. In a few cases developers who undertake conversions may supply more or less equity for a conversion
venture.

Commercial banks make most interim loans and charge interest rates varying from one-half to four points above the prime interest rate. When interest rates rose rapidly in 1979/80, some banks stopped making interim loans for conversions, and others added points 17/ to the overall cost of the loan. The term of the loan generally ranges from three months to three years, depending on the anticipated time required to complete a building's conversion. A clause in the loan instrument usually permits the borrower to repay the interim loan before it is due, although a lender may charge a prepayment penalty for this privilege. Since the interim loan is repaid with funds from the sale of individual units, the borrower has a strong incentive to quickly sell a sufficient number of units to repay the interim loan and thereby reduce the overall carrying costs. To ensure rapid sales, units may be offered to tenants -- and sometimes to outside purchasers -- at discounts averaging from 10 to 20 percent. 18/ Once the interim loan is repaid, the price of the remaining units may be increased, because the proceeds from selling these units represent profits from the conversion venture.

Generally, savings and loan associations, mortgage banks, and mutual savings banks provide the long-term or permanent mortgage loans for individual units. Conversion managers frequently pay a particular lending institution from one-half to two points to ensure that the lender will make all mortgage loans. 19/ Until the prime rate increased substantially in 1979/80, it was also possible to pay an additional point or two to lock-in a set interest rate. Few lenders now follow this practice. 20/

---

17/ A "point" is a payment made to a lender at the time a loan is made and is equal to one percent of the loan amount. The usual reason for charging points is to increase the return to the lender, so that the loan is competitive with other types of loans the lender could make.

18/ Field Interviews, op. cit. In New York, where state law requires that a certain proportion of tenants buy before the conversion proceeds, in a few cases discounts as high as 50 percent have been given to tenants, presumably to induce them to buy units and meet the legal requirement.

19/ Field Interviews, op. cit. Commercial banks make few condominium mortgage loans because most of their funds are concentrated in demand deposits which are not available for long-term mortgage loans. There are exceptions. For example, in Texas, the same commercial bank may provide both interim and long term financing.

20/ U.S. Department of Housing and Urban Development, Telephone Interviews with Developers and Lending Institution Officials in 28 Central Cities, April 1980.

Financial institutions making mortgage loans usually require that the conversion manager have non-binding agreements from a certain percentage of people (usually representing 60 to 80 percent of all units) indicating they wish to buy units in the converted building. A small, refundable payment is typically made by potential purchasers when they enter into the agreement. Not until this "pre-sale" requirement is met will mortgage lenders provide individual borrowers with funds to finalize unit sales. Financial institutions request the pre-sale so that unit mortgages may be sold either to the Federal Home Loan Mortgage Corporation (FHLMC) or the Federal National Mortgage Association (FNMA). Each organization has a pre-sale requirement (usually in the 70 percent range) which must be reached before either one will agree to buy long-term mortgages.

Loans made by mortgage banks may be sold to FNMA for resale in the secondary mortgage market. In addition to the pre-sale requirement, a converted building must comply with FNMA's building condition standards before individual unit mortgages will be bought. One of FNMA's most important requirements is that a substantial majority of the units in a building be owner occupied. This represents an attempt by FNMA to limit investor purchase and subsequent rental of condominiums, which, it is believed, may have a negative effect on the quality of the project.

FHLMC has a role similar to that of FNMA, but FHLMC buys conventional mortgages from savings and loan associations instead of mortgage banks To determine a converted condominium's likelihood of success, FHLMC inspects the building to be converted and its neighborhood. If FHLMC's criteria are not met, it may not buy the mortgages for the building.

It is estimated that from 10 to 15 percent of all condominium mortgages bought by FNMA and FHLMC are for converted condominiums. 21/ Although such mortgages are a small share of total volume for the two organizations, FNMA and FHLMC play an important role in the conversion process. Criteria they establish to reduce their risk in buying condominium mortgages have become, in effect, the industry standards in the field of condominium conversions. (Chapter X presents additional information on FNMA and FHLMC.)

If developers performing condominium conversions are favorably known to local lenders, they usually have no difficulty in obtaining interim or long-term financing. An exception may occur if the developer is carrying out a major rehabilitation (and virtually all conversions needing substantial renovation are performed by developers). Lenders may charge a slightly higher interest rate or add

---

21/ Neither FNMA nor FHLMC maintains records which distinguish between the mortgages they buy for new condominium units and those they buy for converted units. The estimate used was provided by officials of the two organizations in February 1980.

points to the cost of the interim loan because of the developer's greater financial risk. For example, the discovery of unanticipated structural defects may delay the conversion and add to the carrying costs on the interim loan and to the overall expense of the project. If these costs are high, lenders fear the developer may default on the interim loan.

When tenants first began converting buildings to condominiums, lenders in Washington D.C. (where nearly all tenant-managed condominium conversions have occurred) sometimes hesitated in making loans. As the concept proved successful, however, financial institutions became willing to provide both short-term and long-term financing. Tenants who carry out condominium conversions are usually assisted by well known local developers and financial consultants, which tends to reduce lender reluctance. In addition, since tenants convert buildings as nonprofit ventures, the prices tenant-purchasers pay for units are generally below those for other comparable units in the same market. Therefore, the long-term mortgages many tenants require are less than those needed for developer- or landlord-managed conversions of similar buildings. Tenant groups note that this factor helps considerably in obtaining both short-term and long-term financing.

Besides these conventional means of obtaining financing, many tenant associations stage various types of fundraisers to collect money. The proceeds are typically used to cover certain front-end soft costs, such as lawyer and consultant fees. Tenant associations may also accept financial expressions of interest from individuals who are not residents of the building but who wish to purchase units following conversion.

In cooperative conversions, an interim loan may be secured if the conversion is undertaken by a developer or landlord. This loan finances a developer's acquisition and renovation of a building or, in the case of a landlord, only the rehabilitation expenses. When shares are purchased and the building is turned over to the cooperative corporation, the interim loan and any mortgage held by the landlord is usually repaid.

Two forms of long-term financing are needed in cooperative conversions. The first type of loan is obtained by the cooperative corporation and finances that portion of the acquisition costs which are not covered by down payments for shares or the actual sale of shares. If the conversion is being managed by tenants, proceeds from the loan may also cover renovation costs and the retirement of existing mortgages on the building. This long-term loan is secured by a blanket mortgage on the entire building, and the cooperative corporation is the mortgagor.

The second type of long-term financing required is permanent or mortgage loans for the purchase of individual shares in the cooperative. Cooperative mortgages are common only in New York, where state law has permitted them since 1971. 22/ Without a cooperative mortgage, a purchaser must pay cash, make a consumer loan, or when allowed, make installment payments for the share to the cooperative corporation. This lack of mortgage loans is one reason why cooperative ownership has been so rare outside of New York State.

New York lenders are authorized to make cooperative loans at one percentage point above the state usury ceiling (11-1/4 percent as of January 1980). This has, of course, contributed to the popularity of cooperative mortgages. However, when the state usury ceiling was preempted by the Federal government in 1980 because of rapidly increasing interest rates, the cooperative mortgage market came to a virtual halt in New York. Lenders in New York noted that, while they could charge an interest rate which matched the prime rate, many potential borrowers could not qualify for mortgage loans at the higher interest rate. 23/ Since neither FHLMC nor FNMA may purchase cooperative mortgages for resale in the secondary mortgage market, New York lenders who make mortgage loans need not meet any presale requirements or other standards imposed on condominium conversion projects by either of these organizations. 24/

Developers who have converted units to cooperatives have usually done so because of stringent regulation of condominium conversions in their areas of operation. Because these developers often had local reputations as condominium converters, they had little difficulty in obtaining either long-term or short-term financing for the cooperative conversions, despite lender's lack of familiarity with the cooperative form of ownership.

Landlords who convert to cooperatives are almost exclusively located in New York. In obtaining financing, landlord/sponsors must ensure that all requirements of New York State law -- particularly those

---

22/ The Federal Home Loan Bank Board authorized the country's savings and loan associations to make cooperative mortgages in August 1979; however, little use has been made of this authority since it coincided with the rapid rise in interest rates.

23/ Telephone Interviews with Developers and Lending Institutions, op. cit.

24/ The Housing and Community Development Act Amendments of 1979 gave FHLMC authority to study the feasibility of buying cooperative mortgages for resale in the secondary market. FNMA has not yet received a similar authority.

related to the portion of tenants which must agree to purchase shares -- are met. One factor in landlord sponsored cooperative conversions that is increasingly subject to negotiation between landlords and tenants is the degree of renovation made during the conversion process. If landlords perform less work, the size of the blanket mortgage and the cost of individual shares may be reduced considerably.

Tenants who manage conversions to market-rate cooperatives (as opposed to limited equity cooperatives) sometimes experience difficulty in obtaining financing, particularly outside of New York State. The reason for lenders' reluctance may be attributed to either their ignorance of the cooperative concept or their fear that mortgage default is a greater possibility when tenants manage a conversion. An additional factor is that financial institutions cannot sell cooperative mortgages on the secondary mortgage market, because such loans are not technically mortgages. Lenders may have to hold the loans for their full terms, a practice that prudent financial institutions do not favor.

Financing for tenant managed conversion to limited equity cooperatives differs significantly from other types of cooperatives. Government entities and private groups -- principally community organizations, church groups, and nonprofit housing organizations -- frequently help with financing. Assistance has been in the form of below market interest rates for the blanket mortgage, down payment assistance for tenants to buy shares, and grants to finance renovations.

Further, because shares in limited equity cooperatives are priced very low relative to market rate cooperatives (average sales prices range from $500 to $3,000), low-income purchasers usually do not require long-term financing to buy shares. In many instances, too, government programs finance a large portion of the share's purchase price.

During interviews conducted for this study, managers of conversion projects and those who provide professional or governmental assistance frequently mentioned that obtaining financing is the most crucial feature of the conversion process. An illustration of this step's importance occurred during the 1979/80 period of rapidly rising interest rates when few conversion ventures were initiated unless conversion managers already had commitments from lenders for interim and long-term financing at favorable terms. 25/

---

25/ Telephone Interviews with Developers and Lending Institution Officials, op. cit.

2. <u>Selecting and Renovating the Building</u>. Selecting a building
may appear unnecessary in a landlord- or tenant-managed conversion;
however, tenants and landlords examine a building's location and
other features just as a developer does to ensure that it is suitable
for conversion. The following elements are typically considered
in building selection:

**Factors Considered in Selecting a
Building for Conversion**

- ☑ Location
- ☑ Quality of Construction
- ☑ Number of Bedrooms and
     Size of Rooms
- ☑ Age of Building
- ☑ Amenities
- ☑ Remodeling Costs

a. <u>Location</u>: According to conversion managers, an appropriate
location is one with access to public transportation, business dis-
tricts, and shopping. Buildings situated in an historic part of
the city or in a neighborhood with some special ambiance are also
desirable for conversion. This feature is so important to some
developers that they will choose even poor quality buildings for
conversion if they offer superior locations.

b. <u>Quality of Construction</u>: The conversion manager, engineers or
architects usually make a preliminary inspection of a building to
determine if it is sound enough to be converted. If the building
is judged suitable, detailed architectural and engineering studies
are made of its structural and mechanical elements. Problems
discovered in these examinations may eliminate a building from
consideration, particularly if the conversion manager plans a
rapid, relatively inexpensive conversion process.

c. <u>Number of Bedrooms and Size of Rooms</u>: The importance of this
feature varies with the market. In areas where young professionals
comprise a major market segment, buildings with a high proportion of
one bedroom and efficiency units will sell rapidly. Units with two
bedrooms or more are popular in the suburban and retirement

communities because buyers have larger households or want extra
space for guests or for hobby rooms. Smaller rooms are acceptable
if other features -- principally location -- are outstanding. In
other cases, large rooms may be a strong selling point.

d. <u>Age of Building</u>: New buildings (say, less than 20 years old)
are sometimes favored for conversion because their appliances,
mechanical systems, and structural components are more likely to be
in good condition. However, older buildings are selected if they
have been well maintained and if regular repairs or renovations have
been made by the landlord. An additional selection factor for older
buildings is that they may enjoy more favorable locations, be better
constructed, or have more architectural appeal than newer buildings.

e. <u>Amenities</u>: Again, the particular market determines the importance of features such as swimming pools, party rooms, putting greens,
health spas, and saunas. While a swimming pool may be a "must" for
a successful conversion in southern California, a converter operating
in a northeastern city may not consider this amenity to be important.

f. <u>Remodeling Costs</u>: Conversion managers carefully consider the
extent of rehabilitation needed so that the sale prices of units
will not be prohibitive to their intended purchasers.

Developers who specialize in major rehabilitations may choose buildings which would be rejected by other converters. Selection criteria
are different in that these developers often select small, vacant,
abandoned, or dilapidated buildings which can be bought cheaply.
However, developers ensure that the buildings or their neighborhood
offer some aesthetic feature or distinctive charm which will justify
the extremely expensive renovation required. (Chapter VIII discusses
in more detail the types of buildings selected for conversion and
the neighborhoods in which they are located.)

A large share of buildings chosen for conversion require only minor
rehabilitation. Usually, renovations are carried out by subcontract-
ing firms under the direction of a general contractor, the conversion
manager, or developers and brokers hired to assist landlords and
tenant groups. Besides the renovations described earlier, interior
and exterior designers sometimes create a more home-like atmosphere
by placing comfortable furniture, plants, and colorful paintings in
sterile lobbies and by placing shrubbery near parking lots, patio
furniture around swimming pool areas, and picnic tables on grounds
surrounding the building. In garden-style and townhouse complexes,
exterior work sometimes includes minor architectural changes, such
as varied doorways, to give each unit an individualized appearance.

Although renovation is an important part of the conversion process,
purchasers are sometimes given the option of having little renovation
done to reduce the selling price of a unit. When this occurs, the
exterior of the building is refurbished, but individual units are
repaired only to meet local building code standards. Purchasers
decide what improvements they want and pay accordingly.

The speed and care with which rehabilitation is done is important to conversion managers, to tenants (whether buying or moving), and to outside purchasers. If rehabilitation is accomplished rapidly and well, units can be sold sooner, thus reducing the carrying cost of any interim financing.

In addition, tenants who are buying will frequently not endure a pro- tracted remodeling period which might lead to ill-feeling toward the conversion manager. Developers and landlords find, too, that sales to tenants increase after they see first-hand what the rehabilitation is accomplishing. This is desirable since high tenant purchase helps to reduce carrying costs on interim loans and marketing expenses A further benefit to the conversion manager is that tenants who intend to move after conversion may stay in their units as long as possible rather than move when renovation begins. Rent collected from these tenants will bolster a conversion manager's cash flow during periods of heavy outlays. (Chapter IX contains more infor- mation regarding the experiences of tenants living in buildings being converted.)

3. Complying with Government Regulations. The degree to which con- dominium and cooperative conversions are regulated varies across jurisdictions and states. All states have adopted laws related to condominiums (newly built or converted) and one-half impose some additional regulation on conversions. State laws generally also govern the formation of cooperative corporations, although few states or localities regulate cooperative conversions. (Chapters XI and XII contain a description of laws concerning condominium and cooperative conversions.)

Conversion managers generally hire an attorney to ensure that proper legal documentation is filed and that all legal requirements are observed. To legally convert a building to condominium ownership a state or jurisdiction usually requires that a Master Deed or Declara- tion be recorded. A record plat, which describes and graphically depicts the way in which the property is subdivided, and the bylaws for the condominium association generally are filed with the Master Deed. Other legal documents which will be needed at various stages of the conversion process are: purchase agreements for those buying units; individual unit deeds; and a management agreement with the firm operating the building during and after conversion.

Many jurisdictions and states have enacted measures which attempt to restrict condominium conversions or to protect existing tenants and purchasers of units. To comply with these laws, conversion managers often must obtain various government approvals before proceeding with a conversion. It may also be necessary to file a registration statement, offering plan, or disclosure statement before converted units may be sold. 26/

These documents are provided to unit purchasers and sometimes to existing tenants as a form of buyer protection. The most common form of tenant protection offered by law is a notice to tenants that their building is to be converted. Such notices usually indicate a time by which tenants must vacate the unit they occupy. The conversion manager must provide all legal notices in writing; and, although usually not required by law, many developers follow such a notice with a meeting for tenants. During these meetings, a tenant's rights regarding the unit, and any legally mandated form of relocation assistance or financial aid, are explained.

State or local laws sometimes require a conversion manager to provide relocation assistance to tenants moving from converted building. For example, in the Los Angeles SMSA, conversion managers comply with ordinances of some municipalities by providing monetary payments to tenants who move or by helping them to find new housing. One large developer employs a full-time relocation team to assist tenants with moves. Where relocation assistance is not legally required, some conversion managers voluntarily provide this service to tenants. In St. Paul, for example, one developer gave tenants 90 days of free rent in lieu of direct financial aid; and in Hartford, a developer helped a few tenants locate new housing, pay for their move, and make new security deposits.

Besides tenant and consumer protections, several governments have passed statutes aimed at slowing or halting conversions. Some California municipalities prohibit conversion of a building until a certain proportion of existing tenants either agree to the conversion or execute agreements to buy units. New York State has a similar law. Other jurisdictions, again predominantly in California, forbid conversions if the rental vacancy rate falls below a level established by law, or allow only a certain number of units or a set proportion of the multi-family rental supply to be converted each year. The effect of these restrictions may be a delay in the conversion process. For this reason, conversion managers note that complying with government regulations may increase the cost of conversion, particularly by adding to the carrying charges on interim financing.

---

26/ These three documents are similar in that each describes the property being converted and provides information on the individuals carrying out the conversion, unit selling prices, down payment requirements and financing arrangements. Especially in the case of a disclosure statement, details are given on the nature of the defects found in engineering inspections of the building.

In a tenant-managed condominium conversion, the tenant association must incorporate as a legal entity capable of buying real estate. Tenant associations are then responsible for complying with all regulations. Even though the tenant association may be in daily contact with tenants, its board of directors must formally transmit all notices required by law. The tenant association is also responsible for providing any legally mandated relocation assistance to tenants.

To legally convert a building to cooperative ownership, the conversion manager must first organize a cooperative corporation composed of all households buying shares in the cooperative. The households then incorporate in accordance with the appropriate state corporation laws. This procedure involves preparation of legal documents, such as organizational minutes, share certificates, and occupancy agreements or proprietary leases for each member; a corporate charter; and bylaws for the corporation.

Tenant-sponsored cooperative conversions are growing in popularity, principally in the New York and Washington, D.C. SMSAs. In these areas, tenant groups must legally incorporate as a tenant association able to own real estate before proceeding with the planned conversion However, in some limited equity cooperatives with heavy government involvement, tenant groups do not incorporate until they legally form the cooperative corporation. This is because a government entity, rather than a tenant group, is purchasing the building which will eventually be sold to the tenant cooperative corporation.

Most buildings selected for cooperative ownership require and receive only minor renovation. New York State's Offering Plan for converted cooperatives requires a sponsor to disclose every defect in a building planned for conversion, whether discovered by inspectors or engineers employed by the state, the tenants, or the sponsor. Defects do not have to be corrected, but most sponsors repair at least those needed to meet building code standards. Some New York purchasers, especially existing tenants, are willing to accept buildings in "as is" condition in return for a lower sales price.

4. <u>Marketing Units and Relinquishing Control</u>. Many conversion managers aim at a high rate of tenant purchase and market buildings accordingly. If a large proportion of tenants buy units, the pre-sale requirement often needed for financing will be easier to meet; units may be sold faster, reducing the length of the conversion process and the overall carrying cost on any interim loan; and tenants will be less likely to oppose the conversion and take actions which could delay and add to the cost of the conversion process. To ensure high rates of tenant purchase, developers and landlords frequently offer discounts ranging from an average of 10 to 20 percent.

Tenant discounts have benefited many tenants by allowing them to buy units at below-market prices and realize substantial appreciation in the unit's value very quickly. Increasingly, individuals are moving into rental buildings which they believe may convert in order to take advantage of tenant discounts. In some high demand markets where prices of converted units have been appreciating rapidly, real estate investors rent units in a number of buildings in anticipation of conversion. Units are sublet until conversion when the investor, as lessee, may buy the unit at the tenant rate. To avoid this situation, landlords contemplating conversions sometimes stop renting vacant units, rent only on a month-to-month basis, forbid subleases, or limit discounts to those with a tenancy of a set duration. 27/

Conversion managers vary in their marketing approaches to investors. Some developers, especially in the vacation states of Florida and Hawaii, actively seek investor participation. Investors may also be a marketing target if state or local law requires that a number of units be retained for rental by elderly, handicapped or other classes of tenants who may rent investor-held units. Other conversion managers avoid purchases by investors, because they fear potential problems between owner-occupants and an investor's tenants. A second reason for having few investors is the FHLMC and FNMA standard of 80 percent owner occupancy.

Until recently, few cooperative shares were sold to investors because cooperative housing corporations believed tenants to whom investors rented would detract from the cooperative aim of shared housing responsibility. As the distinction between condominiums and cooperatives has blurred in some markets (most notably Washington, D.C.), investor participation has increased. In some instances, cooperative developers have even secured financing for investor purchasers.

The local demand for condominium and cooperatives, of course, greatly affects the marketing stage. In "soft" markets, such as Baltimore and Milwaukee, it is more difficult to sell units to either tenants (despite discounts) or nontenants. Where demand is greater, potential purchasers need few inducements to buy. In a suburb of Washington, D.C., for example, a developer converted a large garden-style complex but was able to keep sales prices relatively low by limiting renovations. It was necessary to hold a lottery so that potential purchasers could be culled from the long list of nontenants wishing to buy.

In areas such as Houston, where rental townhouses have been converted to condominium ownership, conversion managers market the units in the same way as non-condominium townhouses. Since competition is

---

27/  Field Interviews, op. cit.

strong between the two types of townhouses, the condominium concept is underplayed in the marketing phase so that this somewhat different form of ownership does not discourage potential purchasers.

Marketing strategies also differ between individual buildings and townhouse or garden-style complexes. In a single structure, all units usually are marketed simultaneously and sold over a short (say, one-year) period. Garden or townhouse complexes are generally converted and marketed in several phases, with the overall process sometimes spanning five years or more. Often, several units in the complex are renovated and advertised as models to test market public acceptance of the planned conversion. Response to the model units permits the conversion manager to determine the pace at which the remainder of the complex is converted and the households to which advertising and marketing efforts are subsequently directed.

As part of the marketing strategy, most developers and landlords open a sales office on the premises immediately following the announcement of a conversion. They also use meetings and social gatherings with tenants as an opportunity to market units. Emphasis is placed on tenant discounts and the tax advantages of homeownership, while discussion of increased monthly housing costs is minimized. These conversion managers and the sales firms they employ tend to use low-key sales approaches. Tenants note, however, that more forceful tactics (such as repeated telephone calls or false reports on the number of units actually sold) may be used if sales are lagging or if the developer wants a very rapid sellout.

Marketing problems are more likely to occur in a major rehabilitation project than in a conversion requiring only minor repairs. Unforeseen rehabilitation expenses can push the planned sales prices beyond the cost of comparable housing, and it is difficult to show and sell individual units before most renovation is finished. In markets with a heavy demand for totally rehabilitated units, however, developers report that people wishing to buy the units routinely drive through city neighborhoods looking for newly begun conversions. When a building is located, interested parties follow its progress and often make bids for a unit before a firm sales price is set.

Developers and landlords who convert to cooperatives, particularly outside the New York metropolitan area, may have to market the cooperative concept as well as individual shares. Cooperative ownership raises suspicions among potential purchasers who are unfamiliar with it or who prefer buying real estate rather than a share of stock. Conversion managers sometimes attempt to overcome any concern by deemphasizing certain cooperative features and marketing the units as a type of condominium.

In a tenant-managed conversion, very little marketing may be required. Most tenants try to purchase units since the nonprofit nature of tenant-managed conversion allows units to be sold at below-market prices. However, a few units are usually available to nontenant purchasers, and the balance between tenant and nontenant buyers has become a volatile issue in tenant-managed conversions. An example illustrates this point. In a rental building of 40 one-bedroom units, the total acquisition and conversion cost is, say, $2 million. Each unit could then be priced at $50,000 for tenants. (This figure is below the 1979 average price of $71,000 for a condominium in Washington, D.C., where most tenant-managed conversions are occurring.) If 30 tenants wish to buy units, the other 10 units could be sold to outside buyers at a higher price. If the outsider price were increased to $70,000, the selling price to the 30 tenant purchasers could be lowered to about $43,000. Problems have arisen when tenants who have the funds to buy a unit pressure (however subtly) tenants with only a marginal ability to buy to surrender their right to purchase.

Marketing is a minor part of a limited equity cooperative conversion, since members tend to be either tenants living in the building or individuals chosen by government or private organizations to live in the cooperative.

State and local condominium laws specify the time at which the conversion manager must relinquish control of a building to the condominium owners association. Generally, however, when all units are sold and a large percentage of them have gone to closing, the turnover will occur. These same laws also indicate organizing principles for the condominium association, such as the duties and responsibilities of the board of directors. It is typically left to the discretion of individual boards of directors to determine whether households renting in the converted building may join the owners association, as well as their voting powers.

Most developers, it appears, readily complete the turnover at the appropriate time; but there have been a few cases where condominium associations have had to struggle with the developer for control of an association. There are also examples of condominium owners who have lost leverage over a developer once the formal relationship was severed. Promised work was not finished, or it was difficult to have the developer meet certain financial responsibilities. However, in jurisdictions with strong consumer protection regulations, developers generally establish a mechanism for handling problems with items they repaired or replaced during the conversion process.

In a cooperative, a sponsor may relinquish control when the converted building is sold to the cooperative corporation; or, as sometimes happens in New York City, the sponsor may control the corporation for several years following conversion. A sponsor retains control by placing himself or other non-shareholders on the cooperative board before the building is sold to the cooperative corporation.

Since some terms run as long as three years, the sponsor, in effect, can exercise some control over the cooperative even after the conversion is completed. Tenant associations which manage cooperative conversions must dissolve as a legal entity and reincorporate as a cooperative corporation to govern the converted building. Control in many limited equity cooperatives is not fully turned over to the cooperative members but, rather, is shared with government or other sponsoring agencies.

* * *

Multi-family rental buildings are converted to condominium or cooperative ownership in a process which involves at least the four steps just described. Each conversion venture is a unique project, however, which is heavily influenced by elements external to the actual process. Variations within each phase of the conversion process may result from the ownership arrangement, the extent of renovation, and the individual or organization managing the conversion process.

# 2

# Conversions and
# the Housing Market

# Chapter IV
# The Volume and Location
# of Conversion Activity

Both supply and demand factors contribute to condominium and cooperative conversions.  Part II of this report addresses several related
issues concerning these supply and demand relationships.  This chapter
describes the extent and location of conversion activity both in
absolute numbers and as a proportion of the rental supply.  Housing
demand and supply, housing market, and financial conditions which
contribute to the level of conversion activity are examined in chapter
V.  Chapter VI focuses on the composition of demand for conversions,
that is, the types of households who own and rent converted units.
Finally, chapter VII integrates both demand and supply factors in an
analysis of the effect conversions have on the owner and rental
supply and in projecting future conversion activity throughout the
1980-85 period.

The analysis here is based on the most extensive efforts to date to
document the national number of rental housing units converted to
condominium or cooperative ownership between 1970 and 1979.  A brief
description of the methodology and problems encountered in constructing the estimate is given first, followed by a presentation of
national and subnational conversion estimates.  These figures are
then used to compute the proportion of the Nation's rental housing
supply which has, thus far, been converted.

Determining the Number of Conversions

In the past, little reliable information has been available concerning the number of rental units converted to condominium and cooperative ownership throughout the Nation.  A few studies have attempted
to construct national data, but their reliability is questionable.
Accurate information on the extent of conversion activity has been
collected for only a few specific cities or SMSAs, primarily those
with high levels of conversion activity.  This lack of national data
reflects both the great variation in ways state and local governments,
developers and other observers define a converted unit, and the fact
that large-scale conversion activity is such a recent phenomenon that
national norms (particularly with respect to record keeping practices)
have not yet been developed.

Governmental bodies sometimes consider an application to convert a
building the equivalent of a completed conversion.  As a result, units
may be considered converted well before they are actually marketed as

such. In addition, if factors such as a lack of financing cause a developer to delay or cancel a planned conversion, the units may be counted as conversions even though they remain rental. The State of California, for example, maintains records on applications received to convert buildings. These records have been used by observers as a basis for estimating the volume of conversion activity in that state. Applying for conversion, however, is only the first step in a complex, often lengthy process which must be followed before a converted unit is actually sold. Therefore, using application figures as a surrogate for completed conversions overestimates the actual volume of conversions in this state.

Another reason national estimates are difficult to make is that many states and localities do not maintain detailed records of properties which have been converted. In some instances, records do not distinguish between newly built and converted condominiums, making an accurate count of conversions nearly impossible. For example, conversions in Texas and Illinois are recorded by filing a Declaration of Condominium with the appropriate County Clerk's Office; the same procedure and form are used to record newly built condominiums.

Since many governments outside of New York State either do not regulate or regulate only slightly the conversion of rental units to cooperatives, it is even more difficult to collect data on this type of conversion. For example, in Washington, D.C. it is not necessary to formally register a converted cooperative unit with the government as would be the case with a condominium unit. A further complication arises in New York (where cooperatives are prevalent) because a building is not considered a converted cooperative until a certain percentage of tenants agrees to purchase units.

Aside from specific state and local differences, some developers consider a building converted at the time they inform tenants that their units will no longer be available for rent. From this point, developers may even advertise the building as a condominium. Other developers may not consider building converted until enough purchase and mortgage commitments have been obtained to judge the feasibility of conversion.

Differing conversion processes, definitions, and methods of record keeping contribute to the problem of merging information collected from separate jurisdictions into a national estimate of conversion activity. However, by developing a standard definition of conversion and by undertaking an intensive review of documents and records maintained by state and local governments, it is now possible to reliably estimate the number of conversions carried out between 1970 and 1979.

## Previous Estimates of National Conversion Activity

Of the few previous efforts to determine the national volume of conversion activity, two are notable.  First is the 1975 HUD Condominium-
Cooperative Study 1/ which examines the potential impact of new and
converted condominium and cooperative units on the nation's housing
supply.  Since relatively little conversion activity had occurred
prior to 1975, the study, in general, did not treat converted units
as a separate phenomenon.  However, an estimate was made of the
number of condominium and cooperative conversions that had occurred
between 1970 and 1975. 2/

The second, and most widely cited source of information on national
conversion activity, is contained in occasional issues of U.S.
Housing Markets, 3/ a publication of Citicorp, Inc.  To arrive at
its national estimates, Citicorp representatives regularly contact
one or more knowledgeable persons in a limited number of major
metropolitan areas and ask them to report on conversion activity

---

1/ U.S., Department of Housing and Urban Development, HUD Condominium
Cooperative Study, 3 vols., (Washington, D.C.:  Government Printing
Office, 1975).

2/  The 1975 estimate was based on HUD's 1974 Annual Housing Survey
and information developed by HUD Area Offices.  The latter were asked
to determine conversion activity in their jurisdictions, but no
standardized time frame was provided for the estimates.  Consequently,
the 1975 report first noted that the HUD Area Offices reported 60,000
conversions had occurred "in recent years."  The report later expanded
the figure to 125,000 condominium and cooperative conversions, but no
explanation was offered for the second, higher figure.  Although the
exact time period covered by the 1975 estimate is not clear, it seems
to be based on 1970 through 1974 data, with projections made from
these data for 1975.  In the course of the current study, it was
estimated that only 85,000 units were converted to condominium or
cooperative ownership between 1970 and 1975.  One reason for the
discrepancy between the two sets of figures may be the varying quality of the data provided by the HUD Area Offices and the difficulty
of making national estimates from data collected locally without a
consistent definition of "conversion."  Another reason may be that
approximately 20 percent of the conversions begun between 1970 and
1975 were never completed during the period.  Economic conditions,
particularly during the 1973-74 recession, caused a number of buildings planned for conversion to revert to rental when they could not
be sold.  Second attempts to convert some of these buildings were
successful in the late 1970s when the economy improved.

3/ Advance Mortgage Corporation/Citicorp, Inc., U.S. Housing Markets
(New York:  Advance Mortgage Corporation/Citicorp, Inc., 1979-80).

within their particular housing market. In making their estimates, the contacts sometimes use local or state records or data collected by private market research firms, but also rely on their personal knowledge of the local housing market. The problems associated with these types of data gathering have been previously discussed. 4/

Since most conversion activity occurred after 1975, this report substantially updates the data contained in HUD's earlier report on conversions. In addition, the information presented in this report is for the entire country, rather than for selected metropolitan areas.


## Constructing National Estimates

For purposes of this study, a property is considered converted if a single unit in a rental building or complex has been sold as a condominium. Establishing a definition of a cooperative conversion is somewhat more problematic because the vast majority of cooperative conversions occur in the State of New York where very specific requirements govern when a conversion can occur. Specifically, either 35 percent or 15 percent of the tenants must purchase, depending on whether tenants will be evicted as a result of conversion. 5/ Should the sponsor of the conversion fail to obtain purchase agreements from the required percentage of tenants, the conversion remains a rental. Therefore, in the State of New York, a cooperative conversion is considered to occur only when the necessary numbers of tenants have purchased. However, outside of New York, a building is considered converted to cooperative ownership if it has been legally established as a cooperative and if one share (representing one unit) has been sold. 6/ Using these definitions, a coordinated effort was undertaken to collect data on conversion activity throughout the country.

When this study was initiated in late 1979, available literature indicated that the majority of conversions occurred in or near the country's largest metropolitan areas. To ensure that all units converted were counted, incorporated cities, towns and villages

---

4/ In addition, Citicorp's figures are subject to revision. For example, one Citicorp report noted that conversions in 1980 would be similar to the 1979 level of conversions which was previously set at 145,000 units. A subsequent report projected at least 100,000 units would be converted in 1980. For further details, see Appendix 2.

5/ For a more complete explanation of these regulations, see chapter XI.

6/ For the purpose of estimating the number of rental units converted to condominiums and cooperatives, a building is not considered converted if it has never been occupied as a rental or if it was previously nonresidential.

as well as counties and unincorporated jurisdictions within the
37 largest SMSAs were canvassed to determine how many units had been
converted since 1970. 7/ Data for areas outside these 37 SMSAs were
collected on a sample basis in such a way that when combined with
information from the 37 SMSAs, reliable generalizations could be
made to the entire country. 8/ (Additional details on the data
collection procedures are contained in chapter II and Appendix 2.)


## The Volume of Conversion Activity: 1970-1979

Throughout the country, approximately 366,000 rental units were
converted to condominium or cooperative ownership between 1970 and
1979. (See tables IV-1 and IV-2.) Most of this activity occurred in
the latter half of the 1970s. For the five years between 1970 and
1975, 86,000 rental units were converted. During the next four
years, 280,000 units were converted, with dramatic increases occurring annually. Converted units totaled 20,000 in 1976; in 1977,
they numbered 45,000; in 1978, the figure had reached 80,000; and by
1979, the total was 135,000 units.

**Total Number of Rental Units Converted Per Year**

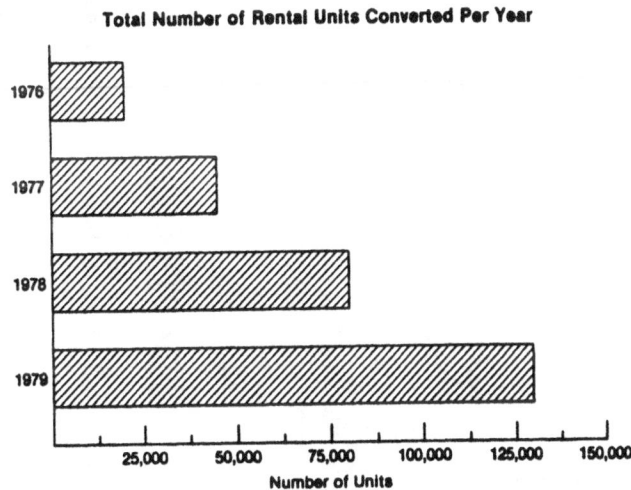

7/ In 1977, the latest date for which SMSA population data are
available, each of these 37 SMSAs had one million or more residents.

8/ Local data sources were used in every area of the country.
However, it was frequently necessary to cross-check private and
public data sources, to follow up on individual buildings or complexes,
and to do additional tracking. When it was impossible to refine or
redefine local data to correspond with the definition used in this study,
local figures which closely approximated the definition were used.
Appendix 2 describes in detail the methods and procedures used to obtain
these data.

## TABLE IV-1

### CONDOMINIUM AND COOPERATIVE CONVERSIONS AND PERCENT OF OCCUPIED RENTAL UNITS CONVERTED, BY LOCATION: 1970-1979

| | 1970-75 | 1976 | 1977 | 1978 | 3 Quarters of 1979 | Total 1970-79 | Total 1977-79 | Total 1970-79 Percentage | Total 1977-79 Percentag |
|---|---|---|---|---|---|---|---|---|---|
| **Total U.S.** | 85,746 | 19,976 | 45,527 | 80,334 | 114,493 | 346,476 | 240,754 | 100.0 | 100.0 |
| Condominium | 82,540 | 19,452 | 43,546 | 74,462 | 108,370 | 328,370 | 226,378 | 94.8 | 94.0 |
| Cooperative | 3,206 | 524 | 1,981 | 5,872 | 6,523 | 18,106 | 14,376 | 5.2 | 6.0 |
| **37 Largest Metro Areas** | | | | | | | | | |
| **12 High Conversion Activity SMSAs** | 55,916 | 10,679 | 31,670 | 50,886 | 54,346 | 203,497 | 136,902 | 58.7 | 56.9 |
| Condominium | 54,099 | 10,175 | 30,050 | 45,521 | 48,108 | 187,953 | 123,679 | 54.2 | 51.4 |
| Cooperative | 1,817 | 504 | 1,620 | 5,365 | 6,238 | 15,544 | 13,223 | 4.5 | 5.5 |
| **Remaining 25 SMSAs** | 14,308 | 3,408 | 8,761 | 14,996 | 20,221 | 61,694 | 43,978 | 17.8 | 18.3 |
| Condominium | 13,188 | 3,408 | 8,441 | 14,509 | 20,084 | 59,630 | 43,034 | 17.2 | 17.9 |
| Cooperative | 1,120 | 0 | 320 | 487 | 137 | 2,064 | 944 | 0.6 | 0.4 |
| **Balance of U.S.** | 15,522 | 5,889 | 5,096 | 14,452 | 40,326 2/ | 81,286 | 59,874 | 23.5 | 24.9 |
| Condominium | 15,253 | 5,869 | 5,055 | 14,432 | 40,178 | 80,778 | 59,656 | 22.3 | 24.8 |
| Cooperative | 269 | 20 | 41 | 20 | 148 | 498 | 209 | 0.2 | 0.1 |
| **Percent Rental Converted, Total U.S.** | 0.32 | 0.08 | 0.17 | 0.30 | 0.43 | 1.31 | 0.91 | | |
| **Percent Rental Converted 12 High Activity SMSAs 1/** | 0.75 | 0.14 | 0.42 | 0.68 | 0.72 | 2.71 | 1.83 | | |
| **Percent Rental Converted 25 Moderate Activity SMSAs 3/** | 0.30 | 0.07 | 0.18 | 0.32 | 0.43 | 1.30 | 0.93 | | |
| **Percent Rental Converted Balance of U.S. 4/** | 0.11 | 0.04 | 0.04 | 0.10 | 0.28 | 0.57 | 0.42 | | |

1/ The 12 SMSAs accounted for 28.3 percent of U.S. occupied rentals in the 1977 Annual Housing Survey.
2/ For all 12 months of 1979.
3/ The 25 SMSAs accounted for 17.9 percent of U.S. occupied rentals in the 1977 Annual Housing Survey.
4/ The balance of the U.S. accounted for 53.8 percent of U.S. occupied rental in 1977, by subtraction.

## TABLE IV-2

### PERCENT OF OCCUPIED RENTAL HOUSING UNITS CONVERTED
### TO CONDOMINIUM AND COOPERATIVE OWNERSHIP
### BETWEEN 1970 and 1979

| Location | Total Percent Rentals Converted | SMSA Central City | SMSA Non-Central City |
|---|---|---|---|
| Total United States | 1.31 | N/A | N/A |
| 37 Largest SMSAs | 2.22 | 1.86 1/ | 2.67 2/ 3/ |
| 12 High Activity SMSAs | 2.71 | 2.10 | 3.76 3/ |
| Boston | 2.37 | 2.20 | 2.46 |
| Chicago | 6.75 | 5.37 | 9.30 |
| Denver-Boulder | 6.96 | 8.79 4/ | 5.19 |
| Houston | 5.38 | 7.27 | 0 5/ |
| Los Angeles-Long Beach | 0.64 | 0.30 | 1.04 |
| Miami | 1.46 | 1.33 | 1.63 |
| Minneapolis-St. Paul | 3.42 | 1.41 | 6.25 |
| New York City | 0.72 | 0.58 | 1.55 |
| San Francisco-Oakland | 1.39 | 0.51 | 2.19 |
| Seattle-Everett | 2.00 | 1.29 | 3.92 |
| Tampa-St. Petersburg | N/A | 3.26 6/ | N/A |
| Washington, D.C. | 7.73 | 6.86 | 8.22 |
| Remaining 25 SMSAs | 1.30 | 1.27 1/ | 1.33 2/ |
| Balance of United States | 0.57 | N/A | N/A |

---

1/  Denominator includes units in Nassau and Suffolk counties, New York.

2/  Not included in the denominator are rental units in suburbs of the Hartford, San Antonio and San Jose SMSAs, or Nassau and Suffolk counties.

3/  Denominator does not include rental units outside of the central city for the Tampa-St. Petersburg SMSA.

4/  Boulder's share of rental housing is based on HUD Housing Assistance Plan estimates of the total amount of rental occupied housing in 1978.

5/  Negligible amount of suburban conversions.

6/  There was no SMSA Annual Housing Survey for Tampa-St. Petersburg.  The SMSA central city percentage is based on the city's Housing Assistance Plan estimates of the total amount of rental occupied housing in 1978.

Condominium conversions far exceed cooperative conversions. Most converted cooperative units are located in the metropolitan areas of New York City, Washington, D.C., and San Francisco-Oakland. Seventy percent of the cooperative conversion activity nationally took place in the New York City SMSA. During the entire decade, 18,000 units were converted to cooperative ownership, which represents only 7 percent of all conversion activity.

Although condominium and cooperative conversion activity has been relatively concentrated in and around the 37 largest SMSAs, some evidence suggests that the phenomenon may be spreading to or increasing in smaller metropolitan areas. Past concentration is evident from the fact that 76 percent of the conversions undertaken in the 1970s occurred in the Nation's 37 largest SMSAs. Broken down further, 59 percent of all conversions took place in 12 of the 37 SMSAs, while the Chicago and Washington, D.C. SMSAs together accounted for 31 percent of all activity. In the Chicago SMSA, this amounted to 70,000 units (20 percent of the U.S. total), and in Washington it totaled 39,000 units (11 percent of national activity).

In the other 25 SMSAs, over 61,000 units were converted. This figure accounts for 18 percent of all conversions carried out from 1970 to 1979. In the remaining parts of the country, 81,000 units (or 23 percent of the national total) were converted during the same time.

In this regard, a trend appears to be emerging. Between 1970 and 1976, 63 percent of all converted units were located in the 12 high activity metropolitan areas; this proportion fell slightly to 57 percent between 1977 and 1979. Concurrently, during the 1970 to 1976 period, 20 percent of all conversions occurred outside the 37 largest SMSAs. By the 1977 to 1979 period, this proportion rose slightly to 25 percent. These shifts are not substantial, yet they do suggest a dispersal of activity from the largest metropolitan areas to other locations. This trend has been gathering strength recently: nearly half of all conversions in areas outside the 37 largest SMSAs occurred in 1979, a sharp expansion in a very short time.

City and Suburban Conversion Activity. Between 1970 and 1979, the country's 37 largest SMSAs experienced 248,000 condominium conversions. Central cities accounted for 49 percent (121,000 units) of these conversions, while 51 percent (127,000 units) occurred in suburban jurisdictions. It appears that condominium conversion activity is a larger element in suburban housing markets than most observers had believed.

A number of SMSAs approximate this nearly even split between central city and suburban conversions. Among these are the Chicago, Pittsburgh, Atlanta, Baltimore, Milwaukee, and Miami SMSAs. Metropolitan areas where suburban conversions are much higher than those in central cities include include Minneapolis-St. Paul, Hartford, Los Angeles-Long Beach, Detroit, San Francisco, Cleveland, and Washington, D.C.

On the other hand, central city conversions far outweigh suburban
activity in the Denver-Boulder, San Diego, Dallas-Fort Worth, San
Antonio, and Houston SMSAs. The jurisdictional pattern in the Texas
SMSAs is due primarily to the state's liberal annexation policies
which have allowed central cities to grow to such an extent that there
are few densely populated noncentral city areas.

<u>Conversions as a Proportion of the Rental Housing Supply</u>. The propor-
tion of the Nation's total rental stock which has been converted to
condominium or cooperative ownership is, to this point, very low,
but there is wide variation among localities.

Conversions between 1970 and 1979 represented 1.31 percent of all
occupied rental housing units in the United States in 1977. <u>9/</u>
Most of this activity (69%) occurred during the last three years of
the decade, reflecting the accelerated pace of conversions since
1977. (Table IV-1 presents a detailed breakdown of the proportion
of the rental stock which was converted during the 1970-1979 period.)

Conversion proportions range from 2.71 percent in the 12 high activity
SMSAs to .57 percent in the part of the country outside of the 37
largest SMSAs (Table IV-2). Among the 12 high activity SMSAs, there
are considerable differences across metropolitan areas and between
central city and non-central city locations. For example, in the
New York City and Los Angeles SMSAs, one percent of all rental units
were converted during the 1970s, compared to eight percent in the
Washington, D.C. SMSA. When considering only central cities, the
conversion proportion was nine percent for Denver-Boulder, seven
percent for Houston and Washington, D.C. and six percent for Chicago.
Among suburban areas, the highest percentages of conversion are in
the Chicago (9%), Washington, D.C. (8%), Minneapolis-St. Paul (6%),
and Denver-Boulder (5%) SMSAs.

While these examples highlight variations among the suburban areas of
SMSAs taken collectively, there is also variation among the specific
suburban communities in any one SMSA.

> <u>In Walnut Creek, California</u>, an outlying
> suburb of Oakland, 18 percent of the
> city's rental stock has been converted
> since 1973 and most has occurred in 1979.

---

<u>9/</u> U.S. Bureau of Census, <u>Annual Housing Survey</u>, Part A, Series
H-150-77. If the 1970-79 conversions are calculated as a percent of
all units in rental buildings of five or more units, 3.56 percent of
the units have been converted. The figure 1.31 percent is based on
all occupied rental units, including single family homes and units
in buildings with less than 5 units.

In Connecticut, a report by the State Department of
Housing indicates that one community had 60 units
converted, but this was 36 percent of its total rental
stock.  Another community had 328 units in the process of
being converted, constituting 29 percent of its rental
supply.

* * *

Between 1970 and 1979, 366,000 rental housing units were converted to
condominium or cooperative ownership.  Conversions have occurred most
frequently in 12 large SMSAs, but there are indications that conversion activity is expanding to other, sometimes smaller metropolitan
areas.

Conversion activity has had only a slight impact on the Nation's
overall rental housing supply.  Units converted between 1970 and
1979 represent 1.31 percent of the country's occupied rental housing,
but 2.71 percent of the aggregate rental supply in the 12 areas with
the highest level of activity.  Specific cities, however, have experienced higher proportions of conversion, with Denver-Boulder, Chicago,
Houston, and Washington, D.C. each having conversion proportions
exceeding five percent.  There are also a few smaller cities and
neighborhoods within cities which have experienced higher levels of
conversion activity.

# Chapter V
# Factors that Drive Conversion: Housing Supply, Market Conditions, and Ownership Demand

Growing numbers of condominium and cooperative conversions within certain housing markets reflect the interplay and changing character of the demand and supply relationships that exist within those markets. The number of conversions that occur and their effects on the rental housing supply depend on factors such as the sources, types, and ultimate disposition of rental units that are converted, and the types of households which buy them.

Alternative explanations have been put forth by researchers, market analysts, local observers and public officials to explain the conversion phenomenon. Some have emphasized, exclusively, supply and market characteristics, demand forces, or financial conditions as having the most significant direct bearing on conversions. This chapter systematically and empirically examines and begins to sort out these various factors in order to understand better the forces that drive the conversion of rental housing to condominiums and cooperatives.

Two Views of Why Conversions Occur. Two distinct lines of argument have been advanced to explain why and where conversions occur. One is that conversions are products of distressed rental markets, in which landlords sell for conversion as a response to declining profitability. 1/ On the demand side, rental market distress would be evidenced by slow growth or decline in population or the rate of new household formation, lack of competition for available units and net out-migration of population. On the supply side, distress would be indicated by a combination of high rental vacancy rates, depressed rent levels, low rates of new rental construction, and high rates of rental losses from inventory.

Another explanation for conversions is that they respond to a strong and growing demand for ownership produced largely by rapid inflation. Strong demand and inflation tend to price traditional single-family homes beyond the reach of some new, younger households and other middle-income people who would otherwise be in the market. On the demand side, evidence of growing preferences for ownership would include strong sales of single-family homes, as well as condominiums, and relatively low

---

1/ The concept of profitability here refers both to current cash flow and to net return on investment. Further discussion of these concepts is provided in a later section of this chapter.

vacancy rates in certain neighborhoods or communities. A large pool
of younger, relatively more affluent renter households might indicate
that an area has great potential demand for multi-family ownership,
including ownership of converted properties. On the supply side,
strong ownership demand would be reflected by relatively high levels
of new construction of both single-family homes and condominiums.

---

## Prevailing Views of Why Conversions Occur

- Distressed Rental Markets
- Strong Demand for Ownership

---

These two views of why conversions occur can be reconciled in either
of two ways. First, it is possible that, within the same market,
rental properties are beginning to experience decreasing cash flow
which, if trends continue, could lead to distress. Decreasing
cash flows result from relatively greater increases in operating
costs compared to rental incomes. In these same markets, however,
ownership demand can be growing. Thus, conversions both allow the
property owner to obtain a significant return on investment (by
selling to a converter) and a shift in the use of the existing
housing supply to meet a shift in housing demand. Second, it is
possible that, within a given market, both explanations are important
but at different stages in the growth of the conversion phenomenon.
It is, for instance, plausible that overbuilding of rental properties
produces distressed rental conditions that stimulate a first wave
of conversions or that induce property owners to seek ways of
minimizing investments in rental properties. Subsequently, rising
ownership demand could account for continuing conversions even as
rental markets tighten. 2/

---

2/ The unit of analysis in this chapter is an SMSA-wide housing market
The chapter does not concentrate on the characteristics of specific
buildings or on buildings actually converted but, rather, describes
the housing markets within which conversions are occurring. The
following types of data are employed here: the views of housing
market experts in the 37 largest U.S. metropolitan areas (SMSAs);
results of a survey of 443 public officials in local jurisdictions
across the nation; and other data on supply, demand, and market
variables in the 37 SMSAs. These data are drawn from such sources
as the Annual Housing Survey and the Housing Assistance Plans
prepared by cities in connection with their Community Development
Block Grant applications.

The analysis below represents the first step in sorting out the available data in order to address the two views of why conversions occur. Various supply and demand characteristics are examined to determine what relationships, if any, exist between them and levels of conversions, including: (1) housing stock characteristics, such as the rental proportion of the total housing stock, the age of the multi-family stock, multi-family building sizes, rents, and prices; (2) new housing construction; (3) removals from an area's housing inventory; (4) rental vacancy rates; (5) rent levels; (6) rent regulation; (7) rental operating margins and profitability; (8) financial conditions, including interest rates and mortgage fund availability; and (9) household characteristics. 3/ As will be evident, the analysis suggests that conversions are associated with strong housing markets characterized by increasing demand for homeownership. Although the most visible cause of conversion is the profit realized by rental property owners and by converters, the availability of households willing to buy converted units represents the most direct cause of conversion.

## Housing Market Conditions and Housing Stock Characteristics

The character of an SMSA's housing market and its housing stock may partially determine the amount of conversion activity which takes place within it. The characteristics discussed below are intended to describe the SMSAs in which conversions are occurring and to shed light on those characteristics of the housing markets and housing stocks that may indicate increased conversion activity. This section

---

3/ Although most available data are at a metropolitan level, some of the posited relationships between housing supply characteristics and conversion levels are likely to be stronger at a neighborhood or community level, while others are likely to be stronger at a metropolitan or SMSA-wide level. Unfortunately, little or no uniform data on neighborhood or community housing market characteristics are gathered between U.S. Censuses and, therefore, the following analyses may not point up certain relationships that exist at the community or neighborhood level. The most recent Census data are ten years old and, consequently, not considered reliable for this analytic purpose. Unless otherwise noted, therefore, the relationships described in this chapter are at a metropolitan level. While these factors are discussed separately, they are interrelated in many ways. For example, the profits to be made by owners of rental properties by selling to converters, as one posited cause of conversions, are related to the tax benefits that are associated with the demand for homeownership, another posited cause of conversions. It is, in fact, the combination of such factors that produces a given level of conversion activity. These interrelationships are examined in the chapter's concluding section.

addresses the two views of why conversions occur by focusing on those conditions and characteristics that determine relatively strong or distressed housing markets.

New Housing Construction.  Converted condominiums compete for home buyers' dollars with newly-constructed condominiums and single-family homes.  Therefore, the level of such new construction in a metropolitan area may influence the volume of conversion activity.  If single-family construction is insufficient to meet total ownership demand, or is not responsive to the nature of demand (vis-a-vis the types of units desired), or is distant from locations where many want to purchase, there may be increased demand for converted units.  There is some degree of direct competition between conversions and new single-family construction, especially in a few of the more rapidly growing, less densely populated western and southern SMSAs.  There is even more direct competition in most metropolitan areas between converted and newly constructed condominiums.

---

### Market Conditions That May Determine Conversion Levels

- New Multi-Family Construction
- New Single-Family Construction
- Cost of Single-Family Units
- Removals From Inventory

---

New rental construction may also influence the level of conversion activity, as well as ameliorate the impact of conversions on the rental housing market.  New multi-family rental construction may provide rental opportunities for persons moving out of conversions and also provide a new source for potential conversions in the future Some analysts argue that conversion will be more frequent in those places where more multi-family building is occurring.  The overall strength of the investment market is seen as the controlling factor, as both converters and investors in new multi-family properties perceive the market to have sufficient strength to generate acceptable returns.  In fact, it is asserted that some new rentals may be constructed with the intent to convert after a relatively brief period. 4/  Other experts argue, however, that conversion may be greater in places where there is greater disinvestment in multi-

---

4/ See U. S. General Accounting Office, Rental Housing:  A National Problem That Needs Immediate Attention (Washington, D.C.:  General Accounting Office, 1979), p. 18; and Donald H. Haider, "Economics, Housing, and Condominium Development," in The Economics of Condominium Development (Chicago:  Center for Urban Affairs, Northwestern University, December 1979).

family housing. In these areas, insufficient returns on multi-family investment could influence current owners to divest as well as discourage new investment. The corollary to this argument is that higher levels of new rental construction will soften ownership demand (for converted units) and result in a negative relationship between new rental construction and conversion activity.

There is a positive relationship across SMSAs between the level of new single-family construction and the amount of conversion activity. (See table V-1.) This means that as the level of new single-family construction increases, so do the number of conversions. This relationship may be, in part, a function of the relative rates of growth in metropolitan areas. Those areas experiencing high levels of both new, single-family construction and conversions may be those areas that are also experiencing growth in the rate of new household formation. In this sense, construction activity and conversions may be supply-side responses to increases in the demand for housing. Important also is that the relationship does not hold inside the central cities where the level of single-family construction can be expected to be low. The SMSA-wide relationship, however, provides evidence that conversions are associated with strong, active housing markets.

New multi-family construction statistics combine both new condominiums and new rental construction. Although nationally, the bulk of new multi-family units are initially rented rather than sold 5/, in some SMSAs new construction of condominium units represents a fairly large share of new multi-family construction. For example, in the Miami SMSA, 20 percent of the multi-family units built since 1970 were intended for condominium or cooperative ownership. In the New York City suburbs, 30 percent of the multi-family units built since the 1970s are owner-occupied.

There is reason to believe that direct competition from new condominium construction influences conversion activity levels. Local public officials in jurisdictions experiencing conversions since 1970 were asked to identify which of several factors accounted for observed

---

5/ In 1978, about 15 percent of all newly constructed apartment units in buildings of five or more units were offered for sale as condominiums or cooperatives. About four-fifths of these were built in the South and the West. See "Market Absorptions of Apartments; Annual 1979 Absorptions," Current Housing Reports (Washington, D.C.: U.S. Department of Commerce, Bureau of the Census, April 1980). At present, little construction of any type of multi-family housing is occurring.

## TABLE V-1

### MEASURES OF ASSOCIATION BETWEEN CONVERSION LEVELS AND SELECTED MARKET CONDITIONS AND CHARACTERISTICS 1/

| Characteristic | SMSA | Central City | Outside Central City |
|---|---|---|---|
| 1970 Population | .590 | N/A | N/A |
| 1977 Population | .619 | N/A | N/A |
| Change in Population | .357 | N/A | N/A |
| Net In-migration | .302 | N/A | N/A |
| Median Rent, 1975 | .329 | N/A | N/A |
| Median Rent, 1980 | .260 | N/A | N/A |
| Multi-family Const., 1976 | .388 | .362 | .423 |
| Multi-family Const., 1977 | .330 | .326 | .266 |
| Multi-family Const., 1978 | * | .337 | * |
| Three Year Average Const. | .309 | .352 | .270 |
| Single-family Const., 1976 | .512 | * | .575 |
| Single-family Const., 1978 | .282 | * | .301 |
| Three Year Average Const. | .372 | * | .412 |
| Value/SF Permit, 1976 | * | * | * |
| Value/SF Permit, 1978 | * | * | * |

Source: Bureau of the Census, 1970 Census of Population (Washington, D.C.: U.S. Department of Commerce); U.S. Department of Housing and Urban Development, Annual Housing Survey: 1974, 1975, 1976 (Washington, D.C.: U.S. Department of Commerce, Bureau of the Census); Bureau of the Census, Housing Authorized by Building Permits and Public Contracts, Construction Reports C40-76-13, C40, 77-13, (Washington, D.C.: U.S. Department of Commerce, 1977, 1978, 1979).

1/ The table values are Pearson correlation coefficients between the amount of conversion in 37 SMSAs (between 1977 and 1979) and the absolute value of the selected characteristics. Each coefficient is significant at least at the .10 level. Most are significant at .05.

N/A = Not available

* = Insignificant coefficient.

year-to-year decreases in conversion activity. A majority said
that competition from new condominium construction had accounted
for these decreases -- more than those who named any other single
factor. 6/ It could be expected, therefore, that in some jurisdictions, new condominium construction decreases the amount of conversion activity.

At the metropolitan level, there is a significant relationship between 1977-79 conversion volume and new multi-family construction
from 1976 through 1978. (See table V-1.) Most of the SMSAs with
the greatest amount of conversion are the same places with the greatest amount of new multi-family construction in the very recent
past. 7/ These SMSAs appear to have recovered more quickly from the
general overbuilding that existed in the early 1970s indicating that
the housing markets in these places are relatively strong.

The latest data available indicate that new multi-family housing
starts have diminished sharply and it is estimated that starts will
remain low through 1980. Estimates of new, unsubsidized rental
starts for all of 1980 range between 100,000 and 120,000 units --
roughly a 50 percent decrease over 1979 starts, and single-family
construction has decreased sharply in the first quarter of 1980. At
the same time, conversion levels have fallen dramatically. 8/ This
is further evidence that condominium conversion and new construction
respond similarly to varying market conditions, and that both construction and conversion rates may be proxies for, or symptomatic
of, increasing demands for housing in relatively strong housing
markets.

---

6/ Department of Housing and Urban Development, Telephone Survey of
443 Local Officials, February 1980.

7/ The proportion of new construction in these SMSAs which is Federally supported is unknown. There is evidence to suggest that
Federally subsidized programs using conventional financing replace
private sector investments in similar housing; see Rochelle L.
Stanfield, "HUD Gets More Money for Housing -- But is it Enough for
the Poor?" National Journal 12 (March 1, 1980), p. 360. If this is
the case, private sector funds may be freed for other investment,
including conversion. The relationship reported here is a comparison of one absolute number (the level of conversion) with another
absolute number (the level of multi-family construction). Other
relationships examine proportions such as the percent of households
that are renters or the percent of all multi-family buildings with
at least 20 units. In these cases, the conversion variable is given
as a percent of the total multi-family housing stock.

8/ See "Unsubsidized Rental Starts to Drop 50%," Housing and Urban
Affairs Daily 74 (March 28, 1980), p. 155; and U.S. Housing Markets
(New York: Citicorp/Advance Mortgage Corporation, March 1980).

The Cost of New Construction. Many developers and market analysts believe that prices of single-family houses have risen beyond the means of many households and that this explains a significant portion of the conversion phenomenon. Developers have found that single-family units are now too expensive for many who desire to own and that converted condominiums can meet homeownership demand at a lower price than either new single-family houses or newly constructed condominiums. The issue, therefore, is the degree to which the rising price of single-family housing has shifted both development and demand toward condominiums and cooperatives -- especially those converted from rentals.

Between 80 and 90 percent of local public officials representing jurisdictions where at least some conversion activity has occurred attribute increases in local conversion volume to the increasing price of single-family housing in their localities. 9/ This suggests that the level of condominium conversion may be higher in those metropolitan areas with higher or more rapidly rising single-family prices. In fact, across the 37 largest SMSAs, this does not appear to be the case. (See table V-1.) The available data show that rising single-family prices during the 1976-1978 period are not associated with rising levels of conversions in the same period. (See table V-1 App. for construction and cost data.) It appears, therefore, that converted condominiums are meeting the homeownership demands of a segment of the population that is not in the single-family market and that converted units are not substitutes for single-family homes.

Removals from Inventory. Removals from the housing inventory involve such actions as abandonment, the boarding up of structures, demolition, disaster losses, changes to non-residential use, or taking units off the market for any purpose. 10/ These removals may be related to conversions in several respects. On the one hand, the conversion option may provide incentives to apartment owners and investors to maintain properties for eventual conversion to condomi-

_____

9/ Those data are from the survey of local officials conducted for this study. The only other factor mentioned by so many officials as responsible for rising conversion volume is the opportunity for profit from conversion. More than 90 percent of officials who expect increased conversions between 1980 and 1985 in their jurisdictions believe increased single-family housing costs will be an important driving factor.

10/ Removals do not refer to conversions to ownership status or to physically moving a unit to another location. Some removals may return to the housing inventory at a later date, as when an apartment building first becomes a transient hotel and, later, a permanent residential facility.

niums or cooperatives. On the other hand, these incentives may apply only to buildings where occupancy rates are already high and where buildings are in fairly good shape. Those properties that are too expensive to rehabilitate, are not in choice locations, or are otherwise inappropriate for conversion may receive little or no additional maintenance or investment as a result of the conversion phenomenon. Thus, the potential for conversion profits may be reason for some, but not all, rental buildings to continue to be maintained rather than be lost to the rental inventory. 11/

The metropolitan areas with the highest volumes of conversion activity tend to be those with lower annual losses from inventory. (See table V-2 App.) This suggests that conversion is not a phenomenon associated with distressed rental housing markets, as indicated by relatively high rates of rental losses due to abandonment or demolition. 12/ Unfortunately, there are no data which can be used to determine rates of rental losses in the immediate neighborhoods where conversions are concentrated.

Rental Vacancy Rates. The combination of changes in total demand for, and total supply of, rental units in an area produces a change in the balance of rental supply and demand in that area. One indicator of this balance is the rental vacancy rate. 13/

---

11/ It is also possible that previous conversions will have a later, secondary impact on the rate of removals. This depends on (1) whether renters leave converted buildings to occupy units they would not have considered before, and (2) the extent to which converted unit buyers come from these and other rental buildings. As a result of the net shift in occupancy, some buildings which normally would continue to decay and be lost to the rental inventory may become more financially stable. See chapter VII for a full discussion of the impact of conversions on rental occupancy.

12/ Although there is widespread concern over the perceived decrease in rental stocks due to conversion, removals from the inventory due to abandonment, demolition, and other factors account for a greater total loss in at least 8 of the 12 SMSAs experiencing the greatest levels of conversion through the 1970s. In the other four SMSAs, new multi-family construction has led to net increases in the rental stock that numerically overshadow the losses due to conversion.

13/ The rental vacancy rate by itself is sometimes unreliable as an indicator of supply-demand balance. Turnover rate, i.e., the rate at which rental units are occupied by new households, provides a useful, though often unavailable, supplementary indicator of the balance of supply and demand. The duration of vacancies is also a useful supplementary indicator.

Conversion may be both a function of, and an influence on, rental vacancy rates. In the short run, high vacancy rates may produce depressed rent levels and operating margins which, in turn, stimulate some apartment owners to sell their properties for conversion. However, owners of these kinds of properties may not always find buyers -- especially converters. Many market experts and developers say that unsuccessful rental properties rarely make profitable conversions.

High vacancy rates signal potential builders of rental apartments that an oversupply exists, thus dampening new rental construction. In many metropolitan areas, overbuilding of rentals in the early-to-middle 1970s produced a substantial oversupply of units. However, a dropoff in new construction in the mid-1970s, combined with conversions toward the end of the decade and losses to the rental inventory through abandonment, has reversed the market picture in many areas which are now experiencing record low average vacancy rates. In these same areas, demand has grown in the recent past to support both new construction and conversions.

---

**Other Market Conditions That May
Determine Conversion Levels**

- Vacancy Rates
- Rent Levels
- Rent Controls

---

Within a metropolitan area, vacancy rates may vary dramatically depending on the strength of demand at different income levels, renters' locational preferences, and changes in the supply of rentals in a particular neighborhood or community. Thus, conversions can have a substantial effect on rental vacancy rates within a small area if many renters in the converting buildings move to other rental apartments within the immediate area.

Statistical evidence that conversions are concentrated in metropolitan areas with below-average rental vacancy rates should be interpreted cautiously. It may be that conversions are more likely to occur in areas where vacancy rates are already low for other reasons -- for instance, in prime residential areas where demand is high and supply fixed. Such conditions not only permit landlords to keep their buildings full and perhaps raise rents; they may also signal developers that a market exists for multi-unit ownership, thus triggering conversions. 14/  It appears that although high vacancy rates encourage apartment owners to sell properties either for conversion or continued rental operation by others, low vacancy rates indicate market conditions that favor sales of converted units, and are more likely, other things being equal, to interest converters.

There is no consistent relationship between vacancy rates and the proportion of the rental stock that has been converted across the 37 largest SMSAs.  This means that on an SMSA-wide basis, levels of conversion may not be associated with either high or low vacancy rates.  (See tables V-2 and V-2 App.)  When central cities are categorized as having high, medium, or low conversion levels, however, those which had higher conversion rates from 1977 through 1979, had higher vacancy rates in the mid-1970s.  Rental vacancy rates in these high conversion central cities have fallen, according to local estimates, to levels similar to those in cities with fewer conversions. 15/  As a result, by the late 1970s there was virtually no difference in average rental vacancy rates between central cities with high and low volumes of conversion activity.  In Miami and Tampa/St. Petersburg, for example, vacancy rates in the late-1970s were above the national norm, but by 1979 they had plummeted to one percent.  Conversions increased dramatically in those cities at almost the same time.

Local public officials in just under 50 percent of jurisdictions with conversion activity since 1970 say that rental vacancy rates contributed importantly to increased conversions in their communities. 16/  These data again suggest that conversions are not concentrated in areas with distressed rental markets but, rather, in areas characterized by tightening rental markets and strong ownership demand.

---

14/  These conditions do not necessarily produce higher operating margins for rental properties.  This is discussed more fully below.

15/  Estimates for late 1979 are from the most recently available Housing Assistance Plans prepared by cities in conjunction with their Community Development Block Grant applications.  Estimates for the middle 1970s are from the 1974, 1975, and 1976 Annual Housing Surveys.

16/  About 18 percent of jurisdictions with some kind of local conversion ordinance have pegged conversion limitations to the rental vacancy rate.  (See chapter XII.)

TABLE V-2

MEASURES OF ASSOCIATION BETWEEN THE PROPORTION OF RENTAL STOCK CONVERTED
AND SELECTED MARKET CONDITIONS AND CHARACTERISTICS GIVEN AS PERCENTS OF ALL
HOUSEHOLDS OR ALL MULTI-FAMILY UNITS 1/

| Characteristic | SMSA | Central City | Outside Central City |
|---|---|---|---|
| Percent of households with 2 or fewer persons, 1970 | * | * | * |
| Percent of households with 2 or fewer persons, 1975 | .321 | .241 | .432 |
| Change in percent, 1970-1975 | .549 | .313 | .497 |
| | | | |
| Percent of households with head less than 36 years, 1970 2/ | .395 | * | * |
| Percent of households with head less than 36 years, 1975 2/ | .429 | .302 | * |
| Change in percent | .302 | * | * |
| Percent of households with head less than 36 years, 1975 3/ | .285 | * | * |
| | | | |
| Percent of households with income off at least $25,000, 1975 | .322 | .349 | * |
| Percent of households paying at least $250/month rent, 1975 | .377 | .416 | .243 |
| | | | |
| Renter-owner ratio, 1975 | N/A | * | N/A |
| Renter-owner ratio, 1979 | N/A | * | N/A |
| | | | |
| Vacancy rate 1975 | * | * | * |
| Change in vacancy rate 1975-1979 | * | * | * |
| | | | |
| Change in median rent, 1975-1980 | * | N/A | N/A |
| | | | |
| Percent of buildings with at least 5 units | .440 | .394 | .505 |
| Percent of buildings with at least 20 units | .443 | .348 | .596 |
| | | | |
| Percent of buildings constructed since 1970 | * | .414 | * |
| Percent of buildings constructed since 1960 | .383 | .349 | .367 |

Source: Bureau of the Census, 1970 Census of Housing (Washington, D.C.:
U.S. Department of Commerce); Housing Assistance Plans for selected cities
submitted with HUD Community Development Block Grant applications; 1979 Census
of Population, op. cit.; Annual Housing Survey: 1974, 1975, 1976, op. cit.

1/ The table values are Pearson correlation coefficients between the proportions
of the rental stock converted (between 1977-1979) and the selected characteristics.
Each coefficient is significant at least at the .10 level. Most are significant at
.05.

2/ All Households.

3/ Renter households only.
N/A = Not Available.  * = Insignificant coefficient.

However, the fact that some high conversion markets had slightly higher-than-average rental vacancy rates in the mid-1970s may indicate that overbuilding of rentals played a role in the initial conversions in those areas.

It is also helpful to look at the relationship of conversion to variations in vacancy rates within metropolitan areas and within central cities.  It appears to many local market experts and other observers that the neighborhoods where most conversions occur have vacancy rates at or below the citywide or metropolitan averages.

> In Atlanta, for example, vacancy rates are lowest in the area north of the central business district where virtually all of the city's conversions have occurred.

> Similarly, in San Diego, Orange County (California), Phoenix, and Chicago, conversions have been concentrated in areas with below-average rental vacancy rates.

Because vacancy rates are likely to influence rent levels and, in turn, the operating margins of rental properties, an examination of how the latter relate to conversion volume will shed additional light on the relationship between vacancy rates and levels of conversion activity.

Rent Levels.  According to many observers, rent increases have not kept pace with the rise in the costs of operating rentals.  As both inflation and real dollar increases in income continue, more households seek to become homeowners, in part, to take advantage of tax benefits.  Those that remain as renters are often less able to support the higher rent schedules necessary to cover rapidly increasing operating costs.  The median income for owner households rose by 143 percent between 1974 and 1979 while median income for renters rose by only 127 percent.  The median owner income in 1979 was almost double the renter median.  Many rental property owners maintain that these conditions prevent them from passing along to tenants the increasing differences between costs and rental income. 17/ The supply side consideration here is the extent to which depressed rent levels have induced rental property owners to disinvest, either by walking away, selling to other operators, or selling for conversions.

If depressed rent levels are one stimulus to conversion, then cities or metropolitan areas which have experienced higher volumes of conversion should have lower average rent levels than cities or SMSAs with lower levels of conversion activity. However, the data show just the opposite pattern across SMSAs. (See tables V-1, V-2, and V-2 App.) Interestingly, those metropolitan areas with higher volumes of conversion from 1977 to 1979 appear to have higher median gross rents both in the mid-1970s and in 1980 than metropolitan areas with fewer conversions. 18/ None of the 12 SMSAs experiencing the greatest volumes of conversion through 1979 were below the national median rent level for unsubsidized units in the mid-1970s. 19/

---

17/ Using 1967 as a base year, the Congressional Research Service of the Library of Congress shows that by 1979, fuel and oil costs rose by over 350 percent and gas and electricity costs by 179 percent; in contrast, residential rents rose only 79 percent. See E. Richard Bourdon, "Condominium Conversions; Possible Changes in Federal Tax Laws to Discourage Conversions and Assist Rental Housing" (Washington: Congressional Research Service, 1980). See also W. Paul O'Mara, "The Future of Rental Housing", Urban Land (December 1979), p. 19. Other analysts offer evidence indicating that, because rents have risen less rapidly than other consumer price index components, renters in at least one SMSA are voluntarily contributing larger shares of their incomes for rent in order to purchase better housing. Cf. John Kain, et al. "Condominium Conversion in Massachusetts: An Evaluation of its Benefits and Costs," unpublished document, April 1980, pp. 88-92.

18/ Most of the 37 largest SMSAs had median rent levels above the national median during this period.

19/ In a recently completed national survey of 600 managers of multi-family properties, almost 30 percent of the units in the survey renting for at least $400 per month were being considered for conversion, compared to 24 percent of the units renting for between $300 and $399; 14 percent of units between $200 and $299; and 7 percent of units renting for less than $200 per month. The percentage distribution for units in the suburbs was similar but the sample size is too small for generalizeability. The survey was conducted for HUD by the Survey Research Center, University of Michigan, Ann Arbor, Michigan. The findings support the conclusion that conversions are associated with both relatively strong housing markets and buildings renting at above average levels.

To Recap. Combining this information with the previous discussion of
rental vacancy rates, it appears that conversions are not a phenomenon
of soft housing market areas where rental vacancies are high and rent
levels are depressed. Rather, conversions seem to be associated with
healthy, perhaps tightening rental markets characterized by strong
demands for homeownership and by higher-than-average rent levels.

Rent Regulation. Rent control and milder forms of government rent
regulations are commonly included on the list of factors contributing
to depressed rent levels and, thus, to lower operating margins for
rental properties and to owners' desire to sell. Even the possibility
of future rent control is said to discourage new rental construction
and to make landlords reluctant to raise rents at rates necessary
to maintain operating margins. 20/ One consequence of rent control
or the fear of future rent control may be heightened willingness
of apartment owners to sell their buildings for conversion.

---

20/ Thomas R. Harter, "Rent Controls Forcing Condo Conversion; The
Mortgage Banker 39 (July 1979) p. 46. For additional arguments
concerning possible negative effects of rent control, see George
Sternlieb, The Urban Housing Dilemma (New York: City of New York
Housing and Development Administration, 1972); Department of
Economics and Research, National Association of Realtors, Rent
Control: A Non-Solution (Chicago: The Association, 1977); Cogen,
Holt and Associates, Housing and Local Government: An Evaluation
of Policy-Related Research in the Field of Municipal Housing Services
(New Haven: Cogen, Holt and Associates, 1975); Jeffrey Palmer,
The Effect of Rent Control on New Construction (Philadelphia,
1977); University of Southern California, Center for the Study of
Financial Institutions, Rent Control: A Survey of the Theoretical
and Empirical Findings, (October 1977); Urban Land Institute,
New Housing Production in the District of Columbia: Toward Possible
Solutions to a Public Policy Dilemma (Washington: Federal City
Council, 1975). Other analysts take a more positive view of rent
controls and their effects. For example, see John Gilderbloom,
The Impact of Moderate Rent Control in the United States: A Review
and Critique of the Literature (Sacramento: Department of Housing
and Community Development, 1978); Emily P. Achtenberg, "The Social
Utility of Rent Control," Housing Urban America, John Pynoos,
Robert Schafer, and Chester W. Hartman, eds. (Chicago: Aldine
Publishing Company, 1973), 434-447; Monica R. Lett, "Rent Control:
The Potential for Equity," American Real Estate and Urban Economics
Association Journal 4 (Spring 1976), p. 57-81; and Community Research
and Publications Group, Less Rent, More Control in Massachusetts:
A Tenant's Guide to Rent Control in Massachusetts (Cambridge:
Urban Planning Aid, Inc., 1973). See also unpublished document,
Report of the Temporary State Commission on Rental Housing, New York
State Temporary Commission on Rental Housing, August 15, 1979.

Only seven of the 37 largest SMSAs include jurisdictions which have enacted some form of rent control.  These are the Boston, Los Angeles, Newark, New York City, San Francisco, San Jose, and Washington, D.C., metropolitan areas.  On a national scale, less than seven percent of local officials in jurisdictions with some conversion activity reported enactment of local rent control measures.

---

## Relationship of Market Conditions to Conversion

|  | Relationship | | |
|---|:---:|:---:|:---:|
|  | Positive | Variable | None |
| New MF Const. | ✔ |  |  |
| New SF Const. | ✔ |  |  |
| Cost of SF Unit |  |  | ✔ |
| Removals | ✔ |  |  |
| Vacancy Rates |  | ✔ |  |
| Rent Levels | ✔ |  |  |
| Rent Controls |  |  | ✔ |

---

Because of the small number of jurisdictions with any type of rent control and given the variations in local regulation, it is not possible to establish a statistical association between such controls and conversion volume.  Some of the jurisdictions which have enacted rent control -- such as New York, Boston, and Washington, D.C. -- are among those with the highest numbers of conversions.  On the other hand, Chicago, which has by far the largest number of conversions of any city, has had no form of rent control.  The same is true of other cities with high conversion volumes such as Denver and Houston.  Interestingly only 10 percent of local government officials in communities wih rent control believe that rent control is an important factor in accounting for increases in local conversion activity. [21] This is in contrast, for instance, to the overwhelming majority of these officials who see the declining profitability of rental properties as a major cause of conversion in their jurisdictions.

---

[21] Telephone Survey of Local Officials, op. cit.

It may be concluded, therefore, that rent controls -- whatever their direct effects on rental operations -- are not necessary conditions or leading causes of condominium and cooperative conversions, if for no other reason than that so few of the jurisdictions with conversions have enacted such measures.

## Operating Margins, Cash Flow, Profits, and Alternatives

There appears to be no question that rising operating costs, the surplus of relatively new luxury and middle-income apartments remaining in some markets as a result of overbuilding in the early to middle 1970s, strong ownership demand and other factors have combined to depress both components of the profitability equation for landlords -- cash flow and return on investment. More than three-fourths of local officials, representing communities with some conversion activity, attribute increased conversion in part to the reduced incentives for landlords to continue operating. Almost 90 percent of these officials say that opportunities for profit from conversion help to account for increased conversions in their jurisdictions. 22/

---

**Profitability Is Major Concern of Property Owner. It Is Composed of**

- Cash Flow (Current Income)
- Return on Investment
  The Importance of These Components Varies by Housing Market

---

Apartment owners considering whether to sell their properties for conversion will compare the estimated short- and long-term returns from: (1) continuing rental operations; (2) sale of their buildings to another for rental operation; and (3) sale for conversion. In this regard, it is useful to distinguish between the operating margins of rental properties and the return to the apartment owner from the capital that is tied up in that property. In calculating profitability, it is necessary to consider not only the current and expected cash flow from the property -- including such variables as operating expenses, property taxes, and tax depreciation -- but also the other aspects of the owner's situation, including other sources of income that determine return on capital invested in the property. A rental property generating negative cash flow may be retained because it is

---

22/ Ibid.

appreciating rapidly in market value or because it is used to shelter other taxable income. Also, a rental property generating a positive cash flow may be sold if the owner receives a purchase price significantly above the market price of the property as a rental.

In some markets, the first part of the equation, operating margins, does not appear to be an important stimulus for conversions, and in other markets it appears to be more controlling. A market expert in Chicago, for instance, noted that "better properties are converted first" and that "conversion never solves the problem of bad property." 23/ Similar comments were made by a New York analyst who claimed that the most profitable rentals were being converted there and that most were operating in the black prior to conversion. A Miami market expert also reported that most conversions in that area had been more profitable than the average rental property and that declining rental operating margins were of "no importance" in motivating owners to sell. In these markets, profitable rentals and successful conversions are suggestive of strong homeownership demand.

However, market experts in several other metropolitan areas claimed that declining operating margins were important in stimulating conversions in their areas. In Tampa/St. Petersburg, a real estate analyst reported that the "vast majority" of converted properties were just breaking even and that declining operating margins were a major motive for sales to converters. In Atlanta, some real estate experts went so far as to claim that none of the converted properties had been in the black. In Houston, a conversion specialist stated that all properties he had been involved with were very minimally in the black and that declining operating margins were a major motive to sell. In the Buffalo SMSA, two multi-family complexes converted after foreclosure that was induced by negative cash flow and vacancy problems. Finally, a San Diego real estate researcher described most converted properties there as having been more profitable than other area rentals "although many had current or expected cash flow problems."

Such evidence suggests that the degree to which distress, caused by a profit squeeze, drives the conversion process varies from one metropolitan area to another and even from building to building.

---

23/ The former owner of a "bad" property will have his/her problems solved on sale.

In all cases, however, it is the greater market value of certain
properties as condominiums or cooperatives than as rentals, that
directly motivates the sale of rental property for conversion.

To Recap. All of this evidence suggests that conversion is more a
sign of market strength and, more directly, a response to profit
opportunities presented by healthy market conditions than to
worsening operating margins or declining return on investment from
rental operation. Although worsening operating margins are, in some
markets, the most visible factor motivating the sale of rental
properties for conversion, the greater market values of buildings
when sold for conversion than when sold for continued rental operation
appears to be of at least comparable importance. This increased
market value is driven by strong homeownership demands and high rent
levels. Rental vacancy rates do not appear to be associated with
concentrations of conversion activity. Moreover, other evidence
indicates that conversions are associated with relatively strong
housing markets, as indicated by higher levels of new single-family
and multi-family construction. Finally, the particular buildings,
within markets, chosen for conversion have most often supported
rents above the market average.

Other Characteristics. The last few factors to be discussed in
this section concern market conditions and housing stock characteristics that some market experts have advanced as being associated
with conversions. For example, some observers suggest that building
age and the number of conversions are inversely related. 24/ The
data provide partial corroboration. (See table V-2.) 25/ Across the
37 largest SMSAs, those places where multi-family properties less
than 20 years old comprise a greater percentage of the total

---

24/ Basically, the argument is that newer properties make more
successful conversions, due to superior quality and less need for
rehabilitation, (see chapter III.) The average age of an SMSA's
rental buildings, therefore, may partially determine both the suitability of the rental stock for conversion and its attractiveness to
buyers, thus influencing the amount of conversion activity that
takes place.

25/ In other words, those SMSAs with newer rental stocks are somewhat
more likely than other places to have high conversion volumes. (See
table V-2). Evidence presented elsewhere in this report suggests
that, within SMSAs, conversions are concentrated in particular
jurisdictions and neighborhoods and that, within these, newer properties
are often converted first. Exceptions to this occur in areas where
architecturally interesting older buildings are selected for conversion.
This is particularly true in some northeastern states. In the National
Survey of Managers conducted for HUD by the Survey Research Center,
a greater percentage of units constructed between 1960 and 1969 were
being considered for conversion than units built in the 1970s.

multi-family stock tend to have higher percentages of that stock converted.

Some market experts contend that small properties (with few units) rarely make profitable conversions. Economies of scale are said to produce a greater return on investment from larger building conversions. Therefore, the sizes of rental buildings in an SMSA should affect the volume of conversions in that area, and, in fact, this is the case. The higher the proportion of a metropolitan area's rental stock which is in larger buildings the greater the proportion of multi-family buildings converted in the 1977-1979 period. (See table V-2 App.). 26/

```
┌─────────────────────────────────────────┐
│                                          │
│    Characteristics of the Housing Stock  │
│    That May Determine Conversion Levels  │
│                                          │
│      • Renter/Owner Ratio                │
│      • Building Age                       │
│      • Building Size                      │
│      • Number of "Luxury" Buildings      │
│                                          │
└─────────────────────────────────────────┘
```

Some housing specialists suggest that in those areas where rentals represent relatively larger shares of the total housing stock, there will be larger "pools" of households accustomed to multi-family living and, therefore, a higher potential demand for converted units. If this is correct, the metropolitan areas with higher renter-owner ratios should have more conversions, which, in fact, they do.

---

26/ Although the properties actually converted are, in large measure, above the median size for their metropolitan area, considerable variation in building sizes does exist. In Houston, over 80 percent of converted projects had 20 or more units. In Minneapolis, one-fourth of all converted buildings had fewer than five units. In Boston, many converted properties had less than ten units. These data suggest that no one size of building is necessarily more suited to conversion and that the sizes selected for conversion will vary depending on the nature of an area's housing stock and market conditions.

Within the central cities of these SMSAs, there is a positive relationship between the renter ratio in the mid-1970s and the absolute number of conversions in the 1977-1979 period: as the percentage of rentals in the stock increases, so does the number of conversions.

Finally, market experts and developers often argue that luxury buildings make the most successful conversions, since they are usually in good condition, in preferred locations, and can most easily satisfy demand induced by the tax advantages of homeowner-ship. This should mean that conversions are likely to occur in greater volume in metropolitan areas with higher proportions of luxury buildings in their rental inventories. Across the 37 SMSAs, there is a positive relationship between the proportion of multi-family buildings converted in the 1977-1979 period and the propor-tion of luxury rentals in the housing stock, i.e., the 1974-76 percentage of renter households paying $250 or more for rent in 1974-1976. (See table V-2). In addition, the proportion of renter households earning $25,000 or more in the 1974-1975 period is also positively associated with conversions. Moreover, it was noted earlier that there is a consistent relationship, across the 37 largest SMSAs, between 1974-1975 SMSA-wide median rent levels and conversion (see page V-11). This suggests that conversions tend to occur with greater frequency in places where renters have higher-than-average incomes, where luxury rentals comprise relatively greater proportions of the rental stock, and where SMSA-wide rent levels are higher than elsewhere.

## Relationship of Housing Stock Characteristics to Conversion

|  | Relationship | | |
| --- | --- | --- | --- |
|  | Positive | Variable | None |
| Rent/Own Ratio |  | ✔ |  |
| Building Age | ✔ |  |  |
| Building Size | ✔ |  |  |
| Number of "Luxury" Buildings | ✔ |  |  |

To Recap. Available data confirm some but not all expectations regarding the relationship between housing stock characteristics and conversions. SMSAs with greater proportions of rental housing and SMSAs whose rental housing is in larger and higher rent buildings have had higher proportions of their rental stock converted.

Financial Conditions

Whatever relationship an area's housing stock and its housing market conditions have to conversion, the condition of, and changes in, the nation's financial markets can have important impacts on the extent and rate of condominium conversion. 27/ For instance, changes in the cost and availability of mortgage money to support the purchase of converted units can exert significant influence over conversions. Inflation, the interest rates charged on loans to converters for acquisition or rehabilitation, and expected appreciation are other examples of such financial influences. These financial considerations are discussed below from three perspectives: the converted unit buyer; the converter/developer; and the rental property owner.

The Unit Buyer. 28/ The interaction between money market conditions and conversions, from the unit buyer's perspective, is indirect and complex. In a vacuum, higher interest rates or a decline in the availability of mortgage money (perhaps as a result of usury ceilings) can result in a decreased demand for any particular unit type or a decrease in the supply of the unit type. It is more common, however, that interest rate changes and alterations in the supply of mortgage funds serve to change the competitive position of one unit type relative to others. Rising interest rates tend to make less expensive condominium units more attractive than single-family, detached units and converted condominium units may become attractive than new

---

**Financial Conditions That May Affect Conversion Levels**

- Inflation
- Interest Rate for Buyers
- Interest Rate for Converters
- Mortgage Fund Availability
- Asking Prices for Rentals

---

27/ When changes in money market conditions occur, they tend to affect all of the Nation's metropolitan housing markets similarly.

28/ Chapter VI discusses the composition of demand for converted condominiums. The financial considerations are discussed here because a major financial condition, interest rates, impacts on "supplies" of converted units in a manner similar to the impact on unit buyers.

condominiums by virtue of their lower cost, on average and, therefore, by virtue of their lower mortgage requirements.  In addition, rising interest rates are usually accompanied by stricter credit require- ments and it may be that some homebuyers can qualify for a mortgage on a converted unit but not for a loan on more expensive shelter. Many homebuyers may be unable or unwilling to bear the higher burdens associated with more expensive housing.  Interest rates could rise to a level where few, if any, homebuyers could qualify and demand would decline sharply.

The general availability of mortgage money, regardless of interest rates, tends to impact uniformly on all segments of the housing market and across all unit types.  If mortgage money is not available, potential unit buyers will be affected regardless of whether they intend to buy a detached unit or a condominium.  However, when mort- gage funds are in short supply, lending institutions will increase downpayment requirements (to insure greater equity participation by the buyer) and under these conditions, less expensive, converted units may become more attractive since, if purchased, they would require lower front-end capital.  Those at the lower end of the income scale will be more sensitive to changes, even small ones, in interest rates or in the availability of mortgage funds.  Conse- quently, increased downpayment requirements may drive some potential unit buyers out of the market.

There is conflicting evidence on the actual impacts of rising interest rates and changes in the supply of mortgage funds on demand for converted condominiums.  Most developers or market analysts indicated that in late 1979, the prevailing interest rates had not severely affected the sales of converted units (perhaps because many converters had secured end-loan packages) and many of these experts also predicted a decline in interest rates by Summer, 1980.  In March 1980, these same observers indicated that condominium sales had either decreased considerably or were non-existent in some areas. Record high interest rates, ranging between 13 and 18 percent, were cited as the main cause of the slowdown.  Condominium or cooperative resales were usually affected first and most sharply.  Sales at the time of conversion were still doing well in other areas. 29/  Some of the reasons for this may include the discounts offered to current tenants, which, in New York City, may be as high as 50 percent. 30/

___

29/  See "Interest Rates Pose High Buyer Hurdle, "Professional Builder 45 (February 1980), p. 18.

30/  In other areas, discounts may be as high as 25 percent.  See Daivd Sutter, "Getting Rich Quick in the Condo Market", Venture (August 1979), p. 50.

Additionally, some developers were either paying points themselves
in order to increase unit closings (this reduces the effective inter
est cost to the buyer) or were financing part of the unit purchases
themselves, through first or second mortgages. In many of these
latter cases, the mortgages are for short terms and the developers
expect that unit buyers will be able to qualify for conventional
loans when the terms end. In addition, many converters secured
end-loan package commitments prior to the very recent escalation in
interest rates and, therefore, were able to offer a product whose
"real" costs were below prevailing market rates.

Whatever the actual level of demand for converted condominiums and
cooperatives, there is little doubt that it is driven by expected
inflation (and a concomitant expected appreciation in property
value), the unaffordable costs (to many) of single-family, detached
units, and the desire for equity build-up in real estate -- all of
which are demand related. 31/

Since the tax subsidy associated with homeownership serves to lower
the "real" interest rate of homeownership and since inflation
increases the marginal tax brackets of households, homeownership
becomes more attractive, all else being equal. However, if the rate
of inflation plus the real interest rate exceeds the mortgage rate,
it is desirable to own regardless of the nominal interest rate. In
fact, these conditions existed throughout 1979 and provided a significant, demand-driven impetus for conversions.

---

31/ In fact, it is probably the case that inflation greatly enhances
the advantage of owning versus renting, and this may be one of the
major reasons for conversion and demand for converted units. Since
house prices move with inflation, houses become a good store of
wealth, and keep the real purchasing power of wealth from falling.
It is also the case that the tax system, inadvertently, stimulates
the demand for homeownership.

Consider a world of zero inflation and a 6 percent mortgage interest
rate. The mortgage interest payment on a $50,000 house with a 20
percent downpayment will be $2,400 per year. Then the total "cost"
of ownership, so far, is $5,400.

But homeowners can deduct mortgage interest on Federal income tax
returns. In the example, a homeowner in the 30 percent tax bracket
would have an after-tax interest cost of only $1,680. To this, how-
ever, must be added the opportunity cost on equity investment, i.e.,
the $10,000 downpayment. If it is assumed that the homeowner could
have earned 4 percent on equity (and would have paid tax on it),

The Converter Developer.  Changes in the money market affect con-
verter/developers in many of the same ways as unit buyers.  As the
cost of money increases, the number of conversion projects undertaken
will generally decrease.  Also, as interest rates rise, lending
institutions require either greater developer equity or a greater
percentage of presales before granting acquisition, rehabilitation,
or interim mortgage financing for conversion.

---

the after-tax opportunity cost is (.7)(.04) ($10,000) or $280, making
the total cost $1,680 + $280 + $3,000 or $4,960 per year.  Since
there is no inflation in the example, there are no offsetting expected
capital gains.

Now, take the same situation but assume an inflation rate of 6 percent
It has been the case that interest rates have tended to move roughly,
point for point with inflation, so that it is appropriate to assume
mortgage rates to be 12 percent (the original 6 percent + 6 "inflation
percentage points) and opportunity cost on equity to be 10 percent.
The after-tax mortgage interest cost of the $50,000 house will now
be (.7) (.12) ($40,000) or $3,360; the equity cost will be (.7)
(.10) ($10,000) or $700; and other costs will still be $3,000.  But
now the owner is expecting capital gains on the house and these
are, in all likelihood, tax free.  If the expectation is that house
prices will grow at 6 percent, the homeowner will expect to "earn"
$3,000 in capital gains.  This must be deducted from other costs
resulting in a net cost of $4,060 -- ($3,360 + $700 + $3,000 - $3,000)
In other words, inflation leads to an actual reduction in ownership
costs.

What this means is that a buyer will now be willing to pay a good
deal more than $50,000 ($61,084 to be exact) for the same house in
order to keep cost constant.  That is, the anticipation of inflation
will bid up house prices.  Essentially, this is because inflation
bids up interest rates, which are deducted at ordinary rates, but
gives capital gains that are not taxed.  The higher the inflation
rate and the higher the tax bracket, the more the homeowner is
willing to pay.

Landlords, however, are not taxed in the same manner as homeowners.
They do get the benefit of deducting interest rates, but they are
likely to have to pay some capital gains tax.  Furthermore, when
they deduct depreciation, it is at historical rather than current
prices, so that the value of this deduction diminishes as inflation
increases.  There are, of course, other tax breaks that landlords
get, but they do not vary directly with inflation.  The result is
that the price an owner-occupier is willing to pay for a unit rises

There is probably some range of interest rates, however, that make conversion more attractive than other real estate investments even though the rates may actually be rising. In essence, rising interest rates may increase the proportion of buyers preferring converted units; and, therefore, converters may be willing to invest in conversion projects to meet this demand. Activity in the real estate market during the last half of 1979 provides some support for this hypothesis.

Although interest rates were rising during this period, some new conversion projects were undertaken and most of those that were on the market were selling well. At the same time, investment in new single-family developments was slowing. Most market experts in the largest SMSAs indicated that a combination of high purchase prices and high interest rates accounted for the slowdown, and that the relative, and increasing price advantage enjoyed by converted condominium units accounted for the successful marketing of most conversions

In the first quarter of 1980, however, the cost of money had risen sufficiently to cause many converters to abandon or postpone conversion projects or to operate acquired properties as rentals until interest rates decreased. A developer in Seattle, for example, reported a 70 percent decrease in converted unit sales in March 1980, and that properties were returning to the rental stock. Other projects have been cancelled in San Francisco, San Antonio,

---

relative to what a landlord is willing to pay for the same unit. Hence, as inflation increases, the demand for ownership increases and the pressure for condominium conversion rises.

This will not be case for all potential owners. Some households in low tax brackets may still benefit more from renting after accounting for tax bracket shifts resulting from inflation (if the landlord is in a higher bracket than the potential owner). Furthermore, the rise in the standard deduction has cancelled out some of the advantages to changing tenure. Nonetheless, the above example does illustrate that there is likely to be a good deal of pressure for owner-occupancy as inflation rises to levels like those in the first quarter of 1980 (especially if inflation is expected to last for some time).

Again, the importance of the tax system in all of this should be clear. If instead of taxing (and allowing deductions) on nominal interest rates, taxes were levied on real or inflation-adjusted interest rates (interest rates minus inflation rates), inflation would not have changed homeowner costs in the illustration and the implied impetus for condominium conversion would vanish.

Portland, and Cincinnati, and most other places have experienced a slowdown in conversion during the same time period. A developer in Miami advised tenants in acquired properties to remain as renters until interest rates receded to 13 percent. This developer helped qualify his tenants for mortgage loans at that rate and offers leases until the rate declines. One major developer in Pittsburgh has gone out of business altogether.

From the converter's perspective, the above scenarios argue that there is some upper limit on interest rates above which developers are less willing to absorb the carrying costs associated with conversion regardless of how quickly they expect to sell-out and regardless of the extent to which inflation and tax subsidies reduce the costs of homeownership for buyers. In addition to the high cost of interim loans, the ability to secure end-loan financing for prospective unit buyers decreases as interest rates rise and this, too, lowers the attractiveness of the typical conversion. Pre-arranged financing is one of the attractions of condominiums and cooperatives for buyers; it is also attractive to converters because it permits a more rapid sell-out. Without it, the carrying costs of a conversion project may seriously undercut profitability if interest rates rise. 32/

Another financial consideration faced by converter/developers is the cost of acquiring rental properties. As the conversion phenomenon has grown, property owners have begun to take advantage of the demand by raising prices. These increased costs impact on profitability in several ways. Increased acquisition costs mean increased interest charges for wrap-around or other acquisition mortgages. In fact, larger acquisition loans may require greater equity participation by the converter and a more expensive pre-sale campaign -- both of which increase developer risk. In addition, higher acquisition cost can result in either increased unit price -- which may decrease the potential buyer pool and, therefore, increase the sell-out period -- or in reduced profit margins if unit prices remain constant.

If interest rates remain high and if asking prices for rental properties suitable for conversion also remain high, it could be expected that only larger firms, perhaps those doing business on a national basis, will remain active in the conversion market. Smaller firms may not be able to marshal the resources necessary to acquire and/or rehabilitate properties or to qualify for acquisition and interim financing loans. As noted, interest rates during the first quarter

---

32/ Donald H. Haider, "Economics, Housing, and Community Development, op. cit.

of 1980 (averaging 14 percent for home mortgages and two points over prime for most developers) may have stopped almost all conversion (and other housing) activity; few firms could either pay cash for acquisitions or finance their own purchases.  Some are using land contracts, but this practice is not widespread.

It has been suggested that converters attempt to earn between 10 and 30 percent of gross sales as profit. 33/  Clearly, the money market conditions described above impact on profitability and may be largely responsible for the sharp cutback in conversion activity in the first quarter of 1980.  Even if demand for converted units remains very high, it is unclear that many firms can afford to undertake conversion projects when the carrying costs are as high as 20 to 22 percent (two points over prime, on average).  Those potential conversion projects requiring substantial rehabilitation are likely to be the most seriously affected since they will have significant carrying costs associated with them.

Actual returns on conversion projects already completed have, in some cases, significantly exceeded the 10-30 percent figure.  In fact, if developer equity or "exposure" is used as the base from which to calculate returns, the percentage can be enormous.  A rather large complex in Houston was converted earning the developer a before tax, 40 percent profit on gross sales (using the cost of acquisition and rehabilitation as the base for calculation). 34/ In San Francisco, a developer expected to at least double his money ($30 million purchase price plus $5 million in rehabilitation) on a project already begun. 35/  In Los Angeles, a group of investors expect a before-tax return of $2 million on a conversion project that required only $50,000 of their own money as equity. 36/  That is a return of almost $40 for every dollar of equity exposed for a relatively short period of time.  The potential for returns of this magnitude may account for the fact that some conversion projects are still undertaken despite the large carrying costs associated with current high interest rates.

Rental Property Owner.  Most market specialists agree that the rental property owner is motivated by two major concerns:  the cost of operating rental property versus rental income (cash flow) and the

---

33/  As noted below, however, profit margins often exceed 30 percent. The key is the base upon which profit is calculated.

34/  E. Richard Bourdon, "Condominium Conversions:  Possible Changes in Federal Tax Law," op. cit.

35/  David Sutton, "Getting Rich Quick in the Condo Market," op. cit.

36/  Ibid.

return received on investment (as measured by equity appreciation, tax brackets, debt service, and the like). Most also agree that investment in rental property has generally become a poor alternative relative to most other investments. Recent changes in financial conditions reinforce this difference.

Basically, a rental property as an investment is worth what the building can sell for as a rental plus any tax shelter advantages and depreciation benefits accruing to owners. The "real" value of these additions depends, to a large extent, on the tax bracket of the owner. 37/ In general, the higher the tax bracket, the greater the value of such things as accelerated depreciation. In essence, more income can be written off to depreciation resulting in a net decrease in current tax liability.

A critical factor, however, is that no amount of allowable depreciation or expected appreciation can equal the return received on the sale of rental property to converters. 38/ In the recent past, high interest rates have diminished the utility of refinancing as a mechanism to allow the recovery of accrued equity, and this serves as a further impetus to divest, rather than hold, investment in rental properties. Even though the Tax Reform Act of 1976 eliminated some of the tax benefits associated with the early sale of a rental property (including the elimination of the excess depreciation recapture credit), a combination of greatly increased values of rental properties as owned units and real or perceived constraints on operating margins provides strong inducement for property owners to sell and reinvest elsewhere. The choice is made more advantageous by the fact that profits on the sale of an entire building, regardless of the intended use of the structure, are taxed at capital gain rates and not as ordinary income. Moreover, the capital gains tax rate was recently reduced, allowing an owner to keep a greater share of profits regardless of tax bracket. The capital gains treatment

---

37/ The following sources provide details on the profitability of rental ownership: "Legislating to Restrain Co-ops and Condos," Business Week 18 (February 1980); Rental Housing: A National Problem That Needs Immediate Attention, op. cit.; William Brueggeman, Tax Reform, Tax Incentives and Investment Return on Rental Housing (Columbus: Ohio State University, 1977); Condominium Conversions: Possible Changes in Federal Tax Laws, op. cit.; and Leonard G. Sahling and Rona B. Stein, "Co-op Fever in New York City," Federal Reserve Bank of New York Quarterly Review 5 (Spring 1980), pp. 12-19.

38/ Condominium Conversions: Possible Changes in Federal Tax Laws, op. cit.

of profits is the prime reason most property owners sell to converters.  If they undertook conversions themselves, the profits would
be taxed as ordinary income.

To Recap.  Interest rates and the availability of mortgage money
play major roles in determining the extent of conversion.  Rising
interest rates may shift both demand and supply factors in favor of
converted condominiums, relative to other unit types.  Very high
interest rates, however, cause a decrease in virtually all real
estate actions.  Rental property owners have benefited from conversion in a number of ways including rapidly rising asking prices for
properties, a strong demand for the product, and changes in the tax
laws that allow owners to retain a significant portion of the proceeds on sales of properties to converters.


Household Characteristics

Conversions are seen by some as driven primarily by the shift in
housing demand from rental to ownership.  This shift is occurring
among some middle-income households, for whom the marginal financial
advantage of owning vs. renting has recently become greater.  The
shift is largely a result of actual and expected future inflation
(including future appreciation of housing values and the greater tax
advantages of ownership for households pushed by inflation into
higher marginal income tax brackets). 39/  Inflation of housing
prices has, at the same time, placed traditional single-family
homes beyond the financial reach of more middle income households.
Thus, inflation -- combined with Federal tax laws -- works both to
increase ownership demand and to reduce the ability of many households
to purchase single-family homes.  Condominiums and cooperatives --
including those converted from rentals -- offer a less expensive
ownership alternative at a time when more are seeking to own rather
than to rent.  For this reason, if for no other, demand for converted
condominiums and cooperatives would be expected to grow and to create
new profit opportunities for converters.

If demand drives conversions, then those housing markets with relatively large proportions of middle-income renter households in the
early 1970s will be those with the greatest volumes of conversions.
As noted earlier, there is a positive relationship between the percentage of renter households in a metropolitan area earning $25,000
or more in the mid-1970s and the likelihood that this area had a

---

39/  See Footnote 31, page V-24.

high level of conversion activity from 1977 through 1979. For these households, the tax subsidy and increases in marginal tax brackets are sufficient to induce increases in the demand for ownership. This supports the argument that conversions are driven by a shift of housing demand from renting to owning.

Further evidence of the demand hypothesis is that conversions are positively associated with change in SMSA population and with net in-migration. (See table V-1). Those areas experiencing relatively greater growth, as measured by percent change in population and percent net in-migration, have greater proportions of their multi-family stock being converted. The change in the percent of house-holds containing two or fewer persons (between 1970 and 1975) and the change in the percent of households headed by persons aged 35 years or less (in the same time period) are both positively associated with the proportion of the rental stock that has been converted. (See table V-2). Nationally, the percentage of all central city renter households comprised of two or fewer people rose from 60.3 percent in 1970 to 66.8 percent by the mid-1970s. Similarly, the percentage of all central city households headed by persons 35 years old or less rose from 27.6 percent to 32 percent in the same time period. These two types of households comprise a large share of the demand for condominiums (see chapter VI) and provide strong evidence of the demand-driven nature of conversions.

* * *

The profit made by rental property owners on sales to converter/ developers is the proximate cause of conversions. The most direct cause is the availability of households willing to buy from the converter/developer. Market values of rental properties have increased dramatically due to the conversion option, and property owners have been receiving purchase prices far in excess of the resale values of these properties as rentals. There is evidence that in some, and perhaps all, markets, the difference in market values is also a function of decreasing operating margins. There is even stronger evidence that the difference reflects a shifting of some middle-income housing demand from rental to ownership.

Therefore, with regard to the two views of why conversions occur, summarized at the beginning of this chapter, little can be found to suggest that conversions are a response to softening rental markets. Although declining operating margins for many rental properties throughout the nation have provided incentives for conver-sion, the major reason for the substantially higher market values of many apartments as condominiums or cooperatives than as rentals is the substantial and growing demand for this form of ownership.

This conclusion is based on the circumstantial evidence that conversions are more likely to occur in SMSAs with stronger housing markets. The metropolitan areas with highest volumes of conversion activity appear to have relatively vigorous housing markets characterized by higher volumes of new single-family and multi-family construction, higher than average rent levels, and lower than average rates of rental inventory losses from abandonment or demolition. Rental vacancy rates in these metropolitan areas are similar to those in areas with fewer conversions. Moreover, these areas have higher proportions of affluent renter households likely to be the major source of demand for converted condominiums and cooperatives. Within metropolitan areas, the particular buildings chosen for conversion tend to be larger and to support higher average rents than other rental buildings in the same markets.

Chapter VI examines the composition of demand for converted condominiums and cooperatives and the reasons for purchase given by those who buy. Chapter VII includes an analysis of the occupancy shifts resulting from conversion. Together, these two chapters provide further evidence on the role that demand plays in driving the conversion of rental property to ownership.

# Chapter VI
# Demand for Conversions: Who Buys, Who Doesn't, and Why

The previous chapter emphasized the importance of homeownership demand as a major factor driving conversions.  This chapter discusses the characteristics and motivational bases of that demand. 1/

It is important to profile the socioeconomic and demographic characteristics of buyers and non-buyers to determine the degree to which conversions draw from the traditional pool of single-family home buyers or "create" a new set of owners.  To complement these profiles, the various reasons people buy or do not buy are also examined.  A primary question is whether converted condominiums or cooperatives are a preferred housing choice.  Ownership per se is an indication of the effective demand for conversions, but it is not always indicative of a strong desire to own such units. Some buyers might prefer to own other types of housing, other than a condominium or cooperative, but buy converted units because they cannot afford their first choice; some may buy because they cannot find suitable rental units; and others may buy because they simply do not wish to move from their units when they are converted.  Knowing why people buy, rent, or move out of a converted building helps to explain the basis for the effective demand for condominium and cooperative conversions.

## Four Types of Occupants

At any point in time, a housing market may contain buildings which have been fully converted (i.e., all units have been sold as condominiums or cooperatives) and buildings which are in the process of conversion (i.e., at least one, but not all of the units have been sold).  Of all of the households who had occupied units in buildings whose conversion began after January 1977 in the 12 high conversion

---

1/ The information sources for this chapter include survey responses from both people currently in converted buildings and those who moved out of these buildings; field interviews with tenant representatives, developers, market experts, and local officials in the nation's 37 largest SMSAs; and a review of existing research.  The survey of households was conducted in December 1979 and January 1980 in 12 SMSAs with high levels of conversion activity over the period 1977 through 1979.

activity SMSAs, 58 percent had moved out as of January 1980. 2/  The remaining 42 percent continued as either owners or renters, along with new occupants who had moved in since the conversion.  Converted and converting building occupants, therefore, consist of the following types of households:

## Table VI-1

### Residents of Converted Buildings

|  | Continuing Residents | New Residents | Total |
|---|---|---|---|
|  | % | % | % |
| Owner Occupied Units | 22 | 41 | 63 |
| Renter Occupied Units | 20 | 17 | 37 |
| Total | 42 | 58 | 100 |

## Owner-Occupiers of Converted Units

This section profiles the characteristics of owner-occupiers of converted units and discusses their reasons for buying.  In addition, owner-occupiers are compared to their counterparts who reside in other types of owner-occupied housing throughout the nation, showing dramatic differences between the two owning groups.  Then, converted unit owners are disaggregated into two types, as indicated in the table above:  tenant buyers, who lived in the building prior to conversion; and outside buyers, who lived in other types of housing before conversion.  The characteristics of each group and the reasons they purchased are contrasted.

Socioeconomic and Demographic Characteristics.  While owners of converted units come from all age, income, racial, and occupational groups, they are mostly white, have professional or managerial occupations, have relatively high incomes, and are smaller households with younger heads.

---

2/ These 12 SMSAs are identified in chapter 2; they account for 59 percent of all conversions in the U. S. during 1977-1979.

VI-3

**Household Income of Owners**

Less Than $12,500 ▇ (12%)

$12,500-21,500 ▇▇ (25%)

$21,500-30,000 ▇▇ (24%)

Greater Than $30,000 ▇▇▇ (39%)

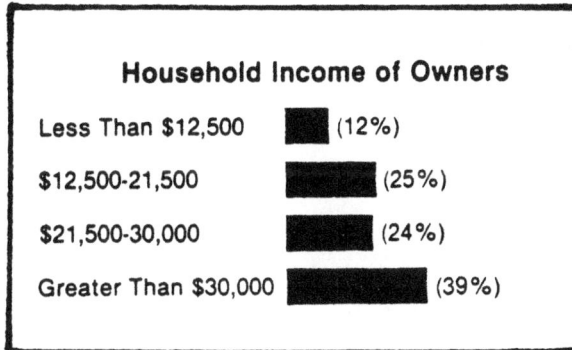

About one-half of the owners are less than 36 years of age; while only one-fifth are over 55, and only 9 percent are over 65. Those over 55 without children constitute only 19 percent of all owners.

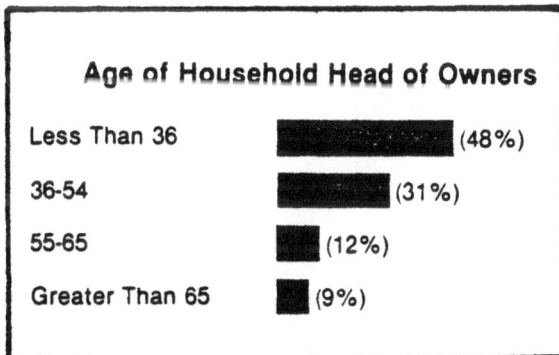

**Age of Household Head of Owners**

Less Than 36 ▇▇▇▇ (48%)

36-54 ▇▇▇ (31%)

55-65 ▇ (12%)

Greater Than 65 ▇ (9%)

Sixty-three percent have incomes greater than $21,500; and 39 percent earn more than $30,000 annually. Furthermore, their incomes can be expected to rise in the future because many are young and professionally employed. On the other hand, only 12 percent have incomes of less than $12,500.

**Household Head's Employment of Owners**

| | | |
|---|---|---|
| Professional, Managerial | ████████████ | (65%) |
| Clerical, Sales | ████ | (13%) |
| Skilled, Service | ██ | (7%) |
| Homemaker | ██ | (5%) |
| Retired | ██ | (10%) |

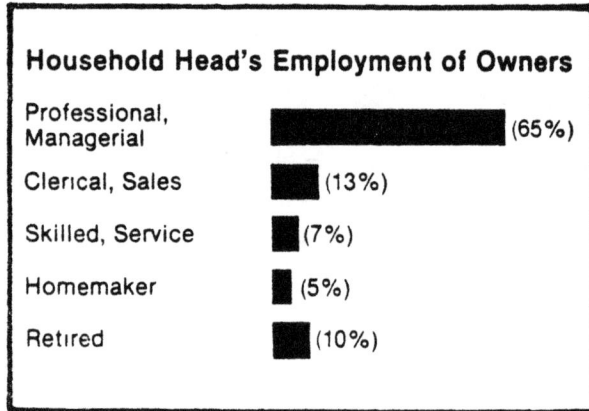

Ten percent of the owners are black, and two percent are Hispanic.
Close to two-thirds of the household heads hold professional or
managerial positions, and 40 percent of the spouses hold similar
jobs.

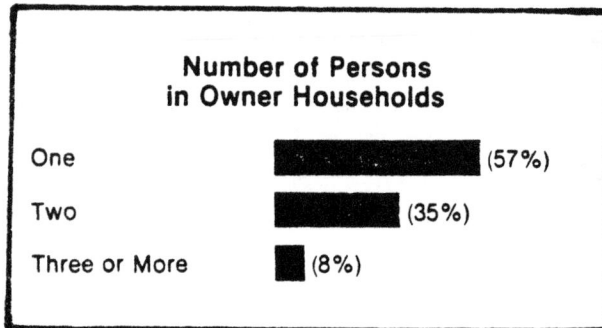

**Number of Persons in Owner Households**

| | | |
|---|---|---|
| One | ████████ | (57%) |
| Two | █████ | (35%) |
| Three or More | ██ | (8%) |

Most households in converted units are small:  57 percent have only
one person; and, of those, nearly two-thirds are female.  Thus, 36
percent of the owners are single females, while 21 percent of the
owners are single males.  Most of these single-person households
are under 55 years of age. 3/  From these statistics, a profile of
condominium and cooperative owners emerges:  owners are predominantly

---

3/ The remaining 43 percent of households are married couples with or
without children (31 percent) and male or female heads with dependents
(12 percent).

young, single, professionals with higher-than-average incomes. They
are not typical purchasers of single family homes. As the chart below
depicts, when the characteristics of owners of converted units are
compared with the characteristics of all homeowners, nationally, one
finds that single males, single females, and, to a lesser extent,
blacks represent a greater proportion of the owners of converted
units than they do of other owner-occupied housing units in the
nation. 4/ Conversely, elderly persons and lower income persons
represent a smaller portion of the owners of converted units than
they do of other types of housing.

Table VI-2

Profile of Owner-Occupiers:
All Owner-Occupied Housing and Owner-Occupied Converted Units

| Population Characteristics | All Owner- a/ Occupied Housing | Owner-Occupied b/ Converted Units |
|---|---|---|
| | % | % |
| One person, male | 4 | 21 |
| One person, female | 10 | 36 |
| Black | 7 | 10 |
| Hispanic | 2 | 2 |
| Age 65 and over | 22 | 9 |
| Income less than $12,500 | 39 | 12 |

a/ U.S. Department of Housing and Urban Development, Annual
Housing Survey, 1977.

b/ U.S. Department of Housing and Urban Development, Survey of
Current and Former Residents of Converted Buildings, December
1979 and January 1980.

Most owners of converted condominium and cooperative units are not
new to the neighborhoods in which they buy. Forty percent have been
in the neighborhood for at least six years, while only nine percent

4/ The proportion of single female owners is notably high. Further
comparisons show that only 12 percent of all owners of newly built
condominiums, which are primarily townhouse and garden style units,
are single females. See Michael Sumichrast, Robert J. Shehan, Gopal
Ahluwalia, Profile of a Condominium Buyer (Washington, D.C.: National
Association of Home Builders), 1978, p. 45.

lived in the neighborhood for less than one year. Of the buyers who
lived in the building prior to conversion, over 60 percent lived in
the neighborhood for six years or more. The relatively long periods
of residence in the area suggest a preference for and familiarity
with the particular location in which they buy.

To this point, all owner-occupants of converted units have been
discussed as an entity in order to describe who they are and to show
their distinctiveness from owner-occupiers of other types of housing.
However, owners of converted units consist of renters in the buildings prior to conversion (35%) and outside buyers who lived elsewhere
prior to conversion (65%). These buyers differ in two basic ways:
tenant buyers are more likely to be older and to have higher incomes
than outside buyers. 5/

While 56 percent of outside buyers are under age 36, only 35 percent
of tenant buyers are in that age category. With regard to older
purchasers, 29 percent of tenant buyers are 55 years of age or older
compared to 16 percent of outside purchasers. Almost one-half of
tenant buyers have incomes of over $30,000, compared to 35 percent
of outside buyers.

These statistics highlight the fact that outside buyers are, on average, younger and have slightly lower incomes than tenant buyers. However, given their young age and employment in the professions, their
incomes are likely to rise over time. On the other hand, tenant
buyers are distributed nearly equally among younger, middle, and
older households.

When outside buyers of converted units are compared to recent movers
into all types of owner-occupied housing nationally, strong contrasts
emerge. Elderly persons move to converted units in the same proportions as they do to other homes, but for minorities, converted units
are slightly more popular. Most noteworthy is the fact that single
males and single females move more frequently into converted units
than into other owner-occupied housing; and persons with low incomes
move to converted units far less frequently.

---

5/ All relationships reported in this chapter are statistically
significant at the .05 level unless otherwise indicated.

Table VI-3

Profile of Owners-Occupiers:
All Recent Movers and Outside Buyers of Converted Units

| Population Characteristics | Recent Movers into a/ Owner-Occupied Housing % | Outside Buyers of b/ Converted Units % |
|---|---|---|
| One person, male | 6 | 28 |
| One person, female | 5 | 29 |
| Black | 5 | 9 |
| Hispanic | 1 | 2 |
| Age 65 and over | 6 | 5 |
| Income less than $12,500 | 39 | 14 |

a/ U.S. Department of Housing and Urban Development, Annual Housing Survey, 1977.

b/ Survey of Current and Former Residents, op. cit.

Reasons for Buying. The literature on condominium and cooperative conversions suggests several reasons why people buy converted units. One portion of the literature posits essentially negative reasons, such as that people buy because: there is a lack of acceptable rental housing; there is a lack of affordable single-family homes (the converted unit, sometimes, constituting a "starter home" used to build equity in order to buy a single-family home in the future); or, they simply do not want to move when their rental homes are converted.

Another portion of the literature posits essentially positive reasons, such as economic advantages. Those who were previously renting may purchase to receive the tax and investment benefits of homeownership, to stabilize monthly housing costs, or to obtain a discount offered by the converter. Those who were previously single-family homeowners may purchase a converted unit in order to reduce maintenance and utility expenses.

Others may want to live in a particular location because of its proximity to the downtown area, their job, public transportation, or other attractions. Retirees and those with leisure time interests may choose to purchase converted units, especially in resort areas, as permanent residences or vacation homes. Finally, younger buyers and elderly persons may prefer the lifestyle of a converted unit in which security, maintenance, and services are provided.

The literature does not make clear which of these reasons is most important, or whether negative or positive reasons dominate. Hence, owners were asked to indicate the single most important reason they decided to buy. 6/

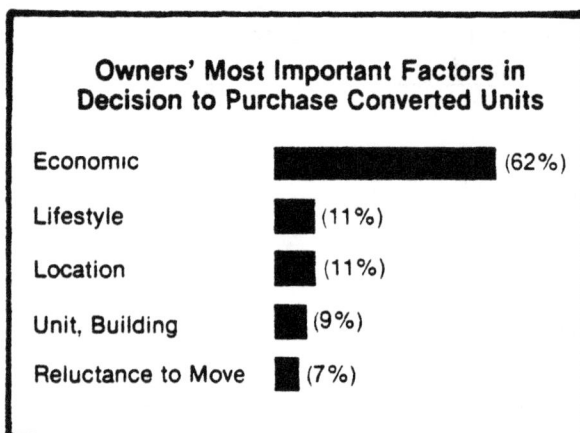

**Owners' Most Important Factors in Decision to Purchase Converted Units**

| | |
|---|---|
| Economic | (62%) |
| Lifestyle | (11%) |
| Location | (11%) |
| Unit, Building | (9%) |
| Reluctance to Move | (7%) |

Owner occupiers, as a group, express all the reasons given in the literature for purchasing converted units; however, most cite economic factors as primarily important. Nearly two-thirds of all owner-occupants decided to purchase their unit for essentially economic reasons such as the following: to provide a hedge against inflation; to stabilize their rising housing costs; to obtain tax shelters and investments; to purchase in lieu of the higher costs of single-family homes; and to take advantage of the discount on the price of the unit offered by the converter (for tenant buyers only). Eleven percent of all owner-occupants bought units principally because of their location. Another 11 percent were attracted to selected character-istics of condominium or cooperative living, such as ease of mainte-nance. Nine percent simply liked the building or unit.

Some buyers cited essentially negative reasons for buying, but they constituted a minority of all purchasers. Seven percent of all buyers bought because they did not want to move; this, however, constitutes fully 23 percent of all tenant buyers, as outside buyers were not in residence. Four percent bought mainly because of a lack of acceptable rental units in their desired area.

---

6/ Respondents were read a list of many possible factors and asked if any were important motives in their decision to buy. Then, they were asked to choose one of the thirteen as the single most important factor in their decision. It is the response to the latter question which is described above.

By and large, this type of multi-family housing is providing ownership benefits to people who have not previously been homeowners. It is important to note, however, that while economic benefits are perceived as positive reasons for buying converted units, these units are not considered to be the final or ultimate type of housing in which most current owners plan to reside: 56 percent of all owner occupants say they plan to buy one-family houses or townhouses next; and 5 percent say they plan to rent at their next move. Thus, a majority of converted condominium and cooperative owners see their unit as interim housing.

Differences Between Tenant Buyers and Outside Buyers. Reasons for purchasing a unit vary by whether the owner lived in or outside the building prior to conversion. Tenants who eventually bought a unit in the building were initially more uncertain than outside buyers about whether they wanted to own or rent anywhere. Unlike tenants in the building who must decide whether or not to buy at the time of conversion, outside buyers initiate the purchase.

Ninety-one percent of all outside buyers began their housing search with the intention of buying rather than renting, and 98 percent prefer to buy the next time they move. On the other hand, when the prospective conversion was announced to tenants in the building who eventually bought, only one-half were sure they wanted to purchase initially. The remaining half were either undecided or did not want to buy.

Most tenant buyers, who initially were reluctant to buy, apparently did not feel under pressure to do so. Four of every five households who finally purchased after initial uncertainty did not attribute their decision to perceived pressure. There are different reasons why these households ultimately bought, including the following: after a search for other housing, some did not find another unit they liked as well; others were persuaded to purchase because they became convinced of the advantages of homeownership over renting; and others, particularly elderly persons, were subsequently assisted in purchasing a unit by family members. However, the comments of persons who felt pressured express at least two types of pressure. Some persons objected to "hard sell" tactics. Others felt pressured by a perceived lack of housing alternatives.

When the motives of tenant and outside buyers are compared, economic incentives still dominate other considerations for both groups; but they are relatively more important for outside buyers. For less than one-half of tenant buyers, but for 69 percent of outside buyers, economic factors are the primary motivation.

**Outside Buyers' Most Important Factors in Decision to Purchase Converted Units**

Economic ████████████ (69%)

Lifestyle ███ (16%)

Location ██ (8%)

Unit, Building ██ (7%)

**Tenant Buyers' Most Important Factors in Decision to Purchase Converted Units**

Economic ████████ (47%)

Lifestyle █ (2%)

Location ███ (16%)

Unit, Building ██ (12%)

Reluctance to Move ████ (23%)

Twenty-three percent of tenant buyers purchase because they do not want to move; and tenant buyers are also more likely to buy because they like their unit, building, or location (28 percent vs. 15 percent for outside buyers). Condominium or cooperative lifestyle character-istics play an insignificant role in the purchase decision of tenant buyers, although 16 percent of the outside buyers cited this factor as primarily important.

Socioeconomic and Demographic Differences. Buyers' decisions to purchase converted units also vary by age and income. Buyers over 65 are less concerned about economic factors than are those between 55 and 65, and both of these age groups emphasize economic factors less so than those under age 36. Buyers over 65 tend to emphasize either the desire not to move (32 percent) or lifestyle and locational factors (30 percent). Also, people earning incomes below $12,500 are less motivated by economic considerations than higher income groups. The decisions of middle income buyers -- those earning between $12,500 and $21,500 -- depend more on economic factors than do the purchase decisions of lower or higher income groups.

To Recap. Condominiums and cooperatives provide a hybrid form of housing, combining the economic benefits of ownership associated with detached or semidetached homes with the locational and lifestyle benefits of renting. These units appeal, in particular, to the rising numbers of small households with above-average incomes who, in the past (i.e., prior to the popularity of condominiums or coopera-tives), may have rented since no alternative to single family owner-ship was available. Both outside buyers and tenant buyers are prin-cipally small households with good incomes, although tenant buyers have higher incomes. Therefore, while outside buyers are most likely to cite economic reasons for purchase, tenant buyers, desiring to avoid a move and to retain their location and unit, cite reasons other than economic ones for purchasing. In particular, elderly tenants bought primarily because they did not want to move from their unit or neighborhood.

Investors In Converted Units

Not all owners of converted units reside in them. Nineteen percent
of all converted units are owned by investors who derive rental
income by leasing them. 6/

The conversion of rental buildings increases real estate investment
opportunities, particularly for investors who do not have large
amounts of capital needed for many other real estate investments.
However, there are two major limitations on the extent to which
investor ownership occurs. First, ceilings on the number of
investor-held units may be imposed by mortgagees as a risk-reduction
mechanism. In addition, any building whose individual unit mortgages
are to be sold on the secondary mortgage market are allowed a
maximum of 20 percent investor-owners. 7/ However, in the case
of mortgages sold to the Federal Home Loan Mortgage Corporation
(FHLMC), this maximum increases to 40 percent after two years of
successful operation as a condominium. Second, most cooperatives
generally have no or very few investor-owners because cooperative
corporations prefer to have only the owners in the building and
because banks making cooperative loans often refuse to finance
investors. Most investors, therefore, own condominiums rather than
cooperatives; although there are indications that investor participation in cooperatives may be increasing, particularly in areas with
active housing markets.

Even though the secondary market does not buy all converted unit
mortgages, the overall proportion of investor units (19 percent) is
very close to the 20 percent limit that the Federal National
Mortgage Association (FNMA) and FHLMC place on the proportion of
investment units in any converted building. However, this 19 percent
varies considerably among housing markets. For instance, investors
may own as high as 40 percent of the units in Miami, where few
mortgages are sold on the secondary market, and as low as 1 or 2
percent in New York City, where cooperatives dominate. More importantly, the proportion of investor-owned units depends on selling
prices. Units in luxury buildings will, more than likely, not be
sold on the secondary market because the unit sales prices exceed
the loan-to-value limits set by FNMA or FHLMC.

---

6/ For this chapter, an investor is one who purchases a converted
unit in which rental income is produced. Others who enter into
limited partnerships with developers are discussed in chapter III.

7/ See chapter X for a more complete discussion of the relationship
of the secondary mortgage market to conversions.

Investors include several types of individuals or groups, as follows: 8/

1. Converters or landlords and associates. 9/ Some developers retain units in converted buildings after they have relinquished control to the condominium association. They are held as investments and rented to persons new to the building or to people who lived in the building prior to conversion. Other developers give rental preference to elderly or handicapped persons who lived in the building previously. Developers may also sell units at below market prices to their staff members or associates who then rent these units to new or existing tenants. This can occur especially when the developer desires to complete all sales and pay off interim financing.

2. Outside individuals or groups. Individual or group investors purchase converted units and make them available for rent. While some of these investor-owners rent to new tenants, others act as landlords for tenants who wish to stay on as renters after the conversion is completed.

3. Family members. Family members purchase for their parents or children. For instance, there are cases in which parents of students purchase converted condominiums located near their children's college or university. Some elderly persons are aided in purchasing their converting unit by their family.

4. Former residents. Four percent of all former residents purchased a unit which they, in turn, rented to a third party.

5. Part-time owner-occupants. Some converted units are purchased by individuals or groups who use them primarily as vacation homes; but, while they are not in residence, they rent the units to other vacationers.

Obviously, the reasons why investors purchase converted units are primarily economic. In many ways, the economic benefits of owning condominiums are similar for both investors and owner-occupiers.

---

8/ Investor owners were not included in the sample of unit owners surveyed for this study; information on who they are and why they buy comes from interviews conducted with a variety of housing market experts, real estate representatives, and from those households living in converted buildings who rent from these investors.

9/ These are not included in the previous calculation of investor-held units. They provide an additional 18 percent.

Both benefit, especially in periods of inflation, by deducting high interest payments and by paying the lower capital gains tax rate on the attendant capital gains at sale. In some cases, people buy a unit for their elderly parents or children or to maintain a vacation residence; but, even then, they receive certain financial benefits.

The economic incentives for purchase include appreciation of value to be realized at the time of sale of the unit and income tax bene-fits associated with investment in rental properties. According to many market experts across the nation, in most areas the resale value of converted units in the fall of 1979 was still strong, and owners could continue to expect a good return on their invest-ment. 10/

Individually or in limited partnership, investors also receive tax benefits on their investment while units are held. They are allowed several deductions from their gross taxable income. These include the following: 11/ (1) mortgage interest -- a maximum interest deduction of $10,000 plus the net investment income is allowed; (2) real estate taxes -- owners deduct real estate taxes assessed on the property; (3) maintenance, repairs, insurance -- expenses for repairs, maintenance, insurance, garbage removal, and similar costs, are deductible when these are paid directly or through association fees; and (4) depreci-ation -- investors use accelerated depreciation methods for new units (constructed after July 24, 1969). Used units are limited to depreci-ation at the 125% declining balance rate. The sum of these deductions allows investors to reduce their taxable incomes, thereby entering lower tax brackets. The benefits are greatest during the first 7 to 12 years the units are held. After that time, mortgage interest and depreciation deductions decrease substantially.

Tax regulations can sometimes result in benefits to tenants who rent from an investor. Some investors seek primarily to shelter their incomes, rather than gain profits; and, therefore, the rents charged need not always include a substantial profit margin. In such cases, rents in converted buildings can be competitive with other types of rental units in the area.

---

10/ For a more complete discussion of the impact of interest rates on conversions, see chapter V.

11/ See the Internal Revenue Code Sections 162, 163(d), 164, 167, 167(j)(2) and (5), and 212.

While the effect of tax regulations is to discourage high rent levels, other factors can increase rents. For instance, extensive rehabilitation to the building at the time of conversion contributes to higher rents. In addition, rent controls, which apply to multifamily rental units in some jurisdictions, do not apply to the condominium or cooperative units held by investors in the same area. Therefore, while the presence of investors means that units are retained in the rental inventory, the rents charged for these units often exceed the amount previously charged for the same unit.

## Renters In Converted Units

Not all residents of converted buildings are owners. In New York, for example, many buildings are converted without tenant evictions; and tenants can renew their leases indefinitely. In Brookline, Massachusetts, tenants cannot be evicted even though their unit is sold. Renters may also live in a building not because of statutory protections but as tenants in units held by investor(s).

Thirty-seven percent of all occupants in converted buildings are renters. About 19 percent lease from an investor(s); the other 18 percent rent from the landlord or developer. 12/ Both groups of renters (those in the developer/landlord held units and those in investor-owned units) include people who were tenants in the building before conversion, as well as those who have moved in since the conversion. Usually, however, newer tenants lease from someone other than the converter of the building.

When renters of converted units are compared to buyers, they are similar in race, household size, occupation, age, and length of residency in the neighborhood. The only significant difference is between income levels of renters and owners. Seventy-three percent of owners have annual incomes of over $21,500; however, only 46 percent of all renters are in this group. On the other hand, 22 percent of renters (but only 12 percent of the owners) earn less than $12,500 annually.

Renters in Converted Units versus All Renters: When renters of converted units are compared to all renters nationally, the former have higher incomes and smaller households. Sixty-nine percent of all renters nationally, but less than one-fourth of those in converted units, make less than $12,500. Similarly, while 37 percent of all renter households nationally have three or more persons, only 15 percent of renters in converted buildings are this large.

---

12/ The household survey included both buildings in the process of conversion and buildings in which sales were completed. In the former, a higher percentage of residents are renters who may leave the building when their lease expires.

## Table VI-5

### Profile of Renters:
### All Renters and Renters of Converted Units

| Population Characteristics | All Renter-Occupied Housing a/ | Renter-Occupied Converted Units b/ |
|---|---|---|
| | % | % |
| One person, male | 15 | 18 |
| One person, female | 19 | 29 |
| Black | 17 | 15 |
| Hispanic | 8 | 4 |
| Age 65 and over | 17 | 17 |
| Income less than $12,500 | 69 | 22 |
| Three or more person household | 37 | 15 |

a/ U.S. Department of Housing and Urban Development, Annual Housing Survey, 1977.

b/ Survey of Current and Former Residents, op. cit.

In addition, the table illustrates that elderly persons lease converted units as often as they lease other rental units. Black and Hispanic persons rent in converted units less often, and single males and single females lease converted units more often than other rental units nationally. Therefore, except for similar representation of elderly persons, renters in converted units are quite different from other renters.

Continuing Tenants versus New Renters. When renters are considered as a single entity, they are more similar to owner-occupiers of converted units than other renters nationally. However, disaggregation into continuing renter and previous renter groups provides additional information.

Elderly persons are more likely to be continuing renters than to move to the units and rent. New renters tend to be younger and have higher incomes than continuing renters. Furthermore since more of them are professionally employed, their future incomes will probably increase faster than the incomes of continuing renters.

More than twice as many new renters (69 percent) are under 36 years of age, compared to roughly one-third of all continuing tenants. More than one-half of the new renters, versus 39 percent of continuing renters, have incomes greater than $21,500. 13/

13/ The income differences between new renters and continuing renters are not significantly different.

As the table below illustrates, the characteristics of new renters
in converted units contrast sharply on several dimensions with those
of all recent renters, nationally, in other types of rental housing.
Higher proportions of single males and single females move, as renters,
into converted units more often than other types of rental housing.
A comparatively small proportion of lower income persons rent in
converted units. Again, these findings indicate that converted units
are providing housing for persons of higher-than-average income and
single persons.

## Table VI-6

### Profile of New Renters:
### All Renters and Renters in Converted Units

| Population Characteristics | Recent Movers into Rental Housing a/ | New Renters in Converted Units b/ |
|---|---|---|
| | % | % |
| One person, male | 17 | 23 |
| One person, female | 15 | 23 |
| Black | 13 | 14 |
| Hispanic | 8 | 5 |
| Age 65 and over | 6 | 5 |
| Income less than $12,500 | 70 | 17 |

a/ U.S. Department of Housing and Urban Development, Annual
Housing Survey, 1977

b/ Survey of Current and Former Residents, op.cit.

Reasons for Renting. The vast majority (80 percent) of all renters in
converted buildings simply prefer to rent, rather than to buy, for
whatever reason. Furthermore, they wish to rent only in the neighborhood where they are currently living.

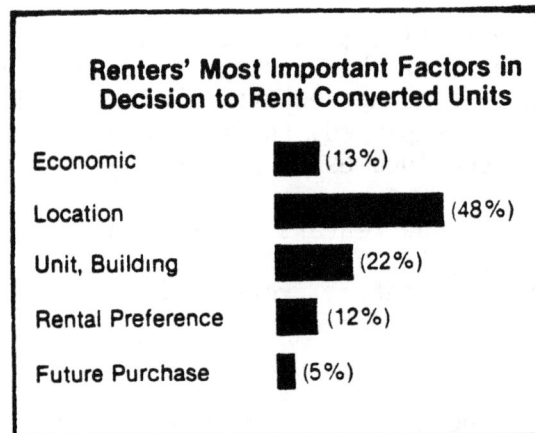

**Renters' Most Important Factors in Decision to Rent Converted Units**

| | |
|---|---|
| Economic | (13%) |
| Location | (48%) |
| Unit, Building | (22%) |
| Rental Preference | (12%) |
| Future Purchase | (5%) |

For one-half of all the renters in converted buildings, the most important factor in their decision to rent was location, although location was much more important to new tenants (58%) than to existing renters (39%). About one-fifth of the renters do so primarily because of the attractiveness of the unit or building. Seventeen percent rent because they were allowed to remain in the building and have an option to buy, or simply because they can rent for a long time before they have to move. Thirteen percent rented because there was little or no increase over previous housing costs.

In contrast to buyers, therefore, renters' decisions depend less on economic factors, such as the cost of renting, than on locational or unit preferences. However, the decision to continue renting in the building must be examined along with the decision not to purchase, which is discussed in the following section.

Those Who Do Not Buy

The previous sections examined the types of owners and renters who live in converted units, as well as their reasons for choosing either form of tenure. This section discusses those residents in the building before conversion who did not buy, first, examining the characteristics of former residents who moved elsewhere and, second, the reasons why these former residents as well as continuing renters in the converted building did not buy.

Most, but not all, of a converted building's former residents go elsewhere to rent. Eighteen percent moved out and purchased another housing unit, 9 percent more (for a total of 27 percent) wanted to buy, but did not. Interestingly, 4 percent of former residents actually purchased their converted units and then moved elsewhere; they are, in effect, investor-owners who rent their units to other households. 14/

Former residents exhibit considerable variation in their incomes, occupations, and ages: there is no overwhelming proportion of old

_____

14/ These figures are based on the first move made by those households which left converted buildings. In Chapter IX (page IX-23), the data on the current residence (that is, the residence where the former resident lived at the time of the interview) are presented. They show that 26 percent of the former residents are currently living in owner-occupied units -- an increase of 8 percent over the percentage of owners at the time of the first move or young, low-income or high-income households. For example, 43 percent of all former residents are under age 36, which is larger than the comparable figure for continuing renters (35 percnt) and tenant buyers (35 percent). While those over 65 constitute one-fifth of all former residents, 60 percent of all those who earn under $12,500 are elderly. Therefore, about 12 percent of all those who move from converted buildings are elderly households with incomes of less than $12,500. Fifty-four percent of the former residents have incomes over $21,500 annually, while only 20 percent make under $12,500. One-half of the households have two persons and almost one-quarter have three or more. Eleven percent are black; 1 percent are Hispanic.

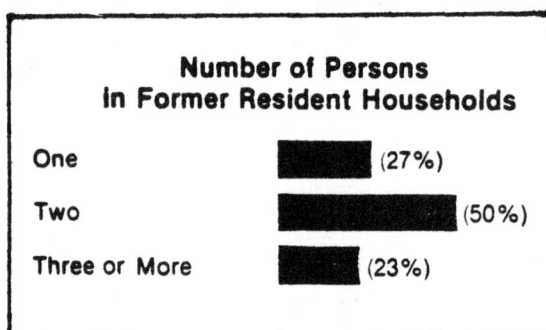

**Number of Persons in Former Resident Households**

| | |
|---|---|
| One | (27%) |
| Two | (50%) |
| Three or More | (23%) |

Former residents of converted buildings do not differ significantly from renters and differ only somewhat from owners, the latter having higher incomes and smaller households. Thirty-nine percent of owners versus 30 percent of former residents earn over $30,000 annually. Fifty-seven percent of owners but only 27 percent of former residents are single persons.

To Recap. The majority of former residents do not have low incomes, in large part because most buildings converted, to date, are at the middle to upper end of the rental market. Rents in the buildings prior to conversion were high enough, in many cases, to have precluded low income households from renting there. However, it is important to remember that these results represent the average of 12 SMSAs. Significant variation can exist from area to area and building to building in the characteristics and experiences of those affected by conversion.

Reasons For Not Buying. Former residents and continuing renters could have purchased their converted units, often at a discounted price. Although they did not do so for several reasons, two reasons dominate all others: tenure choice and affordability.

Overwhelmingly, continuing renters and former residents prefer to
rent or to purchase a single-family home rather than a condominium
or cooperative. About three-fourths of these persons wanted to
continue renting; a few said they were too old to purchase, and a
few said there were too many legal problems with ownership. Former
residents (29%) were more likely than continuing renters (15%) to
prefer to purchase a house.

Affordability was an issue for many during the purchase decision; 47
percent said they could not afford to buy the unit. Fifty-eight
percent could have afforded the purchase costs, but they decided not
to buy either because they did not like the unit well enough to
purchase or they wanted to buy a house. Further discussion of
affordability is given in chapter IX.

Other factors such as the type or location of the unit also played
a role in decisions not to purchase, but these occurred less frequently than rental preference and financial considerations.
Although less than half of these persons were critical of the unit or
location, former residents were twice as likely as continuing renters
to suggest displeasure with the unit or the neighborhood.

* * *

The discussion of demand for conversions has been organized around
three major groups of people: those who buy converted units, those
who rent in converted units, and those who decide not to buy converted units and move from their buildings. Purchasers who occupy
their condominium or cooperative are mostly white, relatively
young, small households. These households have higher than average
incomes and are usually employed in managerial and professional
occupations. Only 19 percent can be considered "empty nesters,"
that is, over 55 and without children living with them. Single
persons, especially single females, and higher income persons
represent a larger share of converted unit owners than of owners
of other housing nationwide. Conversely, fewer elderly or lower
income persons own condominium or cooperative units than own all
forms of housing nationally. Two-thirds of the owners who live in
converted units buy for the economic benefits of ownership, although
economic factors are relatively less important for tenant and
elderly buyers than outside or younger buyers. One in ten of the
owner-occupiers purchases either because of a reluctance to move
or because of a lack of an acceptable rental unit in a desired area.
Tenant buyers more often cite the attraction for the location and
the building or unit as well as a reluctance to move in their
decision to buy.

Nineteen percent of the units are bought by a variety of investors who lease these units to renters.  In the long run, some of these will be sold to owner-occupiers; on the other hand, some units currently owned by owner-occupiers may be sold to investors in the future.

Renters of converted units are newer to the neighborhood than are owners.  They are also less often professionals, have lower incomes, have larger households (more than one person), and are slightly less likely to be white.  However, when compared to renters nationally, renters of converted units have higher incomes and are smaller households.  New renters to the building are twice as likely to be under 36 and have better incomes than continuing renters.  Renters choose to rent in the converted buildings usually because they like the building and/or neighborhood.  A few others wish to buy at some time in the future.

Former residents are found in all age, income, and occupational groups.  They are not primarily elderly or low-income households.  They and continuing renters do not buy in the converted building simply because they wish to rent rather than to own.  One-half cannot afford to purchase, while almost one-third prefer to own single-family homes rather than a condominium or cooperative.

# Chapter VII
# The Interaction of Supply and Demand: Market Effects and Future Volume

Condominium and cooperative conversions have certain obvious effects: housing units once occupied by renters change to owner-occupied status; other rental units are converted to condominiums or cooperatives but continue to be rented rather than occupied by their owners; and some households which once rented housing become owners of converted units. Thus, the effect of these conversions on rental supply or rental demand is not a one-to-one relationship. When rental units are converted to homeowner units, the supply of rental units in the housing market changes; similarly, when renters become homeowners, the demand for rental units is reduced. Previous renters in the converted property who do not purchase or who are unable to continue renting must locate housing elsewhere. The net effect of conversion in the housing market depends upon changes in both the tenure status of households and the occupancy status of housing units.

This chapter considers the interaction of supply and demand in the rental housing market. In the first section, an assessment is made of changes in owner and rental supply and demand based on conversion activity between 1977 and 1979 in the country's 37 largest SMSAs. From this assessment, an index is developed which measures the net effect of conversions on the rental housing market. Following this, three projections of conversion activity between 1980 and 1985 are presented. The first estimate is the sum of 38 separate trend-line projections, based on conversion activity between 1977 and 1979 in the 37 largest SMSAs and the balance of the nation. To determine the second estimate, the trend-line projection is modified to account for constraints on the supply of rental units appropriate for conversion. The trend-line projection is further modified to consider the effect of 1980s high interest rates and related financial conditions on future conversion activity. From this modification, the third estimate of future activity is determined.

These three projections are subject to further changes, depending on factors such as the extent of new multi-family housing construction. This and other factors likely to affect future conversions are discussed briefly. In the final section of the chapter, three scenarios describe what is "least likely" and "most likely" to occur with respect to future conversion activitiy.

## The Net Effect of Rental Conversions on the Housing Market

This section presents the basic elements of a model of the effect of
conversions on the rental market. 1/ Its purpose is to assess changes
in owner and renter supply and demand resulting from conversions
and, consequently, to develop an index indicating the net effect
of conversions on the housing market.

The model is based upon a single-point-in-time analysis (January
1980) of the supply and demand changes occurring between 1977 and
1979 in 12 SMSAs (considered as a group) as a result of condominium
and cooperative conversions. 2/ These SMSAs had high levels of conversion activity during the 1977-79 period, and the model is designed
to estimate the effect of this activity on the collective housing
markets of these SMSAs.  Since 57 percent of all conversion activity
during this period occurred in these 12 SMSAs, it is reasonable to
assume that these effects will be representative of conversions
taking place in the nation as a whole, but not individual markets
of SMSAs.

Although the model and index of net effect may be used with market-
specific data to assess the conversion effect in particular local
areas, the data collected for this study do not permit market-specific
analysis.  It should be noted that the effect of conversions is likely
to differ from market to market and, therefore, the national aggregated
effect may not adequately describe the results of conversion activity
in any particular locality.

---

1/ The model is presented in charts VII-1 and VII-2.  This analysis
is based on information generated from the Survey of Current and Former
Residents described in chapter II.

2/ At present, no information is available to indicate changes in
tenure over time; for example, converted units which are occupied by
their owners may be subsequently rented, or investor-held units may
be sold or occupied by their investor-owners.  It is known that these
and other tenure changes occur, but this cross-sectional study of
recently converted units does not permit an assessment of such changes.
Since the accelerated pace of conversions is a relatively recent
phenomenon, further time and research are required before these tenure
changes can be adequately specified.

# Chart VII-1

**Pre and Post Conversion Status of Households Purchasing Conversions and Former Conversion Residents, With Resulting Changes in the Housing Market Components, as per Each 100 Units Converted, 1977-1979**

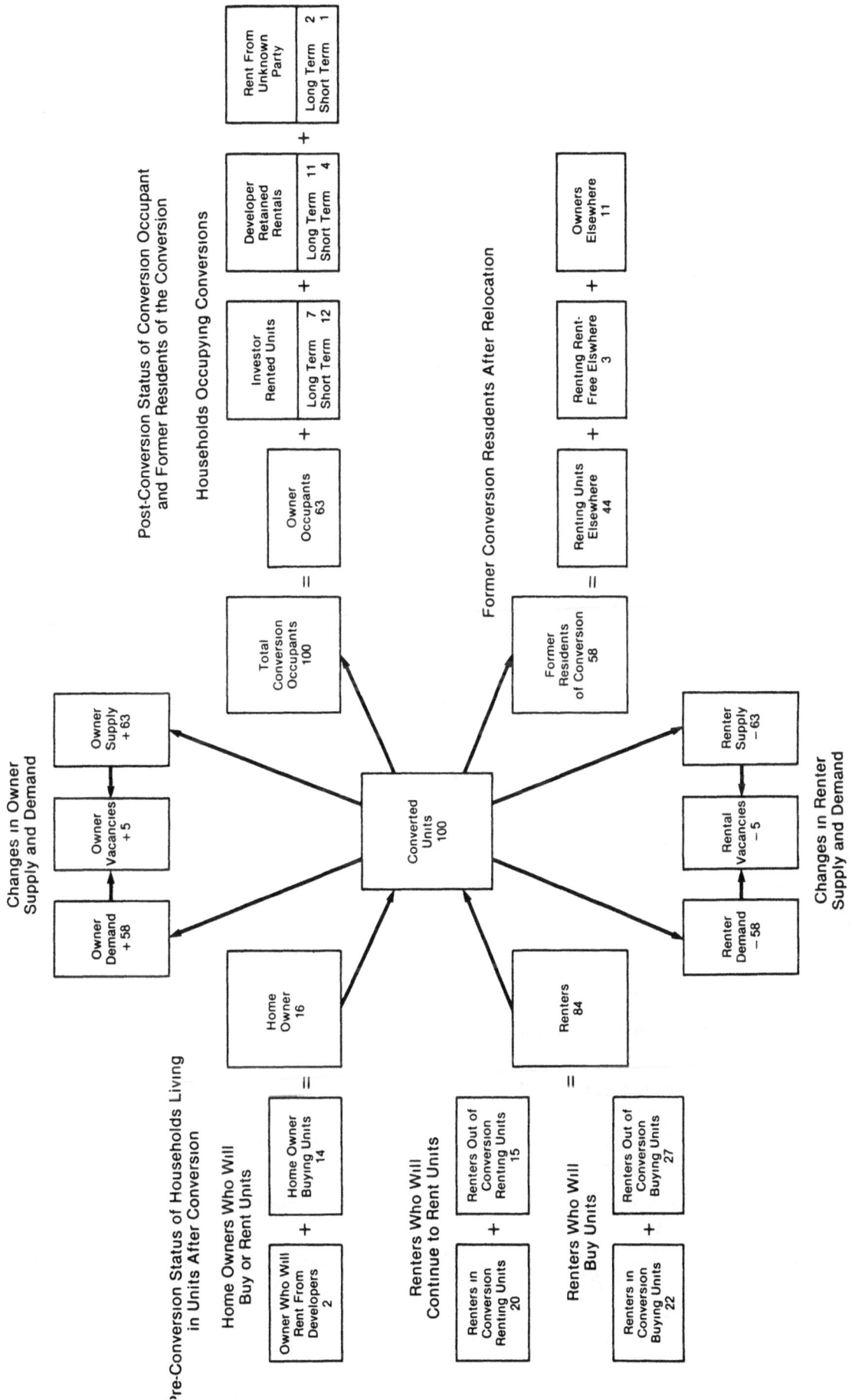

Post-Conversion Status of Conversion Occupant and Former Residents of the Conversion

Households Occupying Conversions

| Rent From Unknown Party | |
|---|---|
| Long Term | 2 |
| Short Term | 1 |

+

| Developer Retained Rentals | |
|---|---|
| Long Term | 11 |
| Short Term | 4 |

+

| Investor Rented Units | |
|---|---|
| Long Term | 7 |
| Short Term | 12 |

+

Owner Occupants 63

=

Total Conversion Occupants 100

Former Conversion Residents After Relocation

Owners Elsewhere 11

+

Renting Rent-Free Elsewhere 3

+

Renting Units Elsewhere 44

=

Former Residents of Conversion 58

Changes in Owner Supply and Demand

Owner Supply + 63

Owner Vacancies + 5

Owner Demand + 58

Converted Units 100

Changes in Renter Supply and Demand

Renter Supply − 63

Rental Vacancies − 5

Renter Demand − 58

Home Owner 16

Renters 84

Pre-Conversion Status of Households Living in Units After Conversion

Home Owners Who Will Buy or Rent Units

Owner Who Will Rent From Developers 2

+

Home Owner Buying Units 14

=

Renters Who Will Continue to Rent Units

Renters in Conversion Renting Units 20

+

Renters Out of Conversion Renting Units 15

=

Renters Who Will Buy Units

Renters in Conversion Buying Units 22

+

Renters Out of Conversion Buying Units 27

Chart VII-2

# Components of Change in the Housing Market Attributable to Conversions

### Changes in Owner Housing Market Attributable to Conversions, as per Each 100 Units Converted

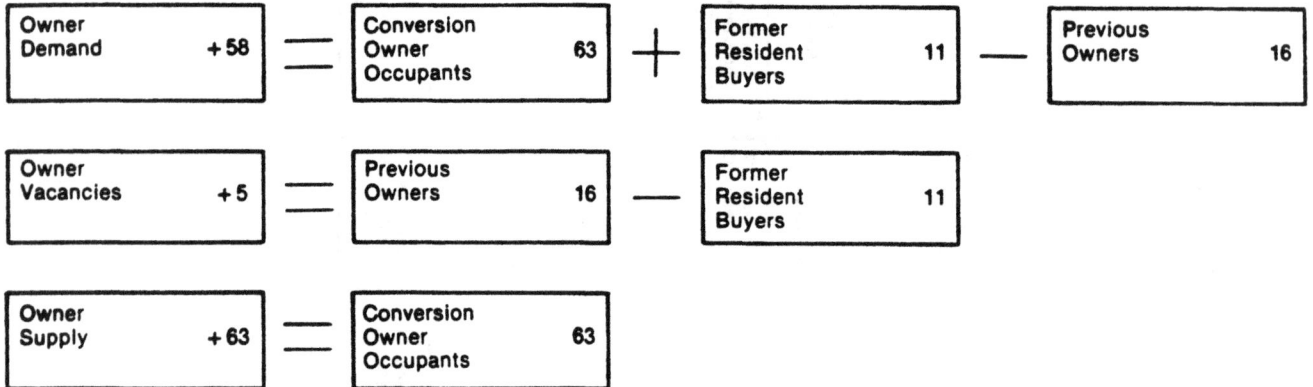

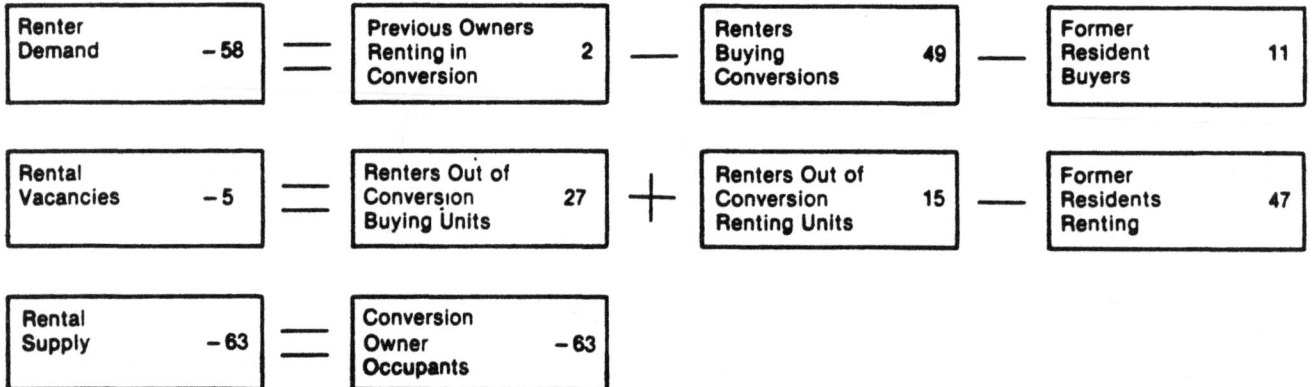

| Owner Demand +58 | = | Conversion Owner Occupants 63 | + | Former Resident Buyers 11 | − | Previous Owners 16 |

| Owner Vacancies +5 | = | Previous Owners 16 | − | Former Resident Buyers 11 |

| Owner Supply +63 | = | Conversion Owner Occupants 63 |

### Changes in Rental Housing Market Attributable to Conversions, as per Each 100 Units Converted

| Renter Demand −58 | = | Previous Owners Renting in Conversion 2 | − | Renters Buying Conversions 49 | − | Former Resident Buyers 11 |

| Rental Vacancies −5 | = | Renters Out of Conversion Buying Units 27 | + | Renters Out of Conversion Renting Units 15 | − | Former Residents Renting 47 |

| Rental Supply −63 | = | Conversion Owner Occupants −63 |

## Definitions

Conversion Owner Occupants Are Households Which Have Purchased Units and Are Living in Them.

Former Resident Buyers Are Households Which Moved Out of the Conversion and Purchased Units in the Area.

Former Residents Renting Refers to Households Which Moved From the Conversion and Continue to Rent Units.

Previous Owners Refers to Households Which Formerly Owned Units in the Area and Now Reside in the Conversions as Owner or Renter.

Renters Buying Conversions Are Households Which Formerly Rented Units, Inside or Outside the Conversio and Bought Converted Units.

Renters Out of Conversion Refers to Households Not Residing in the Units at Time of Conversion; They Ma Currently Be Either Owner or Renter Occupants in the Conversion.

## Pre and Postconversion Status of Households

To assess fully the effect of conversions on the housing market, it is first necessary to determine the preconversion and postconversion status of households which move to and from converted units.

Preconversion Status. The first part of the analysis concerns the previous tenure of households which will move to the converted property. When units are converted to condominiums or cooperatives, their new occupants consist of previous renter and homeowner households. The housing units that are vacated by these households are presumably available for other households to rent or buy. 3/

For every 100 rental housing units converted to condominium or cooperative ownership, 58 are occupied by households who were not occupants of the building before conversion. The following is known about these households: 4/

   o  14 of them are former homeowners who buy 5/
      (24% of 58);

---

The model is simplified to convey the immediate effect of households moving into converted units, households living in such units, and households moving from converted units. For example, no attempt is made to estimate the rents previously paid by renters moving into converted units and to relate them to the rent-paying capacity of tenants leaving the converted units. It is also assumed that no persons moving into or out of converted buildings are from outside the SMSA in which the unit is located; these type of cases were not found in the household survey, but they are likely to occur in some areas and should, therefore, be considered. Further, this model excludes all exogenous factors related to the households moving into, living in, or moving from converted units.

3/ This can be assumed unless the household was newly formed, including recently divorced or separated persons or young adults leaving home. For purposes of this analysis, it is assumed that households moving into converted units do not represent new household formations. The survey did not determine whether the household was newly formed or not.

4/ To simplify the discussion, and to standardize comparisons, a base of 100 converted units will be used for each comparison.

5/ Three of these households who were occupying owner units were not the owner nor did they pay rent. As a result, the tenure status of these units is uncertain. These households may have resulted from new household formations, or households whose employer provided housing, or other circumstances. For the purposes of this analysis, it was assumed that the units which were vacated will continue as owner units rather than rental units.

o  2 of them are former homeowners who rent from
   the converter (3% of 58);

o  27 of them are former renters who buy (47% of
   58): and

o  15 of them are former renters, who rent from
   various parties including investor-owners (26%
   of 58).

Postconversion Status.  Following conversion, unit occupants consist
of renters and owners.  For every 100 rental housing units converted
to condominiums and cooperatives, 63 are occupied by owners and 37
by renters. 6/

Of the 63 owners:

o  14 are previous homeowners from outside the
   converted building (22% of 63);

o  27 are former renters from outside the converted
   building (43% of 63); and

o  22 are former tenants of the converted building
   (35% of 63).

Of the 37 renter households, 20 rented units in the converted building
prior to the conversion; and 17 moved into the building from outside
following the conversion.

The 20 households who were previous tenants in the building include:

o  11 who rent from the building's developer or
   converter (55% of 20);

o  7 who rent from investor-owners (35% of 20);
   and

o  2 who rent from other, unidentified parties
   (10% of 20).

_____

6/ These consist of tenants who rent from investor-purchasers of
converted units and those who rent from landlords and developers,
either while conversion is occurring or after its completion.  For
a discussion of the possible future tenure status of renters in
the converted building, see page VII-38, footnote 39.

The 17 households who moved into the converted building from outside consist of:

- o 4 who rent from the building's developer or converter (23% of 17);

- o 12 who rent from investor-owners (71% of 17); and

- o 1 who rents from an unidentified party (6% of 17).

Following the conversion of 100 units, 58 households move out.  Of these:

- o 44 move to other rental units (76% of 58);

- o 3 move to units as independent renter households and live rent free (5% of 58); and

- o 11 purchase a housing unit elsewhere within the metropolitan area (19% of 58).


Changes in Supply and Demand

Given these changes in pre and postconversion status following the conversion of each 100 units of rental housing, it is possible to determine the changes in owner and rental supply as well as owner and rental demand attributed to conversions.

For purposes of this analysis, owner demand consists of the total number of owner-occupied housing units in the housing market and renter demand consists of the total number of renter-occupied units in the housing market.  Conversely, owner supply consists of all housing units occupied by an owner or for sale for owner occupancy, and renter supply consists of all housing units occupied by a renter or vacant units which are for rent.

Renter Supply and Demand.  For every 100 rental units converted to condominiums and cooperatives, the following is known:

- o 63 units are lost to the rental supply because they are occupied by purchasers;

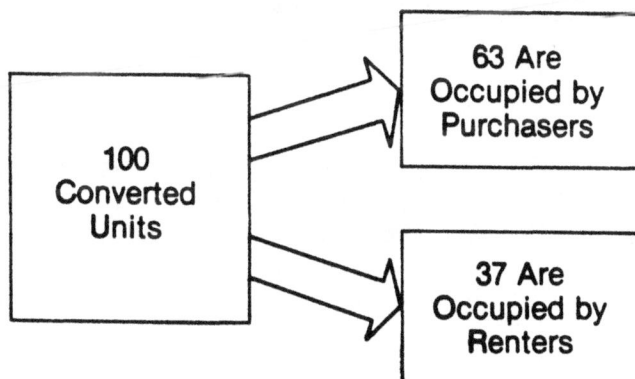

o   of the 63 households who bought and occupy converted units,
    49 were previous renters.  In addition, of 58 former tenants
    in the converted building who moved out, 47 continued to
    rent and 11 bought other housing units.  Considering these
    changes, renter demand is decreased by 60 households, i.e.,
    the 49 renter households who purchased converted units
    and the 11 former tenants who bought housing after moving
    from converted units.  However, since two previous homeowners
    moved to converted units as renters, two households are
    added to renter demand.  Consequently, renter demand is
    actually decreased by 58 households as a result of the
    conversion of 100 units. 7/

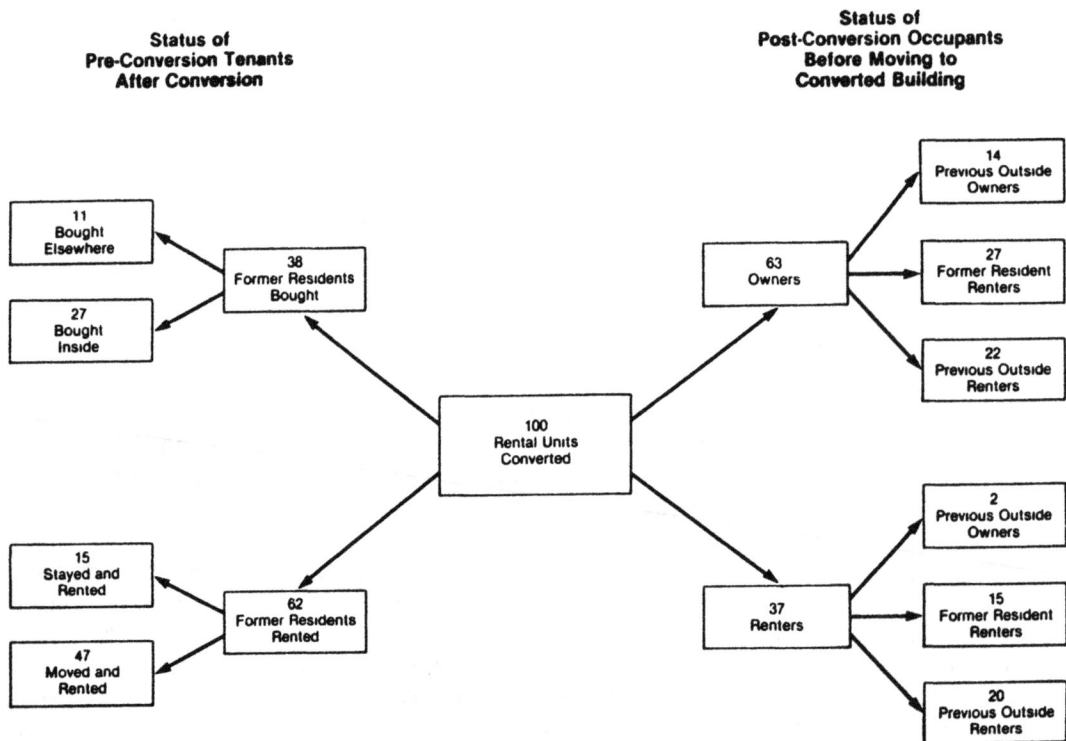

**Status of Pre-Conversion Tenants After Conversion**

**Status of Post-Conversion Occupants Before Moving to Converted Building**

| | |
|---|---|
| 11 Bought Elsewhere | 14 Previous Outside Owners |
| 27 Bought Inside | 27 Former Resident Renters |
| 38 Former Residents Bought | 22 Previous Outside Renters |
| 100 Rental Units Converted | 63 Owners |
| 15 Stayed and Rented | 2 Previous Outside Owners |
| 47 Moved and Rented | 15 Former Resident Renters |
| 62 Former Residents Rented | 37 Renters |
| | 20 Previous Outside Renters |

Again, there is a difference in the degree of change in supply and
demand factors.  The supply of rental units decreases more than
renter demand for this reason:  27 former renters from outside the
converted building move to the building and buy units; 15 former
renters move to a converted building where they will continue to rent
units; hence, 42 rental vacancies occur outside of the converted building.  Forty-seven former tenants of a converted building move elsewhere

_____

7/  This consists of both renters who rent from investor-purchasers
or converters, either while conversion is occuring or after it is
completed.  (See chapter VI for additional information.)

but continue to rent. Although 42 vacant units resulted from conversion, 47 vacant units were needed. Thus, for every 100 units converted, a net of 5 previously vacant units in the rental housing market became occupied.

Owner Supply and Demand. For every 100 rental housing units converted to condominiums or cooperatives, the following is known:

o  63 of these units are occupied by owners. Thus, the supply of owner occupied units in the housing market is increased by 63; and

o  of all converted units, 16 of them (consisting of 14 owners of converted units and 2 renters of converted units) are occupied by previous homeowners. Since these 16 are former homeowners not adding to owner demand, there is an increase of 47 units (63 minus 16) in owner demand. An additional 11 former residents of units that were converted moved out and bought housing elsewhere, therefore adding to the amount of owner demand in the housing market. Consequently, owner demand is increased by 58 households as a result of of converting 100 rental units.

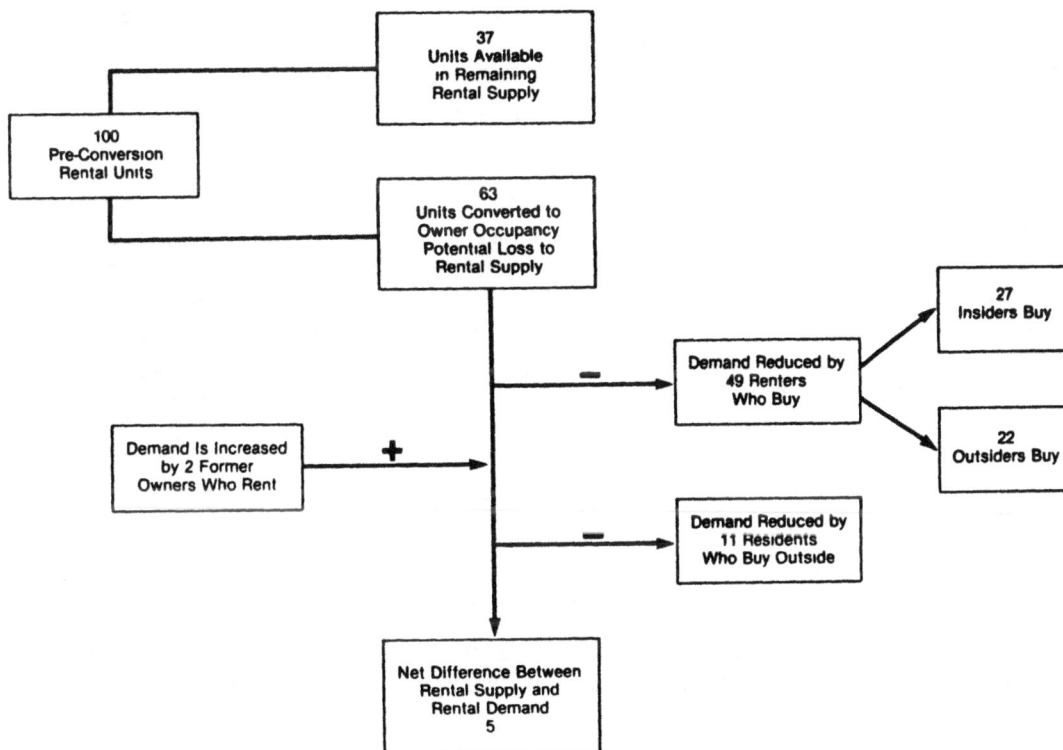

After conversion owner supply (63) increased more than owner demand
(58) because more owner units were available for purchase than there
were households to buy them. That is, 16 previous homeowners bought
converted units and their former housing became vacant. Simultaneously, 11 households which formerly rented in the converted building
bought vacant owner units. As a result, a net of 5 vacant owner units
are created in the housing market by the conversion of 100 units.

In summary, the conversion of 100 rental units results in a net number
of 58 households changing from renter to owner status: 63 rental units
changing to owner units; a net addition of five vacant units for sale,
and 5 less vacant rental units. In each area, the change in the
rental part of the market is mirrored by changes in the owner section
of the housing market.


## An Index of Conversion's Effects on The Housing Market

For every 100 units of rental housing that are converted to condominiums and cooperatives, the net effect on the housing market is an
increase of 5 vacant owner units and a decrease of 5 vacant rental
units. This change in the housing market is an index of the effect
of condominium and cooperative conversion on that market. Depending
on whether the owner or renter portion of the market is being discussed, the aggregate index for the 12 housing markets included
in this analysis is +5 (owner units) or -5 (rental units). As indicated above, this index can be expected to vary from place to place
according to local market conditions, and can also be expected to
vary with time.

The index of net conversion effects must be related to the supply of
rental housing units in order to estimate the absolute amount of loss
to the rental housing stock which can be attributed to condominium
and cooperative conversions. 8/  If it is assumed that the conversion
effect observed in the 12 SMSAs with high activity between 1977 and
1979 is similar to what occurred nationally during the 1970s, the
following took place:  between 1970 and 1979, 366,000 units were
converted; the Nation's rental housing supply was reduced by 231,000
units; renter demand fell by 212,000 households; and a net total
of 18,000 previously vacant rental units were occupied by former
tenants of converted buildings. 9/

---

8/ Chart VII-1 presents the components of the model of housing market
changes resulting from conversion as they affect the rental housing
market.

9/ This assumption is supported by the data, since 69 percent of all
conversions occurred between 1977 and 1979 and, of these conversions,
57 percent took place in the 12 high activity SMSAs.

VII-11

## TABLE VII-1

### PERCENT OF RENTAL HOUSING CONVERTED, WITH CHANGES IN COMPONENTS OF RENTAL HOUSING MARKET RESULTING FROM CONVERSIONS

| | 1970-75 | 1976 | 1977 | 1978 | 1979 (3 Quarters) | Total 1970-79 | Total 1977-79 |
|---|---|---|---|---|---|---|---|
| Occupied Rental Housing 1/ | 25,656,000 | 26,101,000 | 26,515,000 | 26,515,000 | 26,515,000 | 26,515,000 | 26,515,000 |
| Total Conversion 2/ | 85,746 | 19,976 | 45,527 | 80,334 | 114,893 | 346,476 | 240,754 |
| Percent Converted | .32 | .08 | .17 | .30 | .43 | 1.31 | .91 |
| Loss of Units to Rental Supply 3/ | 54,020 | 12,585 | 28,682 | 50,610 | 72,383 | 218,280 | 151,675 |
| Drop in Renter Demand 4/ | 49,733 | 11,586 | 26,406 | 46,594 | 66,638 | 200,956 | 139,637 |
| Net Shortfall of Rental Supply 5/ | 4,287 | 999 | 2,276 | 4,017 | 5,745 | 17,324 | 12,038 |
| Net Shortfall of Rental Supply as Percent of Rental Supply | .017 | .004 | .009 | .016 | .022 | .065 | .045 |

1/ Annual Housing Survey, Series H-150-75,-76,-77, Bureau of the Census, Washington, D.C., 1976-77-78. The 1977 figure is used for 1978 and 1979.

2/ Department of Housing and Urban Development, Field Interviews in 37 SMSAs Conducted by HUD Staff, September and November 1979.

3/ Sixty-three percent of the converted units were owner-occupied after conversion. The remaining 37 percent were rented out by their owners. Field Interviews, Ibid.

4/ Forty-nine percent of those who bought converted units had previously rented, and 11 percent of the renters who moved from the converted building bought housing elsewhere. However, 2 percent of those who moved into the converted building as renters were former homeowners; hence renter demand has dropped by 58 percent of the total units converted. Field Interviews, Ibid.

5/ Forty-two percent of the current residents had rented units elsewhere; 27 percent are now owners and 15 percent are renters in the converted building. However, 47 percent of all former residents now rent outside of the converted building, resulting in a net shortfall of rental supply equal to 5 percent of all converted units.

The figure of 18,000 represents the net number of renter households moving from converted units to rental units elsewhere. Eighteen thousand units represent .065 percent of the Nation's occupied rental housing supply. Thus, the net effect of all conversion activity occurring between 1970 and 1979 has been to increase the Nation's occupied rental supply by 18,000 units and to decrease the Nation's rental vacancies by a corresponding 18,000 units. 10/

## Conversion and Other Changes in the Rental Market

The influence on conversions may also be related to the other components of change in the rental housing market. In order to illustrate this relationship, these changes will be discussed for the 1977 rental housing market. (See table VII-2.)

The rental housing supply experienced several major changes in 1977. There were an additional 567,000 rental units built, but the rental supply decreased by 481,000 units, including 51,000 units converted to condominium or cooperative ownership. Therefore, the net result is an increase of 86,000 rental units (567,000 new units minus 481,000 units removed from the rental stock). The 86,000 figure represents only .31 percent of the 1977 rental supply, and converted units accounted for 11 percent of the total decline in the 1977 rental stock. 11/

The 1977 demand for rental housing increased by the 595,000 new households formed that year, while demand for rentals decreased by the net number of 202,000 former renter households which bought housing in 1977. Of the net number of former renter households

---

10/ The U.S. rental housing stock figure is for 1977, the last year for which reliable national housing estimates are available.

11/ According to the Survey of Current and Former Residents, 63 percent of all converted units were owner occupied; 19 percent were occupied by households renting from an investor-purchaser, and 18 percent were occupied by households renting from a converter. Because the future tenure status of the households renting from a converter is uncertain, this analysis assumes that the proportion of units rented from converters (18%) are in an interim stage of the conversion process and will soon become owner occupied. Therefore, it is assumed that 81 percent of all converted units are owner occupied. As a result of these two assumptions, the analysis overstates by 11,000 owner-occupied units the actual number of such units converted in the 1977 period.

purchasing housing, 51,000 (25%) bought converted units. Therefore the net increase in rental demand for 1977 is 393,000 households, or 1.48 percent of all households renting units in 1977.

The net result of changes in the supply of and demand for rental housing is an insufficient number of rental units to meet renter demand. A net total of 307,000 units were required to meet new rental demand (393,000, the net increase in rental demand, minus 86,000, the net increase in rental units). The 307,000 units represent 1.09 percent of the 1977 rental housing supply. Thus, the overall net effect of conversions on the 1977 national rental market was 11 percent of the reductions in the overall rental stock; 25 percent of the total reduction in rental demand; and 17 percent of the shortfall in the supply of rental housing units. 12/

## Strategy for Projecting Conversion Activity

The interaction of supply and demand also has a significant impact on the number of conversions likely to occur. In the following section, the number of rental housing units which will be converted between 1980 and 1985 is projected. The projection accounts for the supply of rental housing units suitable for conversion and the extent of owner demand for converted units by different types of households. While the preceding analysis focuses on the direct influence of conversions on housing units and households in the recent past, the analysis here considers the effect of converted units in the larger context of the overall housing market between 1980 and 1985.

Several factors make it difficult to project conversion activity. First, large-scale conversions are a relatively recent real estate phenomenon. Before 1970, isolated conversions occurred, but most growth took place after that year, with the bulk occurring since 1976. Second, no major studies describe the influence of various housing market changes, such as rising interest rates, on conversion activity. Third, the relative lack of knowledge about conversion activity over time and under various market conditions means that any model or procedure for projecting conversions must be based upon reasonable, but

---

12/ If it is assumed that 63 percent (rather than 81 percent) of all converted units are owner occupied, the net effect of conversion on the 1977 national rental market is 9 percent of the reduction in the overall rental supply, 20 percent of the reduction in renter demand, and 14 percent of the shortfall in the supply of rental housing.

## TABLE VII-2

### INFLUENCE OF CONVERSIONS ON THE U.S. RENTAL HOUSING MARKET, 1977

| Components of Rental Housing Market | Renter Demand Due New Household Formation | New Rental Units | Conversions to Condo/Co-op Ownership | Renter to Owner Tenure Shift | Rental Removals From Inventory | Net Change for 1977 Total Rental Housing Number | Percent | Percent Change Due to Conversions |
|---|---|---|---|---|---|---|---|---|
| 1977 rental market aggregate estimates | 595,000 1/ | 567,000 2/ | 51,000 3/ | 151,000 4/ | 430,000 5/ | - | - |  |
| Rental housing supply |  | +567,000 | -51,000 |  | -430,000 | +86,000 | +.31 | -10.60 6/ |
| Renter household demand | +595,000 |  | -51,000 | -151,000 |  | +393,000 | +1.48 | -25.25 7/ |
| Shortfall of rental housing units compared to rental demand | - | - | - | - | - | 307,000 | 1.09 | 16.61 8/ |

Source: U.S. Bureau of Census, Series H-150-77, Annual Housing Survey, Part A, GPO, Washington, D.C., 1979; Field Interviews/Study, op. cit.

1/ There was an average increase of 1,691,000 households per year in the 1970-77 period. In 1977, renter households were 35.2 percent of all households. Thus, 1,691,00 multiplied by 35.2 percent results in 595,000 additional rental households in 1977.

2/ There were a total of 4,539,000 rental units built between 1970-77, or an average of 567,000 per year. This total includes single-family units built since 1970 and now occupied as rentals.

3/ There were 45,000 conversions in 1977 and 80,000 conversions in 1978, for an average of 63,000 converted units. The two years are averaged to make the 1977 conversion total more representative of the 1977-79 period of conversion units. Also, 19 percent are owned by investors and will remain renters, for a total of 51,000 owner occupied units.

4/ This figure is from the table on changes in household composition, formation, and tenure; a net total of 202,000 households per year (in the 1970-77 period) shifted from renter to owner status. If 51,000 renter to owner shifts are due to conversions, 151,000 renter to owner shifts occur outside of conversions.

5/ There are a total of 1,721,000 rental units which existed in 1973 and were removed from the housing inventory by 1977, or an average of 430,000 units per year.

6/ Conversions are 11 percent of the total loss of rental stock, including both conversions and removals from the rental inventory.

7/ Conversions account for 25 percent of the decrease in renter demand, including that due to conversions and other factors.

8/ Conversions account for 17 percent of the total amount of shortfall of rental housing units compared to the increase in renter household demand.

necessarily arbitrary, assumptions concerning the role conversions will play in the 1980-85 housing market. Fourth, although national projections should be based on the sum of projected conversions at all local levels, this is a very complex process, and necessary data are lacking. To project conversion activity from 1980 "o 1985, these approaches are used.

o   A trend-line projection is developed, based upon 1977-79 conversion trends for the 37 largest SMSAs and the remaining areas of the Nation. The resulting projection is based on the recent expansion of conversion activity, exclusive of any supply or demand constraints.

o   Following this, the trend-line projection is modified by considering (at the SMSA level) possible limits on the potential supply of rental units appropriate for conversion. This illustrates the effect of a diminishing supply of suitable rental units on future conversion activity.

o   In a third step, the trend-line projections are related to demand considerations. These factors include the types of households which buy converted units and the income restrictions households face in purchasing housing.

o   Next, estimates of future conversion activity provided by local government officials in jurisdictions outside the 37 largest SMSAs allow an evaluation of future activity in the balance of the Nation.

o   Factors other than the supply of and demand for converted units are considered, too. The political or legal actions of governments, general economic constraints, and demographic issues are taken into account in this step.

o   Finally, future conversion activity is described in terms of "most likely" and "least likely" scenarios.


## A Trend-Line Projection of Conversion Activity: 1980-85

The first step in projecting conversion activity is to examine local trends throughout the country from 1977 to 1979, a period in which conversion activity expanded greatly. Since a few areas experienced

TABLE VII-3

TREND-LINE PROJECTION OF CONVERSION ACTIVITY,
1980-85 BASED ON 1977-79 LOCAL TRENDS

| Projection Years | 37 Largest SMSAs | | Balance of United States | Total United States |
| | 12 High Activity SMSAs | 25 Other Large SMSAs | | |
| --- | --- | --- | --- | --- |
| 1980 | 67,150 | 26,227 | 37,573 | 130,950 |
| 1981 | 84,634 | 35,548 | 55,188 | 175,370 |
| 1982 | 102,018 | 44,869 | 72,803 | 219,690 |
| 1983 | 119,787 | 54,190 | 90,418 | 264,395 |
| 1984 | 138,452 | 63,779 | 108,033 | 310,264 |
| 1985 | 157,117 | 73,406 | 125,648 | 356,171 |
| 1980-85 Total | 669,158 | 298,019 | 489,663 | 1,456,840 |

a decrease in the pace of conversions during this time 13/, a projection of these trends suggests that the number of units likely to be converted in 1980 is 4,000 units less than the 135,000 converted during 1979. 14/ In 1981, conversions will increase by an average of 45,000 units per year until 1985. These projections are derived from 38 separate trends, one for each of the 37 largest SMSAs and one for the balance of the United States. Based on the projected annual increases (exclusive of supply, demand, or other considerations), it is estimated that 1,457,000 rental units will be converted to condominium or cooperative ownership between 1980 and 1985. This compares to 366,000 units converted between 1970 and 1979.

---

13/ The trend-line projection for each of the 37 SMSAs and the areas outside the 37 SMSAs uses as a base the 1977-79 average number of conversions. Each year, the 1977-79 average number of conversions is increased or decreased by the average change in the level of conversion activity from 1977 to 1978 and from 1978 to 1979, where the 1979 figure is inflated to reflect a full 12 months of conversion activity. In most cases, this results in the highest number of conversions likely to occur in an SMSA, reflecting the continuation of recent trends. Table VII-3 presents, in summary form, the results for the 37 largest SMSAs and the balance of the U.S.

14/ The February 1, 1980 issue of U.S. Housing Markets, published by Citicorp, predicts the same level of conversion activity for 1980 as for 1979, i.e., 145,000 units. The Citicorp estimate is 10,000 units more than the projection presented here.

Among the 12 SMSAs with high levels of conversion activity, an annual increase of about 18,000 conversions over the 1977-79 base is projected through 1985. This means 669,000 units will be converted in the 1980-85 period in these areas. During the 1977-79 period, conversions declined in three central cities of these SMSAs, 15/ and, therefore, projected conversion activity in each of these cities is reduced by a number which corresponds to the annual declines in 1977, 1978, and 1979. In each case, however, it is expected that units will continue to be converted in suburban areas after activity has slowed in the central city.

Conversion activity in 25 other large SMSAs is projected to rise at the rate of 9,000 units per year over the 1977-79 annual average for a total of 298,000 conversions from 1980 to 1985. Although conversion activity in these 25 areas has been generally moderate, several central cities and suburbs experienced declines in 1977-79. As a result, conversions may cease before 1985 in these low activity locations. 16/

The most noteworthy growth in recent years occurred outside the 37 largest SMSAs. Conversions in the balance of the nation increased from 5,000 in 1977 to 40,000 in 1979, representing an annual growth rate of 18,000 units. From 1980 to 1985, it is projected that 490,000 units will be converted in these areas.

To Recap. Based on trend-line projections, it is estimated that between 1980 and 1985, 1,457,000 rental units will be converted to condominium or cooperative ownership. Of these units, 669,000 will be located in the 12 SMSAs with high levels of conversion activity; 298,000 will be in the 25 other large SMSAs and 490,000 units will be in the remaining areas of the nation.


Constraints on Future Conversions Related to the Supply of Rental Units Suitable for Conversion

To determine the effect of supply constraints, an estimate is first made of the occupied rental housing supply appropriate for conversion. This estimate is then compared to the number of conversions projected for 1980-85. Based on this comparison, any necessary adjustments are made to the trend-line projection.

-------------------

15/ The central cities with declining activity are Houston, Los Angeles-Long Beach, and San Francisco-Oakland.

16/ The central cities with declining activity between 1977 and 1979 are San Diego and Riverside, California. Suburbs with declining activity are located in the Buffalo, Milwaukee, Newark, and Pittsburgh SMSAs.

By examining the remaining rental housing stock, it is possible to estimate the proportion of the housing stock with characteristics similar to buildings converted in the past. This proportion is considered "convertible."

Two attributes of rental properties are particularly significant in selecting candidates for conversion: (1) the condition of the structure; and (2) the desirability of, or demand for, the units. 17/ Well-maintained rental properties with relatively new mechanical systems and structural components are usually considered the most suitable for conversion. Likewise, buildings with desirable locations, sought after amenities, and status or prestige are appropriate conversion candidates. To measure the condition and desirability of the Nation's rental housing stock, two reasonable surrogates are used. A rental building's age serves as a proxy for its condition, and the rent level (relative to the median rent in the community) is a proxy for a building's desirability. For purposes of this analysis, these measures are used to distinguish among three types of rental units (See table VII-4.):

o Prime buildings. Buildings with prime conversion potential have units which rent for 150 percent or more of the local median rent and were built after 1965. The buildings have relatively modern, good quality mechanical systems and structural components; are in excellent locations; and have desirable amenities. Units in such buildings now comprise 5.5 percent of the Nation's occupied rental stock as of 1977.

o Marginal buildings. Buildings with marginal conversion potential have units which rent for 125 to 150 percent of the local median rent and were built after 1965. Their condition is probably as good as buildings in the "prime" category, but various factors make them slightly less desirable than the more expensive rentals. This category contains 5.4 percent of the Nation's 1977 occupied rental stock.

o Rehabilitation buildings. Buildings which have conversion potential only after rehabilitation were built before 1965 and have units which rent for 125 percent or more of local median rent. They are likely to be desirable rental properties,

_____

17/ These factors emerged during extensive discussions with persons who are associated with condominium and cooperative conversions across the Nation. They are corroborated in many local studies on the topic and in numerous accounts of conversion which appear in the printed media. Appendix 1 provides an annotated bibliography of the printed material.

### TABLE VII-4
### 1977 NATIONAL RENTAL HOUSING SUPPLY OF POTENTIAL
### CONVERTIBLE UNITS AND PERCENT OF OCCUPIED RENTAL UNITS 1/

| United States | Single Family Attached | | 2 to 4 Units | | 5 or More Units | | Total | |
|---|---|---|---|---|---|---|---|---|
| | Number | % of Rental | Number | % of Rentals | Number | % of Rentals | Number | % of Rental |
| Prime Potential Conversions (150% or more of Median Rent) | 136,653 | 0.52 | 309,959 | 1.17 | 1,012,602 | 3.82 | 1,459,214 | 5.50 |
| Built Since 1970 | 97,142 | 0.37 | 207,817 | 0.78 | 675,900 | 2.55 | 980,859 | 3.70 |
| Built 1965-1970 | 39,511 | 0.15 | 102,142 | 0.39 | 336,702 | 1.27 | 478,355 | 1.80 |
| Marginal Potential Conversions (125 to 150% of Median Rent) | 55,923 | 0.21 | 265,609 | 1.00 | 1,102,229 | 4.16 | 1,423,761 | 5.37 |
| Built Since 1970 | 24,445 | 0.09 | 171,877 | 0.65 | 675,374 | 2.55 | 871,696 | 3.29 |
| Built 1965-1970 | 31,478 | 0.12 | 93,732 | 0.35 | 426,855 | 1.61 | 552,065 | 2.08 |
| Rehabilitation Potential Conversions (Built Before 1965) | 161,050 | 0.61 | 1,047,275 | 3.95 | 1,293,081 | 4.88 | 2,501,406 | 9.43 |
| 150% or more of Median Rent | 83,571 | 0.32 | 476,573 | 1.80 | 621,615 | 2.34 | 1,181,759 | 4.46 |
| 125-150% of Median Rent | 77,479 | 0.29 | 570,702 | 2.15 | 671,466 | 2.53 | 1,319,647 | 4.98 |
| Total Potential Conversions | 353,626 | 1.33 | 1,622,843 | 6.12 | 3,407,912 | 12.85 | 5,384,381 | 20.31 |

Source: 1977 National Annual Housing Survey Tape, U.S. Department of Commerce, Bureau of Census, Washington, D.C.

1/ Renter occupied units in 1977 numbered 26,515,000.

but they may require replacement or substantial repair
of some of their major structural components and mechanical systems, parking areas, and grounds.  To convert
these buildings generally requires more knowledge of
rehabilitation techniques than is needed for the "as
is" conversions usually performed in prime and marginal
buildings.  Therefore, it takes longer and costs more to
convert these buildings.  This last type of housing stock
constitutes the principal source of convertible units in
older cities such as Boston and Hartford.  Rehabilitation
units constitutes 9.4 percent of the Nation's occupied
rental stock.  (See table VII-4.)

Together, these categories represent 20.3 percent of the Nation's total
rental supply suitable for conversion. 18/ (See table V11-4.)  When
the proportion of the rental stock which was converted between 1977
and 1979 (.9 %) is subtracted from this percentage, 19.4 percent of
the remaining rental stock is "convertible." As of January 1980, 19.4
percent is equal to 5,134,400 rental units.  Within this group, 11
SMSAs with high conversion activity contain 1,376,100 convertible
units.  This number represents 27 percent of all units with conversion
potential and 19 percent of the rental housing supply in the 11 SMSAs.
It is estimated that the remaining 21 large SMSAs have 779,500 rental

---

18/ This may be disaggregated as follows:  1.3 percent are single-family
attached units; 6.1 percent of the units are in buildings of two to
four units; and 12.9 percent are in buildings with five or more units.
Single-family attached units refer to row houses or townhouses, where
no other units are above or below the unit.  These conversions have
been quite popular in many areas.  Other additional factors should
be considered concerning the potential for future conversions.  First,
some developers are building multi-family rentals with the intention
of renting them for several years, depreciating the building, and
then converting the units to condominiums or cooperatives.  To the
extent that this occurs, these newly built multifamily rentals will
provide stock for future conversions.  Second, as the cost of purchasing
newer rental properties continues to escalate relative to the potential
profit from a conversion, rental units which are now considered undesir-
able, e.g., low rent buildings in revitalizing areas, may become attractive candidates for conversion.  The potential for conversion is limited
only by the ingenuity and skill of developers and, of course, by the
demand for converted units.

units appropriate for conversion; this is equivalent to 17 percent of the rental stock in these areas and 15 percent of the country's convertible rental housing. 19/

**Percentage of the Nation's Total
Rental Stock Suitable for Conversion**

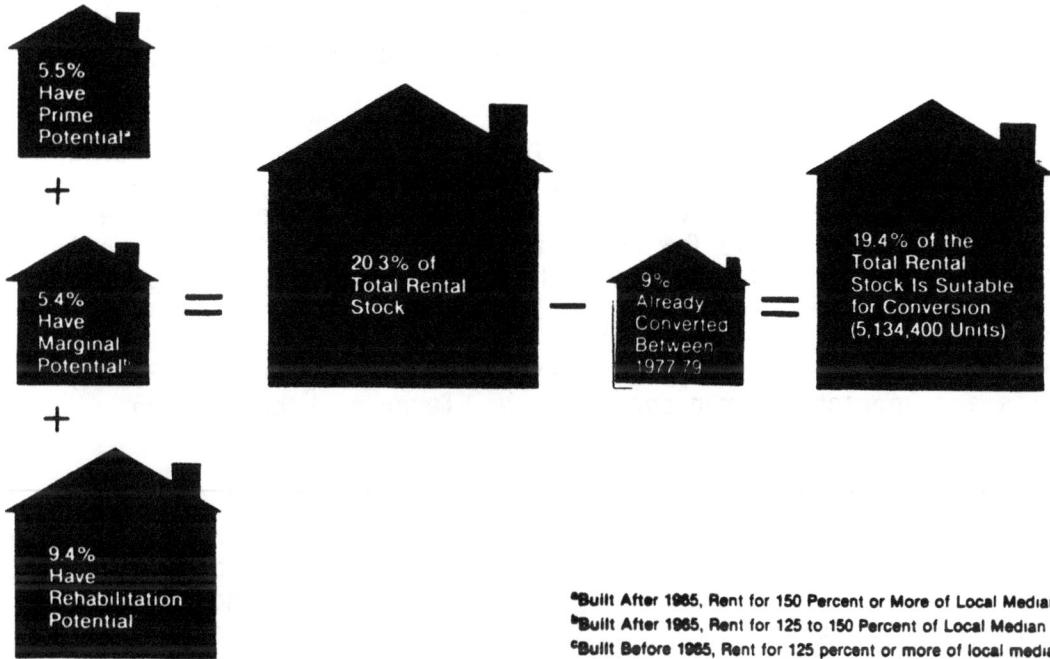

5.5%
Have
Prime
Potential*

+

5.4%
Have
Marginal
Potential*

+

9.4%
Have
Rehabilitation
Potential

=

20.3% of
Total Rental
Stock

−

9%
Already
Converted
Between
1977-79

=

19.4% of the
Total Rental
Stock Is Suitable
for Conversion
(5,134,400 Units)

*Built After 1965, Rent for 150 Percent or More of Local Median
*Built After 1965, Rent for 125 to 150 Percent of Local Median
*Built Before 1965, Rent for 125 percent or more of local median

Among units located outside of these 32 SMSAs, 2,978,800 (or 20.5% of the occupied rental stock in these areas) have conversion potential. Overall, 58 percent of the Nation's convertible rental units are located outside of the 32 largest metropolitan areas. The likelihood that these units will actually be converted to condominiums and cooperatives depends on whether the conversion trend, which began in and around the largest cities of the Nation, diffuses to the remainder of the country. Evidence indicates this may already be happening. Local observers in smaller metropolitan areas such

---

19/ During the 1973-76 period, Annual Housing Surveys were not conducted in the SMSAs for Hartford, Nassau-Suffolk, San Antonio, San Jose, and Tampa-St. Petersburg. Therefore, data are not available to estimate the convertible rental stock in these areas. In addition, Fort Worth was not part of the Dallas-Fort Worth SMSA during this period. Information presented is only for Dallas.

as Lansing, Michigan; Madison, Wisconsin; Raleigh, North Carolina; and Eugene, Oregon, report that conversions have begun there and will increase in the near future. 20/

Although there is no way to determine how widespread conversions will ultimately become, these data suggest that it will be some time before the Nation's supply of convertible rental units is exhausted. In some localities, however, that supply is already low and may be nearly exhausted by 1985. Developers in some communities, such as Houston, believe that the convertible supply is nearly depleted. 21/

Similarly, as SMSAs exhaust their supply of units with conversion potential, large-scale converters, in particular, may move to markets where the supply of rental buildings suitable for conversion is more plentiful. The few remaining convertible units will be left to smaller converters. To some extent, this has already happened in areas such as Denver and Chicago. 22/

To Recap. Of the Nation's occupied rental housing supply, 5,134,400 units are appropriate for conversion. Eleven high conversion

---

20/ U.S. Department of Housing and Urban Development, Field Interviews in 37 SMSAs Conducted by HUD staff, September and November 1979. In addition, a survey of apartment managers in the U.S. indicates that about 5 percent of the apartment units in smaller cities (less than 50,000 people) are currently being considered for conversion. Four percent of the units are considered somewhat likely to be converted. In larger cities (50,000 to 250,000 people), 15 percent of the apartment units are being considered for conversion, and 4 percent are somewhat likely to be converted. About 12 percent of the apartment units in the largest cities (more than 250,000 people) are being considered for conversion, and 9 percent are very or somewhat likely to be converted. Suburbs of the largest cities are expecting the most conversions: 21 percent of the units are being considered for conversion, and 21 percent are very or somewhat likely to be converted. See table VII-3 Appendix for details.

21/ Although some local developers in Houston believe that the supply of converted units has become depleted, the analysis contained herein suggests that there are a large number of additional convertible units in that city. This apparent contradiction reflects a strong rental housing market, high demand for newer rentals, extensive in-migration, and a vigorous competition between converted units and new, lower priced, single-family homes. Thus, a large share of the rental stock appropriate for conversion is still subject to demand from renters willing to pay higher rents and to competition from builders of new condominiums and single-family homes.

22/ See footnote 20.

activity SMSAs have 1,376,100 of these units; the 21 other large SMSAs have 779,500 of these units; and the balance of the nation has 2,978,800 units with conversion potential.

If the projected number of converted units is compared to the number of units suitable for conversion, it is estimated that five SMSAs will exhaust their stock of convertible housing before the end of 1985. However, since the number of convertible units is based on Annual Housing Surveys conducted between 1974 and 1976, it is likely that multi-family units built since the Surveys will become additional candidates for conversion. In this analysis, it is assumed that all multi-family rental units built between 1976 and 1980 will be consider ed for conversion within five years of their construction if an SMSA's supply of convertible units is otherwise exhausted. After adding these newly built units to the supply of convertible units in these five SMSAs, it is estimated that three of them will have a sufficient supply of units to continue their 1977-79 rate of conver- sion. The remaining SMSAs will be unable to sustain the 1977-79 conversion pace.

It should be noted that in some metropolitan areas, few unsubsidized multi-family rental units have been constructed in recent years. Therefore, in these particular markets, this source of potential conversions may be limited. In addition, once the supply of poten- tial conversions is exhausted in an SMSA, it is possible that the perception of what type of unit is suitable for conversion may change. If this occurs, more modest, less desirable units not considered in this analysis may be converted.

Based on the preceding analysis of supply constraints, conversion activity between 1980 and 1985 cannot proceed at the 1977-79 rate in the 12 high activity SMSAs, taken in the aggregate. In the other 25 SMSAs, and in the balance of the country, conversions could continue at their 1977-79 pace through 1985.

When limits on the supply of convertible units are considered, the modified trend-line projection indicates that 1,374,000 units will be converted between 1980 and 1985. (See table VII-5.) This amounts to 5 percent of the country's occupied rental stock. Among the 12 SMSAs with high conversion activity, about 8 percent of the rental stock can be expected to convert. This compares to 6 percent of the stock for the 25 other large SMSAs and 4 percent of the stock for the balance of the nation.

To Recap. After modifying the trend-line projection to account for limits in the supply of convertible units, it is estimated that 1,374,000 rental units will be converted between 1980 and 1985. Of these units, 586,000 are located in the 12 SMSAs which have had high conversion activty; 298,000 are located in 25 other large SMSAs; and 490,000 are located in the remainder of the country.

## TABLE VII-5

### TREND-LINE PROJECTION OF CONVERSION ACTIVITY, 1980-85
### MODIFIED BY LIMITS IN THE SUPPLY OF CONVERTIBLE UNITS

| Projection Year | 12 High Activity SMSA | 25 Other Large SMSAs | Balance of U.S. | Total U.S. |
|---|---|---|---|---|
| 1980 | 67,150 | 26,227 | 37,573 | 130,950 |
| 1981 | 77,982 | 35,548 | 55,188 | 168,718 |
| 1982 | 74,794 | 44,869 | 72,803 | 192,466 |
| 1983 | 107,853 | 54,190 | 90,418 | 252,461 |
| 1984 | 121,942 | 63,779 | 108,033 | 293,754 |
| 1985 | 136,227 | 73,406 | 125,648 | 335,281 |
| 1980-85 Total | 585,948 | 298,019 | 489,663 | 1,373,613 |

## Constraints on Future Conversions Related to Household Demand

Thus far, the discussion has proceeded under the assumption that conversion activity will continue at the 1977-79 rate, with some modification to allow for supply constraints. However, it is not self-evident that the demand for converted units will sustain this projected level of activity. If, for example, the rate of household formation and tenure changes from renter to owner status should differ from recent trends, the number of households wishing to buy converted units could increase or decrease.

Possible constraints on future demand for converted units are determined, as follows:

o First, owner and renter demand and the characteristics of that demand over the 1980 to 1985 period are estimated. This provides information on the types of households expected to purchase housing in the 1980-85 period.

o Second, the number and characteristics of households purchasing converted units between 1977 and 1979 are used to predict the number and type of households expected to buy converted units from 1980 to 1985.

o Third, a comparison is made between the estimated number of households expected to buy any housing unit and those expected to purchase units projected for conversion. This comparison produces the "share of the new home buyers market" (by household type)

which converted units must attract if all
units projected for conversion are to be
sold.

Estimation of Household Formation and Owner Demand by Household Type
and Income. The estimated total housing demand for 1980 to 1985 is
88,808,000 occupied housing units. 23/ Of this number, 59,147,000
units (67 percent) are projected to be owner occupied and 29,661,000
units (33 percent) are projected to be renter occupied. 24/ The components of this projected demand are extrapolated from the average
annual amount of new household formation between 1970 and 1977
(1,691,000 yearly) and from the shifts of renter to owner status
which have occurred during the same period (202,000 yearly).

---

23/ The estimated demand for occupied housing units between 1980
and 1985 is extrapolated from the average annual increase in the
number of households. Census projections are not utilized because
they do not include tenure status and household types, which are
necessary for this analysis. However, the parameters of these projections are generally in agreement with Census projections, as they
are used by other housing demand projections. See Footnote 24 for
more details. A more detailed explanation of the procedure used may
be found in Appendix 2. Table VII-6 presents the results of this
analysis for different household types, after projecting the 1970-77
trends to 1985, an eight year period. A table presenting projections
in demand for units by household income is contained in table VII-1
Appendix.

24/ In general, the results of this study are comparable to other
recently developed housing demand projections. In a 1979 report by
Pitkin and Masnick (see Appendix 2), the projected number of households, homeowners, and renters are very similar to those found in
this study. On the other hand, there is a 21 percent difference
between the two studies in the number of projected cooperative owners.
This variation may be explained by the striking differences between
demand for multi-family ownership in the 1970-75 period studied by
Pitkin and Masnick and the 1977-79 period used in this study. Other
studies (more fully described in Appendix 2) contain estimates of
total demand, or renter and owner demand, which are also comparable
to those in this study. Marcin (1977) describes the types of households which will demand multi-family owner units, but concludes that
such households will continue to buy single-family units. A study
by Sternlieb and Burchell (1978) estimates a total renter demand
which is comparable to this study. However, their findings differ
on the distribution of household types which will rent housing in
the 1980-85 period. Another study by Weicher, et al. (1980), develops
a series of owner demand projections which seem to be closely related
to the projections contained herein. These studies are described in
greater detail in Appendix 2.

TABLE VII-6

CHANGES IN HOUSEHOLD COMPOSITION, HOUSING FORMATION, AND HOUSING
TENURE BY HOUSEHOLD COMPOSITION, 1970-1977, PROJECTIONS TO 1985,
UNITED STATES 1/

(In Thousands)

| Household Composition by Tenure Total United States | 1970 Number | 1970 Percent | 1977 Number | 1977 Percent | 1977 Expected Number 1/ | Annual Net Shift | 1985 Projection Net Change Since 1977 | 1985 Projection Total Household |
|---|---|---|---|---|---|---|---|---|
| Total Occupied Units | 63,445 | 100.0 | 75,280 | 100.0 | 75,280 | +1691 | 13,528 | 88,808 |
| Owner | 39,886 | 62.9 | 48,765 | 64.8 | 47,351 | + 202 | 10,382 | 59,147 |
| Renter | 23,560 | 37.1 | 26,515 | 35.2 | 27,929 | - 202 | 3,416 | 29,661 |
| 2 or More Person Households | 52,295 | 100.0 | 59,483 | 100.0 | 59,483 | +1027 | 8,216 | 67,699 |
| Owner | 35,124 | 67.2 | 42,088 | 70.8 | 39,973 | + 302 | 8,233 | 50,321 |
| Renter | 17,171 | 32.8 | 17,395 | 29.2 | 19,510 | - 302 | - 17 | 17,378 |
| Male-Headed, Wife Present | 43,565 | 100.0 | 47,022 | 100.0 | 47,022 | + 494 | 3,952 | 50,974 |
| Owner | 30,806 | 70.7 | 36,274 | 77.1 | 33,245 | + 433 | 6,511 | 42,785 |
| Renter | 12,759 | 29.3 | 10,748 | 22.9 | 13,777 | - 433 | -2,559 | 8,189 |
| Other Male Head | 2,441 | 100.0 | 3,718 | 100.0 | 3,718 | + 182 | 1,456 | 5,174 |
| Owner | 1,298 | 53.2 | 1,775 | 47.7 | 1,978 | - 29 | 463 | 2,238 |
| Renter | 1,143 | 46.8 | 1,943 | 52.3 | 1,740 | + 29 | 993 | 2,936 |
| Female Head | 6,289 | 100.0 | 8,744 | 100.0 | 8,744 | + 351 | 2,808 | 11,552 |
| Owner | 3,019 | 48.0 | 4,039 | 46.2 | 4,197 | - 23 | 1,113 | 5,152 |
| Renter | 3,270 | 52.0 | 4,705 | 53.8 | 4,547 | + 23 | 1,695 | 6,400 |
| One Person Household | 11,151 | 100.0 | 15,796 | 100.0 | 15,796 | + 664 | 5,312 | 21,108 |
| Owner | 4,762 | 42.7 | 6,677 | 42.3 | 6,745 | - 10 | 2,167 | 8,844 |
| Renter | 6,389 | 57.3 | 9,119 | 57.7 | 9,051 | + 10 | 3,145 | 12,264 |

1/ 1970 percentage applied to 1977 total.

## TABLE VII-6, Cont'd.

### CHANGES IN HOUSEHOLD COMPOSITION, HOUSEHOLD FORMATION, AND HOUSING TENURE BY HOUSEHOLD COMPOSITION, 1970-1977, WITH PROJECTIONS TO 1985, UNITED STATES 1/

(In Thousands)

| Household Composition by Tenure Total United States | 1970 Number | 1970 Percent | 1977 Number | 1977 Percent | 1977 Expected Number 1/ | Annual Net Shift | 1985 Projection Net Change Since 1977 | 1985 Projection Total Household |
|---|---|---|---|---|---|---|---|---|
| Male Head | 3,933 | 100.0 | 6,036 | 100.0 | 6,036 | +300 | 2,400 | 8,436 |
| Owner | 1,329 | 33.8 | 1,988 | 32.9 | 2,040 | - 7 | 734 | 2,722 |
| Renter | 2,604 | 66.2 | 4,048 | 67.1 | 3,996 | + 7 | 1,666 | 5,714 |
| Female Head | 7,218 | 100.0 | 9,760 | 100.0 | 9,760 | +363 | 2,904 | 12,664 |
| Owner | 3,433 | 47.6 | 4,689 | 48.0 | 4,646 | + 6 | 1,442 | 6,131 |
| Renter | 3,785 | 52.4 | 5,071 | 52.0 | 5,114 | - 6 | 1,462 | 6,533 |
| 2 or More Person Household Male Head, Wife Present Under 25 Years | 3,082 | 100.0 | 3,010 | 100.0 | 3,010 | - 10 | - 80 | 2,930 |
| Owner | 800 | 26.0 | 1,064 | 35.3 | 783 | + 40 | 292 | 1,356 |
| Renter | 2,282 | 74.0 | 1,946 | 64.7 | 2,227 | - 40 | - 372 | 1,574 |
| 25 to 34 Years | 9,129 | 100.0 | 11,236 | 100.0 | 11,236 | +301 | 2,408 | 13,644 |
| Owner | 5,190 | 56.9 | 7,400 | 65.9 | 6,392 | +144 | 2,739 | 10,140 |
| Renter | 3,939 | 43.1 | 3,835 | 34.1 | 4,844 | -144 | - 331 | 3,504 |
| 35 to 44 Years | 9,251 | 100.0 | 9,397 | 100.0 | 9,397 | + 21 | 168 | 9,565 |
| Owner | 7,097 | 76.7 | 7,754 | 82.5 | 7,207 | + 78 | 763 | 8,517 |
| Renter | 2,154 | 23.3 | 1,643 | 17.5 | 2,190 | - 78 | - 595 | 1,048 |

1/ 1970 percentage applied to 1977 total.

## TABLE VII-6, Cont'd.

### CHANGES IN HOUSEHOLD COMPOSITION, HOUSING FORMATION, AND HOUSING TENURE BY HOUSEHOLD COMPOSITION, 1970-1977, WITH PROJECTIONS TO 1985, UNITED STATES

(In Thousands)

| Household Composition by Tenure Total United States | 1970 Number | 1970 Percent | 1977 Number | 1977 Percent | 1977 Expected Number 1/ | Annual Net Shift | 1985 Projection Net Change Since 1977 | 1985 Projection Total Household |
|---|---|---|---|---|---|---|---|---|
| 45 to 64 Years | 16,378 | 100.0 | 16,710 | 100.0 | 16,710 | + 47 | 376 | 17,086 |
| Owner | 13,230 | 80.8 | 14,505 | 86.8 | 13,502 | + 143 | 1,470 | 15,975 |
| Renter | 3,148 | 19.2 | 2,205 | 13.2 | 3,208 | - 143 | -1,094 | 1,111 |
| 65 Years and Over | 5,726 | 100.0 | 6,670 | 100.0 | 6,670 | + 135 | 1,080 | 7,750 |
| Owner | 4,490 | 78.4 | 5,551 | 83.2 | 5,229 | + 46 | 1,267 | 6,818 |
| Renter | 1,236 | 21.6 | 1,119 | 16.8 | 1,441 | - 46 | - 187 | 932 |
| 2 or More Person Households Other Male Head Under 65 Years | 1,984 | 100.0 | 3,231 | 100.0 | 3,231 | + 178 | 1,424 | 4,655 |
| Owner | 974 | 49.1 | 1,385 | 42.9 | 1,586 | - 29 | 379 | 1,764 |
| Renter | 1,010 | 50.9 | 1,846 | 57.1 | 1,645 | + 29 | 1,045 | 2,891 |
| 65 Years and Older | 456 | 100.0 | 487 | 100.0 | 487 | + 4 | 32 | 519 |
| Owner | 324 | 71.1 | 390 | 80.1 | 346 | - 6 | - 22 | 368 |
| Renter | 132 | 28.9 | 97 | 19.9 | 141 | + 6 | 54 | 151 |
| Female Head Under 65 Years | 5,058 | 100.0 | 7,407 | 100.0 | 7,407 | + 336 | 2,688 | 10,095 |
| Owner | 2,159 | 42.7 | 3,086 | 41.7 | 3,163 | - 11 | 1,033 | 4,119 |
| Renter | 2,899 | 57.3 | 4,321 | 58.3 | 4,244 | + 11 | 1,729 | 5,973 |

1/ 1970 percentage applied to 1977 total.

TABLE VII-6, Cont'd.

CHANGES IN HOUSEHOLD COMPOSITION, HOUSING FORMATION, AND HOUSING TENURE BY HOUSEHOLD COMPOSITION, 1970-1977, WITH PROJECTIONS TO 1985, UNITED STATES

(In Thousands)

| Household Composition by Tenure Total United States | 1970 | | 1977 | | Expected 1977 Number 1/ | Annual Net Shift | 1985 Projection Net Change Since 1977 | Total Household |
|---|---|---|---|---|---|---|---|---|
| | Number | Percent | Number | Percent | | | | |
| 65 Years and Older | 1,230 | 100.0 | 1,336 | 100.0 | 1,336 | + 15 | 120 | 1,456 |
| Owner | 860 | 69.9 | 952 | 71.3 | 934 | + 3 | 110 | 1,062 |
| Renter | 370 | 30.1 | 384 | 28.7 | 402 | - 3 | 10 | 394 |
| Single Person Household | | | | | | | | |
| Under 65 | 6,184 | 100.0 | 9,254 | 100.0 | 9,254 | + 439 | 3,512 | 12,766 |
| Owner | 2,075 | 33.6 | 2,939 | 31.8 | 3,109 | - 24 | 925 | 3,864 |
| Renter | 4,109 | 66.4 | 6,315 | 68.2 | 6,145 | + 24 | 2,587 | 8,902 |
| 65 Years and Older | 10,421 | 100.0 | 11,980 | 100.0 | 11,980 | + 223 | 1,784 | 13,764 |
| Owner | 6,822 | 65.5 | 8,086 | 67.5 | 7,847 | + 34 | 1,476 | 9,562 |
| Renter | 3,599 | 34.5 | 3,894 | 32.5 | 4,133 | - 34 | 308 | 4,202 |

Source: U.S. Census Bureau, Annual Housing Survey, Series H-150-77, U.S. Government Printing Office, Washington, D.C., 1979.

1/ 1970 percentage applied to 1977 total.

Trends in household formation and tenure change between 1970 and 1977
provide insights into factors which may be related to the demand for
converted units.  Among two-or-more person households, only the
married couple group has had a net yearly shift from renter to owner
status, and the same type of shift has occurred among one person
households headed by women.  Net yearly shifts from owner to renter
status have occurred in two-or-more-person households (with unmarried
male heads and female heads) and in one-person male households.

When these household tenure trends are disaggregated by age of household head, the results are even clearer.  All married couple groups,
despite their age, experienced a net yearly shift from renter to owner
status.  Among other types of households, only those with female heads
over the age of 65 and those comprised of one person, over the age of
65, had a yearly net shift from renter to owner status in the 1970-77
period.

The fastest growing household types between 1970 and 1977 were:

> (1) married couples between the ages of 25 and
> 35 years -i.e., the "baby boom" cohort (301,000
> additional households per year);

> (2) female heads under age 65 -- i.e., women with
> children or other dependents (336,000 additional
> households per year);

> (3) one-person households under the age of 65
> (439,000 additional households per year); and

> (4) one-person households, aged 65 or older
> (223,000 additional households per year).
> Together, these four groups account for 77
> percent of all household growth in the 1970-77
> period.

These changes in household tenure by income status indicate inflationary effects on both household earnings and on a household's
financial capacity to maintain an owner-occupied unit.  Between 1970
and 1977, the number of households with incomes less than $15,000
per year decreased at the rate of 1,338,000 households annually,
while the group earning over $15,000 per year increased by 3,033,000
households each year.  Households with annual incomes below $15,000
shifted from owner to renter status at the rate of 438,000 households
per year, while those earning $15,000 to $24,999 per year shifted
from owner to renter status at the annual rate of 128,000 households.
Only in the household category with yearly incomes over $25,000 is
there a net annual change from renter to owner status.

When changes in household formation are the basis for projecting net demand for all types of housing, it is estimated that 10,263,000 households will comprise the net new owner demand for the 1978-85 period. 25/ Analysis by age of household head places net new owner demand during the same period at 10,432,000 households. 26/ In considering income, the estimate of net new owner demand increases to 10,645,000 households. This indicates that households with annual incomes below $15,000 either will be changing from owner to renter status or their incomes will increase, shifting them into higher income categories. Renter households earning below $15,000 yearly will decline by 8,702,000 households between 1978 and 1985; and, during the same period, it is expected that 19,347,000 additional households will either become owners, or, if they already own housing, their incomes will rise above $15,000. Thus, a net increase of 10,645,000 owner households can be expected between 1978 and 1985.

It is also estimated that households changing to owner status will number 10,382,000 between 1978 and 1985. This projection falls between the estimate developed for changes by household formation (10,263,000) and that based on the age of household head (10,432,000). Although the estimates may vary by the type of comparison being made, the projection that 10,382,000 households will comprise net new owner demand is probably the most representative overall estimate for the 1978-85 period.

Demand for Converted Units by Household Type and Income: 1980-85. The preceding analysis for the 1978-85 period provides estimates of growth or decline among various household types as well as estimates of net shifts in household tenure status. 27/ The next step in the analysis is to estimate the types of households which will demand converted units in the future.

---

25/ Net new owner demand is for an eight year period (1978-85), rather than the six year period of 1980-85.

26/ This is a slightly higher estimate than that for household formation and is caused by differences in trends within some age groups. Because it cancels out fewer differences in household types, the second estimate (10,432,000 households) is more accurate.

27/ In order to relate these estimates to the 1980-85 period, only six of the eight years of projected change will be used for the household demand projections. Therefore each estimate is reduced by one-fourth of its value.

By using a percentage distribution of past buyer characteristics, 28/
it is possible to project the types of households likely to purchase
converted units between 1980 and 1985. This projection is then compared to net new owner demand, and the result provides an indication
of whether the units projected for conversion can be marketed to each
type of household. 29/

Using this procedure, it is estimated that 722,000 converted units
will be purchased by male-headed households, and 685,000 by female-
headed households. 30/ If these two projections are related to the
net new owner demand, converted units will have to "capture" 19 percent of the entire net new home buying market between 1980-85. This
represents 13 percent of the net new owner demand for male-headed
households and 36 percent of the net new owner demand for female-
headed households.

---

28/ According to the Survey of Current and Former Residents conducted
for this study, recent purchasers of converted units have these house
hold characteristics: income - about 29 percent earn between $17,500
and $25,999 yearly and 48 percent earn over $26,000 per year; household composition - 53 percent are headed by males and 47 percent are
headed by females; 58 percent are one-person households; 30 percent
are married couples (with or without children); 12 percent are single
male or single female headed households living with children or
other dependents; age groups - 38 percent are in the 25 to 34 year
old group; 25 percent are in the 45 to 64 year old group; 19 percent
are in the 35 to 44 year old group; 11 percent are in the over 65
year old group, and 7 percent are in the under 25 year old group.
(See table VII-2 Appendix.)

As mentioned earlier, the household types buying a large share of
converted units are similar to the household categories which grew
rapidly during 1970-77. These include married couples between 25
and 34 years old, female headed households under age 65, and one-
person households. (See chapter VI for additional details on household characteristics.)

29/ Table VII-7 provides the information required for this comparison
of total estimated owner demand and the demand required to sell the
units projected for conversion, by households characteristics.

30/ The total units projected for conversion, with no limits on the
supply of convertible units (i.e., 1,456,840 units), is used for this
comparison.

TABLE VII-7

NET NEW OWNERS HOUSEHOLDS PROJECTED CONVERSIONS, AND PROJECTED CONVERSIONS
AS A PERCENT OF NET NEW OWNER HOUSEHOLDS, WITH THREE DIFFERENT CONDITIONS, 1980-1985

| Household Characteristics | Net New Owner Households 1980-1985 1/ | Projected Conversions 1980-1985 2/ | Projected Conversions as Percent of Net New Owner Households 1980-1985 | Projected Owner Occupied Conversions 1980-1985 3/ | Projected Owner Conversions as Percent Net New Owner Households 1980-1985 | Revised Projection Owner Occupied Conversions 1980-1985 4/ | Revised Projection Owner Occupied Conversions as Percent Net New Owner Households 1980-1985 |
|---|---|---|---|---|---|---|---|
| Household Income 5/ | | | | | | | |
| Total | 7,983,750 | 1,456,840 | 18.2 | 917,809 | 11.5 | 718,044 | 9.0 |
| Less than $5,249 | -2,554,500 | 58,274 | -2.3 | 36,712 | -1.4 | 28,722 | -1.1 |
| $5,250 to $12,449 | -2,492,250 | 116,547 | -4.7 | 73,425 | -2.9 | 57,443 | -2.3 |
| $12,500 to $16,999 | -1,479,750 | 160,252 | -10.8 | 100,959 | -6.8 | 78,985 | -5.3 |
| $17,000 to $25,999 | 6,204,000 | 422,484 | 6.8 | 266,165 | 4.3 | 208,233 | 3.4 |
| $26,000 or more | 8,306,250 | 699,283 | 8.4 | 440,548 | 5.3 | 344,661 | 4.1 |
| Household Composition | | | | | | | |
| Total | 7,697,250 | 1,456,840 | 18.9 | 917,809 | 11.9 | 718,044 | 9.3 |
| Married Couple | 4,883,250 | 437,052 | 8.9 | 275,343 | 5.6 | 215,413 | 4.4 |
| Other Male or Female | 1,182,000 | 174,821 | 14.8 | 110,137 | 9.3 | 86,165 | 7.3 |
| Single Males | 550,500 | 320,505 | 58.2 | 201,918 | 37.2 | 157,970 | 28.7 |
| Single Females | 1,081,500 | 524,462 | 48.5 | 330,411 | 30.6 | 258,496 | 23.9 |
| Sex of Head | | | | | | | |
| Total | 7,697,250 | 1,456,840 | 18.9 | 917,809 | 11.9 | 718,044 | 9.3 |
| Male | 5,781,000 | 772,125 | 13.4 | 486,439 | 8.4 | 380,563 | 6.1 |
| Female | 1,916,250 | 684,715 | 35.7 | 431,370 | 22.5 | 337,481 | 17.6 |
| Age of Head | | | | | | | |
| Total | 7,824,000 6/ | 1,456,840 | 18.6 | 917,809 | 11.7 | 718,044 | 9.2 |
| Under 25 | 316,500 | 101,979 | 32.2 | 64,247 | 20.3 | 50,263 | 15.9 |
| 25-34 | 2,966,250 | 553,599 | 18.7 | 348,767 | 11.8 | 272,857 | 9.2 |
| 35-44 | 825,750 | 276,800 | 33.5 | 174,384 | 21.1 | 136,428 | 16.5 |
| 45-64 | 1,592,250 | 364,210 | 22.9 | 229,452 | 14.4 | 179,511 | 11.3 |
| 65 or older | 2,123,250 | 160,252 | 7.5 | 100,959 | 4.8 | 78,985 | 3.7 |

---

1/ These projections are 75 percent of the 1978-1985 projections, covering only six of the eight years projected. They include the number of new households formed which become owners, and the net number of households shifting from renter to owner tenure status.

2/ These projections are based on the trend line projection. The distribution of household characteristics is from percentages developed in the Department of Housing and Urban Development's 1979 Survey of Condominium and Cooperative Conversions. The figures assume that all converted units will be owner-occupied.

3/ Department of Housing and Urban Development's 1979 Survey of Conversions found 63 percent of all conversions to be owner-occupied.

4/ Based on revised 1980 projections which reflect influence of high interest rates and that 63 percent of all converted units are owner-occupied.

5/ The projected net renter to owner shift used a slightly different distribution of income for the 1970-1977 period; see Table VII-1 App. This table uses slightly higher income categories with 1979 dollars; the two distributions of income are probably comparable.

6/ This total includes 284,250 male heads of households, 774,500 female heads of households, and 693,750 one-person households all "under 65 years of age" for which further age distributions were not available; these represent 31 percent of all households with heads under age 65 which experienced a net shift from renter to owner status. These household characteristics were distributed by the same age proportiuons demonstrated by those households for which distributions were available.

From this same comparison, an estimate is made of that segment of
the net new homebuyer market which converted units must capture if
the 1970-77 rate of conversion is to continue. Of new one-person
households expected to buy housing between 1980 and 1985, over 48
percent of all male-headed households and female-headed households
will buy converted units. 31/

The age distribution of households expected to buy converted units
between 1980 and 1985 is also important. Households in the 25 to 34
year old category would have to buy 554,000 converted units, or 19
percent of all home purchases this group of new homeowners is expected
to make. The second highest number of units are expected to be
bought by the 45 to 64 year old group. The 364,000 units they buy
will account for 23 percent of the housing purchased by those in
their age group. Converted units are expected to be bought by 277,000
households in the 35 to 44 age group, a high percentage (34 percent)
of that group's housing purchases. In the group over 65 years of
age, 160,000 households can be expected to buy converted units,
only 8 percent of the units bought by that particular group. Finally,
households under age 25 are projected to buy only 102,000 converted
units; this figure represents 32 percent of the housing units these
households will buy.

The discussion, thus far, has focused on household types and their
demand for converted units. Still to be considered is whether these
households will be able to afford the price of converted housing
units during the 1980-85 period. The Survey of Current and Former
Residents indicates that about 23 percent of those households which
bought converted units earned less than $17,000 in 1979. Yet, on
the national level, households with annual incomes of $15,000 or
less in 1977 experienced a net shift from owner to renter status
instead of a shift in the opposite direction. 32/ On the basis of
income by tenure status, it is estimated that 7,983,750 households
(including newly formed households and households shifting from
renter to owner status) will demand new housing between 1980 and
1985. This number is slightly larger than the projection of

31/ One factor in this case will be the amount of new condominium
and cooperative construction activity: If new, attractive, and
competitively priced condominium and cooperative units are built
in large quantities, the amount of converted units purchased by
each type of household may be reduced.

32/ The net shift of households from owner to renter status is
signified by a negative sign in the projections presented in table
VII-7.

7,697,250 households derived from the trends for household composition by tenure.

Considering demand shifts to owner status based on income, only households earning over $15,000 per year will be able to purchase any type of housing. 33/ No growth in homeownership is expected to occur among households with incomes below $15,000. The chief consideration concerning future demand for converted units is whether or not the same household types which bought converted units in the past can afford the units offered for sale in the future. For example, it is estimated that one-fourth of the units converted during the 1977 to 1979 period were bought by households earning less than $15,000 annually. If households with similar incomes can no longer afford to buy housing, new effective demand for housing will be reduced by one-fourth, unless higher income households buy a larger share of converted units than they have in the recent past. Reasons why higher income households might demand more converted units include escalating home prices and interest rates; both factors could make the cost of a single family home prohibitive, even to higher income households.

To this point, this chapter's analysis has assumed that all units projected for conversion will be occupied by owners. Yet, according to data presented in chapter VI, 37 percent of the households living in recently converted units are renters (including those renting from investor-owners and from converters). It is therefore necessary to consider only the characteristics of those households which bought and live in converted units, or 63 percent of the residents. When this factor is taken into account, it is estimated that units converted in the future must attract only 11 to 12 percent of total net new owner demand if the market is to continue expanding at the 1977-79 rate during the 1980-85 period. This one-third reduction in demand makes it even more likely that the net new owner demand will be sufficient for the projected number of converted units.

_____

33/ However, this is not to say that the same households which will earn over $17,000 per year (in 1979 dollars) will want to buy converted units. This analysis is not sufficient to determine if the households likely to change from renter to owner status are the same households expected to earn enough to purchase a converted unit. Thus, households which actually can afford to and wish to buy units in the future may differ in composition and age from those households which bought converted units between 1970 and 1977.

## Modifications to Projected Conversions Based on 1980 Financial Conditions

The projected number of conversions (using 1977-79 trends) may be subject to short-term fluctuations in the economy and the housing market.  Interest rate increases during 1979-80 had a major impact on the home buying market, although converted units sales were relatively less influenced in the short-run by high interest rates. The March 1980 issue of U.S. Housing Markets estimates that, compared to 1979, single-family housing starts will decline by more than 25 percent; unsubsidized multi-family starts will decline by 40 percent; and the conversion of multi-family units will decrease by 20 percent. Despite this anticipated reduction in conversion activity, the publication notes that at least 100,000 units will be converted in 1980. 34/

In early 1980, developers in the 12 SMSAs with high levels of conversion activity reported that conversions were proceeding only if financing had been secured prior to the recent rapid increase in interest rates.  Otherwise, both interim financing and permanent mortgage financing were difficult or too costly to obtain. 35/  In view of these financial constraints, it is likely that few buildings were bought in early 1980 for conversion in late 1980 or early 1981. Because of this presumed downturn in the 1980 market, it is estimated that conversion activity in the 37 largest SMSAs will be 20 percent less than previously projected. 36/ The 12 SMSAs with the largest number of converted units are expected to experience 58,000 conversions in 1980 instead of 67,000 based on the trend-line analysis; and in the 25 other large SMSAs, it is expected that 22,000 units will be converted instead of the projected 26,000.  (See table VII-8.)

In the balance of the country, it is estimated that conversion activity will decline by 30 percent in 1980.  Local government officials in these areas estimate that only 27,000 conversions will occur rather than the 38,000 projected previously.  Based on these estimates

---

34/ In its February 1980 issue of U.S. Housing Markets, Citicorp estimated that 145,000 units would be converted in 1980. The March 1980 figure reflects the sharp upward trend in interest rates and its effect on conversions, roughly a 20 percent decline in activity.

35/ U.S. Department of Housing and Urban Development, Telephone Interviews with Developers and Lending Officials in 18 Central Cities, March 1980.

36/  See footnote 34.

jurisdictions with some conversion activity between 1977 and 1979
can be expected to have only 24,000 conv  sions in 1980 instead of
the trend-line projection of 38,000.  Among those areas with no
conversions prior to 1980, local government officials estimate that
3,000 units will be converted in 1980. 37/ These additional units,
however are not sufficient to make up for the 30 percent decrease
caused by higher interest rates.  Considering these lowered estimates
for 1980, the total number of projected conversions for 1980 is
reduced from 131,000 units to 107,000 units.

TABLE VII-8

TREND-LINE PROJECTION OF CONVERSION ACTIVITY, 1980-85
MODIFIED BY SUPPLY LIMITS FOR CONVERTIBLE UNITS AND
EFFECTS OF HIGH INTEREST RATES IN 1980

| Projection Year | 12 High Activity SMSAs | 25 Other Large SMSAs | Balance of U.S. | Total U.S. |
|---|---|---|---|---|
| 1980 | 52,767 | 21,569 | 27,047 | 101,383 |
| 1981 | 67,150 | 26,227 | 37,573 | 130,950 |
| 1982 | 77,982 | 35,548 | 55,188 | 168,718 |
| 1983 | 74,794 | 44,869 | 72,803 | 192,466 |
| 1984 | 107,853 | 54,190 | 90,418 | 252,461 |
| 1985 | 121,942 | 63,779 | 108,033 | 293,754 |
| 1980-85 Total | 502,488 | 246,182 | 391,062 | 1,139,732 |

As a result of these changes, the trend-line projections of conversion
activity between 1980 and 1984 are moved up one year to the 1981-85
period.  That is, the previous 1980 estimate now becomes the 1981
projection, and so forth.  The number of converted units in the entire
country is expected to reach 1,140,000 for the 1980-85 period, instead
of the 1,457,000 units projected through trend-line analysis or the
1,374,000 units estimated after the trend-line was modified to account
for supply limitations. 38/  If it is further assumed that 37 percent
of these units will be rented after conversion, then only 718,000 of

37/ U.S. Department of Housing and Urban Development, Telephone Survey
of 443 Local Officials, February 1980.

38/ This new estimate of 1,140,000 conversions will be valid only if
buildings are converted between 1980 and 1985 at the same rate as in
the 1977-79 period.

the 1,205,000 units will be owner-occupied. 39/ With this further
adjustment, converted units need attract only 9 percent of the total
new households entering the 1980-85 net new home buying market to
continue to expand at the 1977-79 rate.


## Other Factors Which Can Influence Future Conversion Activity

In addition to the demand, supply, and financial considerations
discussed above, there are other factors which can influence the
amount of future condominium and cooperative conversion activity.
The impact of these factors, however, is more difficult to assess
quantitatively.  Each of these may alter the magnitude of projected
conversion rates to an extent that can only be suggested at this
time.  These factors, which are briefly discussed below, are: regulatory actions by all levels of government; the rate of inflation;
potential changes in the federal income tax code; migration patterns
of the population; rates of new housing construction; and the characteristics of developers who convert rental units to condominiums and
cooperatives.

Regulatory actions.  Government regulation of conversion activity
can, of course, have an impact on the direction and magnitude of
future trends.  To date, various states and local jurisdictions have
enacted statutes relating to conversions (see chapters XI and XII),
some of which represent deliberate attempts to alter the rate of
conversions.  For example, a complete moratorium on conversion activity
or one which is triggered by local rental vacancy rates is intended

---

39/ The Survey to Current and Former Residents indicates that for
each 100 units converted, 37 households rent units.  Of these households, 18 rent units from a developer or other non-investor landlord.
It is possible that these 18 units may become owner occupied in the
future as non-investor landlords sell the units.  If this occurs,
the renter occupancy would fall to 19 units.  However, the lower
renter occupancy ratio would not change the overall net effect on
the housing market, as caused by a 37 percent renter occupancy.
(See discussion in text.)  The following demonstrates the effect of
19, rather than 37, percent renter occupancy:  Of 100 units, 19 are
occupied by renters.  Therefore, renter demand is decreased by 76
households; rental supply is decreased by 81 households; and rental
vacancies will be decreased by 5 units.  In addition, owner demand
is increased by 76 households; owner supply is increased by 81 households; and owner vacancies will be increased by 5 units.  Thus, the
net impact of conversions on the housing market remains the same as
previously discussed.

to prevent anticipated growth in the rate of conversions. Although it is not clear what actual effects various regulatory actions have on conversion rates, there are some indications that the anticipation of a moratorium on conversion within a community may, in the short-run, stimulate the pace of conversion. Once enacted, certain types of legal restriction can slow conversion rates or encourage developers and converters to move to other localities where their actions are less strictly regulated. At the opposite extreme, certain government regulations or programs can accelerate the rate of conversion beyond the levels projected from past trends. For example, federal and local programs to provide homeownership opportunities to lower-income tenants could lead to the conversion of units occupied by lower-income groups.

Inflation rates. A significant change in the rate of inflation could have a substantial impact on the number of condominium and cooperative conversions undertaken. For example, higher rates of inflation stimulate more ownership demand, since homeownership can provide a hedge against inflation and a tax benefit to owners. Yet, inflation also causes mortgage interest rates to rise; and, as a result, fewer households may be able to purchase converted units.

Tax code changes. Changes in the Federal tax code which affect mortgage interest deductions or the relative advantages, in higher income brackets, of owning a home as opposed to renting, can alter conversion trends. Various proposals for tax credits or deductions for renters have been put forth, and if these were to be enacted, it would likely reduce the number of tenants who buy converted units primarily for the tax advantages of ownership.

Migration patterns. Changing interregional and interarea migration can also influence future trends in conversion activity, although experience to date indicates that conversions have occurred both in SMSAs which are experiencing inmigration and those experiencing out-migration. 40/ This suggests that any change in migration patterns would primarily affect the distribution of household demand rather than the level of conversion activity. SMSAs with population increases caused by net inmigration may have higher levels of new housing construction; however, the price mix, size, or location of newly built or available housing may not meet present demand. Therefore,

---

40/ During the 1970-77 period, the net gains in households caused by migration were in these SMSAs: Denver-Boulder (+137,600); Houston (+321,600); Miami (+147,400); and Tampa-St. Petersburg (+301,600). The net losses of households caused by migration were in these SMSAs: Chicago (-316,800); Los Angeles-Long Beach (-338,500); and New York City (-189,700).

converted units are likely to compete with other alternatives both
for current residents and new households. In SMSAs with population
decreases with net outmigration, it is likely that a large share of
residents who move are renters. As a result of their leaving,
rental vacancy rates will increase, and this may cause landlords to
convert vacant units as a means of recouping their initial investments.

New construction. The level of future conversion activity may be
affected by the amount of new condominium, cooperative, and unsubsidized multi-family housing constructed nationwide. The segment of
the home buying market which will buy either new or converted condominiums or cooperatives is probably limited, since the population
groups attracted to such units in the past, although growing, will
eventually peak. If newly built condominiums and cooperatives are
priced competitively with converted units, the newly built housing
may cut into the demand for converted units. However, to the extent
that the new units are more expensive than comparable converted
units, this type of competition will be minimized and converted
units will claim their own share of the home buying market.

New construction can have other effects as well. Developers, of
course, may convert recently built multi-family structures, especially
as the local supply of potential conversions becomes depleted.
Depletion has already approached this point in several SMSAs, as
discussed above; conversion of recently constructed properties is
likely to continue in such areas. However, if new, unsubsidized
multi-family construction rates continue to decrease (as is currently
the case in many areas), this source of convertible units will be
limited and conversion rates can be affected as a result.

Developer characteristics. It is possible that, in the future, more
and different types of condominium and cooperative converters may
begin to convert units, and this can influence the amount of future
activity in ways that cannot necessarily be projected from past
trends. Most conversions are now undertaken by professional developers
and landlords with the assistance of real estate experts and lawyers.
If conversions increase in popularity and more firms and individuals
believe there is a good opportunity to make a profit, the "conversion
industry" is likely to expand, resulting in more unit conversions.
Finally, tenants in a few areas are also converting their own buildings, and if more tenant groups choose to convert buildings that would
otherwise have remained rentals, additional increases in conversion
activity will occur.


## Scenarios for Conversion Activity: 1980-1985

Considering the previous discussion, several scenarios of future
conversion activity are possible. These scenarios are divided between
those that are "most likely" and "least likely" to occur.

<u>Most Likely Scenario.</u>  The most likely scenario for the 1980-85 period
is that the number of conversions will increase each year, but that
yearly increases will be at successively smaller rates.  If the
various housing supply, market, and financial conditions discussed
in chapter V continue, then the increases in conversions noted during
the 1977-79 period can be expected to continue into the first half
of the 1980s.  Under this scenario, 1,140,000 units, or 4.3 percent
of the currently occupied rental housing stock, will be converted in
the 1980 to 1985 period.  <u>41</u>/ (See also table VII-9.)

In larger metropolitan areas, the pace of conversion activity probably
will not slow until desirable, high quality units (including those in
recently constructed buildings) are converted.  In the long-run, converted units are likely to become a clearly defined submarket because
they generally cost less than other types of owner-occupied housing.

As the supply of units suitable for conversion in the larger SMSAs
declines, conversions may occur in other areas of the country, although it seems unlikely that conversions will occur in communities
with small populations.  The rental supply in such areas is mainly
comprised of single-family detached houses, which are not appropriate
for conversion.  In addition, these areas probably have an adequate
supply of houses for ownership, usually at lower prices than similar
units in larger cities and SMSAs.

**Scenarios of Conversion Activity Projections: 1980-85**

Scenarios

Projection A—Activity Will End in 1980

Projection B—Activity Decreases After 1979

Projection C—Activity Levels Off After 1979

Projection D—Modified Trend-Line Using National 1976-79 Trends

Projection E—Modified Trend-Line Using 38 1977-79 Trends

Projection F—All Suitable Rental Supply Converted (Not Included on This Chart, Ranges From 478,000 in 1980 to 1,390,000 in 1985)

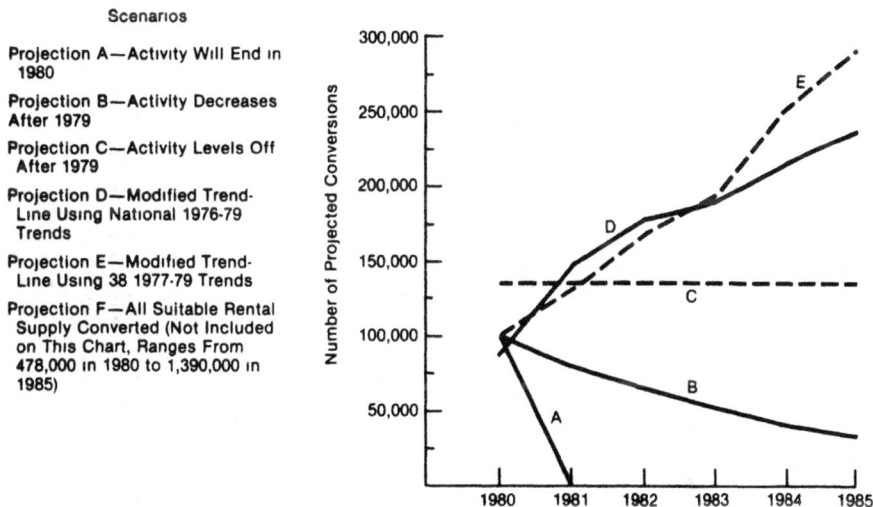

41/ If the 1976-79 national conversion trend is used to estimate
future conversion activity instead of the 1977-79 trend, the projected
number of 1980-85 conversions is 1,056,000 units.  This total is
84,000 units smaller than the estimate using 1977-79 trends.  It
indicates that the use of the data from the 1977-79 period yields
relatively stable estimates of future conversions.

TABLE VII-9
SCENARIOS OF PROJECTED CONVERSION ACTIVITY , 1980-85

| Total United States | 1980 | 1981 | 1982 | 1983 | 1984 | 1985 | Total 1980-855 | Percent of occupied rental housi converted |
|---|---|---|---|---|---|---|---|---|
| Projection A (Activity will end in 1980) | 101,383 | 0 | 0 | 0 | 0 | 0 | 101,383 | 0.4 |
| Projection B (Activity decreased after 1979) 1/ | 101,383 | 81,106 | 64,885 | 51,908 | 41,526 | 33,221 | 374,029 | 1.4 |
| Projection C (Activity levels off after 1979) | 135,000 | 135,000 | 135,000 | 135,000 | 135,000 | 135,000 | 810,000 | 3.1 |
| Projection D (Modified trend-line using national 1976-79 trends) 2/ | 86,840 | 146,891 | 178,580 | 189,697 | 216,104 | 237,935 | 1,056,047 | 4.0 |
| Projection E (Modified trend-line using 38 1977-79 trends) 2/ | 101,383 | 130,950 | 168,718 | 192,466 | 252,461 | 293,754 | 1,139,732 | 4.3 |
| Projection F (All suitable rental supply converted) 3/ | 478,357 | 613,936 | 794,959 | 913,254 | 1,193,565 | 1,390,310 | 5,384,381 | 20.3 |

1/ Decreases at 20 percent per year, after 1980.
2/ Modified by a 20 percent decrease in 1980 and by convertible supply limitation.
3/ Refer to 1977 occupied rental housing supply.

Other Scenarios. There are several other possibilities for conversion activity in the 1980-85 period. The first, and rather unlikely, possibility is that the conversion market will never recover from the tight money market conditions existing during the first half of 1980. If conversions end after 1980, only 101,000 units would be converted in the 1980-85 period, which represents the total for 1980 alone. It is more likely that converters will be able to return to the market place as soon as interest rates fall, because owner demand for their product is high in most areas and existing properties can be rapidly brought to market, as converted condominiums.

Second, and also unlikely, is that conversion activity will decrease or will level off after 1979. If, for example, conversion activity decreases at 20 percent per year, there will be 374,000 conversions in the 1980-85 period rather than 1.2 million. If conversion activity levels off after 1979, there will be 135,000 conversions per year, for a total of 810,000 conversions in the 1980-85 period. These scenarios, however, are unlikely because conversions are expanding into new market areas and there are many units with conversion potential remaining in those markets where relatively high levels of conversion have occurred. In addition, inflation continues to provide incentives for many households to own units, rather than rent, and some of this inflation-driven demand is for condominiums. The supply and demand factors indicate that the amount of yearly conversions will probably increase but at a decreasing rate.

A third possibility is that the bulk of the rental housing supply will be converted, and that publicly owned and subsidized rental housing will be the only remaining multi-family rental properties. As has been shown earlier, however, no more than 20 percent of the existing rental housing stock is considered suitable for conversion, so this scenario is not likely. If the 20 percent suited for conversion is, in fact, converted, 5,384,000 units will experience a tenure change. It is unlikely, however, that the level of demand for converted units will justify the conversion of such a large share of the Nation's rental housing supply. Homeownership demand remains concentrated in the single-family housing market and will remain there unless housing prices reach extraordinary levels or the preferences of homebuyers change drastically.

* * *

It is possible (but not probable) that conversions occurring between 1980 and 1985 will range from one hundred thousand to five million units. The greater likelihood is that conversions will number between 1,056,000 and 1,140,000 units during this period. However, when the net number of rental units which will be needed for tenants moving from converted buildings is considered, the net shortfall of rental

could range from 5,050 to 269,200 units in the extreme scenarios.
In the more likely scenario, the net shortfall of rental units can
be expected to range between 52,800 and 57,000 units.  Thus, the
actual net effect of conversions on the housing market as a direct
result of conversions is relatively small, even though it involves
large numbers of units and the movement of many households.
Although the net effect may be small in general, it is conceivable
that conversions may cause the vacancy rate to "tip over" to an un-
acceptable level.  For example, in some neighborhoods, the impact of
conversions may cause the vacancy rate to drop to marginal levels,
tightening the rental market to the extent that renters leaving
conversions must find rental units in other areas of the city.

# The Impacts
# of Conversion

# Chapter VIII
# Community and Neighborhood Impacts

Conversions of rental properties to condominiums or cooperatives can have various impacts on the communities and neighborhoods in which they occur, on the renters whose units are converted, and on the households that occupy converted units. The latter -- impacts on current households and former residents -- are examined in chapter IX; in this chapter, community and neighborhood effects are analyzed.

The community and neighborhood impacts which are most frequently attributed to conversions are those that relate to the local tax base, the condition and composition of neighborhoods, and the housing stock.

Tax Revenues. To the extent that conversions result in increased property tax revenues resulting from changed assessments or increased numbers of home-owners, conversions can have an impact on the community's fiscal condition. The magnitude of the impact depends on tax and assessment practices and on the level of conversion activity.

Neighborhoods. To the extent that conversions result in changes in building occupancy, they can have an impact on the composition of a neighborhood's population and related characteristics. The size of the impact depends on the level of conversion activity, on mobility patterns of residents affected by conversions, and on the amount of spatial concentration of activity within a community.

Housing. To the extent that conversions involve rehabilitation of buildings, they can have an impact on the quality and character of the housing stock. The degree of the impact depends on the amount and type of repairs undertaken as part of the conversion process.

## The Fiscal Impacts of Conversions

The conversion of rental properties to condominiums and cooperatives can have an impact on the tax revenues and expenditures of
local governments. These impacts, however, can vary widely from
community to community and from building to building within a community.

Potentially, the largest and most direct fiscal impact of conversions is through the property taxes that are assessed on converted
units. 1/ A second impact is on local government expenditures. This
can result from changes in the demand for public services associated
with changes in the characteristics or behavior of postconversion
residents compared to preconversion households.

The Impact on Property Taxes. The impact of conversion on property
tax revenues depends on effective property tax rates and the assessment changes which occur as a result of conversion. During the last
decade, many states have developed property tax relief mechanisms
which take a variety of forms, the most prevalent of which are homestead exemption and circuit breaker laws. All 50 states and the
District of Columbia have programs, for instance, to ease the tax
levy on low-income households with most giving special attention to
elderly households. 2/ Many states provide tax relief to all homeowners, regardless of income or age.

> In Louisiana, for example, up to $5,000 may be
> deducted from the assessed value of all owner-
> occupied housing in the state. Since assessed
> value equals only 10 percent of current market
> value, households in condominiums valued at
> $50,000 or less pay no property taxes.

Other states and other jurisdictions provide different forms of tax
relief which decrease the potential level of local revenues resulting
from conversion.

---

1/ There are other incidental revenues generated by conversions
but, in most cases, these revenues include possible transfer taxes
on real estate transactions, filing fees, and increases in income or
wage receipts resulting from rehabilitation undertaken during conversion.

2/ U. S. Department of Housing and Urban Development, Property Tax
Relief Programs for the Elderly (November 1975).

In New York City, there is a program which provides
a 12 year exemption from increased real estate
assessments due to building improvements and a
90 percent tax abatement of the fair value of
the improvements taken at the rate of 8-1/3%
annually. Substantial rehabilitation done at
the time of conversion does not contribute to
increased property tax revenues.

Property tax relief programs, therefore, mediate the impact of conversions on tax revenues. Since these programs vary widely from state
to state in the number of people and in the extent of coverage, the
the impact of these programs on the potential revenues from conversion
will also vary considerably.

Property assessment practices, like tax relief programs, also condition
the impact of conversions on local revenues. Prior to conversion, a
rental property is typically assessed as a single entity and the assessment is based on the property's income producing capacity or on the recent
sales prices of comparable properties. 3/ After conversion to a condominium, each unit in a converted building or complex is assessed separately
Generally, the aggregate assessment of the individual units in the converted building is greater than the single preconversion assessment. This
increase may be due wholly to the tenure changes of the building and the
value premium associated with ownership, or it may be due to the extensive
renovation which sometimes takes place at the time of conversion, or to
both. Since the methods and frequency of reassessment differ widely among
jurisdictions, the impact of conversion on tax revenues is largely affected
by these local practices. The following examples highlight the variation
among local jurisdictions in assessment practices:

In Los Angeles, the assessed value of all properties,
rental and ownership alike, is equal to 25 percent of
their market value. This, in turn, is determined by
sales price of comparable properties.

In Baltimore, however, a rental property is assessed
at 50 percent of the entire market value and an ownership
property is assessed at the slightly lower figure of 45
percent.

---

3/ Since the prices of rental buildings are closely associated with
their income producing potential, assessments based on the income
potential may be similar to those based on sale prices of other
rental properties.

In Minneapolis, a method is used which assesses more expensive homes at a higher rate than less expensive homes, and both at a lower rate than rental properties. 4/

Perhaps the greatest variation is between Chicago and other cities.

In Chicago (Cook County), Illinois, rental properties are assessed at twice the percentage of market value as ownership properties -- 33 percent versus 16 percent. Therefore, unless assessment of condominiums double, the property taxes collected on buildings after conversion will not exceed the property taxes collected when the buildings were rentals.

Clearly, different local assessment practices mean that the conversion of comparably valued rental properties in each of these cities would show markedly different percentage changes in assessed values and property taxes owed. 5/

The timing of reassessments may also influence the revenue effect produced by conversion.

In Chicago, for example, since properties are reassessed only at specific intervals (and even then only a fraction of all properties are reassessed at any one time), a converted building whose units are reassessed soon after conversion will generate a much greater tax revenue than a comparable property that avoids reassessment for a number of years.

---

4/ Rental properties are assessed at 40 percent of their limited value (a fraction of their market value), and condominiums are assessed at 18 percent of the first $21,000 limited value and 30 percent of the remaining limited value. As a result, the assessed value for a $40,000 rental building would be $16,000, while a condominium of equivalent value would be assessed at $9,480.

5/ Characteristics of local housing markets may affect assessed values and, therefore, revenues. In cities with rent control, a building may experience an increase in value at conversion, since rent control stabilized its previous worth. In cities with high rental vacancy rates, the gap between a building's value as a condominium and as rental building may be wider.

Other cities, such as those in California, reassess only at the
time a property is sold. In these cases, the maximum increases in
assessed values and taxes are likely to be generated soon after
conversion. 6/

Although there is not a large body of data available to assess the
extent, nationally, of changes in postconversion property tax assessments, there is some limited information on this subject. For
instance, a ten year assessment history of 50 converted buildings in
Boston shows that, in the first year after buildings are converted,
valuations increase an average of 40 percent, with higher value
increases in the late 1970s reflecting greater market demand and
renovation. 7/ In contrast, the assessments of similar buildings
which were not converted increased by only 12 percent on average
since 1975. However, over the last five years as the values were
rising rapidly, the city has periodically reduced the percentage of
market value at which condominiums are assessed, making revenue
changes less dramatic than they might otherwise have been.

---

6/ In 1978, the passage of Proposition 13 reduced assessed values to
1975-76 levels and set the maximum rate of taxation to four percent
of assessed value. When properties are sold, assessed values are
based on the current market value (selling price). Therefore, in
California, increases in assessments for condominiums reflect the
difference between the current market value and the market value in
1975-1976.

7/ Condominium Conversions in Boston, No. 97, (Boston: Municipal
Research Bureau, April 1, 1980). During the period of the Boston
study (in 1974), the Massachusetts Supreme Court found a lack of
consistency in local assessment practices in the state. (Sudberry v.
The Commissioner of Corporation and Taxation, 366 Massachusetts
558, 1974.) As a result, Boston and other local governments, were
ordered to implement full valuation equalization assessment practices
Procedures to achieve compliance are underway in Boston, but, it is
unclear whether conclusions reached in this study take into account

The conclusions of other local studies of conversion's tax impacts in Chicago, 8/ Washington, D.C., 9/ and Brookline, Massachusetts, 10/ also support these findings. In Washington, D.C., the average property tax increase of $466 per converted unit per year is estimated to yield additional tax revenues of more than $1.4 million annually. 11/

According to local officials, conversions do provide additional tax revenues but the actual dollar increases are small when compared to a community's total assessments. In only 11 percent of all communities with conversions (especially those between 100,000 and one-half million in population) do local officials believe that increased postconversion assessments have a "major" impact on the local tax base. 12/ Data collected for this study in 13 cities with high levels of conversion activity illustrate the extent of variation in changed assessements that accompany conversion, and the relatively small impact that changed assessments have had on communities. (See table VIII-1.) 13/ Consisting of pre and postconversion assessments

---

8/ Michael S. Young, Michael D. Nicholas and Richard Roddewig, Condominium Conversions in Chicago: Facts and Issues (Chicago: Shlaes and Company, 1979).

9/ Development Economics Group, Condominiums in the District of Columbia. The Impact of Conversions on Washington's Citizens, Neighborhoods, and Housing Stock (Washington: Raymond, Parish and Pine, Inc., 1975).

10/ Condominium Conversions in Brookline: An Analysis of How Conversions Take Place in Brookline, and How They Affect the Town's Residents and Its Fiscal Conditions (Boston: Harbridge House, Inc., 1979).

11/ Condominiums in the District of Columbia, op. cit., p. 260.

12/ U.S. Department of Housing and Urban Development, Telephone Survey of 443 Local Officials, February 1980.

13/ With the exception of Baltimore, data were collected for one large property (with more than ten units) and one small property (with less than ten units). In Baltimore, data were collected only for the small property. Properties were randomly selected from a list of known conversions in the year 1978. Data collected included the assessed value of units after conversion; assessed value of the rental property prior to conversion; and the property tax rate associated with each. The average size of the small property was 6.4 units; the average size of the large property was 48.6 units. These data are shown for illustrative purposes only. They do not comprise a representative sample and, therefore, generalization is limited.

TABLE VIII - 1

PERCENTAGE CHANGE IN ASSESSED VALUES
AND NOMINAL PROPERTY TAX LIABILITIES FOR
SELECTED CONVERSIONS

| SMSA | Percent Change in Assessed Value | Percent Change in Nominal Property Tax Liability |
|------|------------------------------------|--------------------------------------------------|
| Baltimore | + 643 | + 643 |
| Boston | + 28 | + 28 |
| Boston | + 26 | + 26 |
| Chicago | + 49 | + 48 |
| Chicago | + 57 | + 57 |
| Denver | + 225 | + 225 |
| Denver | + 28 | + 28 |
| Houston 1/ | 0 | 0 |
| Houston | + 205 | + 205 |
| Los Angeles | + 294 | + 294 |
| Los Angeles | + 78 | + 78 |
| Miami | + 57 | + 57 |
| Miami | + 6 | + 6 |
| Minneapolis | - 21 | - 21 |
| New Orleans | + 229 | + 229 |
| New Orleans | + 57 | + 57 |
| New York 2/ | + 2 | + 2 |
| New York 2/ | 0 | 0 |
| St. Paul | + 45 | + 45 |
| San Francisco | + 755 | + 755 |
| San Francisco | + 152 | + 152 |
| Seattle | + 110 | + 81 |
| Seattle | + 85 | + 59 |
| Washington, D. C. 1/ | + 1,250 | + 967 |
| Washington, D. C. | + 79 | + 42 |

- - - - - - - - - - - - - - - - - - - - - - - - - - - - - - - - - - - -

| | | |
|------|------|------|
| Mean All Cases (N=23) | + 139 | + 135 |
| Median All Cases | + 57 | + 57 |
| Mean All Condominiums (N=21) | + 152 | + 147 |
| Median All Condominiums | + 78 | + 78 |

1/ Accuracy of these data is questionable so they have been excluded from
   calculations.

2/ Cooperatives.

Source:  Property assessment data from city assessors' offices.

for 23 buildings, these data indicate that the postconversion
percentage change in assessed values ranged from +755 percent
to -21 percent, with an average (mean) increase of 139 percent. 14/ Half of these properties had an increased assessed value
of 57 percent or more. If only condominium conversions are considered, the average (mean) increase is 152 percent, and one-half
of the condominiums had an increased assessed value of 78 percent
or more. 15/

As a result of these changes, the nominal property taxes owed 16/
(i.e., owed before any property tax exclusions or abatements are
taken into account) increased, in most cases, by amounts that were
identical to increases in assessed value. 17/ For example, 8 of
the 23 condominium properties more than doubled in assessed value,
and all but one of these properties also doubled the nominal property tax generated. 18/ Although most jurisdictions experience an
increase in real estate assessments as a result of conversions, the
increase is very small compared to the total assessments existing in
these places. (See table VIII-2.) Among SMSAs with the largest

---

14/ Originally, data were collected on 25 buildings, but this calculation excludes one Washington, D.C. building and one Houston, Texas
property because data from these are questionable.

15/ This excludes two New York cooperative buildings.

16/ Nominal property taxes were used because data on the amount of
exclusions granted for each building in all cities were unavailable.
Using nominal property taxes exaggerates somewhat the net tax effect
of conversion. However, the average nominal tax increase in those
cities for which both the nominal and net tax are available is only
13 percent greater than the net tax increase:  96 percent versus 83
percent.

17/ Only in 2 of the 12 high conversion volume cities were the percentage changes in nominal taxes levied different from the percentage
changes in assessed values. In one city, the change occurred because
of a decrease in the tax rate charged to all classes of property. In
the other, a lower tax rate is applied to owner-occupied converted
units than is applied to rental properties. Even there, the increase
in assessed value was so great that the nominal tax owed still
increased.

18/ It is unreasonable to assume that increases of the magnitude
found in this report and in other studies occur in all conversions.
Those considered here are far too few to make such quantitative
estimates. They can be used, however, to illustrate general trends.

amounts of conversion, only San Francisco experienced a net increase
in assessed values greater than two one-hundredths of one percent
(.0002%) of total real property assessments as result of conversions
occurring in 1978 and subsequent reassessment. 19/  While the totals
are very small, they represent additional tax revenues to be collected
year-after-year and conceivably, could amount to a significant sum in
the future.  The net impact is dependent, in part, on the number of
conversions occurring and the mitigating effects of special property
tax relief measures such as homestead, elderly, and disability exemptions.

---

In addition, it would be unwise to attribute all of the increases
noted above to the change in use of the property, i.e., from rental
to condominium or cooperative.  A rental property that remained
rental after undergoing rehabilitation, comparable to that in many
conversions, would also show some increase in assessed value and
property tax.  Furthermore, the undetermined time lag between the
last date the property was assessed before the conversion, together
with the general rate of inflation, no doubt accounts for some of the
increase in many of the cases.  Attributing as much as one-half of
the increase to these factors does not diminish the general thrust
of the point; conversions substantially increase assessed values
and property taxes.

19/ This percentage assumes that the largest per-city increase in
assessed value resulting from conversion (as indicated by the very
small sample of buildings used to generate these data) represents
the increases to be expected from all conversions.  If the average
increase is used, the increases in total assessed values resulting
from conversions would be much smaller.  (See table VIII-2.)  The
fiscal impacts of cooperative conversions do not appear to be greater
than those generated by condominium conversions.  The only cooperative
conversions included in this analysis were two properties in New York
City where most of the cooperative conversions have taken place.
In one building, there was no increase in assessed value or nominal
property tax generated.  In the other building, only a two percent
increase occurred after conversion.  Cooperatives in New York are
taxed at the same rate as a rental buildings, and, unlike condominiums, which have separate assessments on each unit, cooperatives
have only one blanket assessment on the entire building.  A court
case, now pending in New York, has important implications for future
tax treatment given to cooperatives:  the case involves a cooperative in Bronxville, known as River House, which is challenging the
town and village assessments for the years 1976 through 1978 on the
grounds that they were overvalued.

## TABLE VIII-2

### ESTIMATED ASSESSMENT INCREASES DUE TO CONVERSION AS A PERCENT OF TOTAL ASSESSMENTS, SELECTED SMSAs

| SMSA | 1978 SMSA Real Property Assessed Values (In Billions) | Conversions in 1978 | Largest Per Unit Increase Assessed Value 1/ | Total Increase as Percent of Total Assessment 2/ | Per Unit 3/ Average Increase | Average Increase as Percent of Total Assessments |
|---|---|---|---|---|---|---|
| Baltimore | $ 11.74 | 762 | $ 1,604 | .0001 | - | |
| Boston | 19.32 | 2,224 | 486 | .0001 | 310 | .00004 |
| Chicago | 30.54 | 11,355 | 474 | .0002 | 422 | .00016 |
| Denver | 4.95 | 6,743 | 94 | .0001 | 33 | .00004 |
| Houston | 12.60 | 5,615 | 83 | * | 25 | ** |
| Los Angeles | 25.87 | 4,506 | 1,235 | .0002 | 1,205 | .00019 |
| Miami | 20.03 | 1,970 | 401 | * | 208 | .00003 |
| Minneapolis-St. Paul | 7.89 | 1,703 | 146 | * | -340 | -.00008 |
| San Francisco-Oakland | 15.78 | 2,639 | 6,141 | .0010 | 2,004 | .00032 |
| Seattle | 21.32 | 2,828 | 446 | * | 427 | .00005 |
| Washington, D.C. | 10.69 | 3,761 | 356 | .0001 | | |

Source: Property Values Subject to Local General Property Taxation In the United States; 1978, U.S. Bureau of the Census, Series GSS No. 92, Washington, D.C. 1979.

* = Less than one one-hundreth of 1 percent.
** = Less than .00001

1/ Of 2 buildings sampled; one building in Baltimore.

2/ Using the largest per unit increase as the basis for calculation.

3/ Average of 2 buildings sampled.

To Recap. With some exceptions, conversions do not appear to
generate substantial tax windfalls for local jurisdictions. Changes
in nominal property taxes closely parallel changes in assessed values
following conversion from rental to condominium status, and both tend
to increase substantially. It is not possible to separate out what
portion of the increase is due to substantial improvements in the
building and what portion is simply a result of the increase in the
value of the building due to conversion per se. However, although
in most cases, the majority of buildings converted to date have not
undergone substantial rehabilitation, it cannot be presumed that in
most cases, building improvements are not the primary cause of
assessment increases.

Impacts on Local Expenditures. Condominium and cooperative conversions may have additional fiscal impacts not measured by changes in
assessed values and property taxes. Changes in the characteristics
of the households who occupy converted buildings may generate new
levels of demand for public services which entail changes in the
level of local expenditures. The following section examines
differences between pre and postconversion residents, as well as the
mobility patterns of those households who buy into or move out of
converting buildings. If those mobility patterns are constrained
primarily within the same local jurisdiction, then the net effect
on demand for services may not change. It is also possible that the
fact of ownership per se affects demand for public services, i.e., the
same household has different public service demands as an owner then
it has as a renter. This potential shift in demand, however, is not
addressed empirically.

---

Historically, the fair market value of a cooperative is estimated
by treating the property as an income producing rental building
and comparing it to similar rental buildings in the neighborhood.
For River House, the two municipalities ascertained fair market
value by analyzing recent sales of units in River House and similar
cooperatives in its vicinity.

As a result, the municipal figures on which the assessments were
based were considerably greater than those developed by the cooperative using rental values. Should the municipalities prevail in this
case, an important precedent of using sales prices for cooperative
assessments may be set.

Relatively few cooperative conversions have taken place outside of New
York State. The New York SMSA accounts for 70 percent of cooperative
units converted since 1970, and the neighboring Nassau-Suffolk SMSA
accounts for 6 percent of all such conversions.

## Three Types of Conversion Neighborhoods

In the remainder of this chapter, postconversion changes in the socioeconomic characteristics of residents and in the overall condition of the neighborhood housing stock are examined. Conversions occur most frequently in three types of neighborhoods distinguished both by their location (whether in a central city or its suburbs) and stage of development (whether revitalizing or nonrevitalizing): central city nonrevitalizing; central city revitalizing; and suburban nonrevitalizing. (See exhibit VIII-1.) 20/ Different types of buildings, based on the degree of renovation at the time of conversion, are associated with these neighborhood types. As discussed in chapter III, conversions can be distinguished by whether they involve minor or major renovation; those involving major renovation are more frequently found in central city revitalizing neighborhoods than in the other two neighborhoods. Each of the three neighborhood types is discussed, in turn, below.

**Exhibit VIII-1**
**Three Types of Conversion Neighborhoods and the**
**Building Condition Associated With Each**

| Types | Location | Description | Pre Conversion Building Condition | Level of Repairs |
|---|---|---|---|---|
| Central City Non-revitalizing | Central City | Economically Viable Due to Continued Private Reinvestment | Most Are in Good Condition | Minor Cosmetic Changes (i e , Painting or Carpeting) or Sold "As Is " |
| Central City Revitalizing | Central City | Have Experienced Decline but Are Beginning to Revitalize Due to Increased Private/Public Reinvestment | Most Are in Good Condition but a Significant Number Are Substandard | Most Undergo Minor Repair but a Significant Number Undergo Major Repairs Prior to Sale |
| Suburban Non-revitalizing | Outside of Central City | Economically Viable Due to Continued Private Reinvestment | Most Are in Good Condition | Minor Cosmetic Changes (i e , Painting or Carpeting) or Sold "As Is " |

**Central City Nonrevitalizing Neighborhoods.** Nonrevitalizing neighborhoods are those which are experiencing steady and continued private investment and are economically viable. 21/ Generally, the

---

20/ This is determined by the relative levels of private investment and local public funds targeted to these neighborhoods, based on information provided by local housing and planning experts and Community Development Block Grant applications.

21/ According to local observers, a few of these nonrevitalizing neighborhoods may receive allocations from local Community Development Block Grant (CDBG) or Section 8 new or existing housing programs. Most frequently, CDBG funds are used for public improvements such as streets, sidewalks, or lighting.

housing stock is well maintained, and these areas have not experienced significant socioeconomic shifts in population during the last decade.

The Nation's 37 largest SMSAs contain 48 central cities. According to local planning officials, conversions have occurred in nonrevitalizing neighborhoods in 30 of these cities. (See exhibit VIII-2.) 22/ Studies of conversion activity in San Francisco and the District of Columbia, for example, have shown that a substantial number of the conversions in these localities have occurred in economically stable neighborhoods. 23/ The median incomes, rents, and housing values in these neighborhoods are higher than citywide, and local observers indicate that vacancy rates in nonrevitalizing conversion neighborhoods tend to be equal to or below city averages. Although reliable information is not available for turnover rates in individual neighborhoods, the low vacancy rates suggest fairly tight rental housing markets in most of these areas. 24/ The ovewhelming majority of the neighborhoods surveyed in the Washington, D.C. study did not experience significant changes in racial composition from 1960 to 1972; most conversion neighborhoods were predominantly white in both years.

The demographic profiles of other nonrevitalizing neighborhoods included in this study are similar to those identified in the San Francisco and Washington, D.C. studies. Most residents are middle- or upper-middle-income whites who are employed in white-collar,

---

22/ The Census is generally considered to be the best available data source for neighborhood analysis. However, the 1970 Census may not provide accurate demographic or housing characteristics of neighborhoods in 1979 or 1980. On the other hand, data from more recently conducted Annual Housing Surveys are aggregated at the SMSA (central city/outside central city) level and do not provide an adequate base against which to assess neighborhood characteristics. Therefore, local observers who are familiar with those neighborhoods in which conversions have occurred were interviewed in order to obtain pertinent neighborhood information. In-person interviews were conducted in 37 SMSAs, and a separate round of telephone discussions were held with local planners in 18 central cities which are located in 12 SMSAs with high levels of conversion activity. The telephone interviews were conducted in February 1980, separately from the national telephone survey of local government officials. See Appendix 2 for a description of the method used.

23/ Development Economics Groups, Condominium and Cooperative Conversions in the District of Columbia (Washington: Raymond, Parish and Pine, Inc., 1979); Condominium Conversions in San Francisco (San Francisco: San Francisco Department of City Planning, 1978).

24/ See discussion on relationship between SMSA-wide vacancy rates and conversion activity in chapter V.

Exhibit VIII-2

**Types of Neighborhoods With Significant Amounts of
Conversion Activity Within the Nation's 37 Largest SMSAs**

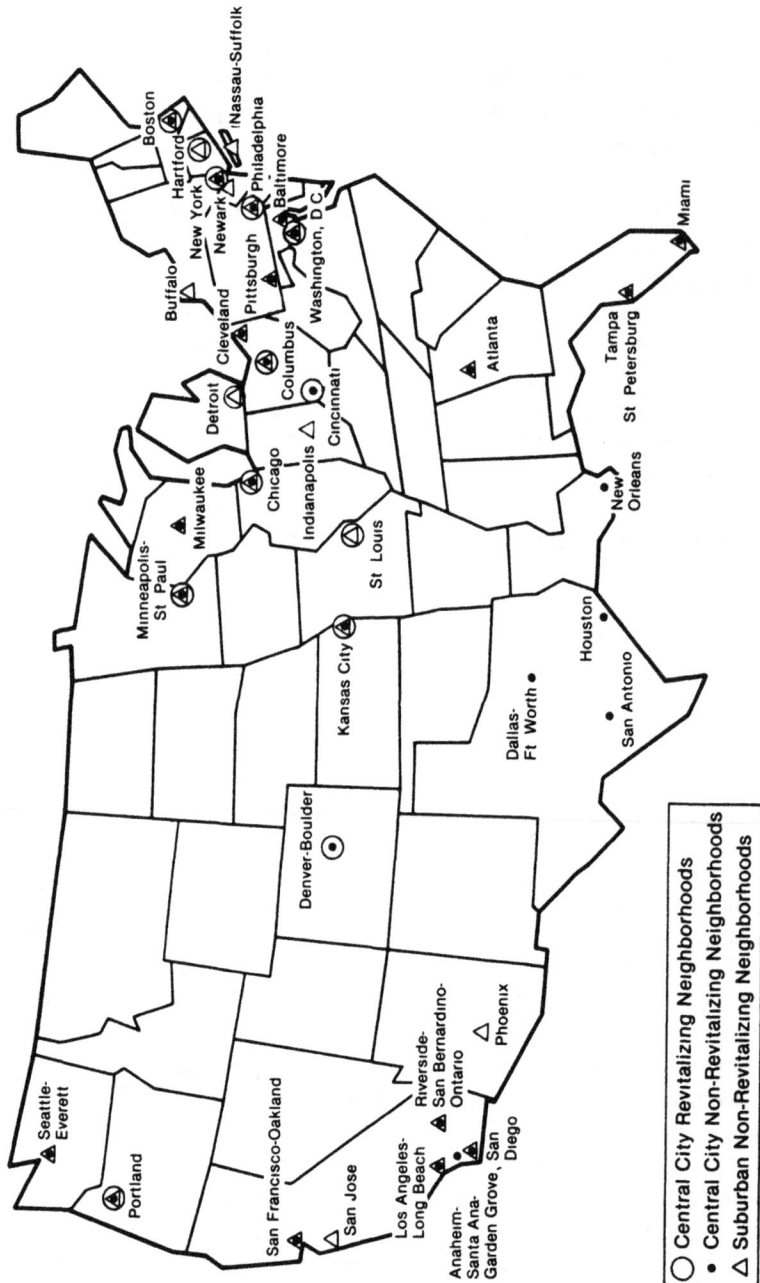

Boston
Nassau-Suffolk
Hartford
New York
Newark
Philadelphia
Baltimore
Washington, D.C.
Miami
Buffalo
Pittsburgh
Cleveland
Columbus
Atlanta
Tampa
St Petersburg
Detroit
Cincinnati
Milwaukee
Chicago
Indianapolis
St Louis
New Orleans
Minneapolis-
St Paul
Kansas City
Houston
San Antonio
Dallas-
Ft Worth
Denver-Boulder
Seattle-
Everett
Portland
San Francisco-Oakland
San Jose
Riverside-
San Bernardino-
Ontario
Phoenix
Los Angeles-
Long Beach
Anaheim-
Santa Ana-
Garden Grove, San
Diego

○ Central City Revitalizing Neighborhoods
• Central City Non-Revitalizing Neighborhoods
△ Suburban Non-Revitalizing Neighborhoods

Source. Field research in the Nation's 37 largest metropolitan areas and indepth discussions with local
planners in 18 central cities with significant conversion activity.

professional, or managerial occupations.  Neighborhood median
incomes are generally well above city averages and, in many cases,
are among the highest in these cities.  Households tend to be
smaller -- singles or couples, most frequently without children.
Many heads of household are concentrated in two age categories --
25 to 35 years and over 65 years old.  Elderly heads of households
are frequently single women with middle or upper middle incomes.

Although most residents of these nonrevitalizing areas tend to be
middle-income, white professionals, there are exceptions.  For
example, the residents of several nonrevitalizing neighborhoods in
Los Angeles, Tampa, and Miami, are predominantly black, Asian, or
Hispanic.  Also, in Everett and Long Beach, most residents of certain high activity conversion neighborhoods are moderate-income
whites who tend to be employed in nonprofessional occupations.

Central City Revitalizing Neighborhoods.  Revitalizing neighborhoods
are those which have undergone sustained decline in the past but
have recently experienced significant private or public reinvestment. 25/  As a result, the overall condition of the residential
housing stock in these areas has generally improved.  Revitalizing
neighborhoods are often among the oldest sections of their respective
metropolitan areas and, in some cities such as Minneapolis, St.
Paul, and Cincinnati, are designated as historic preservation dis-
tricts. 26/  Multi-family residential housing structures in these
areas tend to be small (under 20 units) and many were built between
the late 1800s and the early 1930s.  Although there are a significant
number of substandard or deteriorated structures in these areas, the

---

25/ Local observers indicate that most private reinvestment in these
neighborhoods, is in the form of single-family home renovation,
while public funds are generally from local Community Development
Block Grant (CDBG) or Section 8 allocations.  Frequently, CDBG funds
are used for housing rehabilitation loans or for capital improvements
(streets, sidewalks, lighting).  Also, in New York, HUD has sponsored
several conversions through its multifamily "Sweat Equity" Homestead-
ing program.  Under this program HUD provides funds for the rehabilitation of vacant HUD-held properties that are later converted to
moderately priced cooperatives.

26/ Although historic preservation programs vary, they generally
include loans or grants for housing rehabilitation, capital improvements, the development or improvement of parks and other recreational
facilities, or local tax abatement.

architectural design and the size of units, often have aesthetic appeal. Prior to initial conversion activity, several of these neighborhoods have also experienced dramatic changes in the overall socioeconomic characteristics of their residents; middle- and upper-middle-income, white homeowners have often replaced low- and moderate-income, minority renters.

Conversion activity has occurred in revitalizing neighborhoods in one-third of the 48 cities in the 37 largest SMSAS. (See exhibit VIII-2.) With the exception of Denver, Portland, and Washington, D.C., these cities are older urban centers located in the northeastern or northcentral regions of the country. Similar to nonrevitalizing areas, vacancy rates in revitalizing neighborhoods experiencing conversion tend to be equal to or lower than city averages. Turnover rates vary from "extremely low" to "very high" across jurisdictions, but it appears that rental markets are just as tight in these areas as in nonrevitalizing neighborhoods, given the low vacancy rates.

The Hyde Park section of Chicago provides examples of central city revitalizing neighborhoods which have had conversion activity. Under urban renewal, a substantial number of deteriorated apartment buildings in these neighborhoods were demolished and replaced by townhomes; these were frequently purchased by middle- and upper-middle-income whites while many low-income black households moved out of the area. 27/ The first conversion of rental units to condominiums in Hyde Park coincided with the close-out of urban renewal activities in the area in 1965. The earliest conversions were in small structures (three to six flats) of high quality construction. These buildings generally underwent cosmetic repairs during the conversion process. However, more recent conversions have been in buildings considered to be of lower quality and have required substantial rehabilitation.

During the past decade, revitalizing neighborhoods in other cities have also experienced significant changes in their socioeconomic profile and/or the quality of their residential housing stock. For example, neighborhoods in St. Louis, Cincinnati, St. Paul, and Washington, D.C., which were characterized in the early 1960s as having

---

27/ Peter Adels, Condominium Conversion in Hyde Park, 1965-79 (Chicago: Department of Geography Research Papers, 1977), p. 20.

mostly low- or moderate-income residents, have experienced appreciable in-migration of middle- or upper-middle-income, professionals. 28/ Housing in these areas, which was often considered deteriorated or substandard 20 years ago, has been renovated largely through private reinvestment.

The current socioeconomic profile of revitalizing neighborhoods undergoing conversion is similar to that of nonrevitalizing areas. In general, they tend to be predominantly white neighborhoods whose residents are professionals earning incomes equal to or above the city's median, but there are exceptions. For example, Chicago's South Shore area is a racially mixed neighborhood; and in St. Paul, Minneapolis, and Hartford, most revitalizing neighborhoods experiencing conversion have median incomes below that for the city. In addition, a significant proportion of the residents in St. Paul's revitalizing neighborhoods are service or clerical workers rather than professionals. Households generally tend to be smaller, often without children, and many heads are 25 to 35 years of age, or over 65 years old.

Local observers generally do not perceive a clear relationship between conversion and revitalization in these central city neighborhoods. In most cases, private reinvestment as well as the targeting of local public funds to these neighborhoods occurs at least two to five years before initial conversion activity. In general, it appears that conversion activity lags behind, rather than acts as a catalyst for, revitalization. Often, single-family homes are the first buildings renovated. One developer in Washington, D.C. decided to convert an abandoned apartment building but only after he had rehabilitated a number of single-family houses in the vicinity. On the other hand, in Newark, New Jersey, there is a neighborhood which has experienced decline and disinvestment, but is not yet considered to be "revitalizing." Despite the targeting of a substantial amount of Federal and local housing and community development funds, the neighborhood has yet to experience significant private reinvestment. To encourage additional reinvestment, local agencies have sponsored the conversion of four rental units to condominiums. 29/ Conversions

---

28/ Revitalization does not always entail a change in the racial composition of the neighborhood. In only three cities -- St. Louis, Cincinnati, and Washington, D.C. -- did revitalizing areas experience significant racial change.

29/ This conversion is a unique joint venture between the city government, the Chamber of Commerce, and a local nonprofit housing, rehabilitation and development corporation.

sponsored only by the private sector, however, rarely take place in such neighborhoods.

Demographic Impacts on Central City Neighborhoods.  According to community planners and other knowledgeable local observers, most central city neighborhoods -- both nonrevitalizing and revitalizing -- have undergone little or no change in their overall socioeconomic profile as a direct result of conversion activity:  new residents are believed to resemble former residents with respect to racial, income, age, and employment characteristics.  In those instances where conversions have occurred in revitalizing neighborhoods, local observers generally agree that changes in the neighborhood demographic or housing profiles are more a result of the overall process of revitalization than a direct result of condominium conversion.  Thus, the relative impact of conversion even on these neighborhoods, is perceived by local officials to be minimal.

Most local housing market experts indicate that potential changes in the demographic profiles of central city neighborhoods are minimized since there are sufficient housing alternatives in the immediate vicinity.  Former residents of converted buildings, who move rather than purchase their units, frequently stay in the area.  However, there are exceptions; several local officials in jurisdictions with particularly low rental vacancy rates report that households leaving converted units sometimes have difficulty finding alternative housing in the neighborhood.

For this study, it is not possible to separate the sample of households into those who reside in revitalizing or nonrevitalizing neighborhoods.  However, the survey does provide additional insights about the demographic impacts of conversions on central city neighborhoods in general. 30/  To assess these impacts, those  households living in buildings before and after conversion are compared. 31/

Pre as well as postconversion residents of central city converted buildings tend to be middle- or upper-middle-income whites, aged 25 to 35, who are employed in professional or managerial occupations and who frequently do not have school age children. (See table VIII-3.)  There are, however, some small differences between these two groups as shown in the following table:

---

30/ For a description of the surveys of current and former residents see chapter II.

31/ Obviously, these groups are not mutually exclusive.  Tenant buyers and continuing renters who remain in the building after conversion are considered both pre and postconversion residents.

VIII-19

## Table VIII-3

## Pre and Postconversion Selected Socioeconomic Characteristics

| Selected Socioeconomic Characteristics a/ | Preconversion (%) | Postconversion (%) |
|---|---|---|
| Non-White Households | 21 | 15 |
| Incomes of Less Than $12,500 | 18 | 15 |
| Incomes of $30,000 or more | 31 | 38 |
| Professional/Managerial Occupations | 59 | 63 |
| Retired | 16 | 12 |
| Age 65 or Older | 23 | 17 |
| Households with Children 18 Years Older or Younger | 7 | 7 |

a/ For additional characteristics, see table VIII-9 at end of this chapter.

Therefore, while pre and postconversion residents in converted central city buildings are more similar than dissimilar in their socioeconomic characteristics, small changes have occurred. Postconversion residents are somewhat more likely to be white, non-elderly, and have higher incomes than tenants in the building prior to conversion. The buildings have become a little more homogeneous in terms of race, income, and age. Of course, the extent to which these rather small changes affect the overall neighborhood profile is dependent on the amount of conversion activity in the neighborhood.

The extent to which conversions are concentrated or dispersed varies across cities. 32/ (See, for example, exhibits VIII-3 through VIII-7.) In some communities, such as Boston, conversions are concentrated in certain sections of the city, but the level of conversion activity in any given neighborhood appears to be too low

32/ To determine the degree of concentration of conversion activity, conversions within 18 central cities were mapped by census tract. These conversions occurred between January 1977 and December 1979 and are located in the 12 metropolitan areas with very high levels of conversion activity. These maps are presented in the field reports contained in Appendix 1.

**Condominium/Cooperative Conversions in New York, New York January 1977 to December 1979**

**Range of Converted Units Per Census Tract**

1-50
51-100
101-200
201-500
501-800
801-4000

5736 Numbers are census tract numbers.

# Condominium Conversions in Chicago, Illinois
## January 1977 to December 1979

Exhibit VIII-4

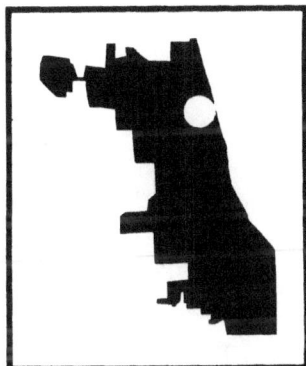

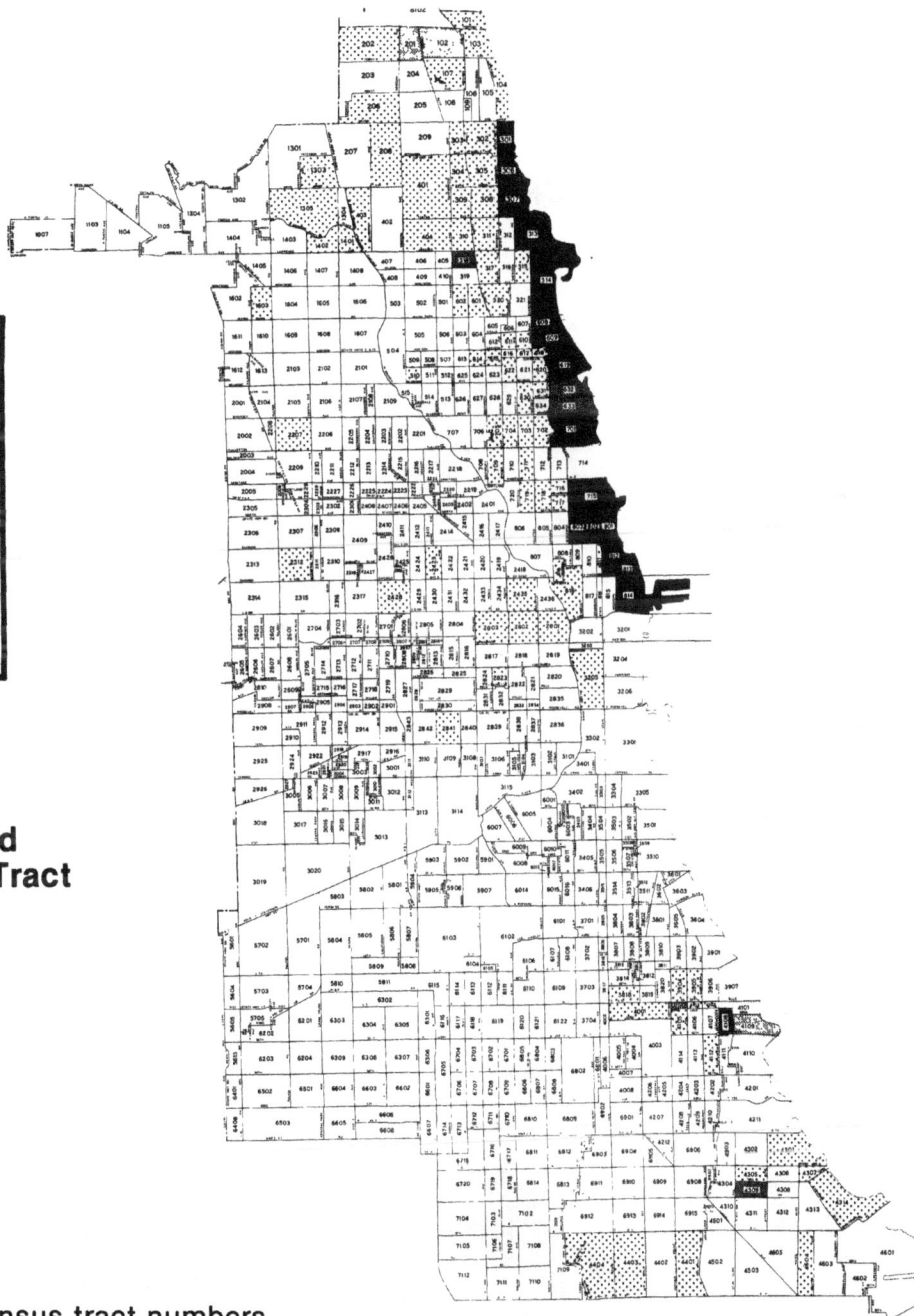

**Range of Converted
Units Per Census Tract**

▨ 1-50
☐ 51-100
▢ 101-200
▣ 201-500
■ 501-800
■ 801-4000

[370] Numbers are census tract numbers.

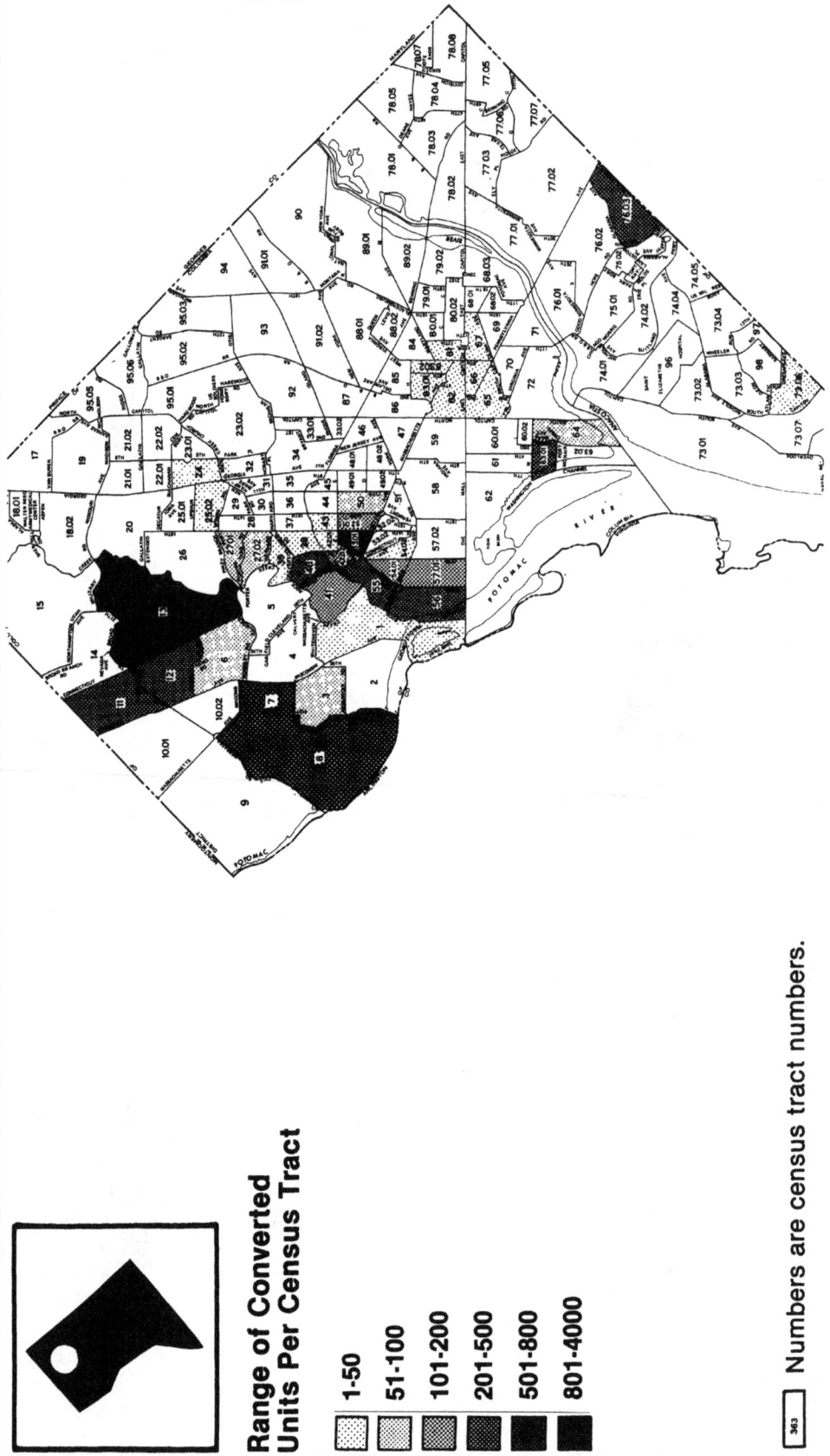

Exhibit VIII-5

# Condominium/Cooperative Conversions in Washington, DC January 1977 to September 1979

**Range of Converted Units Per Census Tract**

- 1-50
- 51-100
- 101-200
- 201-500
- 501-800
- 801-4000

[363] Numbers are census tract numbers.

Exhibit VIII-6

# Condominium Conversions in Boston, Massachusetts
## January 1977 to September 1979

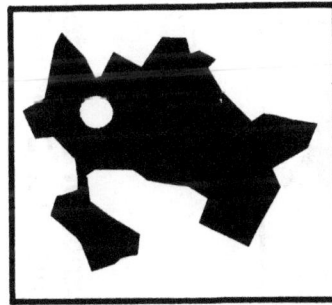

**Range of Converted Units Per Census Tract**

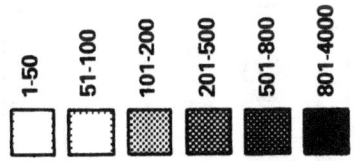

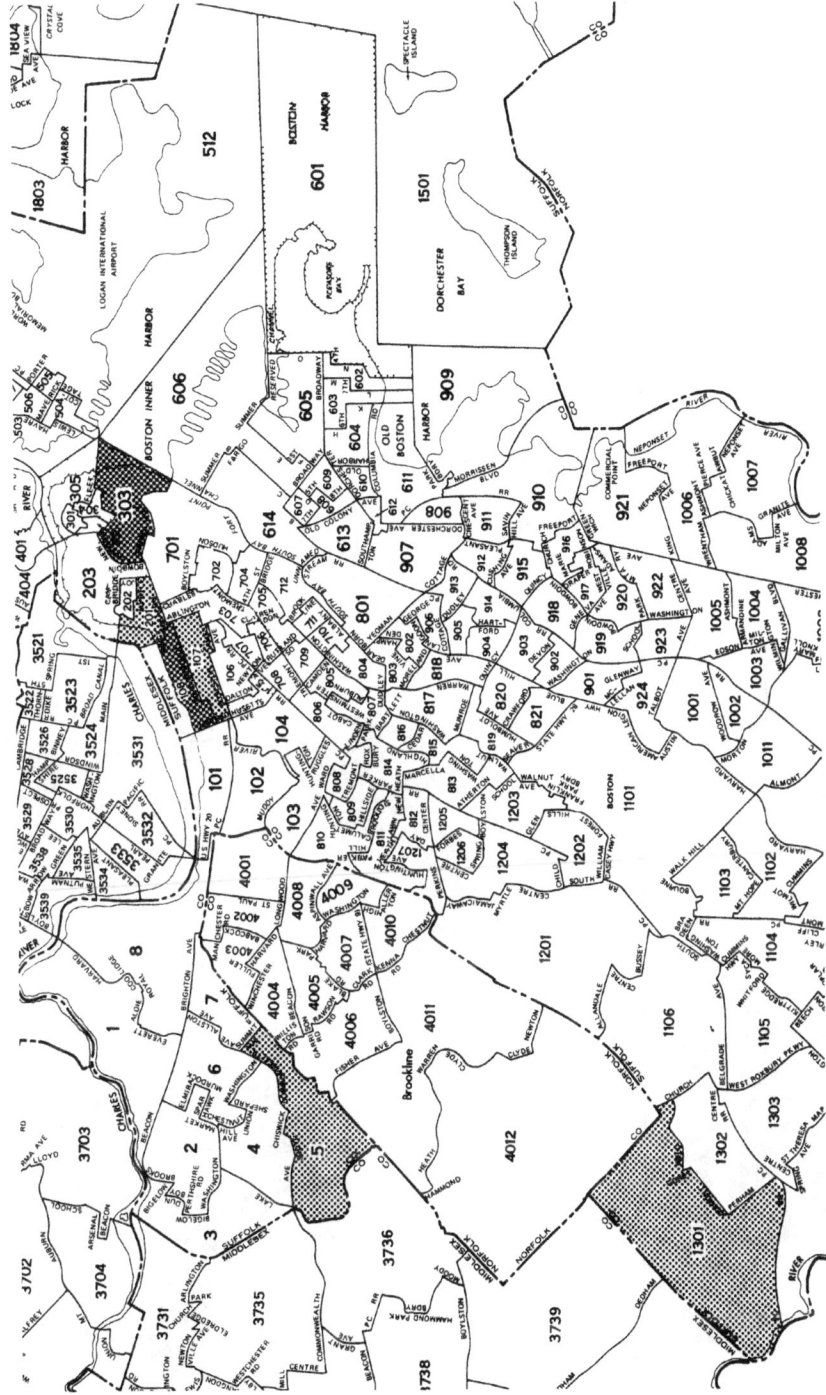

- 1-50
- 51-100
- 101-200
- 201-500
- 501-800
- 801-4000

1708 Numbers are census tract numbers.

Exhibit VIII-7

# Condominium Conversions in Los Angeles, California
## January 1977 to September 1979

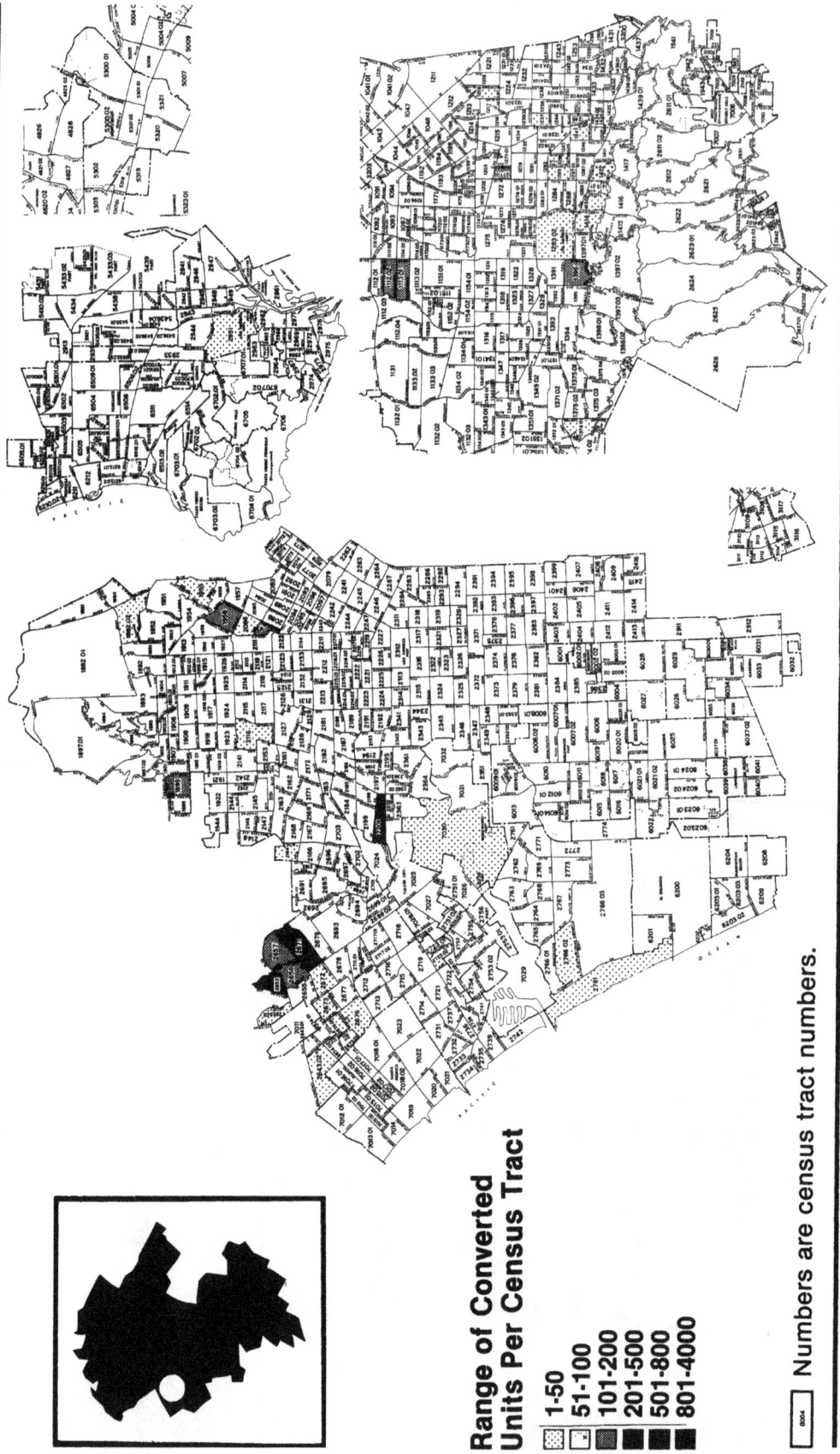

Range of Converted
Units Per Census Tract

1-50
51-100
101-200
201-500
501-800
801-4000

Numbers are census tract numbers.

(1 to 50 units) to have a major impact on neighborhood socioeconomic profiles. Conversions in Chicago are also taking place primarily in several neighborhoods, especially the "Gold Coast" along Lake Michigan. The potential for neighborhood change is greater in these areas since the level of activity per census tract is high (ranging from 800 to 4000 units). At the other extreme, conversions in Los Angeles are dispersed very widely throughout the city. It is less likely, therefore, that they exert a major effect on neighborhood socioeconomic characteristics in that city.

In addition to the degree of concentration, it is necessary to consider other factors when assessing the impact of conversions on neighborhoods: (1) the extent to which former residents of converted buildings move to new residences within the same neighborhood; (2) the extent to which new residents of the converted buildings have previously lived in the same neighborhood as the converted building; and (3) the extent to which "long-term" neighborhood residents initially move to new neighborhoods as a result of conversion activity. The larger the proportion of former residents who move elsewhere within the same neighborhood or the larger the proportion of new residents who come from within the same neighborhood, the smaller the degree of change in the overall neighborhood profile resulting from conversion.

About one-half of all former residents initially moved from a central city converted building to a residence within the same neighborhood. 33/ (See table VIII-4.) However, movers to converted buildings were less likely to have lived in the same neighborhood; 27 percent had previously lived within the conversion neighborhood, while the balance of these households lived in another neighborhood within the city (34%), a suburb of the city (12%), or another city entirely (27%).

Most former residents of these buildings had not lived in the neighborhood more than five years, and almost one-half had lived there three years or less. On the other hand, current residents who were preconversion tenants (continuing residents), were more likely to

___

33/ Only the initial move from the converted building is considered here given the small number of former residents who moved more than once. If subsequent moves made by some of the former residents are also considered, neighborhood turnover is more significant. Overall, 72 percent of the former residents of central city and suburban conversions currently live in new neighborhoods.

## TABLE VIII-4

### NEW LOCATION OF FORMER BUILDING RESIDENTS

|  | Central City % | Suburb % |
|---|---|---|
| Initially Moved Within Neighborhood | 51 | 30 |
| Initially Moved to Different Neighborhood | 49 | 70 |
| Total | 100 | 100 |
| Number | (71) | (110) |

Source:  Survey of Current and Former Residents, op.cit.

## TABLE VIII-5

### PREVIOUS LOCATION OF NEW BUILDING RESIDENTS

| Location of Previous Residence | Central City % | Suburb % |
|---|---|---|
| Same Neighborhood | 27 | 22 |
| Same City | 34 | 29 |
| Suburbs of Same City | 12 | 12 |
| Another City | 27 | 37 |
| Total | 100 | 100 |
| Number | (248) | (241) |

Source:  Survey of Current and Former Residents, op.cit.

have lived in the conversion neighborhood longer: almost 40 percent
of the continuing residents versus 9 percent of former tenants had
lived in the area for more than ten years. (See figure VIII-1.)

## FIGURE VIII-1

**Length of Residency in Neighborhood**

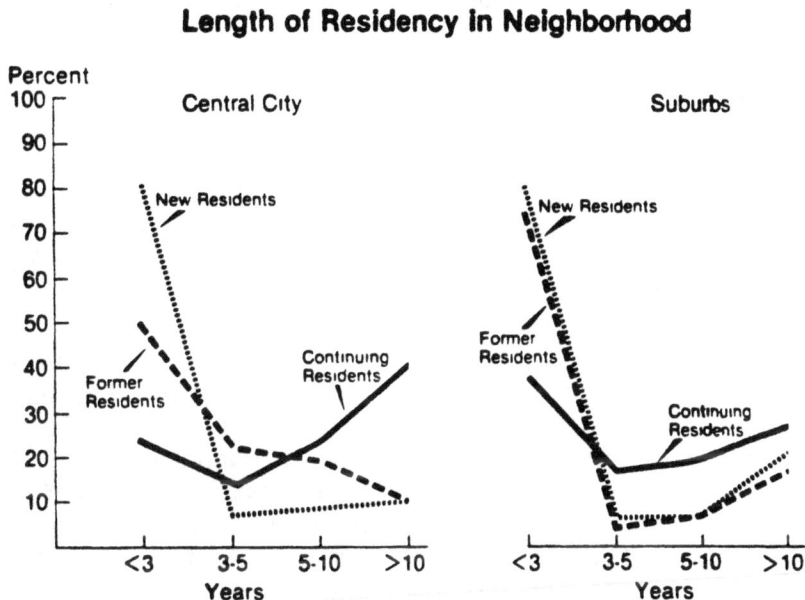

While the survey suggests that conversion does not typically contribute to significant shifts in the profile of neighborhood residents,
interviews with local officials revealed interesting trends. Several
formerly all-white, nonrevitalizing neighborhoods in Houston have
experienced some influx of middle-income black professionals; and in
Boston, middle-income whites and students are being replaced by upper-
middle-income whites in the same neighborhoods. In St. Paul, Washington, D.C., and Hartford, conversions have attracted a number of
upper- or middle-income, white-collar professionals to revitalizing
neighborhoods whose residents were previously low- and moderate-
income, blue-collar households.

Housing Impacts on Central City Buildings and Neighborhoods. Local
housing planners suggest that conversion activity has little short-
term impact on the condition of housing in central city nonrevitalizing or revitalizing neighborhoods: high-quality buildings in sound or
improved condition are frequently the initial targets of central city
conversions. As a result, most conversions in both kinds of neighborhoods undergo minor repairs or cosmetic changes (e.g., painting or
carpeting of common areas) or are offered for sale in "as is" condition. However, buildings selected for conversion in revitalizing
neighborhoods are more often in substandard condition and more often
require major repairs (especially those which are vacant prior to conversion) than those in nonrevitalizing areas. Major repairs may

include substantial work on, or replacement of, heating or air conditioning systems, plumbing, wiring, the roof, elevator(s), or even a "gut rehabilitation" of the building.

Most converted condominium and cooperative units in the Nation's central cities are in high-rise (more than 9 floors) buildings that are between 11 and 20 years old. (See table VIII-6.) These buildings are generally in good condition. Both before and after conversion, most current residents who were also preconversion tenants believe that the building required only minor repairs. About one-third felt that the condition of their building had improved while over one-half reported it to be in the same condition after conversion. In most cases, according to local observers, repairs at the time of conversion are minor or cosmetic in nature. In the minority of cases where major systems are replaced in the buildings or where the buildings are completely rehabilitated, they often are located in revitalizing neighborhoods.

Nonresidential Conversions. While the previous discussion has focused on conversions of rental buildings, a growing phenomenon, particularly in the Northeast, is the conversion of nonresidential buildings to condominiums or, in the case of New York, to cooperatives. Such conversions have been prevalent especially in Boston and New York, but they are becoming popular in many other areas as well, including Washington D.C. and Seattle. In general, the conversion of formerly nonresidential buildings to condominiums and cooperatives requires complete rehabilitation. Often these buildings are located in neighborhoods which are heavily commerical or industrial in character and which have experienced some economic decline due to the out-migration of business and industry. Although these neighborhoods do not precisely fit the central city revitalizing neighborhood described earlier, they are in the process of rejuvenating.

Prior to conversion, many of these structures were vacant hotels, warehouses, schools, or factories. These buildings often have appealing features, such as extensive square footage, large amounts of open space, and high ceilings. Before marketing many of these unconventional conversions, developers undertake major repairs, including installation of plumbing, electrical, heating and air conditioning systems, as well as kitchens and bathrooms. However, some of these conversions, commonly referred to as "residential lofts" in New York, undergo only minor repairs in the conversion process. In these instances, tenants are expected to provide such necessities as bathrooms, kitchens, or dividing walls. 34/

---

34/ Kristina Ford, Housing Policy and the Urban Middle Class (New Brunswick, NJ: Center for Urban Policy Research and the Citizens Housing and Planning Council of New York, 1978). About 90 percent of all loft conversions are "illegal" under local zoning ordinances or building codes.

## TABLE VIII - 6

### AGE AND TYPE OF CONVERTED BUILDINGS AS PERCEIVED BY
### CURRENT RESIDENTS

| Age of Building (years) | Central City % | Suburbs % |
|---|---|---|
| Less than 5 | 1 | 6 |
| 5 to 10 | 23 | 53 |
| 11 to 20 | 50 | 25 |
| 21 to 30 | 4 | 3 |
| 31 to 40 | 2 | 6 |
| 41 to 50 | 9 | 2 |
| Over 50 | 11 | 5 |
| Total | 100 | 100 |
| Number | 381 | 335 |

| Type of Structure | Central City % | Suburbs % |
|---|---|---|
| High-rise | 55 | 11 |
| Mid-rise | 19 | 13 |
| Low-rise | 26 | 68 |
| Townhouse | 0 | 5 |
| Other | 0 | 3 |
| Total | 100 | 100 |
| Number | 455 | 396 |

SOURCE: Survey of Current and Former Residents, op. cit.

## TABLE VIII - 7

### BUILDING/COMPLEX CONDITION AS PERCEIVED BY CONTINUING RESIDENTS

|  | Perceived Condition Before Conversion | | Perceived Condition After Conversion | |
|  | Central City | Suburb | Central City | Suburb |
|---|---|---|---|---|
|  | % | % | % | % |
| Little or no repairs | 28 | 34 | 35 | 39 |
| Minor repairs | 39 | 44 | 37 | 47 |
| Major repairs | 33 | 22 | 28 | 14 |
| Total | 100 | 100 | 100 | 100 |
| Number | 196 | 138 | 193 | 147 |

SOURCE: Survey of Current and Former Residents, op. cit.

## TABLE VIII -8

### CONTINUING RESIDENTS' COMPARISON OF POSTCONVERSION BUILDING CONDITION WITH PRECONVERSION CONDITION

| Condition of Building After Conversion | Central City % | Suburb % |
|---|---|---|
| Much Better | 9 | 4 |
| Somewhat Better | 26 | 29 |
| About the Same | 56 | 60 |
| Somewhat Worse | 8 | 7 |
| Much Worse | 1 | 0 |
| Total | 100 | 100 |
| Number | (197) | (144) |

Source: Survey of Current and Former Residents, op. cit.

Some local observers in New York suggest that nonresidential conversions result in the displacement of various small businesses and jobs to areas outside of the city. Conclusions reached by the Mayor's Task Force on Loft Conversions in 1978 tend to refute this view: it found that loft conversions were not the major cause of the city's loss of manufacturing jobs, 35/ and that the loss of industry from the city had preceded the advent of loft conversions. Nevertheless, continued revitalization of some of these nonresidential neighborhoods and buildings may result in greater competition between demands for commercial and manufacturing space and demands for residential housing within the city.

To Recap. In central city conversions, pre and postconversion residents tend, for the most part, to resemble one another. There is some change, nevertheless: postconversion residents are somewhat more often white, nonelderly, and have slightly higher incomes. The impact on the neighborhood, however, will vary according to the degree of conversion activity and the mobility patterns of new and former residents. Conversions in revitalizing areas usually lead to no more change in the neighborhood's socioeconomic profile than conversions in nonrevitalizing areas. Any dramatic demographic change that occurs usually does so before initial conversion activity.

Most converted buildings in central cities are in sound condition and generally undergo little or no major repairs at the time of conversion. In these cases, there is little short-term impact on the buildings' condition. However, in the longer run, these buildings may be better maintained than if they had remained in the rental stock.

A considerable number of conversions, particularly those in revitalizing neighborhoods, undergo major rather than cosmetic changes at the time of conversion. For these buildings, conversion contributes to structural improvement.

Suburban Nonrevitalizing Neighborhoods. Conversions have occurred in nonrevitalizing suburban neighborhoods in 27 of the Nation's 37 largest SMSAs. In fact, 19 of these metropolitan areas have higher proportions of conversion activity in their suburban areas than they have in the central city. (See exhibit VIII-2.)

---

35/ Report of the Mayor's Task Force on Loft Conversion (New York: City of New York, July 1978).

In almost every case, these neighborhoods are located in close-in suburban jurisdictions and, in several respects, are similar to non-revitalizing neighborhoods in central cities. They tend to be econo-mically stable areas which have experienced neither deterioration nor revitalization. Given their economic vitality, these neighborhoods are seldom targeted for Federal or local funds for housing or commu-nity development, and they generally have not experienced major changes in either their socioeconomic or housing profiles. In most cases, neighborhood residents are typically middle- or upper-middle-income whites, who are employed in white collar professions.

There are, however, differences between the suburban and central city nonrevitalizing neighborhoods other than location. Generally, resi-dential housing in suburban neighborhoods is newer than that of the central city. A large percentage of the suburban stock was built in the 1960s and 1970s, while much of the central city housing was con-structed before 1940. Also, there tends to be a higher percentage of townhouses and garden apartments in these areas than in the central city neighborhoods experiencing conversion.

Demographic Impacts. According to local observers, most residents of suburban neighborhoods where conversions occur are middle- and upper-middle-income whites both before and after conversion. Their con-clusion is based on the understanding that a relatively small propor-tion of the housing stock is being converted in most areas, and that current residents of converted buildings resemble those who lived there before the building was converted. 36/

Results from the household survey support this view. (See table VIII-9.)

---

36/ Suburban conversions were not mapped by census tract (as they were in the 18 central cities) so it is not possible to address the issue of the degree of concentration or dispersion of conversions in suburban areas of the 12 metropolitan areas with extensive conver-sion activity.

Table VIII-9
Pre and Postconversion Selected Socioeconomic Characteristics

| Selected Socioeconomic Characteristics | Preconversion (%) | Postconversion (%) |
|---|---|---|
| Non-White Households | 12 | 17 |
| Incomes of Less Than $12,500 | 27 | 16 |
| Incomes of $30,000 or more | 27 | 27 |
| Professional/Managerial Occupations | 52 | 59 |
| Retired | 21 | 11 |
| Age 65 or Older | 18 | 13 |
| Households with Children 18 Years Old or Younger | 14 | 13 |

a/ For additional characteristics, see table VIII-10.

For the most part, conversions in suburban neighborhoods appear to have a minor effect on the income, age, and racial mix within individual buildings. 37/ When pre and postconversion residents are compared, postconversion buildings are somewhat less racially homogeneous; in terms of income and age of residents, however, converted

37/ Although conversion activity, in most cases, is reported to have little or no effect on demographic profiles of suburban nonrevitalizing neighborhoods, atypical examples were offered by experts in several jurisdictions. One example was the conversion of a large garden apartment complex (3,400 units) in a Washington, D.C. suburb which resulted in significant displacement of low- and moderate-income households. Before conversion, most tenants were low- and moderate-income whites, employed in blue-collar or clerical occupations, but after conversion, there was an almost total turnover of residents. Except for race, new residents are significantly different from former residents. Prior to conversion, households tended to be married couples, frequently with children. As a condominium, the complex tends to attract smaller, one- or two-person, childless households. The household heads are generally middle-income whites who are employed in white-collar professions.

buildings are more homogeneous. A lower proportion of current residents than of preconversion residents have low or moderate incomes, are retired, and are over 65 years of age. Postconversion households, however, are no more likely to have school age children than preconversion households.

As noted earlier, the impact of conversions on a neighborhood is influenced by mobility patterns of both new and former residents. Similar to new residents of central city conversions, those moving to suburban buildings are more likely to have previously lived in another city (37%) than within the conversion neighborhood (22%). On the other hand, most former residents of these buildings (70%), unlike those in central cities, move to new neighborhoods when they first leave their buildings. Former residents of suburban buildings that are converted are even less likely to have lived in the neighborhood a long period of time than are former residents of central city buildings. About 75 percent of the surburban group lived in the neighborhood three years or less, but a somewhat higher proportion of the suburban households compared to those in central cities lived there ten years or more. (See figure VIII-1.) Although the potential for turnover, as a result of conversions, is greater in suburban neighborhoods, those who move are not likely to be long-time neighborhood residents.

Housing Impacts. Thus far, conversions have had a negligible impact on the quality of multi-family housing in suburban nonrevitalizing neighborhoods. Buildings selected for conversion in these areas tend to be newer than those in central cities. They are generally in sound condition and require only minor repairs. 38/ While half of the central city converted buildings are between 11 and 20 years old, slightly more than half of the suburban buildings are 5 to 10 years old. Unlike those in central cities, suburban conversions are more likely to be low-rise (one to four floors), than high-rise structures. (See table VIII-6.) Most current residents who were prior building tenants believe that their building and individual unit needed minor or no repair before conversion, while one-fourth of this group believe that major repairs are now needed and most feel that the postconversion condition of their buildings is the same (60%) or better (33%) than preconversion.

---

38/ There are exceptions. Several conversions in suburbs of Washington, D.C. and Philadelphia were in poor condition and required complete rehabilitation. Consequently, the overall condition of these buildings improved substantially. For further detailed discussion see the field reports contained in Appendix 1.

<u>To Recap.</u>  For the most part, suburban conversion activity has resulted in slight changes in building racial and age mixes, but has not affected overall neighborhood socioeconomic characteristics. Similarly, conversion activity has had little effect on the overall condition of the residential housing stock since buildings selected for conversion are generally in sound condition.

<u>Future Conversion Activity</u>

This chapter has concentrated on conversions which have taken place throughout the 1970s, but the future may bring changes in the character and location of conversion activity.  As noted in chapter VII, the supply of readily convertible rental buildings is already low in a few localities, and it is possible that buildings once considered unsuitable for conversion will, in the future, be converted.  It is also possible that more conversions will occur in revitalizing or yet-to-be revitalized neighborhoods.  For instance, in Evanston, Illinois, local officials report that by late 1979, the "best" buildings had largely been converted and a "second tier" of older, smaller buildings was beginning to be converted.  More nonresidential buildings outside of New York and Boston are also likely to be converted in the future.

If increasing numbers of conversions take place in neighborhoods which are revitalizing, the conversion phenomenon could play a more significant role with respect to neighborhood change.  It is likely that more such conversions would involve "gut" rehabilitation of structures nearing or at the end of their useful lives as rentals.

The restoration of these buildings would result in improving the neighborhood housing stock, but such rehabilitation would also affect a higher proportion of lower income and minority households.  In the future, therefore, conversion is more likely to result in greater numbers of tenants moving from converting buildings, unless the conversion process is managed by the tenants themselves and/or unless it involves some type of special government or private assistance.

* * *

To date, condominium and cooperative conversions have had minimal impact on the fiscal capacity of local communities and on the demographic and housing profiles of most neighborhoods.

Any gain in local property tax revenues from condominium conversion is determined not only by the level of conversion activity within a community but also by tax rates and methods of assessment.  Conversion of a rental building to a condominium may produce a slight revenue gain, because the aggregate assessment of the converted units is generally greater than the assessment of the property as a rental; in New York, where most cooperative conversions have occurred, subsequent reassessments have not been substantial and converted buildings are taxed at the same rate as prior to conversion.  To date, the amount of revenue generated from the sale of converted units is small compared to total assessments in communities experiencing high levels of conversion activity. Thus, the relative impact of conversion on local fiscal capacity has been slight.

Conversions have had little direct impact on the three types of neighborhoods in which most activity has occurred. Although the race, income, and age mix of individual buildings may have changed slightly, the majority of postconversion residents resemble preconversion tenants with respect to these socioeconomic characteristics. In many cases, mobility patterns of new and former residents of converted buildings and the level and concentration of activity per neighborhood, minimize neighborhood change. As a result, the neighborhood demographic profile is basically the same as before. Even in revitalizing neighborhoods, most of the socioeconomic change has occurred gradually, through the revitalization process, rather than as a direct of conversion activity. These similarities in houshold characteristics suggest that the demand for public services in most conversion neighborhoods is basically the same as it was before conversion. For example, in both central city and subruban converted buildings, postconversion households are no more likely to have school age children than preconversion households. Thus, conversions probably have little effect on the demand for or public expenditure for public schools. Although there are undoubtedly expections, by and large, local government expenditures have probably not substantially changes as a result of conversion.

Most conversions are located in central city or suburban neighborhoods which have not experienced decline and are economically viable. Buildings selected for conversion in these areas are generally in sound condition and undergo minimal or no repairs. Therefore, the process of conversion has little short-term impact on the quality of these buildings. On the other hand, a significant number of conversions located in central city neighborhoods which are revitalizing, undergo major repairs; and in these cases, conversion contributes to the improvement of the neighborhood housing stock. Should such conversions become more common, the future impacts of conversion could differ from those measured to date.

Although the impact of condominium and cooperative conversion on communities and neighborhoods has been minor thus far, the potential impact is greater if the level or character of conversion activity should change. The impact on neighborhoods will be greatest in those cases where conversions are concentrated in a small number of neighborhoods rather than dispersed widely throughout a community.

# Chapter IX
# Tenant and Owner Impacts

The conversion of rental housing to condominiums and cooperatives affects communities and neighborhoods in different ways, as described in chapter VIII. Unquestionably, however, their primary impacts are on people -- people who rent or buy units that are converted.

Because of the effects on people who have to decide whether to buy, to move, or to remain as renters, the conversion phenomenon has sometimes become a divisive and emotional issue. In particular, assessment of the human impacts tends to highlight the involuntary relocation that can result. There are ample newspaper headlines that describe individual cases of adverse or even traumatic consequences in communities that have experienced a large number of condominium or cooperative conversions. This chapter documents the extent to which these adverse impacts occur.

Conversion proponents, on the other hand, emphasize various benefits for those who remain in or move to converted buildings. Although the economic benefits of ownership have been discussed earlier in chapter VI, the extent to which other positive impacts also occur is of interest here, as well.

The chapter begins by looking at the impacts on residents during the initial stages when a building is being converted. The proportion of residents who move out of the building once converted and their experiences in locating alternative housing are examined. Conversion related financial impacts on households are estimated in a third section, and the chapter concludes with a discussion of other issues which concern condominium or cooperative ownership. This final issue was not part of the original mandate for this study and consequently, is only briefly discussed; however, it warrants considerably more attention in the future as the social and other implications of tenure changes due to conversion become more apparent.

## Initial Impacts on Tenants Living in Converted Building

Three types of tenant households are directly affected by condominium and cooperative conversions: those that continue to rent in the converted buildings (continuing renters); those that buy their units (tenant buyers), and those that move out of the buildings as a result of conversion (former residents). 1/ All of them are faced with the

---

1/ The primary source of evidence used in this chapter is the U.S. Department of Housing and Urban Development, Survey of Current and Former Residents of Converted Buildings, December 1979 and January 1980. For a more detailed decription of this survey, see chapter II and Appendix 2.

same series of circumstances. As tenants in a building about to be converted, they have received notification that the conversion will occur and must decide how to respond. During the period following notification, they are often the recipients of attractive inducements to purchase, but at the same time, they may feel anxious about the decision which they must make.

As indicated in chapter III, converters benefit if a large number of existing tenants purchase their units. The more units sold to tenants, the lower the marketing costs for unsold units and the greater the certainty that all units will be sold in a shorter period of time. Interim financing for conversion projects is often easier to obtain or is obtained on more favorable terms if a large proportion of tenants decide to buy. Consequently, converters have an incentive to induce tenant purchase. 2/

Although it is usually in the converter's interest to retain renters in the building until the units are sold to provide continuing rental income, a conversion with substantial rehabilitation may be more difficult and costly for the converter if the tenants remain in occupancy. Also, the longer a tenant has a legal right to remain in the unit, the longer the unit remains off the sales market, and this adds to the carrying costs associated with it. In these instances, the converter has an incentive to induce tenants to move out.

In the discussion that follows, examples are given which highlight both positive and negative experiences of tenants at the initial stage of conversion. First, examples of converters' actions to ameliorate some of the adverse effects of conversion are described. Following this, examples are given which highlight negative tenant experiences at this early stage of conversion.

Assistance and Inducements

Most converters offer discounts to tenants as a matter of standard operating procedure. 3/ These discounts are usually in the range of 10 to 20 percent of purchase price. This is done to encourage

---

2/ Some converters will have many potential buyers other than current renters and can sell to these households without discounts. In these cases, they may desire to minimize sales to current renters.

3/ Keith B. Romney, Condominium Development Guide (Boston: Warren, Gorham & Lamont, 1974), X-20 - X-21.

tenant buying and results in some benefit to both converters and buyers.  In some cases, converters offer tenants the option to buy their units in "as is" condition to lower prices even further.  The tenant has, therefore, the option of refurbishing the unit to the extent desired or affordable. In those cities where a percentage of tenants must purchase their units before conversion is approved, discounts can be more substantial.  In New York City, for example, discounts of up to 50 percent have been reported. 4/

Converters in some SMSAs have assisted tenants by allowing them to continue leasing their apartments. 5/  This has often been done by selling the apartment to an investor who in turn leases it to the original occupant.  In other cases, converters do not sell all of the units, but retain a small number of them to rent to certain tenants.  One developer who has converted a large number of units in the Washington, D.C. area has not evicted a single tenant in the last several years.  He does this in several ways, such as providing long-term leases for terms of up to five years, or selling units to the county which then leases them to existing tenants at subsidized rental rates.

Converters occasionally provide help to those tenants who decide to move out of their buildings.  Most often, this aid consists of counseling and assistance in finding a new apartment rather than money to cover moving expenses, yet there are notable exceptions.  In Columbus, Ohio, for example, one converter has, in some cases, volun tarily paid moving costs, forgone a month's rent, and given $100 in cash to households agreeing to terminate their leases and waive their rights to buy under Ohio law.  Voluntary relocation assistance has been provided in the city of Hartford, Connecticut, on a broader scale than found in most other cities.  In three conversions there, two nationally known but locally based insurance companies served as developers and contracted with a private firm to establish and imple ment a relocation program for displaced households.  The program included the following components:

o    Tenants were not given specific dates to vacate;

o    Tenants were given assistance in finding new units;

o    All moving expenses were paid;

_____

4/ See field notes on the New York City SMSA in Appendix 1.

5/ The discussion here focuses on actions taken by converters.  See chapter X for a discussion of tenant assistance programs enacted by local jurisdictions.  In some cases, these programs help tenants to locate and move to new housing.

o    Security deposits for new apartments were paid by the
     developers and the old security deposits for vacated units
     were returned to households;

o    Departing households had to find "comparable" units; and

o    No harassment of tenants was allowed and no work could be
     done in the units while tenants still occupied them.

Local observers familiar with this relocation program estimate that
it costs about $700 per family for moving expenses plus $300 per
family for the new security deposits.

Although the preceding discussion suggests that some of the tenants'
needs are met by actions of the landlord or converter, there is also
evidence of negative tenant experiences.  There are cases in which
landlords attempt to "induce" tenant purchases or moves through the
use of quick eviction or other methods when local regulations
provide tenants with some period of time before eviction can legally
occur. 6/

In one city, for example, a converter issued seven-day notices to
tenants in a building to be converted.  Subsequent tenant complaints,
however, led to the cessation of the conversion project.  A widow in
another city reported that she received numerous phone calls from
the converter of her building urging that she buy her apartment,
which she felt she could not afford.  When she refused, her children
were called to ask why she did not buy.  Unable either to buy or to
continue renting at the newly doubled rent, she moved from the building.  In another city, a resident of a building undergoing conversion
was summoned from a business meeting to accept a "very important
call" that proved to be a sales agent telling him that he had just
two more days in which to decide whether or not to purchase his
unit.

A study in Evanston, Illinois indicates that approximately 35 percent
of all households feel the length of time allowed for decision making
is inadequate. 7/  And, a Cambridge, Massachusetts study finds that
30 percent of the households feel they are harassed into moving. 8/

----

6/ Victor A. Cohen and G. Gregory Handschuh, "Tenant Protection in
Condominium Conversions:  The New York Experiences," St. John's Law
Review 48, (May 1974), pp. 978-93

7/ James L. Fremming and Carla B. Howery, Condominium Conversions in
The City of Evanston, (Evanston, Illinois:  Evanston Human Relations
Commission, 1978).

8/ Condominium Conversions in Cambridge:  A Profile of New Owners and
Former Tenants (Cambridge, December 1978).

If these examples are characteristic, the conversion process will
produce pressure, anxiety, and anger among tenants.  Moreover, low-
income and elderly persons -- those who have fewer options -- are
likely to be particularly anxious when faced with decisions to buy
or move.  One study reports that the aged often feel "out of control"
when they are dealing with the uncertainty and changes that unplan-
ned relocation can bring. 9/

The next section analyzes systematically these tenant experiences for
a large number of households.  The principal sources of information
are the surveys of current and former residents of converted buildings.

Pressures to Move or to Buy

From the tenant's point of view, the conversion process usually
begins with receipt of a notification from the converter/developer.
(See table IX-1 App.)  This notification generally includes a schedule
detailing the amount of time tenants have to decide whether to buy and
the length of time tenants may remain as renters if they choose not
to buy.  Typically, tenants in the 12 metropolitan areas surveyed for
this study are given about 70 days in which to buy, although 20 percent are give 30 days or less.  The median time given tenants to move
is 80 days.  (See table IX-2 App.)

TABLE IX-1
Household Type  1/

| Perception of Pressure: | Tenant Buyers % | Continuing Renters % | Former Residents % |
|---|---|---|---|
| Yes | 21 | 28 | 74 |
| No | 79 | 72 | 26 |
| Total | 100 | 100 | 100 |
| Number | (185) 2/ | (166) 3/ | (298) 4/ |

Source:  Survey of Current and Former Residents, op. cit.

1/ Percentages are based on weighted data.
2/ Perception of pressure to buy.
3/ Perception of pressure to move.
4/ Perception of pressure to move.

9/ Gail Brenner and Richard Schulz, "Relocation of the Aged:  A
Review and Theoretical Analysis," Journal of Gerontology, Vol. 32
(1977), p. 323.

Although these data convey some of the constraints facing tenants whose building are being converted, they do not indicate how tenants perceive the conversion process or whether tenants feel under pressure because their building is converting.

In hindsight, a minority of tenant buyers (21%) and continuing renters (28%) believe that they felt pressure to make their choice, once notified that the building would be converted. However, a large majority (74%) of former residents (those who moved out after conversion) perceived pressure. (See table IX-1.) Sense of pressure, therefore, appears associated with moving from a building which is undergoing conversion; this suggests that those continuing renters, who remain in their buildings only temporarily, may also feel pressure when a move is imminent.

When tenants and former residents discuss these pressures, they are generally not referring to harassing phone calls or to continuing personal confrontations between the new owner and the tenants, but rather to the anxieties and uncertainties that are associated with being told that they must move if they choose not to purchase their units. 10/ The tone of many of the responses suggests that tenants felt pressured by the difficult choice they had to make and if they decided not to buy, they felt pressured by the necessity of moving.

Even if the converter does his or her best to ease the anxiety associated with the decision to buy or move, the choices tenants are asked to make are not without potential for creating stress. A majority of former residents were perceived by interviewers as being angry and resentful about the conversion of their apartment. (See table IX-2.) In contrast, only 11 percent of tenant buyers were perceived as angry. 11/

---

10/ The following are examples of reasons why those choosing not to buy felt pressure: "I could not afford to buy, therefore, I had to move"; "The lease was terminated and I had to buy or move out"; and "I was asked if I wanted to buy; if not, I would have to move. There was no harassment. They were very considerate."

11/ Former residents were profiled as follows in interviewers' notes: "Mrs. _____ felt it was not fair to be forced to make the decision to move"; "Mr. _____ did not want to move, because of children. Housing is just non-existent. They were happy with school and the girl missed her friends"; and "the respondent felt very resentful about having to move, was very satisfied at _____ and went through a lot of worrying to find a suitable place."

TABLE IX-2
Attitude of Former Residents and Tenant Buyers
Towards Conversion as Perceived by Interviewers

| Attitude | Former Residents | Tenant Buyers |
|----------|------------------|---------------|
| | % | % |
| Angry | 56 | 11 |
| Satisfied | 18 | 77 |
| Noncommital | 17 | 7 |
| Other | 9 | 5 |
| | | |
| Total | 100 | 100 |
| Number | 290 | 185 |

Source: Survey of Current and Former Residents, op. cit.

Although the prospect of moving appears to be the main source of pres
sure for former residents, a few tenants do cite instances of harassment. Some complain of overly persistent salespeople, while others
are disturbed by the violation of privacy that accompanies the frequent showing of their apartment to prospective buyers. In one
building, several former residents complained that the converter had
failed to provide adequate heat, had not repaired the elevators when
they were broken, and had not provided hot water.

## Purchase and Relocation Assistance

The most common means used by converters to ease the transition to
condominium or cooperative ownership involves purchase price
discounts to existing tenants. (See table IX-3 App.) 12/ The widespread use of discounts -- about 90 percent of tenant buyers receive
them -- accounts for some decisions to buy, but it is not certain
whether the availability or amount of such discounts significantly
increases the rate of tenant purchase.

Discounts are not the only inducements offered by converters to
increase the rate of tenant purchase. Prearranged, end-loan financing packages secured by the converter sometimes result in mortgage
fund availability below the current market rate. Additionally,
remodelling is often provided as an inducement to buy.

---

12/ As noted earlier, discounting also benefits the converter if it
results in greater sales to existing tenants.

Although converters often provide inducements to tenants who choose
to buy, they rarely provide assistance to those households choosing
to move. Thirteen percent of former residents received some type
of relocation aid, but for only 4 percent did this include financial
assistance. (See table IX-3 App.) Converters, therefore, are more
likely to offer tenants incentives to buy rather than aid them in
their move.

At times, tenants in special circumstances are also offered an
option of continuing to rent. For example, converter developers,
either themselves, or through an arrangement with an investor
owner, may give elderly and handicapped tenants the option of
continued renting. Increases in rent, however, may accompany the
issuance of renewed leases.

Elderly and Nonelderly Persons. It has been reported that elderly
persons are more likely than others to feel the pressure of conversion
and to be anxious about the prospects of relocation or about having
to make a substantial investment in purchasing their unit. 13/
Some have suggested that elderly tenants who ultimately purchase
their units are "distressed purchasers," who buy because they have
no other choice. There is some support for these contentions, but it
appears as if not wanting to move is a more pervasive explanation
than the unavailability of alternative housing or the pressures and
anxieties associated with purchasing.

In terms of perceived pressure, 28 percent of elderly tenant buyers
believed that they were under pressure to buy, compared to 18
percent of nonelderly tenant buyers. (See table IX-4 App.) 14/
However, only 3 percent of the elderly -- compared to 4 percent of
those between the ages of 25 and 35 -- decided to purchase because
they could not find alternative rental accommodations. Although
there are many reasons for purchasing (see chapter VI) such as a
preference for the neighborhood or building, half of all elderly
tenants who purchased did so because they did not want to move out
of their unit, compared to 17 percent of tenant purchasers under
the age of 60.

Among those who do not purchase, elderly tenants are no more
likely than their nonelderly counterparts to have felt pressure
to move: 30 percent of elderly continuing renters felt pressure
compared to 28 percent of their nonelderly counterparts; and 72

---

13/ David Marlin and Erica Wood, Condominium Conversion: Options
for Tenants and Rental Market Protection (Washington, D.C.: National
Council of Senior Citizens, 1979).

14/ This difference is not statistically significant at the .05 level.

percent of elderly former residents felt pressure compared to 74
percent of their nonelderly counterparts. Elderly former residents
however, are more likely to express anger over conversion than those
who are younger. Seventy percent of the former residents 60 and
over were perceived by interviewers as angered by the conversion,
in contrast to 52 percent of the nonelderly. (See table IX-5 App.)
Nonpurchasing elderly households are, however, somewhat less likely
than others to have received either discounts or other inducements
to purchase, and they were no more likely to have received relocation assistance. (See table IX-4 app.) 15/

Income and Racial Differences. Because higher proportions of lower-
income 16/ and nonwhite households are renters rather than homeowners,
it is conceivable that these households are more likely to perceive
greater pressure to relocate, since they are less able to purchase
converted units. 17/ However, the evidence does not strongly support
this expectation. Higher proportions of nonwhite than white former
residents felt pressure to move; but among tenants continuing to
rent, higher proportions of white households felt such pressure.
Similarly, lower-income households were no more likely to feel pressure to move than were other income groups. (See table IX-4 App.)

The extent of assistance provided to these groups for purchase of a
unit or for relocation appears to vary with income and race. Higher
income tenants are more likely to be offered assistance to purchase
their units while lower-income tenants are somewhat more likely to
receive relocation assistance. The situation with regard to race is
again mixed, however. Although nonwhites who continued to rent or
who purchased their units were as likely, or more likely, than whites
to receive purchase incentives; nonwhite former residents were less
likely to receive inducements to purchase. 18/ Nonwhites were no
more likely than whites to receive relocation assistance.

---

15/ The differences between the elderly and nonelderly here are not
statistically significant at the .05 level.

16/ Eighty-nine percent of current residents and 77 percent of
former residents are one or two person households. According to
HUD regulations, two-person families earning less than 64 percent of
the local SMSA median income are considered lower income. Since the
average median income was $19,542 across the 12 SMSAs, lower-income
households are those earning under $12,500.

17/ "Let's Put Some Limits on Condo Conversion," Planning 43 (September
1977), p. 25; U.S. Congress, Senate Committee on Banking, Housing, and
Urban Affairs, Condominium Housing Issues, Hearings before the Sub-
committee on Housing and Urban Affairs on Condominium Conversions and
S.612, Testimony of Marion J. Barry, Jr., 96th Cong., 1st. sess., 1979,
p.4.

18/ These differences, however, are not statistically significant at
the .05 level.

Households with and without Children. Condominiums and cooperatives are typically thought of as appealing to young, single, and smaller households. Therefore, it might be expected that these sorts of tenants are the recipients of more intense marketing efforts than households with children. If this is true, households with children might be more likely to feel pressure to move. However, this is not the case. Furthermore, tenants without children do not show a higher probability of reporting incentives to buy their units. (See table IX-4 App.)

Experiences of Former Residents

Having examined the experiences of tenants during the initial stage of conversion, this next section looks at what happens to those households who move from the building. Following a determination of the number of preconversion tenants who move out rather than stay in the building (either as renters or owners), the remainder of the section describes the former residents' housing search, postconversion housing, and neighborhood quality that results from this search.

Estimating the Proportions of Tenants Who Stay and Who Move. Various studies have estimated that at least two-thirds of the tenants in converted buildings do not purchase their units. (See table IX-3.) Although these studies focus on the rate of tenant purchase, their findings are often interpreted as indicative of the rate of displacement or outmoving. 19/ But rates of tenant purchase do not account for tenants who continue renting in a condominium or cooperative, and hence they underestimate the percentage of tenants who stay and overestimate the percentage who move. As noted in chapter VI, continuing renters sometimes lease their unit from a developer, landlord, investor, family member, or friend. Therefore, it is important to note that the proportion of tenants who stay in the building usually exceeds the proportion who purchase.

According to the household survey conducted for this study, 22 percent of residents in converted buildings purchase their units. Not all of the remaining 78 percent move out, however; some of them rent until a later time when they buy, some rent indefinitely, and some rent temporarily. Sixty percent of all continuing renters have definite plans about either buying (2%), renting indefinitely (42%), or moving in the future (16%) and therefore their plans can be accounted for in estimating the proportion of residents who will eventually move out. Because the other 40 percent are not certain, two different methods are used to measure the proportion of residents who stay or, conversely, the proportion who move out.

---

19/ Gregory Longhini and Daniel Lauber, Condominium Conversion Regulations: Protecting Tenants, (American Planning Association, 1979); and HUD Condominium/Cooperative Study, 1975, op. cit.

TABLE IX-3
Proportion of Tenants Not Purchasing
Converted Units According to Other Studies

| Studies Done in | Percentage of Tenants Who Do Not Purchase |
|---|---|
| Evanston, Illinois, 1978 | 80-88 |
| Washington, D.C., 1978 | 68 |
| Washington, D.C., 1979 | 68 |
| Newton, Massachusetts, 1979 | 63 |
| Seattle, Washington, 1978 | 66 |
| HUD Condominium/Cooperative Study, 1975 | 75-85 |

Source:  Condominium Conversion in the City of Evanston, op. cit.;
Development Economics Group, Survey of Non-Purchasing Tenants in
Apartment Buildings Converted to Condominium (Washington, D.C.:
Development Economics Group, 1978); Development Economics Group,
Condominium and Cooperative Conversions in the District of Columbia
(Washington D.C.:  Development Economics Group, 1979); Newton
Condominium Study, (Newton, Massachusetts:  Newton Mayor's Advisory
Committee on Condominiums, 1975);  Washington Public Interest Research
Group, Wash PIRG Condominium Report (Seattle, Washington:  June, 1978);
U.S. Department of Housing and Urban Development HUD Condominium Coop-
erative Study, Vol. 1, (Washington, D.C.:  Government Printing Office,
1975).

Other studies have attempted to estimate the proportion of
tenant movers by surveying present occupants of converted condominiums
to determine the proportion which were tenants before conversion.  This
method of estimating the proportion of outmovers is subject to error
because it does not include tenant purchasers who bought but who have
subsequently moved.  These studies include Development Economics Group,
Condominiums in the District of Columbia, (Washington, D.C.:  Development
Economics Group, 1975); Metropolitan Washington Council of Governments,
Condominium Housing:  A New Homeownership Alternative for Metropolitan
Washington, (Washington, D.C., 1976); San Francisco Department of City
Planning and Members of the Real Estate Industry, Condominium Conver-
sions in San Francisco, (San Francisco, 1978).  Of all these studies,
only the 1975 HUD study attempts a national estimate of the rate of
outmoving or displacement.  In this case, however, the estimate was
arrived at by asking condominium owners associations to estimate the
percentage of tenants who purchase their units.  Public Interest
Research Group, Wash PIRG Condominium Report (Seattle, Washington:
June, 1978); U.S. Department of Housing and Urban Development HUD
Condominium Cooperative Study, Vol. 1, (Washington, D.C.:  Government
Printing Office, 1975).

Method 1 assumes that all of the uncertain continuing renters will actually move, while Method 2 assumes all will stay indefinitely in their converted buildings as either buyers or renters. Since some will stay and some will move, the estimates reflect the range of possibilities.

Table IX-4 shows that, using Method 1, the estimated proportion of tenants who leave is 69 percent. This method assumes a minimum number of continuing residents and a maximum number of outmovers among the currently uncertain tenants. Using Method 2, the proportion of outmovers is 61 percent. Table IX-5 describes the estimates resulting from Method 2.

Since a small percentage of tenants in converted buildings have bought their units but subsequently moved, they are also subtracted from the proportion of tenants who move out. When this is done, the proportion of tenant outmovers ranges between 58 percent (Method 2) and 66 percent (Method 1). 20/ Thus, the proportion of tenants who leave converted buildings is somewhat lower than what was estimated in some earlier studies, most notably, the 1975 HUD Condominium/Cooperative study.

It is important to note, however, that this range of figures represents an average range around which there is substantial variation among SMSAs, specific localities, or buildings. 21/ In some SMSAs, such as New York City and Chicago, relatively high proportions of tenants, especially in the central cities, purchase their units. In

---

20/ Both of these proportions may overestimate the number of tenants who move because of conversion, since it is possible that many of these former residents would have moved within a year, even if their building had not been converted. Former residents, like other renters, are a fairly mobile population; 35 percent lived at their preconversion residence for less than a year, and only 13 percent for longer than five years. In some areas, however, tenants have lived in converting buildings for long periods of time and hence are less likely to move if there is no conversion. According to a 1975 study of Washington, D.C., for example, 54 percent of the former residents of converted buildings had lived in their residences for more than five years while only 14 percent had lived in their preconversion residences for less than a year.

21/ Figures cited in this and the following paragraph are based on estimates by local market experts, local officials, developers, and tenant representatives in the SMSAs cited.

## TABLE IX-4

### Estimation of Rate of Outmoving
#### Method 1
#### (Assuming a Minimum Number of Stayers)

| Group | N |
|---|---|
| Tenant Buyers | 188 |
| Renters who have already purchased | 3 |
| Renters who can rent indefinitely | 47 |
| Renters in New York and Brookline who have a statutory right to rent indefinitely | 25 |
| Total number of stayers | 263 |

$$\text{Rate of Outmoving} = 1 - \frac{\text{Total Stayers}}{\text{Total Current Residents}} = 1 - \frac{263}{861} = 69.4\%$$

Adjusting for residents who bought their units but who have since moved

$$\text{Rate of Outmoving} = 1 - \frac{293}{861} = 66.0\%$$

\* \* \*

## TABLE IX-5

### Estimation of Rate of Outmoving
#### Method 2
#### (Assuming a Maximum Number of Stayers)

| Group | N |
|---|---|
| Tenant Buyers | 188 |
| Renters who have already purchased | 3 |
| Renters who can rent indefinitely | 47 |
| Renters in New York and Brookline who have a statutory right to rent indefinitely | 25 |
| Renters who plan to purchase | 9 |
| Renters who say they "Have a lease" | 8 |
| Renters who are uncertain | 30 |
| No answer | 22 |
| Total number of stayers | 332 |

$$\text{Rate of Outmoving} = 1 - \frac{\text{Total Stayers}}{\text{Total Current Residents}} = 1 - \frac{332}{861} = 61.4\%$$

Adjusting for residents who bought their unit but who have since moved

$$\text{Rate of Outmoving} = 1 - \frac{362}{861} = 58.0\%$$

New York City, this is partly due to high demand and partly due to the state law that requires at least 35 percent of tenants to purchase their units before a rental building is permitted to convert (in buildings with eviction plans; see chapter III).  In Chicago, the high rate of tenant purchase, especially in luxury buildings along Lake Michigan, is generally attributed to the extremely high demand for units in this area.  In other cities, there have generally been lower rates of tenant purchase.

There is also variation in the rate of tenant purchase from building to building.  For example, in Phoenix there are reports of buildings with tenant purchase rates as low as 10 percent and as high as 65 percent.  Similarly, in Baltimore, these figures range between 20 and 70 percent; in Dallas, between 6 and 60 percent; in Kansas City, between 0 and 50 percent; and in Chicago, between 10 and 80 percent. The high variability among buildings is due to a number of factors, including the way in which the units are marketed, their location, the incomes of tenants, and the cost of units.  According to most market experts, higher rent buildings have higher rates of tenant purchase than do lower rent buildings.

Selected characteristics of the former residents were discussed in chapter VI.  Table IX-6 reviews these findings and compares them to 1977 data on the national renter population.

TABLE IX-6
Comparison of Former Residents of Converted Buildings
to the National Population of Renter Households

|  | Former Residents | U.S. Renter Households |
|---|---|---|
|  | % | % |
| Nonwhite | 17 | 19 |
| Annual Income |  |  |
|  Less than $12,500 | 20 | 69 |
| Age 65 or older | 20 | 17 |

In terms of their race and age, former residents are relatively simi-lar to renters in general.  However, considerably fewer of them have low incomes:  nearly three and one-half times as many renters as former residents have incomes of less than $12,500.

Although these figures indicate that former residents of converted buildings are not more likely to be elderly or low income, other studies show considerable variation in these measures. Reports from Newton, Massachusetts and Baltimore have found that about two thirds of former residents in these communities are 65 years of age or older. 23/ In other communities, the fraction is much closer to 20 percent. The income of former residents also varies from one community to another. Nearly one-third of the former residents in Cambridge, Massachusetts earned less than $10,000 compared to ten percent in Evanston, Illinois. 24/ These data suggest that the character of the former resident population varies considerably from one community to another and thus the impact of conversion on specific population groups will also vary from place to place.

The Search for Other Housing. Because of the low and decreasing vacancy rates that currently characterize rental markets in many cities which have experienced conversions, former residents of converted buildings may experience difficulty in finding substitute housing. The following discussion focuses on this housing search. One indicator of problems in locating alternative housing is the amount of time required. Although this study did not obtain data on this question, several local studies have addressed the issue.

Evidence from Washington, D.C. for 1975 and 1978 shows that an average of one month was required to find new housing; more recent evidence (1979) suggests two months. (See table IX-7.) This may be due to the decline in the absolute number of rental units in Washington, D.C. and to an increase in the number of households since 1970. 25/ Data from Cambridge, Massachusetts, and San Francisco also suggest that the average housing search process takes between two and three months.

23/ Newton Condominium Study, op. cit. and Condominiums: Baltimore City, (Baltimore: Department of Housing and Community Development, City of Baltimore, 1980).

24/ Condominium Conversions in Cambridge: A Profile of New Owners and Former Tenants, op. cit. and Condominium Conversions in The City of Evanston, op. cit.

25/ Council of the District of Columbia, Final Report of the Emergency Condominium and Cooperative Commission (September 1979).

TABLE IX-7
Average Time Needed By Former Residents to
Find New Housing as Reported in Several Local Surveys

| Community and Date | Average Time Needed to Locate New Housing |
|---|---|
| Washington, D.C., 1975 | 1 month |
| Washington, D.C., 1978 | 1 month |
| Washington, D.C., 1979 | 2 months |
| Cambridge, Massachusetts, 1978 | 2-3 months |
| San Francisco, 1978 | 3 months |

Source:  Condominiums in the District of Columbia:  The Impact
of Conversion on Washington's Citizens, Neighborhoods, and Housing
Stock, op. cit.; Survey of Non-Purchasing Tenants in Apartment
Buildings Converted to Condominiums, op. cit.; Condominium and
Cooperative Conversions in the District of Columbia, op. cit.;
Condominium Conversions in Cambridge,  op. cit.; Condominium Conver-
sions in San Francisco op. cit.

As to the cost of moving, the median level of moving expenses for
former residents was approximately $145 (See table IX-6 App.);
30 percent of all former residents considered these costs to be
burdensome.  (See table IX-7 App.)  In contrast, no more than 10
percent of former residents received any kind of monetary relocation assistance either from converters or from government agencies.
(See table IX-3 App.)  Somewhat higher proportions of lower-income
households, the elderly, and households with children consider
their moving costs to have been a burden.  (See table IX-7 App.)

Overall, one-half of all former residents experienced some degree
of difficulty in finding new housing.  Elderly, nonwhite, and to a
lesser degree, lower-income households are more likely than others
to experience such difficulties.  (See table IX-8 App.) 26/

---

26/  These relationships are not statistically significant at the .05
level.

Although about one-half of all former residents had difficulty
finding new housing; the extent to which these difficulties were
overcome and comparable units found remains to be determined.  To
provide a point of reference, former residents' evaluations of
their new housing are compared with the evaluations made by those
who replaced them in converted buildings (outside buyers).  In
other words, are former residents more or less satisfied with
their current housing and neighborhood than outside buyers who
purchased converted units in buildings vacated by the former residents?

Satisfaction with Current Residence. 27/  Ninety percent of all former residents of converted buildings are satisfied with their new
units and buildings.  (See table IX-9 App.)  The remaining 10 percent who are dissatisfied compare with two percent of all tenant
and outside buyers who are dissatisfied.  In their own opinions,
former residents have done nearly as well as buyers of converted
units.  Not only are most former residents satisfied, but four out
of five feel their new residences are as good as, or better than,
those they vacated; 18 percent, on the other hand, consider their
new residences to be inferior to the ones they lived in prior to
conversion.  (See table IX-8.)  In comparison, about 10 percent of
all outside buyers feel their new condominium or cooperative
units are worse than their previous residences. 28/

---

27/ These survey responses reflect former residents' evaluation
of their current residence.  For most, (75%) the current residence
is the first residence since moving from the converted building.
However, for 25 percent of the former residents who have moved
more than once, the current residence is not their first residence.

28/ The majority of former residents also evaluate selected features
in their buildings (e.g., heating, plumbing, air conditioning,
appliances, recreation facilities) as the same or better compared
to preconversion dwellings.  In most cases, there appears to be
little or no difference (see table IX-11 App.) in the way former
residents and outside buyers evaluate the condition of their present
residences relative to preconversion dwellings.  Equally large
proportions of both groups view their new dwellings as the same or
better than their former residences.  The major exception concerns
recreational facilities; 42 percent of all former residents found
them to be worse in their new residences compared with 16 percent
of outside buyers of condominium and cooperative units.  This is
not surprising, since rental buildings with special amenities like
swimming pools are more likely than others to be converted.

TABLE IX-8
Comparison of Present Residence with Preconversion-residence
for Former Residents and Outside Buyers

Household Type a/

| Evaluation of Residence | Former Residents | Outside Buyers | |
|---|---|---|---|
| | | Comparison of Units | Comparison of Buildings |
| | % | % | % |
| Better | 58 | 60 | 54 |
| Same | 24 | 30 | 33 |
| Worse | 18 | 10 | 13 |
| Total | 100 | 100 | 100 |
| Number | (294) | (347) | (347) |

Source: Survey of Current and Former Residents, op. cit.

a/ The former residents were asked to evaluate "The Residence" while the outside buyers were asked to evaluate the unit and the building

Outside buyers of converted units and former residents, therefore, tend to view their current residences similarly. Moreover, elderly households and households with children among former residents are as likely as other households to see their new residences as being as good or better than their preconversion dwelling. (See table IX-10 App.) On the other hand, nonwhite and lower-income households are slightly more likely to find their new residences worse than their previous ones. 29/

Change in Neighborhood. A rather high proportion (72%) of all former residents no longer live in thier preconversion neighborhoods. (See table IX-12 App.) 30/ Also, a significantly higher proportion of nonwhites (88%) than whites (68%) said they presently live in a new neighborhood. 31/ Although it is not known if these households

29/ These relationships are not statistically significant at the .05 level.

30/ No formal definition of neighborhood was provided; respondents defined the term in a manner that seemed appropriate to them. Also, this proportion differs from those reported in chapter VIII, because it refers to the household's current neighborhood, rather than the one it first moved to after conversion.

31/ This relationship is statistically significant at the .05 level. There were no differences among age, income, or family status groups in terms of migration from the neighborhood.

changed neighborhoods voluntarily or if they changed because they could not find comparable housing, it is evident that conversion is associated with a substantial amount of outmigration of former residents from their preconversion neighborhoods. Despite this, 85 percent of those who did switch neighborhoods find that their new one is as good, if not better, than their preconversion neighborhood. (See table IX-9.) In comparison, only 78 percent of the outside buyers perceive their new neighborhood to be as good as their previous one. Judging by their own opinions, then, former residents who change neighborhoods have done as well as, if not better than, condominium or cooperative purchasers in locating higher quality neighborhoods. 32/

TABLE IX-9
Comparison of Present Neighborhood with Preconversion
Neighborhood for Former Residents and Outside Buyers a/

| How Does This Neighborhood Compare With the Preconversion Neighborhood? | Former Residents % | Outside Buyers % |
|---|---|---|
| Better | 55 | 36 |
| Same | 30 | 42 |
| Worse | 15 | 22 |
| Total | 100 | 100 |
| Number | 209 | 260 |

Source:  Survey of Current and Former Residents, op. cit.

a/ Asked only of those households changing neighborhoods.

The high proportion of former residents who leave their preconversion neighborhood may result in frequent disruptions of social ties that were established in the local area. The elderly are especially susceptible in this regard since they are more likely to have lived in the same buildings or neighborhood for a long time.

---

32/ Although overall evaluations and comparisons of present and previous neighborhoods are useful to determine the impact on former residents, they can hide variations in certain aspects of neighborhood quality, such as quietness and safety, proximity to specific services, and the quality of local public services. On almost all of these attributes, at least eight of every ten former residents who moved to a new neighborhood found the new environment to be of the same or higher quality as their preconversion neighborhood.

About one-sixth of all former residents had all or most of their friends and relatives living in their preconversion neighborhoods, but the vast majority do not have social networks which are strictly tied to the local area and thus are able to maintain their preexisting social relations when they move to a new neighborhood. (See table IX-13 App.) Furthermore, eight out of ten former residents live as close, if not closer, to their friends and relatives as they had at their preconversion residences. (See table IX-14 App.) Although lower-income and nonwhite households find it more difficult to visit their friends after their move, the elderly do not. (See table IX-15 App.) 33/

The majority of former residents give good ratings to their new neighborhoods, but this is not the case for low-income and nonwhite tenants. Three times as many lower-income households (31% versus 10%) like their new neighborhood less than they liked their former one. (See table IX-10.) Thus, although only 15 percent of former residents who switch neighborhoods consider their new neighborhood to be worse than their previous one, 40 percent of these are lower-income households.

Nonwhites are more likely than whites to evaluate the general quality of their new neighborhood, and their neighborhood's police protection, safety, medical facilities, and shopping facilities, and proximity to friends or relatives as worse than their preconversion neighborhood. (See table IX-16 App.) 34/ Neither elderly households nor households with children have a higher probability of rating their new neighborhood as worse than their preconversion one. (See table IX-10.)

Finally, advanced age undoubtedly restricts mobility and hence makes accessibility to services dependent upon residential location. Nevertheless, the elderly are as likely, or more likely to perceive their new residence to be as accessible to services as their preconversion location. (See table IX-17 App.)

---

33/ These differences are not statistically significant at the .05 level.

34/ The relation between race and change in overall neighborhood quality is not statistically significant. The relation between income and change in neighborhood quality, and between race and these measures of neighborhood attributes, however, are significant at the .05 level.

TABLE IX-10
Comparison Between New and Old Neighborhoods
By Selected Background Characteristics  a/

| Characteristics | Better % | About the Same % | Worse % | Total % | Number % |
|---|---|---|---|---|---|
| Age | | | | | |
| Less than 60 | 57 | 30 | 13 | 100 | 144 |
| 60 or more | 52 | 33 | 15 | 100 | 63 |
| Race | | | | | |
| Non-white | 62 | 16 | 22 | 100 | 36 |
| White | 54 | 34 | 12 | 100 | 172 |
| Income | | | | | |
| Less than $12,500 | 42 | 27 | 31* | 100 | 42 |
| $12,500 or more | 59 | 31 | 10 | 100 | 150 |
| Family Status | | | | | |
| Has children | 64 | 32 | 4 | 100 | 28 |
| Doesn't have children | 52 | 30 | 18 | 100 | 181 |

Source:  Survey of Current and Former Residents, op. cit.

a/  Asked only of former residents who changed neighborhoods.

*  Statistically significant at .05 level.


Financial Impacts on Former Residents and Continuing Renters

So far, many of the nonfinancial impacts of conversions have been
discussed.  This section examines changes in the costs and quality
of shelter following conversion.  It also assesses how many former
residents could have afforded to purchase their preconversion
residence.

Impacts on Former Residents.  For former residents who continue
to rent, the median change in total costs per household is an
increase of eight percent.  However, 28 percent of all former residents
who still rent pay at least 25 percent more in housing costs than
they did in the converted building, while another 30 percent pay less
than they did prior to conversion.  (See table IX-11.)  For those
former residents who have subsequently purchased a residence, the
median change per household is an increase of 68 percent in housing
costs without tax benefits considered.

### TABLE IX-11
### Percent Change in Total Monthly Costs
### Prior to and Following Conversion

| Percent Change in Total Costs | Former Residents | | Tenant Buyers | Outside Buyers | Continuing Renters | New Renters |
|---|---|---|---|---|---|---|
| | Owners % | Renters % | % | % | % | % |
| Lower Costs | 6 | 30 | 16 | 16 | 2 | 26 |
| No Change | 0 | 5 | 1 | 0 | 47 | 3 |
| +1 to +10 | 6 | 22 | 9 | 25 | 25 | 6 |
| +11 to +25 | 6 | 15 | 11 | 26 | 19 | 16 |
| +26 to +50 | 11 | 22 | 28 | 23 | 5 | 17 |
| > + 50 | 71 | 6 | 35 | 10 | 2 | 32 |
| Total | 100 | 100 | 100 | 100 | 100 | 100 |
| Number | (49) | (164) | (155) | (261) | (155) | (117) |
| Median | +68% | +8% | 36% | +62% | +0.4% | +25% |

Source:   Survey of Current and Former Residents, op. cit.

To obtain a more complete picture of what happens to former residents
of converted buildings, it is necessary to examine changes in both
monthly costs and changes in housing quality. 35/  Figure IX-1 shows
the residential history of former residents since conversion.  Twenty
six percent presently own a house, a cooperative, or a condominium; 36/
70 percent presently rent; and 4 percent live rent free.  The 70 percent who still rent can be classified into four categories depending on the changes in housing quality and cost. 37/

---

35/  To determine whether postconversion housing quality is comparable,
respondents were asked whether they considered their present residence
to be better, the same, or worse than their preconversion residence.

36/ Eighteen percent of all former residents became owners upon their
first move after conversion.  Subsequent moves by former residents
increased this percentage to 26 percent.

37/  In this instance, change in cost is measured by change in rent
for those who maintain the same utility structures, i.e., who either
continue to have utilities included in their rent or have them
excluded both before and after conversion.

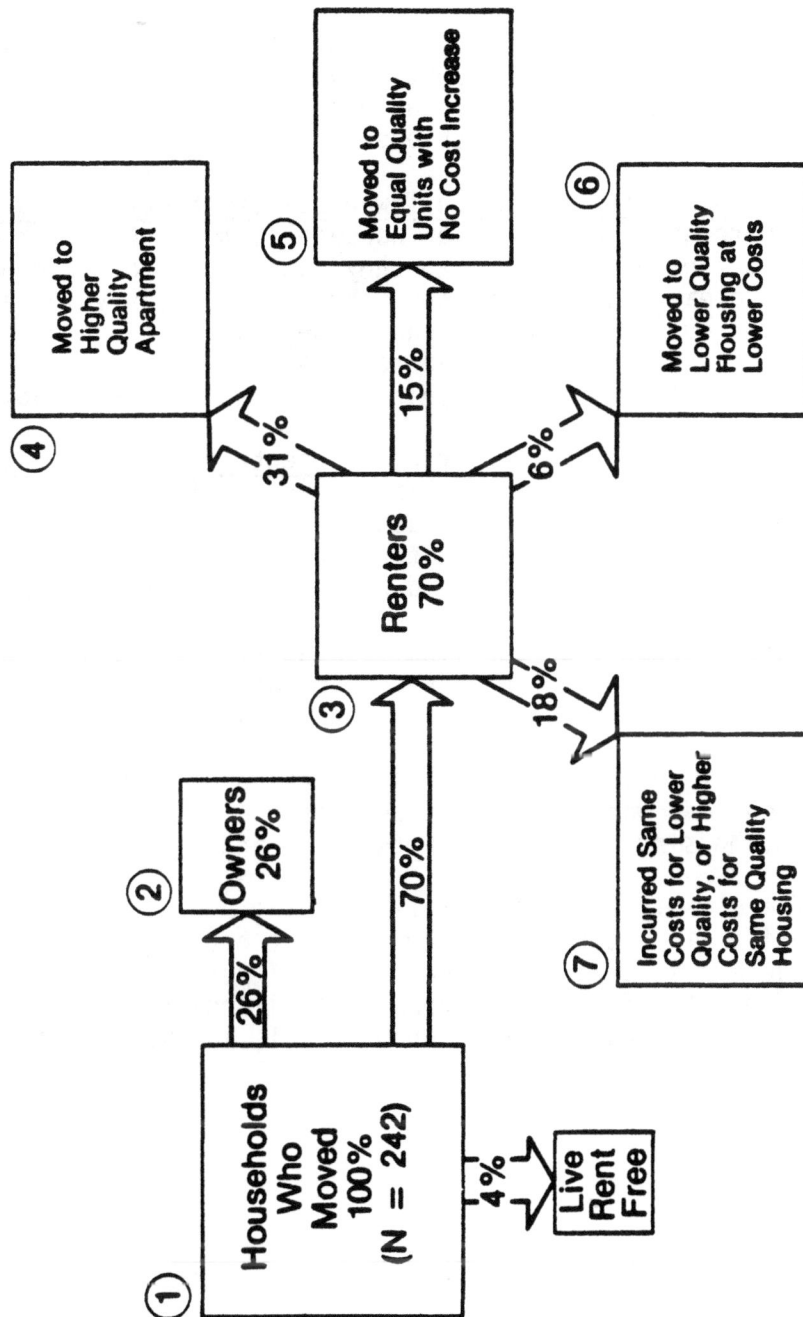

EXHIBIT IX-1

Household Experiences After Moving from Converted Residence

1. <u>Households moving to higher quality rental units</u>: 31 percent of all former residents moved to higher quality rental housing. A little over one-half of these households paid higher costs in order to obtain higher quality housing. <u>38</u>/

2. <u>Households moving to rental housing of equal quality, with no cost increase</u>: 15 percent of all outmovers were able to rent equal quality housing for roughly equal or lower costs. <u>39</u>/ Sixty percent of these households were able to find equal quality housing at lower costs than they had previously paid.

3. <u>Households moving to lower quality rental units at lower cost</u>: 6 percent of all outmover households moved to lower quality housing that rented for less than they had paid prior to conversion. It is not clear, however, whether these households voluntarily accepted lower quality housing because they wanted to reduce housing expenditures or were constrained to choose lower quality units because they could not find comparable housing that was affordable.

4. <u>Households incurring higher rents for equal quality housing or paying as much or more than previously for housing of lower quality</u>: 18 percent of outmover households received less housing value for their dollar compared to their preconversion residence. Of these households, one-fifth paid higher costs for lower quality housing.

Those households receiving less housing value for their dollar (Group 4) can be considered adversely affected by condominium conversion. The effect of conversion on Group 3 depends on whether their acceptance of lower quality housing was voluntary or constrained by lack of choice. Thus, the proportion of former residents who have been made worse off since conversion in terms of housing quality and housing cost ranges between 18 and 24 percent.

The elderly are more likely than the nonelderly to be members of group 4 While 14 percent of former resident households less than 60 years of age are in the group 4 category, 27 percent of those 60 and over are adversely affected in terms of their postconversion housing. This pattern is not repeated when racial, income, and family status differences are examined.

---

<u>38</u>/ "Higher costs" are defined as increases of more than 10 percent above preconversion rents.

<u>39</u>/ "Roughly equal costs" are defined as rents no more than 10 percent higher than previous costs.

Impacts on Continuing Renters. Fifty-one percent of continuing renters experienced an increase in housing costs during the conversion process. In most cases, the increases were small. One-fourth of all continuing renters, however, paid rents that were more than 10 percent higher than they had paid prior to conversion. (See table IX-11.) 40/

The Affordability of Converted Units. Two different approaches are used to determine the actual proportion of former residents who could not afford to buy their units. The first compares tenants' annual incomes to the purchase prices of their units to determine if they would qualify according to traditional lending institution criteria. The second examines tenants' responses when asked directly whether their perceived inability to purchase was a consideration in their decision to move rather than to buy.

To measure a household's ability to afford a unit, the banking and real estate community often uses the following criterion: a buyer can afford to purchase a property that is roughly equal to two-and-one-half times the buyer's annual household income. Application of this formula produces mortgage payments which are approximately equal to 25 percent of monthly income. While this "2-1/2 times" rule works well at lower interest rates, it is less applicable as interest rates rise above 10 percent. At high interest rates, the sales price affordable by prospective buyers must be revised downward. For example, at an interest rate of 13 percent, a buyer can qualify for a loan at two times annual household income if mortgage payments are equal to 25 percent of income. 41/

---

40/ In contrast, 32 percent of all outside renters (households that moved into the building after conversion) paid more than 50 percent above their previous housing costs. (See table IX-11.)

41/ At a 10 percent interest rate with a five percent downpayment, and a mortgage amortized over 30 years, the "2-1/2 times" rule generates a monthly mortgage payment which equals 25 percent of the owner's monthly income. At an 11 percent rate, a household with income of $20,000 could only afford a $46,000 home or 2.3 times their annual income. At a 12 percent interest rate, the maximum affordable price is 2.13 times income. These data are based on standard amortization tables.

Thus, all else being equal, rising interest rates lower the afford-ability of a given unit. 42/

The median purchase price of units vacated by former residents is $43,000 and the distribution is as follows:

| Price of Unit | Percentage of Units |
| --- | --- |
| Under $30,000 | 13 |
| $30,000 to $39,999 | 26 |
| $40,000 to $49,000 | 30 |
| $50,000 to $69,000 | 19 |
| $70,000 and Over | 12 |
| Total | 100 |

Application of the rule indicates that 42 percent of all former residents could not have afforded to buy their converted units. However, the proportion of tenants who could not afford to buy rises dramatically with the price of the unit. (See table IX-18 App.) 43/ While 86 percent of former residents who lived in units selling for less than $30,000 could afford to buy them, only 32 percent could buy when unit prices exceeded $70,000.

A second measure of affordability is the tenant's own opinion of what was possible at the time of conversion. Forty-seven percent of all former residents say that being unable to afford the unit was a factor in their decision to move rather than purchase.

This percentage is somewhat higher than that which would be expected based on the first measure, which compares income to purchase price. The discrepancy between perceived affordability and calculated

42/ This rule may slightly overestimate the affordability of some transactions made near the close of the survey period. Households included in the survey lived in buildings which were converted be-tween 1977 and 1979. According to the Federal Reserve Bulletin, con-ventional mortgage interest rates rose from 8.95 percent in 1977 to 12.5 percent by November 1979.

43/ This does not mean that tenants could not afford to purchase units elsewhere. Rather, it means that tenants could not exercise the option to buy their converted unit.

affordability may be attributed to a variety of factors other than income. 44/ Whatever the explanation, it is clear that, although a substantial number of former residents move because they cannot afford their unit, a majority move for other reasons. These reasons have been discussed in more detail in chapter VI.

Certain types of people are more likely to say one reason they decided to move was because they could not afford to purchase their units. (See table IX-19 App.) For example, younger former residents and those earning less than $12,500 more frequently say that they moved because they could not afford to buy. Interestingly, the elderly (over 65) are no more likely than others to give unaffordability as a reason for moving.

Impacts on Buyers

The Costs and Benefits of Ownership. Total cash outlays for tenant purchasers are typically 36 percent higher than total costs for rent, utilities, and fees prior to conversion. (See table IX-11.) 45/ In comparison, the median percentage increase in monthly costs for outside buyers is 62 percent.

The differences in cost increases for outside buyers versus tenant buyers result from several factors. Tenant buyers are likely to receive discounts and other inducements to purchase that reduce the total costs of owning, while outside buyers more often pay full market value. In addition, since many tenant purchasers buy the same unit which they rented, the size and quality of the unit often remains the same. On the other hand, outside buyers are more likely to purchase units which differ substantially from their previous residences in price, quality, and size.

---

44/ For example, a family's annual income may be sufficient to support the monthly mortgage payments, but the family may not have accumulated enough money to cover the downpayment. Alternately, a household may have additional expenses for medical care, child care, alimony, etc., that affect the ability to pay for housing, but which are not taken into account when affordability is based soley on gross income. Also, there is a possibility that some households may have overestimated the purchase price or the total costs involved in owning a unit.

45/ Total cash outlays for owners are defined as the sum of payments for mortgage (principal and interest), insurance, real estate taxes, condominium and recreation fees, and all utility costs not included in fees.

Although owners' monthly housing fees can increase substantially, the real increase is lessened by tax deductions which are available to homeowners. Owners can deduct real estate taxes and mortgage interest payments on Federal income tax returns and, therefore, reduce income tax liability. The tax savings due to the deduction of mortgage interest for condominium owners purchasing their units between 1977 and 1979 averaged $130 per month. 46/

A condominium or cooperative also has investment potential that can result in profit to the purchaser after resale of the unit. Assuming an annual 10 percent rate of appreciation and a median price of $43,000 (see table IX-20 App.), the benefit to the owner due to appreciation is $4,300 in the first year. Unlike tax asvings, however, this saving is tied up in the value of the dwelling and is captured only on the sale of the unit.

Homeowners' Issues. Given the expenses associated with purchasing a home and the importance of protecting homeowners' investments, consumer protection for condominium buyers has received increased attention in the last few years, both in the press and in state and local

---

46/ The actual dollar value of tax savings realized by owners of condominium units can be estimated from data on household income, household size, and the dollar value of annual interest paid on the mortgage. The average owner of a converted condominium pays $5,555 per year in mortgage interest (30 percent of the 540 tenant and outside buyers surveyed were able to say how much interest they paid). The typical owner also earns between $21,500 and $26,000, thus falling into the 28 percent income tax bracket if there are two persons in the household. At this level, the average yearly savings for a two person household is $1,555 or $130 per month. This calculation is based on the assumption that two person households have deductions totaling at least $3,400 (zero bracket deduction) before taking a homeownership credit. The overwhelming majority of renters in the United States take zero bracket deductions of $2,300 for one person households and $3,400 for married households. Those families taking a zero bracket deduction are likely to have itemized deductions of approximately equal or somewhat lower value than the zero bracket deductions allowed. Since these renter households do not itemize deductions, it is impossible to tell what the actual dollar value of deductions would have been had they submitted itemized accounts. According to the Office of Tax Analysis of the U.S. Department of the Treasury, only 20% of itemized tax returns are submitted by renters. Based on a computer analysis of 1975 tax returns, updated to 1979 levels, approximately 80 percent of taxpayers who submitted itemized return take deductions for mortgage interest and/or real estate taxes.

legislative bodies. 47/ Most real estate specialists contend that, although less scrupulous developers may market buildings in poor physical condition, most developers conscientiously offer buyers high quality homes in basically sound condition. To some extent this is corroborated by the fact that the majority of buildings converted to date have been high quality, middle-income, or luxury buildings which have not needed extensive repairs.

There are, however, instances of purchaser complaints about inferior quality buildings, misrepresentation of building condition, and inadequate renovation or repairs. In Houston, for example, owners of a 300-unit building began to experience roof problems two years after conversion. Since the reserve funds that were maintained were inadequate to meet the costs of replacing the roof, individual owners are bearing the repair costs at an average of $2,000 per unit. In general, complaints are more frequent in older converted buildings or those which, regardless of age, were under-maintained as rentals.

Previous research provides somewhat contradictory findings on the prevalence of unexpected maintenance costs in converted condominiums or cooperatives. A Washington, D.C. study found that 54 percent of the owners of converted units rated the construction quality of their buildings as "good," while only 6 percent rated building quality as "poor." Owners of converted units, in fact, appeared to have fewer complaints about the quality of building construction than owners in newly constructed buildings had. 48/

In this study, over 80 percent of the residents of converted condominiums and cooperatives report that their buildings need no more than minor repairs (see table IX-21 App.), while 17 percent

---

47/ Several cities and a few states have enacted a range of buyer protection measures including requirements that developers meet modern codes, provide engineering reports on the condition of major systems, and provide warranties to assure the quality of the converted unit. Some communities have developed more stringent building codes for condominiums than those which apply to rentals. For example, a few cities require additional sound-proofing, insulation, fireproofing, or separate metering of utilities. See chapters XI and XII for a complete discussion of state and local ordinances.

48/ Metropolitan Washington Council of Governments, Condominium Housing: A New Homeownership Alternative for Metropolitan Washington, op. cit., p. 160. See also chapter X for a discussion of consumer protection provided by secondary mortgage market institutions.

believe that their buildings are in need of "major repairs."
Interestingly, residents new to the buildings are more likely to
rate them as needing fewer repairs than are continuing residents
who lived there prior to conversion.  The low perceived need for
repairs is primarily because better maintained or substantially
rehabilitated buildings are most often candidates for conversion.

Underestimation of Maintenance Costs.  To market units more quickly,
a seller may have incentive to underestimate the costs of homeownership to prospective buyers.  These prospective costs include operating costs for utilities, management, and services; reserves for
capital improvements; or future building repair costs.

The 1975 HUD study on condominiums and cooperatives examined this
issue in great detail.  It reported that 54 percent of homeowner
association executives found developer estimates to be reasonably
accurate, while approximately one-third believed that developers
underestimated the maintenance costs. 49/

As of 1980, converters' estimates of maintenance costs are judged
to be accurate by 67 percent of converted condominium or cooperative
ownrs; 29 percent reported higher-than-estimated costs, and four
percent reported lower-than-estimated costs.  (See table IX-22 App.)

Services, Management, and Renter-Owner Relations.  In general, a
high proportion of converted condominium residents are satisfied
with their units and buildings.  (See table IX-23 App.)  Only two
percent of condominium owners are dissatisfied with their units,
and no more than five percent are dissatisfied with their buildings.
Renters in converted buildings show a greater tendency to be
dissatisfied, but the difference between renters and owners is
small.

One feature of condominium living is the maintenance services provided to residents.  About 90 percent of owners receive services
through membership in a condominium association or through payment
of a service contract or maintenance fee, and most owners and
renters (85%) are pleased with the type and quality of services
provided under these arrangements.  (See tables IX-24 and IX-25
App.)  These findings parallel earlier results from the 1975 study.

An issue of concern to some condominium residents is the relationship
between renters and owners.  Several previous studies have reported
that a number of condominium owners dislike living near renters

---

49/ HUD Condominium/Cooperative Study, op. cit., p. V-52.

because the latter allegedly lack the incentives that owners have to exercise care over their property. 50/

Ten percent of both renters and owners have experienced "confrontations" with members of the opposite tenure group. (See table IX-26 App.) The majority of complaints reported by owners concerned noise, unruly pets, and children; continuing renters more often complained about conflicts engendered by the process of conversion. However, even though only one of every ten condominium owners perceived conflicts between owners and renters, almost one-half would rather live in buildings without renters (see table IX-27 App.). Thus, although most owners of converted condominiums are satisfied with their residences, many of them prefer living near owner-occupants only.

\* \* \*

At the time of conversion, three of every four tenants who move from the building and one in four tenant buyers feel some degree of pressure, primarily because of the choice they must make between buying and moving rather than because of harassment by the converter. There is no strong evidence that elderly or lower income persons, nonwhite households, or households with children are more likely to experience this pressure. Nevertheless the fact that a majority of former residents felt pressure and exhibited anger indicates their emotional stress caused by conversion.

Tenants are provided a variety of inducements and assistance to cushion the effects of conversion. Most tenants in converting buildings are offered incentives to buy, primarily in the form of discounted purchase prices. Additionally, the building's prior tenants are sometimes given the opportunity to continue renting from an investor owner, converter, or another party. The incidence of relocation assistance to former residents is much less. Of those who move, 1 in 8 receives some type of relocation assistance from the converter: 1 in 25 receives actual cash from converters or landlords, with 1 in 4 lower income households receiving this type of assistance.

---

50/ Carl Norcross, Condominiums and Townhouses, (Washington, D.C.: Urban land Institute, 1973); and Condominium Housing: A New Home-ownership Alternative for Metropolitan Washington, op. cit.

Between 58 and 66 percent of residents in converting buildings move rather than stay as renters or owners. However, this percentage will vary, not only from city to city, but from building to building. High rent buildings, for instance, retain higher percentages of their tenants at the time of conversion. The number of tenants who stay will also be higher where regulations prohibit tenant evictions.

One-half of those who move have some difficulty finding new residences, and elderly, non-white, and, to a lesser extent, lower income households are more likely than others to have problems. However, the majority of former residents are satisfied with their postconversion housing, neighborhood, and social environment. Furthermore, they perceive their new dwelling and neighborhood to be equal to, if not better than, their preconversion residences. The probability of locating a comparable neighborhood is not equal for all former residents, however. Lower income and nonwhite former residents' households are significantly more likely to rate their new neighborhood, or some aspect thereof, as inferior to their preconversion neighborhood.

Those who left the building to rent elsewhere typically pay eight percent more for housing each month, while those who buy pay 68 percent more. Once again, these figures vary considerably; for instance, 28 percent of those who rent elsewhere pay 26 percent or more for housing while another one-third pay no more than they did before conversion. For 30 percent, the move itself was a financial burden. Finally, 18-24 percent of the former residents are adversely affected in terms of facing the same or high costs for lower quality housing, or higher costs for the same quality housing.

Financial benefits to condominium or cooperative buyers include tax savings that average $130 a month, while median appreciation is estimated to be $358 per month.

Condominium or cooperative owners generally perceive their buildings to be in good condition, and most are satisfied with the maintenance services received. Nearly one-third, however, say that maintenance costs are higher than expected, although this perception must be interpreted in the context of the ultimate economic benefits they receive through ownership. Finally, although conflict is not very prevalent between renters and owners, one-half of all owners prefer to live in buildings that are entirely owner-occupied.

# 4

# Conversions and the Public Sector

# Chapter X
## Government Programs for, and Federal Regulation of Conversions

The public sector influences the volume and character of conversion
activity and deals with its impacts through regulatory and programmatic actions.

Regulatory actions include legislative, administrative, and judicial
decisions which either specify the manner in which rental property
conversions are to be carried out, or promote or prohibit all or
some categories of condominium and cooperative conversions.

Programmatic actions involve the government as a participant in the
conversion process and include those programs which are specifically
designed for this purpose and those which are intended to accomplish
broader or different objectives but which are adapted to condominium
and cooperative conversions.

A variety of regulatory actions have been undertaken by state and
local governments to deal with conversion activity and these are detailed in chapters XI and XII.

In this chapter, a number of Federal government programs which have
been, or have the potential to be, used in relation to condominium
and cooperative conversions, are briefly discussed. 1/ For example,
the Federal government has occasionally insured or subsidized individual condominium unit mortgages and cooperative shares. Also
described in this chapter are the regulatory effects of programmatic
actions taken by institutions in the Federally established secondary
mortgage market. Underwriting standards set by these institutions
provide certain protections to buyers of converted units. Finally,
selected state and local government programs are discussed. Some
of these programs use Federal government assistance and are designed
to aid tenant groups in converted buildings; subsidize households
which rent or purchase units in converted buildings; and help former
residents of converted buildings relocate.

---

1/ Chapter V discusses the regulatory effects of Federal tax laws
and Internal Revenue Service regulations which are excluded from
this chapter.

The Department of Housing and Urban Development (HUD), the Department
of Agriculture's Farmers Home Administration (FmHA) and the Veterans
Administration (VA) each have housing loan, insurance, and guarantee
programs that could be used in the conversion of rental properties.
However, these programs have played only a minor role in the
acquisition and rehabilitation phase of conversion or in individual
unit purchases.

Conventional financing is available for purchasers of most converted
units.  In this connection, the Federally established secondary mortgage market corporations which buy condominium mortgages appear to
play a significant role in that segment of the conversion market
which is within their program mortgage limits. 2/

Federal condominium or cooperative programs applicable to conversions
are most easily analyzed and understood by distinguishing between
programs related to financing for the overall conversion project and
those related to the financing of individual units.  Some programs
cover only one type of financing, while some combine both types or
work in conjunction with other programs.  Following is a discussion
of these two types of financing.


Condominium Conversion Financing

One Federal program can be used to finance the conversion of a rental
property to a condominium, and several programs can be used to insure
or finance individual unit mortgages.  The latter programs are intended to give homeownership opportunities to households who otherwise could not afford the cost of buying converted condominiums.

HUD's Section 234(d) program insures private loans made by HUD
approved lenders who finance the construction or substantial rehabilitation of multi-family projects of four units or more that result
in homeownership of individual units. 3/   This program may be used
in the rehabilitation phase of conversion.

_____

2/ Appendix 1 provides a detailed description of Federal programs
related to converted rental housing.

3/ Under HUD's definition of substantial rehabilitation, work may
vary in degree from gutting and extensive reconstruction to cosmetic
improvements, coupled with the cure of a substantial accumulation
of deferred maintenance.  Cosmetic improvments alone do not
qualify for substantial rehabilitation.

HUD insures up to 90 percent of the cost of acquiring, refinancing, and rehabilitating a conversion project sponsored by a profit or nonprofit group. Along with meeting minimum property standards and a variety of other requirements, individual units in the building must be eligible for HUD's Section 234(c) mortgage insurance. 4/

In regard to individual unit financing, Section 234(c) authorizes insurance of condominium units in a project that has been finally endorsed by HUD (e.g. Section 207, 221(d)(3), 221(d)(4), 5/ a project that is to be constructed or substantially rehabilitated under 234(d), or a conventionally financed project of 11 units or less. Recent legislation has authorized the use of Section 234(c) insurance in an existing conventionally financed condominium project of 12 or more units which was completed more than a year prior to the application for mortgage insurance. 6/ A regulation change implementing this authority is currently being considered within HUD. Section 234(c) loans are eligible for inclusion in the GNMA Mortgage-Backed Security Program.

Since August 1979, the Veterans Administration has extended its basic home loan guaranty program to existing condominiums, including converted units.

In addition to these insurance and loan guarantee programs, three other Federal programs assist moderate-income households in purchasing units in buildings being converted to condominiums. HUD's

---

4/ A condominium unit purchaser may finance a unit through HUD insured or conventional mortgages if cash is not paid.

5/ Section 213 management style corporations are not eligible. Three Section 221(d)(3) insured projects have been converted to condominiums. No data is currently available on the number of Section 221(d)(4) projects involving condominium conversion.

6/ The authority for this change is contained in the Housing and Community Development Amendments of 1978. In its Report No. 95-1161, the House of Representatives states that this authority should be used to facilitate resales of condominium units and cautions the HUD Secretary not to encourage conversions that would result in displacing low- and moderate-income families.

Section 245 Graduated Payment Mortgage (GPM) 7/ program is available
to eligible condominium purchasers using a mortgage insured under
Section 234(c). A second HUD program provides interest subsidies
for condominium mortgages. The Section 235 program is intended to
help eligible low- and moderate-income families become homeowners.
In 1979, Congress extended coverage under this program to include
eligible households who moved from a rental building converted to
condominiums or cooperatives. 8/ Finally, under the Government
National Mortgage Association's Targeted Tandem Programs, individuals
or organizations holding Section 234(d) or Section 234(c) mortgages
may be eligible for financing at the FHA rate (plus 2-1/2 points).
To qualify for the program, the units must be located in cities
eligible for HUD's Urban Development Action Grant program or in
designated neighborhood strategy areas under HUD's Community Development Block Grant program.


## Cooperative Conversion Financing

Although both HUD and the Farmers Home Administration administer
programs that are applicable to cooperative conversions, little use
has been made of them. Regulations for cooperative conversion financing under the existing authority of Section 221(d)(3) pursuant to
Section 223(f) are currently being considered by HUD.

HUD's Section 213(i) program permits the Department to insure a building's conversion to a cooperative if it is an existing FHA-insured
rental project or if it is a conventionally financed rental building
constructed before September 23, 1959. The Section 221(d)(3) mortgage insurance program also authorizes HUD to finance the substantial
rehabilitation of a rental building converted to a cooperative.
Moreover, Section 213(a)(1) and (3) or Section 221(d)(4) also authorize
financing of substantial rehabilitation of a rental building converting to a cooperative. Under Section 221(i), an existing Section 221(d)
(3) BMIR rental project may convert to a 221(d)(3) BMIR cooperative.

---

7/ Under a graduated payment mortgage, the mortgagor makes low
monthly payments for the first few years of the mortgage term.
The payments gradually increase for the next few years until
they reach a level where they remain for the balance of the
mortgage term.

8/ Prior to the expanded eligibility requirements of Section 235,
provided for in the Housing and Community Development Amendments
of 1979, the program had been limited to families in existing
dwellings who were displaced from an urban renewal area, or
displaced as a result of a major disaster; families with five
or more children; or families living in public housing.

The Farmers Home Administration has the authority, under its Section 515 program, to finance the substantial rehabilitation of a rental property where the owner wishes to convert to cooperative ownership. To date, however, no cooperative conversions have been financed under this authority. The Veterans Administration also has the authority to finance cooperative conversions, but has not become involved in this activity.

In addition to mortgage insurance, HUD's housing subsidy programs are potentially adaptable to cooperative conversions. For example, lower income cooperative members may be subsidized for the monthly carrying charges on their units under the Section 8 program. 9/ If at least 20 percent of the units in a cooperative are assisted in this way, the Government National Mortgage Association (GNMA) may purchase the cooperative's blanket mortgage under its Section 8 Tandem program. When GNMA buys the blanket mortgage, the interest rate is reduced and the cooperative members realize a further savings in their monthly carrying charges. Similarly, in cities eligible for Urban Development Action Grants, GNMA's Targeted Tandem program can be used to purchase HUD-insured mortgages of substantially rehabilitated cooperatives. In this way, a below market interest rate is provided for property converted to cooperative housing. However, it should be noted that these programs are not available to a Section 213(i) project because GNMA requires substantial rehabilitation or new construction and the Section 213(i) program does not involve either.

HUD's Section 203(n) program provides insurance for mortgages made to purchase individual shares in cooperatives whose blanket mortgages are insured by HUD. The program insures only the resale of cooperative units by financing a portion of the seller's equity, i.e., the difference between the HUD-appraised value of the unit and the unpaid balance on that portion of the blanket mortgage covering the unit. At present, HUD is considering a rule change which would permit the use of Section 203(n) to insure individual cooperative mortgages in an existing rental property converting to a cooperative under Section 213(i).

Several approaches are currently being considered for using the authority in HUD's Section 223(f) program to convert existing rental properties to cooperative ownership. The rental properties need not be FHA-insured and may not require substantial rehabilitation. One proposal combines this program's authority to refinance

---

9/ Section 8 of the National Housing Act provides rental assistance payments to landlords on behalf of households whose incomes are less than or equal to 80 percent of an area's median income.

the entire property with conventional savings and loan financing of
individual unit loans. The individual unit mortgages could then be
sold on the new secondary mortgage market for cooperative mortgages
being developed by the Federal Home Loan Mortgage Corporation.

The interest reduction subsidy available under Section 235 may be
used in cooperative conversions, generally under the same terms as
those for condominium conversions.


## HUD's Loan Management and Property Disposition Programs

HUD's Loan Management Program covers all aspects of loan servicing
for HUD-insured (subsidized and unsubsidized) rental properties. In
HUD-insured, unsubsidized, multi-family rental properties, a mortgagor may undertake a conversion without obtaining HUD approval
if he or she prepays in full the outstanding mortgage. Once prepayment is made, HUD's regulatory agreement is cancelled, and the mortgagor may convert the property. If an existing mortgagor wishes to
sell the property to a second party for conversion, and that party
wishes to either assume the existing FHA-insured mortgage because of
its favorable terms or obtain financing or related assistance from
HUD not routinely available, HUD can discourage a conversion by the
second party by denying these requests. Although HUD's present
policy is not to encourage conversions of unsubsidized, multi-family
properties involving mortgage assumptions, requests to HUD concerning
mortgage assumption, and similar issues, are treated on a case-by-case
basis.

Since HUD currently prohibits the prepayment of mortgages on subsidized, multi-family rental properties, the prohibition, in effect,
prevents the conversion of such properties.

HUD's Property Disposition Program deals with the sale of rental
properties acquired by HUD following a mortgagor's default on a HUD-
insured loan. The Department's principal policy concern in these
sales is to prevent the displacement of low- and moderate-income
tenants. Therefore, both previously subsidized and unsubsidized
HUD-owned properties, which house low- and moderate-income tenants,
are sold by HUD only with long-term Section 8 housing assistance
commitments attached to them. Thus, conversion of these properties
for occupancy by indivduals not eligible for Section 8 assistance
is prohibited. If, however, a vast majority of the low- and
moderate-income tenants of a HUD-owned property are interested in
converting the property to a cooperative, HUD will explore this
possibility with them. For example, HUD is managing a demonstration
in Boston designed to help lower income tenants of HUD-owned buildings purchase the buildings and convert them to cooperatives.

are purchased by one or the other organization. 15/

Secondary market programs, therefore, can have two significant effects
on condominium conversions. First, they help to finance the ultimate
sales of units from the converter and resales from the homeowner,
thereby enhancing the marketability of converted units. The availability of the secondary market may also help to underpin a whole set
of financing arrangements necessary to convert a project from rental
status to condominium ownership. Second, since many projects are
developed to qualify for secondary market programs, the legal,
financial, and physical condition standards required by FHLMC and
FNMA have tended to become the industry's minimum standards that
affect the quality of conversion projects. In addition, evidence
of a project's eligibility to participate in one or both corporations'
mortgage programs is viewed as a "seal of approval" concerning the
quality of the individual unit mortgages by other long-term investors.
In particular, a number of these standards afford a measure of consumer
protection to buyers of converted units. 16/ Buyer protection results
from two factors. The secondary market agencies try to protect
consumers within the limits of their primary missions. Thus, for
example, long-term recreational leases and other abuses are prohibited.
Moreover, many of the underwriting standards which reflect what
FHLMC and FNMA believe to be prudent lending practices also rebound
to the benefit of the buyer.

The following discussion reviews a number of FHLMC and FNMA standards
which affect condominium consumers.

---

15/ Stanley M. Taube, "Condominium Conversion Financing" (National
Association of Home Builders' Seminar on Converting to Condominiums),
fall 1979. Taube indicates that, "A further, and perhaps most important, requirement will be that the development meet the underwriting
requirements of the Federal National Mortgage Association (FNMA) and
the Federal Home Loan Mortgage Corporation (FHLMC). . . . At the
time of this writing and for the foreseeable future, no lender will
be interested in making loans that are not readily marketable in the
secondary market. It has been the general practice of the lenders
to sell condominium loans to FHLMC. However, the loan commitments
will normally require that the development meet the standards of
both secondary purchasers."

16/ FHLMC and FNMA do not specify any standards for protecting tenants in condominium conversions but do require that the converter
follow any state and local laws on this matter.

Legal Requirements. Each corporation has a number of standards concerning the form and type of legal documentation required for a project. 17/ There are specific requirements on insurance coverage, condemnation and loss of units, and in the case of FNMA, the transfer of control from the developer to the homeowner association.

Project Condition  FNMA mandates and FHLMC may often require the preparation of an architect's or engineer's report on the condition of structural and major mechanical systems, including their expected useful lives.  Both corporations require that the project be completed as planned, especially the common elements and amenities. 18/

Warranties.  FHLMC does not set warranty standards, but may require information on any warranties provided.  The thrust of FNMA's approach is to provide unit owners and unit mortgagees assurances that the project is in reasonably good physical condition and to bind the developers to the project beyond the sellout period. In this regard, FNMA currently mandates a one year warranty against latent defects in the project.

-----

17/ FNMA reviews all basic project documents, such as the declaration or master deed, bylaws, covenants, conditions and restrictions, articles of incorporation, ground leases, and the anticipated or actual date of document recordation.  FNMA requires information on any state agency review reports, as well as information on any existing or pending litigation or government action on the project.  An attorney's opinion detailing the project's compliance with state law and FNMA standards is required.

18/  FNMA reviews the plans and specifications of the project and tries to ensure that the project is completed as planned.  A certified copy of the proposed or recorded plot plan or plat for the project is required, as are floor plans for the basic unit types. FHLMC also determines whether a project has a sufficient number of units to support the common elements and amenities.  FNMA appears to pay particular attention to current conditions of the project both from an underwriting and borrower's standpoint.  FNMA requires a registered architect's or engineer's opinion to ensure that any rehabilitation is done according to plans and specifications which meet local codes.  Also, the mechanical systems must be adequate to serve the project.  The architect or engineer must also indicate the estimated effective lives of major building features (roofs, heating and cooling systems).  This information is especially important in judging the adequacy of the project's budget for replacement reserves.

Management.  FNMA and FHLMC have substantive requirements on certain kinds of lease or management arrangements involving the developers/ declarants or organizations controlled by them.  In order to avoid long-term management contracts and other abuses, FNMA requires that a management agreement can be terminable for cause upon 30 days written notice by the homeowners association and such agreement may not exceed one year.  FHLMC requires the lender to warrant that any professional management or other contract services to be provided by the developer not exceed three years and that the contract may be terminated without cause or penalty on 90 days or less written notice.

Budget.  FNMA and FHLMC review the proposed budget of a condominium to determine its accuracy and completeness.  In particular, each organization looks at the budget to determine whether an adequate reserve fund for maintenance, repairs and replacement of common elements is present. 19/ FNMA mandates and FHLMC may require an actual income and expense operating statement for the last two years that the project was operated as a rental.  In addition, expenses must be budgeted in regular monthly installments rather than through special assessment.  20/

Presale Requirements.  In order to insure that the project is marketable, each agency generally requires that 70 percent of the units be under sales agreements. 21/

Escrow Funds.  FNMA requires that buyers' deposits must be placed in a special account segregated from other funds of the seller, or in an escrow account maintained by a third party.

---

19/  FNMA requires a detailed analysis of project cash flow and needed working capital.  It also requires information on items not reflected in the budget, but which are expected to be substantial expenses within the next three years, including items requiring replacement or maintenance after the expiration of a warranty.

20/  FNMA tries to avoid a large lump sum assessment occurring in the future by requiring prepayment by developer or by setting up a joint developer-owner escrow arrangement.

21/ FNMA requires that agreements of sale signed by purchasers must total the higher of either 51-70 percent of the total value of all units in the project or 51-70 percent of the total number of units in the project.  The general FNMA rule is 70 percent, unless documentation is presented showing conformity to the practices of other lenders in the area; unless a strong market exists; or unless the developer provides guarantees on common area assessments. FHLMC requires 70 percent of the units in a project to be sold to bona fide purchasers who have closed or who are legally obligated to close.  FHLMC also will waive this requirement to 51 percent if adequate documentation of reasons is presented by a seller.

Owner-Occupant/Investor-Purchasers. Both corporations only purchase
mortgages on units occupied as primary residences by owner-occupants.
FHLMC requires that at least 80 percent of the units in a project must
be sold to individuals for use as their primary year-round residences.
FNMA requires that a "substantial proportion" of the project purchasers
be owner-occupants.

Condominium Resales. Since 1978, FNMA and FHLMC have also had special
standards for purchasing mortgages in existing condominiums, including
converted buildings. These programs were developed to help consumers
who had difficulty in obtaining financing. Subsequent buyers found
that many lenders were reluctant to provide mortgages because of the
burden of reviewing all the project's legal, financial and physical
documentation for only a spot loan. Most of the substantive standards
discussed above also apply to FNMA/FHLMC programs on condominium
resales. However, FNMA standards are generally more detailed
than those of FHLMC. 22/

Cooperative Programs. FHLMC has authority, under its multi-family
mortgage purchase programs, to purchase cooperative project blanket
mortgages. A few cooperative blanket mortgages have been purchased,
but it is unclear whether any have been conversions. The Federal
Home Loan Bank Board (FHLBB) has recently authorized federal savings
and loan associations to make loans for cooperative shares for up to
95 percent of the value of the cooperative unit. FHLMC has recently
been given authority by Congress to develop a secondary market program
for cooperatives, however, the program development process will not
begin until late 1980.

FNMA also has authority to purchase cooperative project mortgages under
its multi-family program. A few HUD-insured cooperative mortgages
have been purchased for the FNMA portfolio. In addition, FNMA has
recently received authorization from HUD to purchase conventionally
financed cooperative project loans, but the program has not yet been
implemented. FNMA also has authority to purchase HUD-insured Section
203(n) loans but, to date, has not done so.

---

22/ FHLMC and FNMA require a project to have been under the control
of a homeowners' association for a period of time and prohibit
future phasing or add-ons. In addition, the project must comply with
state laws, certain insurance requirements, and other legal standards.
FNMA also has a number of additional requirements, such as that the
project be demonstrably well-managed, operated, and maintained. In
addition, FNMA may require that the budget reflect adequate reserves
for replacement of common area components. FNMA and FHLMC each
require that 90 percent of an approved project must be sold to bona
fide purchasers; the remaining 10 percent may be retained by the developer
FNMA requires that these projects must be substantially owner-occupied,
while FHLMC is more specific -- requiring that 60 percent of a project's
units be the primary residences of their owners.

## The Securities and Exchange Commission.

The Securities and Exchange Commission (SEC) has published several
interpretative releases and letters concerning when cooperative and
condominium offerings are to be considered securities subject to
registration requirements. SEC jurisdiction and requirements may
apply to cooperative or condominium conversion offerings which
involve rental pools or time-sharing arrangements. Those cooperative
and condominium offerings which would generally be deemed to be
securities are those which are usually sold with an emphasis on the
investment benefits to be derived from the efforts of a manager or
promoter. However, few, if any, cooperative or condominium conversion
projects have been registered with the SEC. The U.S. Supreme Court
has held that sales of stock in cooperative units do not constitute
the sale of securities within the meaning of the Securities Act of
1933, and thus the SEC has no jurisdiction over cooperative units
sold solely for residential use by a buyer. 23/

## Innovative Local and State Programs Related to Conversion

This section describes some local and state government programs
developed as reponses to conversion (See Appendix 1 for additional
details). A number of these programs have received financial support
from HUD through its State Technical Grants and Innovative Grants
programs. The sources of state and local funds are bond issuance
and general revenues.

The various programs are designed to accomplish one or more of the
following objectives: (1) to provide financial and technical assistance to tenant groups converting their buildings to condominiums or
cooperatives; (2) to subsidize low- to moderate-income persons and/or
current tenants in the rental or purchase of converted units; and
(3) to assist households who are relocating from converted buildings.

Assistance to Tenant Groups. Some state and local governments provide loan insurance, loans, education, or direct technical assistance
to organized tenant groups which desire to purchase and convert
their buildings to cooperatives or condominiums.

For example, the State of California, in an effort to mitigate the
effects of displacement caused by conversions, has three programs to
assist low- and moderate-income households in purchasing converted
units. The first is the homeownership coinvestment concept which
includes provisions for assisting low- and moderate-income households
in purchasing homes through public or private co-investment and
deferring the repayment or servicing of co-investment funds. 24/
The Community Development Block Grants, as well as well as contributions from State Grants Programs, the Innovative Grants Program,
and from the private sector, are among the sources of funding for the

---

23/ United Housing Foundation,Inc. v. Forman ,421 U.S. 837,
95 S.Ct. 2051 (1975).

24/ Repayment is required when the home is sold, refinanced, or the
household is able to assume full responsibility for payments.

program. 25/ Under the Homeownership Loan Program, the California Department of Housing and the California Housing Finance Agency are authorized to assist low- and moderate-income households in obtaining loans for the purchase of condominium and cooperative units. The Agency also administers a program which insures loans to finance limited equity cooperatives and permits priority processing of applications of multi-family developments proposed for conversion to limited equity cooperatives.

Officials in Santa Barbara, California have proposed a similar program to establish limited equity cooperatives for low-income tenants in revitalizing neighborhoods. The program will provide down payment assistance covering from 15 to 35 percent of the amount needed for the entire project. The down payment fund is expected to be replenished when loans are either repaid with mortgage financing provided by the California Housing Finance Agency or through the restructuring of payments made by members for individual shares.

To help tenant associations determine the feasibility of their cooperative conversion proposals, local officials in Washington, D.C. are using an innovative Grant to finance a program offering professional technical assistance. Tenant groups will be able to hire consultants, engineers, and architects to assist them in planning a cooperative conversion.

The Denver city government is also encouraging the formation of housing cooperatives to minimize displacement caused by revitalization. Programs to provide public education as well as technical and financial assistance are being planned in that city.

Subsidies for condominium or cooperative purchase or rental. State and local programs also provide loans or grants to assist individuals to purchase converted units. Other programs subsidize rents so that eligible tenant households can remain in converted buildings. Such programs are targeted to specific groups -- such as the elderly or low- to moderate-income persons -- likely to be adversely affected by conversion.

The Government of King County, Washington (which includes Seattle) plans to prevent displacement of elderly occupants of converting buildings by purchasing units in the buildings. HUD Innovative Grant funds and conventional financing will be used to buy the units, and Section 8 subsidies will help to reduce rents for elderly persons who are eligible for the program.

---

25/ Program development was financed with a $200,000 grant from the state grants program. The state expects to receive $700,000 from HUD's Innovative Grant program and the local government contribution is expected to be $3 to $11 million.

The City of Brookline, Massachusetts plans to use Innovative Grant
funds to provide equity assistance to low-income households for the
purchase of converted units.  The amount of assistance will be
determined on a sliding scale based on what is required to bring a
household's monthly payments in line with the 25 percent-of-income
standard.  The assistance will be secured by a lien on the unit
which will be recovered upon resale.  The Massachusetts Home Mortgage
Finance Agency, which provides financing to low-income households at
interest rates of 1-1/2 to 2 percent below conventional market rates,
is expected to provide the balance of the financing.

With the help of Innovative Grant funds, local officials in Baltimore,
Maryland intend to establish a nonprofit real estate corporation
which will provide homeownership and cooperative housing opportunites
to low- and moderate-income households.  The real estate corporation
will identify, acquire, repair, and sell residential properties.
Its activities will be coordinated with neighborhood organizations
and city agencies to ensure that the city's homeownership programs
and Section 8 subsidies are made available for participants in the
program.

The California Department of Housing and Community Development and
the California Housing Finance Agency have been granted authority to
assist low- and moderate-income households to purchase converted
condominium and coopertive units.  Loan amounts may not exceed 45
percent of the unit's purchase price, and the purchaser must make a
down payment of at least three percent.

Other localities have combined purchase or rent subsidies with other
types of assistance offered to groups which are converting their
buildings to multiple ownership.  For example, Arlington County,
Virginia (a Washington, D.C. suburb) will use Community Development
Block Grant fund to assist tenants in converting their buildings to
cooperatives.  Tenant associations will be eligible for technical
assistance funds of up to $50,000 ($10,000 as a grant and $40,000 as
a loan).  The $40,000 loan must be repaid to the county when final
settlement is made on the permanent purchase loan, although the county
can agree to forgive or defer repayment of the loan.  Section 8
subsidies are expected to be available for low-income cooperative
members.

Officials in Montgomery County, Maryland (another suburb of Washington,
D.C.) plan a multi-faceted approach to lessen the adverse effects of
of conversion on low-income tenants.  The county will rely on the
cooperation and assistance of the State of Maryland and the Federal
government.  The major features of the strategy involve the use of
(1) revenues from a proposed 4 percent transfer tax on the initial
sale of a converted condominium unit to provide rental and down
payment assistance to low-income residents of the County; and (2)
Federal funds to purchase converted units which will be reserved for
sale or rental to low-income households living in converting build-

ings. Developers who set aside 15 percent of the units in a converted building for the second purpose will be exempt from the proposed
4 percent transfer tax. HUD Section 235 mortgage insurance and
interest subsidies will be provided to eligible low-income households
purchasing converted units.

Between August 1978 and July 1979, Minneapolis, Minnesota used revenue bond financing to make eight percent mortgage loans to purchase
converted condominium units and cooperative shares. Over 400 households with incomes below $22,000 purchased condominiums under this
program, and a smaller number of households purchased cooperative
shares. In conjunction with the mortgage loan program, an apartment
homeownerhip team encouraged conversions from rental housing to
condominiumes or cooperatives by providing technical assistance to
the converter.

Assistance to households moving due to conversion. A few localities
have developed programs which aid specific groups of renters who must
move because of conversions. For instance, Montgomery County,
Maryland has instituted a Condominium Conversion Emergency Aid fund.
The fund provides relocation and down payment assistance to elderly
and handicapped renters who are adversely affected by conversions.
Revenue from an existing one percent transfer tax on all real estate
and from the upward reassessment of converted buildings is used to
finance this special fund.

* * *

At present, the Federal government has several housing programs which
may be used to insure or subsidize the conversion of a rental property or to purchase individual condominium units or cooperative
shares. Low-income cooperative members are eligible for rent subsidies under HUD's Section 8 program, and HUD's Community Development
Block Grant funds are provided to local governments for innovative
programs related to conversion. Some state and local governments
also have responded to condominium and cooperative conversions by
developing programs to assist tenants in converting their buildings;
to subsidize the purchase or rental of converted units by tenants; or
to assist low- to moderate-income households to relocate following conversion. The combined effect of these programmatic activities cannot
yet be determined because of the small scale and limited use of the
Federal programs and because of the recent adoption of state and local
programs.

From the regulatory perspective, FNMA's and FHLMC's underwriting
standards for the purchase of condominium mortgages provide some
protection to buyers of converted units. Apart from current legislative proposals to halt or regulate condominum and cooperative
conversions at the national level (none of which has been enacted),
the secondary mortgage market programmatic activity is the primary
way in which the Federal government regulates rental housing

conversions. 26/ State and local governments, on the other hand, have initiated extensive regulatory actions of their own. Their efforts to regulate and control conversion activity are detailed in chapters XI and XII, which follow.

26/ The following legislation has been introduced in either the Senate or the House of Representatives: H.R.975, the "Condominium Act of 1975" is a consumer protection bill which includes national minimum standards to govern condominium conversions; S.612 "Residential Unit Lease Act of 1979," and its House companion bill, H.R. 2792, "Condominium Act of 1979," encourage condominium ownership and the provision of disclosure statements and other types of consumer protection to purchasers of converted units; and H.R. 5175, "Condominium-Cooperative Conversion Moratorium Act of 1979: For Tenant Protection and for the Preservation of Rental Housing," would impose a three-year nationwide moratorium on conversions. In addition, the Senate reported out its version of the Housing and Community Development Amendments of 1980 on May 15, 1980. Title V of this bill, "Condominium and Cooperative Conversion Protection and Abuse Relief Act of 1980" encourages the use of the condominium and cooperative forms of ownership as a way of meeting the shortage of adequate and affordable multi-family housing throughout the country. In addition, the act aims at correcting and preventing the abusive use of long-term recreational and similar leases.

# Chapter XI
# State Regulation of Conversions

Almost half of the states have passed statutes that provide various
types of protection for tenants and buyers in converted condominiums
or cooperatives. 1/  The most frequent protections for tenants are
requirements for notice of conversion or lease extensions, and rights
to purchase units in a converted building.  A number of states have
enacted additional protections -- usually in the form of full disclosure of the legal, financial, and physical condition of the project
-- for all condominium purchasers (newly built and converted) and,
in several instances, special protections for purchasers of converted
condominiums.  In addition, a few states have passed measures to assure
a given level of rental stock, to preserve low- and moderate-income
housing, or to provide special considerations for certain classes of
tenants, such as the elderly, handicapped, or families with children.

The first section of this chapter briefly traces the origins of
state conversion regulation.  Then, the various state regulations
that protect tenants and buyers, the rental supply, and low- and
moderate-income housing are discussed.  Finally, the legality of
government regulations affecting conversion is considered.

## The Origin and Evolution of State Conversion Regulation

The enactment of condominium statutes was begun in the United States
in the early 1960s.  In less than a single decade, such statutes
were passed by every state in the union and the District of Columbia.
Cooperatives, on the other hand, are not a creature of statute but
are based upon a combination of corporate ownership of land and
long-term residential leases given exclusively to the corporation's
stockholders.  The participants in the latter type of common ownership are generally referred to as "cooperators" or "proprietary
lessees." The cooperative form of ownership is confined to a few
major cities -- among them New York, Chicago, Miami, San Francisco,
and the District of Columbia -- but by far, the vast majority of
cooperative housing in the United States is located in New York City
(95 percent).  While some cooperatives originated as new construction
in the post-World War II era, most such ventures stemmed from conver-

---

1/ Most state regulation concerns conversion to condominium rather
than cooperative ownership.

sion of existing rental structures to cooperative housing status. Condominiums, on the other hand, have taken the form of new construction in the past two decades, largely because of the relatively recent passage of enabling legislation and the concentration of new condominium developments in vacation and retirement states. To gain an overview of the conversion field, as well as a grasp of existing state legislation in this field, it is useful to look at the legal, economic, and social factors that gave rise to a steady stream of cooperative conversions in New York State from and after the conclusion of the Second World War.

Following the war, some apartment owners in New York City found it advantageous to market their rent-controlled properties to tenants and outsiders as cooperatives. The aggregate yields from such sales were typically much higher than what could be realized if the buildings were sold to a single investor or successor landlord. The rapid increase in the value of cooperative apartments (as measured by unit resale prices), attractive financing, favorable converter capital gains treatment, the absence of any competing condominium concept, and the absolute control the cooperators have over the person(s) to whom an apartment could be sold all combined to make cooperative conversions an ongoing fact of life in New York City.

Faced with the potential loss of many of the city's desirable apartments through cooperative conversions, authorities charged with administration of the rent control program issued regulations to govern the process. They early established the rule of thumb that the rent-controlled status of apartments of nonpurchasing tenants could not be terminated unless the sponsor of the conversion induced 35 percent of the tenants in occupancy to purchase their apartments within six months after the offering plan was issued. This figure was viewed, not as a tenant referendum, but as a fairly good indication that the offering plan was sound. If the sponsor was willing to make cooperative sales over a long period of time, or failed in the attempt to obtain 35 percent sales to tenants in occupancy, then a "noneviction plan" could be issued; i.e., one that did not seek to terminate the rent-controlled status of tenants who decided not to purchase. Such an offering plan did not require any certain number of sales to occupying tenants before a sponsor could declare the plan effective. Between 1945 and 1965, dozens of high-rise apartment buildings were converted to cooperative status in New York City each year. The passage of a condominium statute in New York State did not alter this trend because of the advantages that the cooperative apartment conversion technique afforded the sponsor, in terms of income tax factors, financing, and marketing.

By 1960, the New York Attorney General's Office had assumed jurisdiction of cooperative apartment conversions, under statutory amendments to the General Business Law, which resembled state laws governing the offering of securities. This jurisdiction, in turn, was rapidly expanded to cover condominiums and homeowner conversions. 26/ State and local governments, on the other hand, have initiated extensive regulatory actions of their own. Their efforts to regulate and control conversion activity are detailed in chapters XI and XII, which follow.

---

26/ The following legislation has been introduced in either the Senate or the House of Representatives: H.R.975, the "Condominium Act of 1975" is a consumer protection bill which includes national minimum standards to govern condominium conversions; S.612 "Residential Unit Lease Act of 1979," and its House companion bill, H.R. 2792, "Condominium Act of 1979," encourage condominium ownership and the provision of disclosure statements and other types of consumer protection to purchasers of converted units; and H.R. 5175, "Condominium-Cooperative Conversion Moratorium Act of 1979: For Tenant Protection and for the Preservation of Rental Housing," would impose a three-year nationwide moratorium on conversions. In addition, the Senate reported out its version of the Housing and Community Development Amendments of 1980 on May 15, 1980. Title V of this bill, "Condominium and Cooperative Conversion Protection and Abuse Relief Act of 1980" encourages the use of the condominium and cooperative forms of ownership as a way of meeting the shortage of adequate and affordable multi-family housing throughout the country. In addition, the act aims at correcting and preventing the abusive use of long-term recreational and similar leases.

associations. Gradually, an elaborate set of disclosure requirements evolved that included both a filing with the Attorney General's
Office and publication of an "Offering Plan" for prospective unit
purchasers (whether tenants in occupancy or third parties). Since
1960, conversion regulation has undergone extensive analysis and
refinement via legislative, judicial, and administrative pronouncements. Consequently, the disclosure requirements and tenant protection measures currently found in New York State are generally recog-
nized as the most comprehensive in the Nation.

With the possible exceptions of California, Florida, and the District
of Columbia, few cooperative conversions of any magnitude have occurred outside of New York State. In the early years of the condominium
boom, developers and state legislatures focused almost exclusively
upon the use of this new-found concept in new construction. By the
1970's individual state legislatures began to enact "second generation
condominium statutes, which were largely designed to solve technical
problems encountered in constructing new condominium units. However,
the advent of the Virginia second generation statute and its model
act counterpart (the Uniform Condominium Act) have started state
governments down the path toward greater regulation and consumer
protection measures. Part of that effort has focused upon condominium conversions. Nevertheless, conversion measures still constitute
only a minor aspect of most state condominium statutes.

When the condominium conversion trend appeared more or less simultaneously in major population centers within the past 5 years, public
officials and affected tenants were taken by surprise. Unlike the
New York situation, there had been no gradual evolution of the conversion process and regulation dating back over 35 years. Moreover,
few of the cities experiencing the wave of conversions had rent
control of any kind. Finally, most state statutes had few if any
provisions relevant to conversion issues. As a result, there emerged
a broad-based demand on the municipal level for regulation or prohibition of residential apartment conversions to condominium status.
Though more extensive state regulation may occur as more experience is
gained with problems associated with conversions, for the foreseeable future, the legislative response will probably take the form of
local ordinances. When these problems do attract attention on a state
wide basis, the New York experience 2/ and the Uniform Condominium Act
provisions 3/ will probably serve as models.

---

2/ Appendix 2 contains the citations to relevant state statutes.
Detailed information on the highly regulated conversion process
in New York state can be found in the Report of the Temporary Commission on Rental Housing submitted to the Governor in the spring 1980.

3/ The Uniform Condominium Act is discussed below.

The next sections categorize state legislation affecting conversions as follows: tenant protections; buyer protections; rental stock protection; preservation of low- and moderate-income housing; and the protecton of elderly and handicapped tenants. In addition, provisions of the Uniform Condominium Act relating to conversions are analyzed.

## Protection Afforded Existing Tenants

Approximately one-half of the states have enacted statutes that afford varying types of protection to tenants of residential buildings that are about to undergo conversion to condominium status. The most significant protection pertains to the notification of intent to convert, with provisions for minimum tenancy. Right of first purchase is also frequent, but requiring relocation assistance is rare. Only three states, New York, Connecticut, and Minnesota, provide special protections for one or more of the following types of tenants: elderly persons; handicapped persons; or families with minor children.

Tenant protection statutes can be separated into the following categories: notification of a proposed conversion and occupancy/eviction requirements; right to quiet enjoyment; minimum tenant-purchase or tenant approval; right of first refusal; relocation plans and assistance; and miscellaneous tenant protections.

The nature and extent of each of these tenant protection measures are discussed below.

Notification of proposed conversion, and occupancy eviction requirements procedures. Most of the states which require notification of tenants specify a minimum period of tenancy following the notice of intent to convert. The tenant may maintain occupancy throughout this period or to the end of the existing lease, whichever is longer Frequently, the tenant must notify the developer in writing of his or her intention to take advantage of the statutory minimum period beyond the expiration of an existing lease. The length of notice varies from state to state. The shortest is 60 days, the longest, 270 days, and the most common is 120 days. 4/

---

4/ Breakdowns by state are as follows:  (1) 60 days -- Tennessee and New Jersey; (2) 90 days -- Colorado, New Hampshire, Oregon, and Virginia; (3) 120 days -- Arizona, California, Illinois (before filing of the condominium declaration), Michigan, Ohio, West Virginia, and wisconsin; (4) 180 days -- Connecticut and Maryland and (5) 270 days -- Florida.

## State Statutes Affording Protection to Tenants in Condominium and Cooperative Conversions[†]

| | Notice of Intent to Convert/Minimum Occupancy (In Days) | Tenant Right to First Refusal (In Days) | Right to Quiet Enjoyment | Relocation Assistance | Other |
|---|---|---|---|---|---|
| Alabama | | | | | |
| Alaska | | | | | |
| Arkansas | | | | | |
| Arizona | 120 | 30 | X | | |
| California | 120 | 60 | | X | X[4] |
| Colorado | 90 | | | X | |
| Connecticut | 180 | 90 | | X | X[5] |
| Delaware | | | | | |
| Florida | 180 - 270 | 90 | | | |
| Georgia | | | | | |
| Hawaii | | | | | |
| Idaho | | | | | |
| Illinois | 120 | 120 | X | | |
| Indiana | | | | | |
| Iowa | | | | | |
| Kansas | | | | | |
| Kentucky | | | | | |
| Louisiana | | | | | |
| Maine | | | | | |
| Maryland | 180 | | | | X[7] |
| Massachusetts | | | | | |
| Michigan | 120 | | | | |
| Minnesota * | 120 | 60 | | | X[7] |
| Mississippi | | | X | | |
| Missouri | | | | | |
| Montana | | | | | |
| Nebraska | | | | | |
| Nevada | | | | | |
| New Hampshire | 90 | 60 | | | |
| New Jersey | 60[1] | 90 | X | X | |
| New Mexico | | | | | |
| New York | *[2] | *[2] | X | | X[6] |
| North Carolina | | | | | |
| North Dakota | | | | | |
| Ohio | 120 | 90 | | | |
| Oklahoma | | | | | |
| Oregon | 90[3] | 30 | X | | |
| Pennsylvania | | | | | |
| Rhode Island | | | | | |
| South Carolina | | | | | |
| South Dakota | | | | | |
| Tennessee | 60 | | | X | |
| Texas | | | | | |
| Utah | | | | | |
| Vermont | | | | | |
| Virginia | 90 | 60 | | | |
| Washington | | | | | |
| West Virginia * | 120 | 60 | | | |
| Wisconsin | 120 | 60 | | | X[7] |
| Wyoming | | | | | |
| Uniform Condominium Act | 120 | 60 | | | X[7] |

[†] Most state protections apply only to condominiums

[1] Notice precedes 3-year notice of intent to institute eviction proceedings

[2] Notice varies for rent control and rent stabilization housing

[3] Does not constitute or include notice to terminate tenancy

[4] 10-day notice of optional public hearing

[5] Prohibits retaliatory eviction for failure to purchase

[6] Prohibits stockpiling empty apartments, tenant harrassment, etc

[7] Right to cancel lease

A few states have more rigorous tenant protections which require separate notices of intent to convert and notice of intent to evict. 5/
These statutes often prohibit evictions of tenants for long periods of time, including extended stays of eviction proceedings in the case of hardship. 6/ A few states provide extended notification periods based upon the tenant's age, physical disability, or family status, 7/ or the tenant's length of residence in the building, 8/ or the presence of a local housing emergency. 9/ Some states have shorter than usual notification periods but include other provisions,

---

5/ New Jersey, in particular, requires that tenants receive 60 days notice of intent to convert before the owner may serve a three-year notice of intent to institute eviction proceedings. Oregon's statute specifically states that the 90-day notice of intent to convert shall not constitute or include a notice of termination. Both states also require that the notice include the plan of conversion and a description of the tenant's rights.

6/ New Jersey law provides for a court ordered stay of evictions after the minimum 3-year period. Connecticut's statute states that if a tenant cannot secure suitable premises in a reasonably comparable neighborhood after searching with due "diligence," the court may grant a stay of the eviction for up to 6 months. The court may further grant an additional 6 months based on the age of the applicant, the size of the applicant's family, the length of tenancy, and the availability of suitable alternative housing.

7/ See the discussion of Connecticut, Minnesota, and New York statutes in a following section on protection of elderly and handicapped individuals, and families with children.

8/ In Florida, a tenant who has been a resident of the building for 6 months or more prior to the notice of intent to convert may extend his or her lease for 270 days. A tenant who has been a resident for less than 6 months prior to the notice of intent to convert may extend his or her lease for 180 days. In both cases, the tenant must notify the developer of his election to extend the lease within 45 days of the notice of intent to convert. Tenants whose leases expire within 45 days may choose to remain (with written notice) for that 45-day period in order to decide whether or not to extend their rental agreement for the 180- or 270-day period.

9/ Florida law provides that a county may further extend the tenant's right to stay for an additional 90 days (a total of 360 days) for tenants in residence for 6 months or more and 270 days for tenants in residence less than 6 months if a county finds that there is a 3 percent or less vacancy rate. A municipality in the county may vote not to have the 90-day extension apply within its boundaries.

such as the right to terminate and be compensated for moving expenses.
10/ Several states authorize considerably less stringent notice of
termination provisions for leases which were entered into after public announcement of the plan to convert the premises. 11/

Right to quiet enjoyment. State statutes contain little treatment of
a tenant's right to quiet enjoyment of the premises during the conversion process. Arizona law prohibits construction or improvement of
the unit without the tenant's express permission, stipulating that
peaceful enjoyment of the premises, including common areas, is not
to be interrupted by unreasonable noise or construction activity.
Minnesota also prohibits repairs or remodeling during the notice
period unless "reasonable precautions" are taken to ensure tenant
safety and security.

A few states limit access to occupied units for the purpose of showing them to prospective purchasers. Illinois, for example, limits
such showings to a reasonable number of times, at appropriate hours
and then only during the last 90 days of an expiring tenancy. The
New Jersey statute provides that, during the first 90 days after
notice of intent to convert, the unit may not be shown to a third
party unless the tenant has, in writing, waived his or her right to
purchase. New York has established severe penalties for landlords
who keep apartments empty or harass tenants in order to speed up the
conversion process. In addition, certain measures require that
after the conversion is completed, the nonpurchasing tenants must be
serviced by the same managing agent who services the apartment purchasers and that the pre-conversion level of services must be maintained. Oregon mandates that a tenant's dwelling unit may not be
shown to a prospective purchaser without the tenant's permission
unless tenancy has been terminated.

----------------------------------------------

10/ See the discussion of Colorado, Florida, and Tennessee in the
following section on moving expenses.

11/ Connecticut allows termination of such leases on 30 days notice.
Florida allows termination on 60 days' notice if the landlord's right
in this regard is conspicuously disclosed in the lease. New Jersey
provides that a statement of intention to convert must be provided for
tenancies begun after the condominium master deed has been filed. If
this notice is given, these tenancies can be terminated on 60 days
notice; if not, the tenants have a right to the regular 3-year
notice. In New York, 60-day notice of termination provisions may be
inserted in new or renewal leases of "rent stabilized" apartments,
from and after the date that the first draft of the conversion offering
plan is distributed to tenants and filed with the appropriate governmental agencies.

Miminum tenant purchase or tenant approval. New York State has the most significant rules regarding this issue. By a combination of statute and administrative regulation, the state mandates that conversion plans in New York City can only proceed if 35 percent of tenants in occupancy sign subscription agreements within a relatively brief period after the plan is accepted for filing by the attorney general. Special state legislation for the counties of Nassau, Westchester and Rockland authorizes local governments to mandate a minimum 35 percent sale to tenants for an eviction plan, as well as a mandatory 15 percent sale to tenants for noneviction plans, if local governments deem it necessary.

The right of first refusal. A number of states require the converter to give tenants in occupancy an unqualified, exclusive option to purchase their units. This option, often called a "right of first - refusal", must be exercised within a specific period of time, usually linked with the notice of intent to convert or notice to vacate. Right-to-purchase periods range from 30 to 120 days in various states. 12/

Some states provided for the possibility of extending notice of intent to convert/right to occupancy depending upon the timing of a developer's offer to the tenant of the right to first refusal, 13/ or disclosure of certain mandated information to the tenant. 14/

Minnesota is the only state which prohibits discrimination based on the age of the lease holder or any resident when offering the right of first refusal. Florida is the only state to limit the right of first refusal to tenants who were in occupancy at least six months prior to the notice of intent to convert.

---

12/ In Oregon, it is 30 days after notice of intent to convert; in Wisconsin and Virginia, it is 60 days after notice to vacate and in California it is at least 60 days after issuance of the Final Subdivision Public Report; in Connecticut and New Jersey, it is 90 days from notice of intent to convert, and in Ohio, 90 days from notice to vacate. Arizona provides a 30 day period which can be given during or after the notice of intent period. In Florida, the right to first purchase lasts 45 days from the receipt of all mandated purchaser information on the housing market, financing, and tax system. New York statute and regulations require each tenant in occupancy be given a 90 day exclusive right to purchase.

13/ Arizona provides a minimum 90-day right to occupy from the offer of the right of first refusal.

14/ Florida stipulates that if a tenant informational package is not provided within 90 days of the notice of intent to convert, the notice period is extended one day for each day the report is late, unless the tenant disclaims this extension in writing.

Relocation Plans and Assistance. A few states require developers to pay moving expenses or establish a relocation assistance program. Three states permit the developer to terminate or shorten the notice period by paying moving expenses or other agreed upon consideration. 15/

Connecticut mandates that low income tenants must receive moving and relocation expenses equal to one month's rent, or up to $500 (as determined by local government). 16/ Connecticut also requires a converter to provide nonpurchasing tenants with relocation assistance which includes information on the availability of alternative housing, financing programs, and Federal, state, and municipal housing assistance

The State of New Jersey has also legislated fairly extensively in this area. It has developed an integrated set of tenant protections and assistance involving moving expenses, relocation assistance, and long-term eviction stays. Specifically, the statute provides that preconversion tenants who are evicted or leave because of the conversion shall receive moving expense compensation equal to one month's rent. The statute also provides for relocation services: tenants in occupancy prior to the recording of the master deed (who received the three-year notice) have a right for 18 months to demand that the landlord offer them a "reasonable opportunity" to examine and rent "comparable housing." 17/

---

15/ Colorado state law allows a developer, with the tenant's consent, to terminate the tenancy in less than the 90-day minimum, if the developer pays all moving expenses or other agreed-upon considerations. A Tennessee statute mandates that if the owner converts without giving tenants two months' actual notice, the occupants may choose to vacate immediately upon receiving a belated notice, and the owner must than pay all reasonable moving expenses. However, if a tenant is in a position to make this choice and does not vacate the premises immediately, the owner is not obligated to pay moving expenses. Florida permits developers to offer tenants entitled to 270 days notice the option of accepting 120 days notice plus one month's rent for moving expenses.

16/ Connecticut limits moving and relocation benefits to households with incomes of less than 175 percent of the Federal Community Services Administration poverty guidelines for nonfarm recipients.

17/ The statute specifically defines "reasonable opportunity" and "comparable housing" and stipulates that a landlord must prove that these requirements were met before eviction proceedings can begin. If a landlord cannot prove this, the court may authorize up to five one-year stays of eviction (with reasonable rent increases), until it is satisfied the tenant has been offered the statutory benefits. If, after at least one such stay has been authorized, the owner gives the tenant "hardship relocation assistance" equal to a waiverr

Miscellaneous tenant protections. Arizona, Maryland, and Minnesota all permit tenants to cancel an existing lease within 30 days of the notice of intent to convert. Connecticut's legislation prohibits retaliation against tenants by an owner wishing to convert.

The statute provides that, where a written lease exists, there can be no retaliatory eviction because a tenant refuses to purchase an apartment. The various New York statutes governing conversion to condominium or cooperative status contain several provisions of a similar nature. Among other things, these statutes prohibit the stockpiling of empty apartments; harassment of tenants to induce them to purchase or move; and reduction of services during or following the conversion process. Finally, these measures mandate that both tenants and purchasers must be serviced, on a nondiscriminatory basis, by the same managing agent, once the conversion is declared effective and title is transferred.

## Protections Afforded Buyers

Almost half of the states have revised their statutes to include more protections for all condominium purchasers. These protections apply to both newly constructed condominiums and conversions, although several states and the Uniform Condominium Act require additional protections in the case of conversions. The most common buyer protection provisions concern to the preparation and publication of a building, property, or engineer's report. This report is often a key element in a full disclosure scheme of consumer protection and usually includes information on the present condition of the property, the useful life of the major structural and mechanical components, the estimated costs of major repairs and replacement, and the project budget and past operating expenses of the building. A few states specify that the developer must provide warranties, post bonds, or establish escrow funds to guarantee the quality or completion of common areas and individual units. Some states give purchasers the right to rescind or cancel the sales contract within a set period of time, usually 10 to 15 days after execution on the contract or receipt of all full disclosure documents.

Buyer protection statutes can be separated into seven distinct categories: building codes; preparation and publication of building, property or engineer's report; full disclosure requirements; warranties; escrow funds to ensure completion or renovation of common elements; purchaser's right to cancel or rescind contracts of purchase; and escrow of purchaser deposits.

The nature and extent of these measures are discussed in greater detail below.

Building codes. There is little regulation of such codes at the state level. Most existing statutes mandate disclosure of the status of compliance with local building codes in the public offering statement or registration. 18/

Preparation and publication of building, property, or engineer's report. Most of the state statutes that require disclosure incorporate these items in a public report that must be given to tenants and other prospective unit buyers. Those states which specifically require that the property report be filed with the relevant state agency prior to the disclosure to the public are reviewed in this section. 19/

A property report requires a statement by the converter as to the present condition of all structural and major mechanical components. Some states further stipulate that the statement be substantiated by an architect or engineer's report, 20/ or that construction details and necessary repairs of components be disclosed. 21/ Florida, for example, requires a property report detailing the date and type of construction; the prior use of the building; and the condition of the roof and structural and mechanical elements, substantiated by an architect or engineer's report. It also requires a substantiated report on the extent and treatment of termite infestation.

Some states also require a statement in the property report which discloses the estimated remaining useful life of the structural and major mechanical components. A few states also require the converter to estimate the cost of replacing structural and major mechanical components. 22/

---

18/ Connecticut, Florida, Hawaii, New Hampshire, Louisiana, Michigan, Minnesota, New Jersey, New York, Ohio, Oregon, Virginia, and West Virginia all require such disclosure. New York regulations also require that building, fire, or other code violations of record be removed before the conversion process is completed.

19/ Connecticut and Louisiana require its inclusion in the Public Offering Statement; Florida and New York in the Prospectus; New Jersey and Virginia, in the Application for Registration; and Oregon, in the Notice of Intention. Hawaii and California require property reports, separate and apart from the disclosure documents.

20/ Florida, Hawaii, Louisiana, New Jersey, and New York require independent verification by an architect or engineer.

21/ Connecticut, Florida, New York, Oregon, and Virginia are among the states which specify details of construction and necessary repairs.

22/ Connecticut, Hawaii, Louisiana, Oregon, and Virginia require estimates of useful life; Connecticut and Virginia include estimated costs of repairs. New York prohibits the inclusion of such cost estimates on the theory that inflation, differences among contractors, differences in the scope of the work and available warranties, make such cost projections unreliable and counter-productive.

## State Statutes Affording Protection to Buyers in Condominium and Cooperative Conversions[†]

| | Reports and Disclosure | | | | | | Warranties | Escrow | | Right to Cancel | | Other | | |
| --- | --- | --- | --- | --- | --- | --- | --- | --- | --- | --- | --- | --- | --- | --- |
| | Building Codes | Property Condition | Useful Life | Estimated Repairs | Budget | Legal Documents | Unit/Common Areas | Work Completion | Deposits | Unconditional | Limited | Notice of Tenant Rights | Schedule of Completion | Other |
| Alabama | | | | | | | | | | | | | | |
| Alaska | | | | | | | | | | | | | | |
| Arkansas | | | | | | | | | | | | | | |
| Arizona | | | | | | | | | | | | | | |
| California | | X | | | | X | | | | | | | | X[3] |
| Colorado | | | | | | X | | | | | | | | |
| Connecticut | X | X | X | X | X | X | X | X | | X | | X | | X[4] |
| Delaware | | | | | | | | | | | | | | |
| Florida | | X | | | X | X | X | X | | X | | | | X[5] |
| Georgia | | | | | X | X | | | X | | X[1] | | | |
| Hawaii | X | X | | | X | X | | X | X | | X[1] | | | X[4] |
| Idaho | | | | | | | | | | | | | | |
| Illinois | | | | | X | X | | | X | X | | X | | |
| Indiana | | | | | | | | | | | | | | |
| Iowa | | | | | | | | | | | | | | |
| Kansas | | | | | | | | | | | | | | |
| Kentucky | | | | | | | | | | | | | | |
| Louisiana | X | X | X | | X | X | | | | X | | | | |
| Maine | | | | | X | X | | | | X | | | | |
| Maryland | | X | | | X | X | | X | | X | | | | |
| Massachusetts | | | | | | | | | | | | | | |
| Michigan | | X | | | X | X | | X | X | X | | | | X[6] |
| Minnesota * | X | X | X[7] | X[8] | X | X | X | | X | X | | | X | |
| Mississippi | | | | | | | | | | | | | | |
| Missouri | | | | | | | | | | | | | | |
| Montana | | | | | | | | X | | | X[1] | | | |
| Nebraska | | | | | | | | | | | | | | |
| Nevada | | | | | | | | | | | | | | |
| New Hampshire | | X | X | X | X | X | | | X | X | | | X | |
| New Jersey | X | X | | | X | X | | | X | X | | X | X | X[3] |
| New Mexico | | | | | | | | | | | | | | |
| New York | X | X | | | X | X | | | | X | | X | | |
| North Carolina | | | | | | | | | | | | | | |
| North Dakota | | | | | | | | | | | | | | |
| Ohio | X | X | | | X | X | X | | | X | X | | | |
| Oklahoma | | | | | | | | | | | | | | |
| Oregon | | X | X | X | X | X | X | | | X | | | X | |
| Pennsylvania | | | | | | | | | | | | | | |
| Rhode Island | | | | | | | | | | | | | | |
| South Carolina | | | | | | | | | | | | | | |
| South Dakota | | | | | X | | | | X | | | | | |
| Tennessee | | | | | | | | | | | | | | |
| Texas | | | | | | | | | | | | | | |
| Utah | | | | | | | | | | | | | | |
| Vermont | | | | | | | | | | | | | | |
| Virginia | X | X | X | X | X | X | X | X | X | X | | | | |
| Washington | | | | | | | | | | | | | | |
| West Virginia * | X | X | X[7] | X[8] | X | X/X | X | | X | | X[2] | | X | |
| Wisconsin | | | | | | X/X | | | | X | | | | |
| Wyoming | | | | | | | | | | | | | | |
| Uniform Condominium Act | X | X | X[7] | X[8] | X | X | X | | X | | X[2] | | X | |

[†] Most state protections apply only to condominiums.

\* Uniform Condominium Act with amendments.

[1] Buyers may cancel if misled by fraud or misrepresentation

[2] Buyer may cancel if Public Offering Statement not disclosed

[3] Property report includes utilities, access, noise and safety, etc.

[4] Design standards

[5] Must disclose prior use of building

[6] Title insurance

[7] Useful life or indication that no representations are made on major systems

[8] List of uncured building violations and cost to repair

In New Jersey and Oregon, the status and schedule of completion of any improvements still under construction must be disclosed.  A statement describing noise and safety conditions, and provisions for sewage disposal and public utilities must be given to tenants and prospective buyers in both California and New Jersey.

Full disclosure requirements.  On the state level, disclosure to prospective purchasers is most frequently accomplishjed by way of the Public Offering Statement or prospectus.  In most cases, this must be filed with the relevant state agency prior to any offerings for sale, and a copy must be given to prospective purchasers, usually at or before the time a contract is executed.  Disclosure requirements generally cover three categories of information, usually included in the offering statement: building reports, budgets, and legal documents.

a.  Building report.  The requirement of full disclosure of the building report is usually satisfied through the building and property reports described above, including condition, useful life, and estimates of repairs. 23/  Some states may limit the reports to conversions, as Maryland does by requiring reports only for buildings completed more than five years before the recording of the condominium declaration.

b.  Projected budget and past operating expenses.  Many states require disclosure of the projected annual budget for the first year of operation as a cooperative or condominium.  Generally, this require ment is phrased in terms of the actual expenditures on all repairs, maintenance, operation or upkeep of the building or buildings. 24/ New Jersey, for example, requires an audited statement of expenses for the past five years, or the ownership period, whichever is less, certified by an independent public accountant.

---

23/  As above, California, Connecticut, Florida, Hawaii, Louisiana, Maryland, Minnesota, New York, Oregon, Ohio, Virginia, and West Virginia require that the Public Offering Statement include a statement by the declarant on the present condition of all structural and major mechanical components.  Michigan's statute refers only to the disclosure of such material information as the administrator may require.  Some states (see footnote 16) also require disclosure of estimates of useful life and repair costs.  Ohio requires an estimate of repair and replacement costs for the next five years.

24/ Connecticut, Florida, Georgia, Hawaii, Illinois, Louisiana, Maryland, Minnesota, New Jersey, New York, Ohio, Oregon and Wisconsin all require a budget statement.  Maine does also, but its disclosure requirements, in general, are only applicable to time-share projects.

## Disclosure Requirements:
## Property Report, Budget, and Legal Documents

| State with Agency Oversight and Disclosure to Prospective Buyers | States Which Mandate Disclosure to Prospective Buyers |
|---|---|
| California — Real Estate Commission[1] | Colorado[2] |
| Connecticut — Dept. of Housing | Georgia |
| Florida — Division of Florida Land Sales and Condominiums | Illinois[3] |
| Hawaii — Real Estate Commission | Maryland |
| Michigan — Corporation and Securities Bureau (Dept. Commerce) | Minnesota |
| New Jersey — Department of Community Affairs | New Hampshire |
| New York — Attorney General | Ohio |
| Oregon — Real Estate Commision | West Virginia |
| Virginia — Real Estate Commission | Wisconsin[2] |

[1] Property report and legal documents only.
[2] Legal documents only.
[3] Legal documents and budget only.

There are several variations in this type of disclosure requirement:
a few states require the disclosure of the actual operating costs
for the past three years (or the maximum period the building has
been occupied, if less than three years.); 25/ some states mandate
that the budgets be presented on a per unit basis; 26/ and, other
states require that the budget to be revised periodically.  In
Hawaii, the budget must be revised every 12 months, in Ohio, every
6 months.  In New York, such changes must be made whenever a change
occurs (such as publication of a new tax bill) that would materially
affect the projected budget for the project's first year of operation.
Finally, some states require a description of the budget provision
(or lack thereof) covering reserves for capital expenditures. 27/

c.  Offering statements.  Most states with disclosure requirements
mandate that prospective purchasers be given a "disclosure package,"
usually consisting of those documents previously filed with the
governing state agency.  Typically, this includes a Public Offering
Statement or Prospectus, which usually contains, at a minimum, the
declaration, bylaws, articles of incorporation of the association,
(these first three being the legal or organizational documents),
management contracts, budget information, recreational leases, and
any encumbrances, easements, liens, or other matters affecting
title. 28/  In addition, some states mandate that prospective
purchasers be informed of the rights of tenants in a residential
building undergoing conversion.  Connecticut requires that purchasers
be given a copy of the notice to tenants.  New Jersey and New York
both mandate that the Prospectus or Public Offering include a statement of the rights of nontenant purchasers of apartments that are
occupied by tenanats who are entitled to remain for a brief or
indefinite period.  Illinois stipulates that the contract conspicuously
disclose the tenant's right of first refusal.

---

25/  Connecticut, New York, Virginia.

26/  Florida, Hawaii, Illinois, Louisiana, Maine (time-shares only),
New Jersey, New York, and Ohio, in particular.

27/  This is required in Connecticut, Louisiana, Maine (time-shares
only), Minnesota, New Hampshire, New Jersey, New York, Ohio, Oregon,
Virginia, and West Virginia (UCA).

28/  California, Connecticut, Florida, Georgia, Hawaii, Illinois,
Louisiana, Maine (time-shares only), Maryland, Michigan, Minnesota,
New Hampshire, New Jersey, New York, Ohio, Oregon, South Dakota,
Virginia, West Virginia, UCA and Wisconsin require disclosure of
most or all of the above to prospective purchasers.  Colorado
requires disclosure only of the bylaws.

Various requirements concern the delivery of the offering statement
Some states do not specify a time when the disclosure information
must be provided, and others stipulate only that it be provided "at
or before" the contract. 29/  Still other states specify that the
disclosure must be delivered prior to closing; others specify one
to two weeks before the contract. 30/

Warranties.  Only a few state statutes require warranties by
condominium declarants or developers. 31/  This coverage usually
extends to both the common areas and the units.  However, conversions
may not be covered by the same provisions as newly constructed
condominiums. 32/  Most condominium statutes were drafted solely with
new construction in mind (as, for example, provisions relating to
condominium developers complying with subdivision laws).  Thus,
although the issue is an open one, in most jurisdictions a compelling
argument can be made that conversions were not intended for inclusion
in the warranty section of the applicable condominium statute.  This
conclusion would be reinforced if there were few or no conversions
in the state at the time the statutory provision in question was
enacted; it would also be supported if warranty statues governing
the sale of real property in general within the state were restricted
in their operation to new construction.

---

29/ California, Connecticut, Florida, Hawaii, Louisiana, Maine, Ohio,
and Virginia do not specify a delivery time.  Colorado and New Jersey
require it be provided "at or before" contract.  Illinois, Oregon,
and South Dakota require it be provided "before" contract.  New York
mandates that tenants in occupancy must receive the "red herring" or
first draft of the Offering Plan, before the same is delivered to
the Attorney General's Office to obtain approval for filing and
issuance.

30/  Maryland, Minnesota, and Wisconsin require that it be provided
at least 15 days before closing.  Georgia requires that it be provided
at least seven days before contract.  Michigan requires that it be
provided 10 days before closing or before the purchase agreement
becomes binding.  Michigan also provides that this time limit may be
waived in writing on an approved form.

31/  Connecticut and Florida provide fairly detailed coverage; Ohio,
Oregon, and Virginia have more limited warranties.

32/  The New Jersey statute specifically provides that the statutory
warranties on construction and fitness for intended use are inapplic-
able to conversions.  In other states this exception may be read
into the statutory scheme by implication.  Oregon specifies that the
declarant shall expressly warrant against defects in plumbing,
electrical, mechanical, structural, and all other components of the
newly constructed common elements, for at least one year from the
first conveyance.

Warranty coverage of the common area generally applies to the roof,
structural, and common mechanical elements for one or two years,
either from the date of completion or conveyance.  Again, these
warranties do not usually apply to conversions.  The most comprehensive and innovative approach for providing guarantees to prospective
purchasers concerning the quality of the converted property is found
in Florida.  A converter must undertake one of the following three
alternatives: establish reserve accounts for capital expenditures
and expenditures for deferred maintenance 33/; provide warranties on
certain building components; 34/ or post a surety bond equal to
reserve account requirements.  35/

Escrow funds to ensure completion or renovation of common elements.
A few states require that when units are contracted for or conveyed
prior to their completion (or completion of the common elements),
the developer must either post a bond or place in escrow some or all
of the purchase price to ensure completion.  Some states also require
that the developer post security to cover all uncompleted work on
the unit or common areas. 36/

---

33/  The Florida statute specifies the creation of reserve accounts
for the air conditioning system, plumbing system (if water is supplied
to the project in galvanized plumbing), and the roof.  A detailed
formula specifies the cost and useful life of the relevant building
components to be used in determining the converter's contribution to
each reserve account.  The reserve accounts are funded on a pro rata
basis upon the sale of each unit.

34/  If the converter does not create reserve accounts or post a
security bond, the statute deems that the converter has granted each
unit purchaser an implied warranty of fitness and merchantability for
the purposes or use intended, as to the roof and structural components
of the improvements and as to the mechanical, electrical, and plumbing
elements serving as improvements (except mechanical elements serving
only one unit).  The time of the warranty runs from the longer of
(but in no event more than 5 years) the following: three years from
the notice of intended conversion; one year after the homeowners
obtain control of the association; or, three years from the recording
of the declaration to condominium.  A developer may satisfy these
responsibilities by obtaining an adequate warranty insurance policy.

35/  A converter may post a surety bond, payable to the association,
to cover the amount specified for reserve accounts.

36/  Virginia, in particular, requires that on uncompleted improvements to common elements, the developer must post a bond equal to
100 percent of the estimated cost of completion.  Hawaii and Montana
provide, that as to units sold before construction is completed,
all monies paid from the sale must be put in escrow.  Montana also
provides that any funds obtained prior to the issuance of the final
report shall be refunded if there is any change in the condominium
building plans subsequent to execution of the contract, unless the
purchaser accepts the change.

Other states require that part or all of any deposit or sales monies must be put in escrow to cover any uncompleted work. 37/ However, because of their scope, these measures are seldom applicable to condominiums arising from a residential conversion. The terms of such measures indicate quite clearly that they were intended to apply to new construction. Moreover, these measures have no application to residential conversions involving property converted to cooperative housing status.

<u>Purchaser's right to cancel or rescind contracts of purchase.</u> The right to rescind or cancel is sometimes provided for a certain number of days after execution of the contract, 38/ or after receipt of all required disclosure documents, whichever is later. The most common provision for cancellation specifies a period of days (after either full disclosure or any amendments or "material changes") during

---

37/ Michigan gives the state administrator power to require an escrow of a portion of the sales price, to cover cost of construction of the recreational facilities and other elements. Maryland mandates that, for any unit uncompleted <u>at contract</u>, the purchaser's deposit must be escrowed or a corporate surety bond, payable to the state, must be obtained. Connecticut requires that a declarant must post a bond or escrow 10 percent of the purchase price to cover uncompleted elements. Florida provides that if a developer contracts to sell before substantial completion of any elements, he must escrow 10 percent of any sale price received.

38/ In Connecticut and Maine, (time-shares only) this right lasts 15 days; in New Jersey, 7; and in Oregon, 3. Michigan addresses only to reservation or subscription agreement, which the prospective purchaser may cancel within 10 days after receipt of required disclosure documents. Virginia allows cancellation within ten days of the later of the contract date or receipt of all disclosure information. Florida gives the buyer 15 days after execution of the contract and receipt of all disclosure information.

which the buyer may rescind a purchase agreement. 39/  New York, for example, affords purchasers the right to cancel for several days after receipt of the public offering statement (up to the time of conveyance).  In addition, purchasers must be afforded a further right to rescind for 10 days whenever a material change is made in the offering plan.  A few states specify that the right to rescind terminates at unit closing.

Escrow of purchaser deposits.  Several states provide that all deposits or payments received from purchasers on a contract or reservation agreement must be held in escrow until closing. 40/  A few states require that a developer escrow all money paid before issuance of the final public report, and if this report is not issued within one year of the preliminary report, the purchaser is entitled to a full refund. 41/

Rental Stock Protection: Preservation of Low- and Moderate-Income Housing

California is the only state with legislation focusing on preservation of the low and moderate income rental stock.  State statutes require that local agencies consider the housing needs of the region when

---

39/ Louisiana permits the purchasers to rescind up to 15 days after full disclosure, or after any material changes up to closing.  Maryland, Minnesota, and West Virginia provide for a 15 day right of rescission after receipt of the required full disclosure information.  In addition, Maryland provides a 5-day right to rescind after any disclosure amendments.  In Wisconsin, the right extends for 5 business days following notice of any material change in those documents (this right terminates if the buyer proceeds to closing).  Illinois and New Hampshire stipulate that, if the disclosure information is not provided at contract, the purchase agreement is voidable within 5 days after the last item of information is received, or until closing, whichever is earlier.  Hawaii and Montana declare that contracts are not final until purchasers have had a full opportunity to read the final public report.  They may obtain refunds if the final report differs in "any material respect" from the preliminary report. Georgia provides that contracts executed within less than 7 days after receipt of all disclosure information are of no force on effect.

40/  California, Florida, Georgia, Illinois, Michigan, New Jersey, New York, Ohio, South Dakota, and Virginia require this.

41/ Hawaii and Montana tie the escrow of funds to issuance of the full disclosure report.

looking at subdivision requests.  In the area of protecting low-
and moderate-income housing, California offers the possibility of
financial assistance to enable conversion households to purchase
their units.  This assistance may not be more than 49 percent of the
purchase price, nor may it reduce the purchaser's down payment to
less than 3 percent of the total purchase price. 42/

## Protection of Elderly and Handicapped Individuals and Families with Minor Children

Three states provide special protections to tenants who are elderly,
handicapped, or have minor children.  Minnesota, for example, permits
all three groups to extend the right-to-occupancy period from 120 to
180 days upon written notice.  Connecticut protects elderly (over 62),
blind, and disabled tenants whose incomes are within certain limits
from eviction without cause until January 1, 1983 provided the landlord does not remove the unit from the rental market or decide to
live in it himself.  This protection applies only to tenants in
buildings containing seven or more units. 43/

New York has extensive provisions designed to safeguard the economic
well being of elderly tenants.  State legislation mandates that
tenants who are 62 years or older when a conversion plan is declared
effective do not have to purchase their apartments.  These measures
apply to conversions in New York City (the most populous portion of
the state) and to municipalities in the surrounding counties (Nassau,

---

42/  Eligibility for such aid is limited to households which meet
the following requirements: an income at or below the median for
the county; the household members must not currently own a residence
and must not have owned any real property for at least three years;
the household must not have previously received assistance under
this chapter; and the household must be unable to acquire the
dwelling unit without this assistance.  The statute mandates that
each recipient of assistance enter into a contract (secured by a
deed of trust on the dwelling unit) under which the state would
receive proceeds proportionate to the percentage of the initial
purchase price which was paid with this financial assistance,
whenever the unit is resold.

43/  Municipalities can set income limits between $13,000 and $21,000
for singles, and $17,000 and $25,000 for couples in regard to this
protection.  The lower limits prevail if a municipality does not
act.  The January 1, 1983 limitation is required by the state's
"sunset" law and the legislature will review this provision in 1982.
In addition, the bar to eviction covers all designated rental units
whether or not a conversion is planned.

Rockland, and Westchester) if such municipalities have implemented the state law by local optional legislation. The three-county and New York City laws afford the nonpurchasing elderly tenant (and his or her spouse) a form of life tenancy, with rents to continue under any applicable regulatory system, or if unregulated, to be judged by a statutory standard based upon comparable premises available for rent in the area.

The New York City measure contains the following statutory prerequisites: the elderly tenant must have resided in the premises for at least two years prior to the time of the conversion; the apartment must be the tenant's primary residence; the annual income of the household must be less than $30,000; and the tenants must state their intention to take advantage of the benefits of this provision by completing forms from the Attorney General's office. This decision, however, can later be rescinded by the tenant. The New York City legislation also differs from its three-county counterpart in that it subtracts elderly tenants who choose to take advantage of this statute from the total number of tenants in the premises when determining whether or not 35 percent of the stabilized tenants have purchased (as required for an eviction plan). If the elderly tenants who are taking advantage of this statute occupy rent-controlled apartments, only one-half of their number is subtracted in determining whether the 35 percent sale to tenants (required for an eviction plan) has been met.

## The Uniform Condominium Act Governing Conversions

The Uniform Condominium Act (UCA), developed after several years of drafting by the National Conference of Commissioners on Uniform Laws, seeks to unify and modernize the law of condominiums. The UCA was adopted by the National Conference in the summer of 1977 and approved by the American Bar Association in the winter of 1978. The act has been promulgated to every state for consideration. A number of states have the act under active consideration, with West Virginia being the first state to enact it on February 15, 1980, followed by Minnesota on April 16, 1980.

The act seeks to remedy inadequacies and inflexibility found in the "first generation" of condominium legislation passed in the 1960s and meet the need for greater consumer protection. The commentary to the UCA indicates that the section on condominium conversions is substantially based on similar provisions in the condominium statutes of Virginia and the District of Columbia. The UCA is, therefore, likely to serve as the basis for future revisions of condominium law in many states with "first generation" statutes. 44/

---

44/ It should also be noted that implementation of the provision of this model statute via its adoption by individual state legislatures would not affect conversion to cooperative housing status, in the absence of the enactment of parallel measures to cover this type of conversion.

Three major aspects of the Uniform Condominium Act relating to conversions are discussed in detail in the following pages. They are protections afforded tenants, buyer protections, and limitations on local government authority to regulate condominiums.

## Protections Afforded Tenants

The UCA provides tenants in condominium conversions with two principal rights. First, a tenant is given 120 days notice of conversion, which also may constitute the notice to vacate. Second, in the notice of conversion, a tenant is given the right of first refusal, i.e., the right to purchase his or her unit on terms equal to those offered the public.

Notice of intent to Convert/Notice to Evict. The act requires a declarant to give tenants and subtenants in possession at least 120 days notice of the conversion. The notice must generally set forth the rights of tenants and subtenants under the conversion section of the act, i.e., rights as to notice and right of first refusal. No tenant or subtenant may be required to vacate on less than 120 days notice, except for cause, and the terms of the tenancy may not be changed during that period. The notice of intent to convert may also constitute the statutory notice to vacate if it specifies a date by which the unit must be vacated.

Right of First Refusal. As to residential units whose dimensions will be substantially the same after the conversion, the declarant must offer tenants the right to purchase their units. The act recommends that this right of purchase be available for 60 days after notice of conversion, and that if a tenant fails to exercise it, the declarant not offer the unit on more favorable to a third party for the following 180 days. If the declarant conveys a unit to a bona fide purchaser without having given the tenant a right to purchase, recording of the deed extinguishes the tenant's right to purchase but does not affect any right the tenant may have to recover damages from the declarant.

## Buyer Protections

The UCA adopts a full disclosure scheme for informing the potential purchaser of all aspects of the building and unit. A public offering statement must be prepared and submitted to a review agency (this is optional under the act) or to the purchase. The opening statement requires information on the developer and his or her overall plans for the project, the legal documentation, the projected budget and monthly assessments, purchaser rights to cancel a contract to purchase, and any warranties offered or disclaimed.

The UCA requires several additions to the offering plan in the case of condominium conversions. A statement prepared by an independent architect or engineer must be included describing the present condition of all structural components and any mechanical and electrical system material to the use and enjoyment of the condominium. In addition, the UCA requires statement on the expected useful life of each structural, mechanical, or electrical component, or a statement that no representations are made in that regard. Finally, the public offering must contain a list of any notices of uncorrected building code violations together with an estimated cost to remedy the violations.

Engineer's Report; Building Code Violations. The Uniform Act mandates that the public offering statement for converted condominiums must contain a statement by the declarant based on an independent architect's or engineer's report covering the present condition of all structural components and mechanical and electrical installations. This additional information is required for conversions because of the difficulty a purchaser would have in determining the condition of an older building. The declarant is also required to make a statement as to the expected useful life of the above items, or a statement that no misrepresentations are made in this regard. In addition, any outstanding notices of building code violations must be listed, as well as the estimated cost to cure the violations.

Budget Provisions. The general provisions of the act governing public offering statements require disclosure of the current balance sheet and a projected budget. The act suggests that these be provided for one year after the first conveyance. The budget must include a statement of the amount reserved for capital repairs and replacement, or a statement that there is no such reserve.

Legal Documents. The declarant must provide purchasers with copies of the public offering statement (which includes the declaration, by-laws, rules and regulations of the condominium, and any contracts or leases to be executed by the purchaser).

Warranties. The act's sections on express and implied warranties apply to all condominiums, with no specific provisions applying only to converted condominiums. The act provides that express warranties of quality may be given by the declarant acting in a way that creates particular expectations in a purchaser. This may be by an affirmation or a promise, or via models, descriptions of physical characteristics, or the plans and specifications. The burden is on the declarant to show that a contracting purchaser did not rely on any such representations.

The act provides an implied warranty that a unit will be in at least as good condition at the time of conveyance or possession as it was at the time of contracting. 45/ The declarant also warrants by implication the suitability of the premises for ordinary use and that improvements will be free from defective materials and legally and soundly constructed. These warranties may be created regarding both the units and the common elements.

Purchaser's Right to Cancel. The act provides that if a purchaser is not given a copy of the public offering statement more than 15 days before execution of a contract, he or she may cancel the contract without penalty within 15 days of receipt of the statement, at any time up to the time of conveyance. Delivery of the public offering statement is not required prior to execution of a "nonbinding reservation agreement", as these agreements may be unilaterally cancelled by a purchaser at any time without penalty.

Escrow of Deposits. The act provides that any reservation deposits made to the purchaser must be held in escrow until closing or until refunded to the purchaser (unless paid to the declarant upon a purchaser's default under the terms of the contract).

Limitations on Local Government Authority to Regulate Condominiums. The UCA contains a significant provision pertaining to the authority of local governments to regulate condominiums, including conversions. Under the UCA, local governments would be barred from using zoning, subdivision, building codes, or real estate regulation to prohibit the condominium form of ownership or to impose any requirement upon a condominium form of ownership which it would not impose upon a physically identical development under a different form of ownership. In the case of a condominium conversion, this section appears to bar local governments from regulating a building in one way for rental use and in another way if it is converted to a condominium.

---

45/ The implied warranties may be excluded or modified by agreement of the parties or by disclaimers; except that, for residential units, the disclaimer must be specific and must be contained in an instrument signed by the purchaser. The act states that the statute of limitations for breach of the express or implied warranties is 6 years, but may be reduced to not less than 2 years by agreement of the parties. As to the unit, the cause of action accrues at the time of first possession or when a non-possessing interest was conveyed. As to the common elements, the cause of action accrues at completion, or at conveyance of the first unit to a bona fide purchaser, whichever is later. If a warranty of quality explicitly extends to future performance, accrual is at the earlier of either discovery of the breach or the end of the explicit warranty period.

West Virginia, the first state to pass the UCA, retained the limitations on local government authority to regulate condominiums. However, Minnesota amended this section of the UCA to provide two significant exceptions to the limitations on local government regulations. First, the general prohibition on local government regulation does not apply to the financing of construction, rehabilitations, or purchases of condominiums through programs established by Federal or state law and operated by state or local governments. Second, a statutory or home rule charter city may prohibit or impose reasonable conditions upon the conversion of buildings to condominium form of ownership in two circumstances: the city must have a significant shortage of suitable rental dwellings available to low- and moderate-income individuals or families; or the city must impose such a prohibition or restriction on conversions in order to maintain eligibility for any Federal or state housing assistance program. A public hearing must be held before enacting any prohibition or restriction on condominium conversions. Finally, it appears that under both exceptions, any regulation is limited to 18 months duration

In the remainder of this chapter, the legal arguments likely to be made concerning government regulation, especially municipal regulation, of condominium and cooperative conversions are considered.

## The Legality of Conversion Regulations and Moratoria Adopted by Local Governments

Various types of conversion regulation have been adopted by municipalities throughout the United States. Because most conversions taking place in these population centers involve a switch from rentals to condominiums (as opposed to cooperatives), these ordinances are invariably addressed to this form of conversion. While most local enactments are designed to broaden consumer protection and to soften the impact of dislocation upon existing tenants (whose occupancy may be abruptly terminated to facilitate conversion and sale of units to prospective purchasers), some have taken the form of a moratorium upon conversion.

Several different types of local regulations of conversions have been subjected to judicial scrutiny. While few state courts of last resort have spoken definitively on the issues involved, local government enactments concerning conversion have generally been sustained. However, generalizations should be approached with caution because different ordinances may present radically different legal issues, ranging from mundane questions concerning home rule, to rent control authorization, equal protection, and substantive due process. Moreover, cases can be gathered from various states, pointing in almost any direction on these questions. Nevertheless, there has been sufficient judicial consideration of these ordinances to enable identification of the types of issues that will be raised in future

The State Preemption Question.  An initial inquiry in many of the
cases reviewed was whether or not the state had expressly or im-
plicitly prohibited local regulation of condominiums.  Since the
condominium is a creature of state enabling legislation (like a
business corporation), and since the public has an interest in statewide uniformity with respect to real property matters, it may be
argued that local governments are prohibited from legislating regarding condominiums.  While a few judicial decisions have reached this
conclusion, most have found that the mere existence of a statewide
condominium statute did not compel a finding of state preemption of
the field.  This conclusion is usually buttressed by the observation
that the local laws in question supplement, rather than contradict,
the statewide enabling legislation.

Of course, where the state legislature reserved to itself the preroga-
tive to legislate in the conversion field (as in New York), local
enactments would be ultra vires 46/ without question.  It should also
be noted that the preemption question would not normally be raised if
the ordinance sought to regulate cooperative conversions, since the
latter are not creatures of state statute.

Rent Control or Other Emergency-Based Ordinances.  Where a local ordinance regulating or prohibiting residential conversions is presented
as a form of rent control legislation, the question may turn upon
whether the organic law of the local government encompasses the
authority to adopt rent control measures.  Questions of state preemption may also be presented if the jurisdiction's history indicates
that the state legislature has reserved to itself the right to legislate in this field, or indicated that it was state policy not to
adopt rent-control type measures.  In most cases, the answer to such
questions might have to be gleaned from inferences and an historical
analysis of state rent control legislation, as opposed to a clear-cut
statement of legislative policy on the matter.

Most local ordinances reviewed avoided the rent control label or format
Instead, they proceeded upon the basis of a finding by the local govern
mental body that a dire housing emergency existed due, in part, to the
sudden upsurge in conversion of residential apartments to condominium
status.  In this connection, property owners could argue that conversions neither increase nor diminish the available housing stock in
any given locality.  Instead, the individuals and families competing
for shelter are reshuffled among the existing facilities; with unit
purchasers undergoing a change in status from renter to owner.

---

46/ Ultra vires is a legal doctrine used to designate acts which are
beyond the scope of the power of a (municipal) corporation.

Thus viewed, conversions do not eliminate housing opportunities but rather shift the legal status of apartments from lessee-occupied to owner-occupied accommodations. Further, the dislocation of tenants who cannot purchase, or choose not to purchase, must be balanced against the opportunity for homeownership; the long-term security of tenure achievable through acquisition of title to one's apartment; the elimination of future landlord profits and potential landlord-tenant disputes; the stabilization of neighborhoods and increased real estate tax base associated with conversions; and the income tax and equity build-up features of homeownership. The value of unit ownership as the average citizen's only real hedge against inflation must also be considered.

While these factors would certainly support a municipality's determination not to regulate or ban conversions, they are seldom discussed in judicial opinions regarding the validity of emergency measures intended to regulate or slow the trend to transform rental stock into condominium unit ownership. If anything, the tendency to sustain local government measures, as an exercise of the policy power is reinforced by the local legislative finding that conversions are adversely affecting the renter population. [Only one court has found this type of finding to lack evidentiary support in the record.]

The Substantive Due Process Argument. Almost invariably, those contesting the validity of local conversion ordinances argue that such measures deprive the affected property owners (the landlord of the apartment building who seeks to convert it, unit buyers who have contracted to purchase an apartment, or both), of their property without substantive due process of law. Occasionally, such arguments are linked with constitutional issues concerning to the impairment of outstanding contractual obligations. Most courts that have considered these questions have concluded that the local regulations or moratoria under review are not so pervasive in scope or duration as to pass the invisible line that separates permissible regulation of property in the public interest from confiscation (or appropriation of private property for a public purpose without payment of just compensation).

The pronouncements of the United States Supreme Court in the last 20 years indicate that arguments based on deprivation of property without due process are seldom fruitful if the ordinance under review does not deprive the complainant of all reasonable use of his or her property. The Supreme Court's recent opinion in the landmark preservation case, Penn Central Transportation Company v. New York City, 438 U.S. 104 (1978), is illustrative. Since conversion ordinances usually operate to control or slow the process of conversion (as opposed to a long-term prohibition against this type of marketing real property), it is extremely difficult to make out a case of complete (or all but complete) frustration of an owner's ability to economically operate or dispose of apartment holdings.

Equal Protection Considerations. In several cases that have arisen to date, it was argued that governmental regulation of conversions or moratoria violate the equal protection clause of state and Federal constitutions. However, in order for this contention to succeed, the complainant would have to carry the burden of demonstrating that the ordinance under attack lacks a rational foundation and constitutes invidious discrimination. Such an argument might be advanced where the ordinance is directed solely toward condiminium conversion (and leaves cooperative conversions wholly unregulated), or where the ordinance is restricted in its operation to certain types of residential real property (as, for example, buildings containing 30 or more units).

However, the courts are prone to allow wide latitude of action to legislative bodies in remedying social problems, and since condo-minium conversions are the most commonplace type of conversions, a local determination to tackle this form of conversion first (or exclusively) would be difficult to overturn. The same could be said for ordinances that reach only the larger projects, since conversion of the latter would have the greatest impact upon the perceived evil of tenant displacement in a tight housing market. Finally, the broad scope of the Supreme Court's opinion in Village of Belle Terre v. Boraas, 416 U.S. 1, 94 S.Ct. 15365 (1974), indicates that the "invidious discrimination" type of argument would probably not impress the members of that Court.

Conversion Moratoria. Most of the local ordinances that have imposed moratoria upon conversions have been of extremely short duration, averaging from 30 days to 6 months. The very brevity of the time span involved is likely to make a court challenge difficult to mount in time, much less succeed. Further, this type of legislation may be difficult to overturn where it is designed as a stop gap measure to enable the local legislature to study the situation and formulate a reasoned response to the housing problems occasioned by a flurry of residential conversions. The precedents in the area of building permits, sewer and water hook-up, and other types of stop gap land use moratoria indicate a willingness by the the courts to sanction short-term moratoria.

In the celebrated case of Golden v. Town of Ramapo, 30 N.Y.2d 359, 334 N.Y.S.2d 138 (1972), the New York Court of Appeals took solace in the fact that the planned growth zoning ordinance at issue would in no event delay development of the property for more than 18 years. Nevertheless, enactment of a prolonged or indefinite moratorium upon condominium conversions, or repeated reenactment of short-term moratoria provisions, would be much more open to attack than a one-time, short-term enactment prohibiting conversions while the local governing body completed deliberations on a plan or regulation.

The foregoing summary of the legal issues presented in this type of litigation is neither exhaustive nor meant to suggest the conclusion that the judiciary would reach in passing upon any given type of ordinance. Instead, it is an outline of the types of legal arguments (constitutional or otherwise) that are prevalent in such cases and a reference to some of the Supreme Court opinions that may influence the result. 47/

* * *

About half of all states have provisions in their condominium statutes which provide protection for tenants in converted buildings and buyers of new or converted units. These states are generally those which contain metropolitan areas experiencing significant amounts of conversion activity. Although most state tenant and buyer protection measures refer only to condominiums, a few states (such as California, Florida, and New York) have similar protections for cooperative tenants and owners.

The most frequent tenant protection measures involves notice to the tenant of the conversion, coupled with a guaranteed minimum tenancy period. Only a few states provide for an extended right to occupancy (over one year), and these states usually limit this protection to the elderly and handicapped. Almost every state with a notification requirement also grants tenants the right to purchase a unit in the conversion.

No state has prohibited conversions and only a few mandate that the converter provide relocation assistance to those tenants who leave the building at the time of conversion. Finally, three states -- New York, Connecticut, and Minnesota -- have enacted special protections which extend the right to occupancy for tenants who are elderly, handicapped or have minor children.

The most common buyer protection is some form of full disclosure of the legal, financial, and physical condition of the project. Another common buyer protection gives the purchasers the right to rescind or cancel the sales contract within a particular period. Only a few states specify that the developer must provide warranties, post surety bonds, or establish escrow funds to guarantee the quality or completion of construction or rehabilitation.

The Uniform Condominium Act (UCA) encompasses the latest effort to unify and modernize condominium regulations. Two states have already passed the UCA with amendments, and several more are actively considering it. The Act has several tenant and buyer protection measures similar to those passed in a number of states.

---

47/ The periodical literature, as well as the selected opinions to date on this subject, are excerpted in Appendix 2.

Although it is possible that more restrictive state regulations may
be enacted in the future which will discourage conversions, it
appears that tenant and consumer protection measures passed to date
have influenced, but not significantly inhibited conversion activity

# Chapter XII
## Local Government's Response to, and Regulation of Conversions

Many cities, towns, villages and counties have also responded to recent increases in the volume of rental conversions by adopting local ordinances which regulate or suspend the conversion process. As with state regulation, these ordinances can be grouped into the following categories: the protection of the rental status of tenants or purchasers (whether tenants or non-tenants at the time of conversion); the maintenance of an adequate supply of rental housing within the community; and the preservation of low- and moderate-income housing.

In this chapter, the national survey of local officials is used to estimate the amount of local regulation which has taken place and to determine the types of communities which have passed them. To illustrate the pattern of, and variation in local regulation, the conversion ordinances of 54 local jurisdictions are analyzed in detail. These include all of the central cities of the Nation's 37 largest SMSAs which have enacted regulations, and selected suburban communities and counties within the same SMSAs. Fully half of these jurisdictions are in California, a state which has had large amounts of conversion activity and, as detailed in chapter XI, has enacted a considerable amount of state-level regulation. The chapter concludes with a discussion of the basic policy preferences of the Nation's local chief executives -- especially, whether they favor or oppose government regulation of conversions.

Community Reaction to Conversions

One of the factors affecting the amount and kind of local government regulation is the community's response to conversion. As reported by local chief executives or their delegates, about one-third of all jurisdictions which have had conversion activity have experienced some negative community response, and organized opposition has occurred in 20 percent of these localities.

> In Philadelphia, for example, tenant groups were instrumental in the enactment of an 18-month moratorium imposed on conversion activity and an ordinance requiring one-year's notice to tenants residing in converting buildings.

The most frequent reaction, however, reported by nearly one-half of local officials, has been complaints from individuals in converted buildings. About one-fifth have also received complaints from purchasers of converted units regarding the quality of the property. (See table XII-1 App.) Of those communities which are experiencing negative community response, 37 percent have ordinances related to conversion, compared to only 7 percent of those communities where

opposition has not been evident.  Even so, nearly two-thirds of the
communities where opposition had been made known to local chief
executives do not have conversion ordinances.  (See table XII-2 App.)

Local Government Response.  Six percent of all the Nation's local
jurisdictions which have had some conversion activity now have some
form of local conversion ordinance. 1/ The rate of conversion enactment is higher, however, in certain types of communities.  For
example, regulation is present or pending in 24 of the 47 central
cities located in the Nation's 37 largest SMSAs. 2/

The likelihood that a particular local government has enacted conversion-related ordinances is related to:  the level and nature of
conversion activity experienced within the community; the kind and
degree of community response to it; actions, if any, taken by state
governments that affect conversions; and their legal authority to
legislate in this area. 3/  There is, therefore, considerable variation in the frequency, as well as the type of response.  (See table
XII-3 App.)

> Variation by amount of activity:  Thirty percent of
> jurisdictions with high amounts of conversion activity
> have enacted ordinances, compared to approximately 11
> percent of jurisdictions with low volumes of activity.
> (See table XII-4 App.)
>
> Variation by region:  Local governments in western
> states (principally California but also Washington)
> are three times more likely to have enacted local
> ordinances concerning conversions than those in
> other regions.  Local governments in southern states
> are least likely to have enacted conversion ordinances.

---

1/ Approximately 36 percent of local officials report some amount
of conversion activity within their jurisdictions.  Less than
one-fifth of these localities have adopted conversion legislation.
In a very few cases, communities which have had no previous
conversions have also enacted a regulatory ordinance.

2/ Conversion ordinances have been enacted in 21 central cities
and are pending in 3 more.  A detailed review of conversion
ordinances in the 37 largest Standard Metropolitan Statistical
Areas is found in exhibit XII-1.

3/ Limited home rule power, preemption of conversion regulation
by state law, or state constitutional limitations may limit local
government authority to enact regulations governing conversions or
homeownership.

Variation by community size:  Smaller cities and counties are less likely than larger jurisdictions to have passed conversion ordinances.

Variation by governmental type:  Twelve percent of all counties with conversion experience have passed ordinances compared to 18 percent of cities which have had conversions.

The type of legislation enacted by local governments has also varied. The most prevalent type of tenant protection ordinance, for example, deals with notification provisions, and the most prevalent type of buyer protection is the filing of a property report which describes the condition of converted buildings.  The extent and nature of this variation is discussed in subsequent sections of this chapter.

Future Regulations by Local Governments.  In addition to communities which have already enacted conversion ordinances, an additional 20 percent of jurisdictions with conversion activity are likely to enact ordinances in the next two years, according to local chief executives.  Furthermore, 10 percent of all local officials in communities which already have conversion ordinances indicate that additional provisions will probably be passed in the coming years. Expectations of future regulatory ordinances are found in roughly the same proportion in all regions of the country and sizes of communities, and in communities with varying amounts of conversion activity.  This suggests that regulation by local governments is likely to continue to grow in future years.

Notification to tenants of an impending conversion is the most frequently anticipated measure, followed by legislation to protect elderly renters.  About two-thirds of those local officials who anticipate future legislation foresee one or both of these require- ments.  (See table XII-5 App.)  Relocation assistance for tenants and special protections for low-income renters are anticipated by about half of these officials.  The next most frequent type of antici pated ordinance is one which would provide public loans or grants to low- and moderate-income renters to assist them in buying their converted units, or would tie conversions to local rental vacancy rates.  Finally, 30 percent of all local officials who predict future legislation expect that moratoria will be enacted; 25 percent expect that evictions from converting buildings will be banned in their jurisdictions.


Types of Local Regulation

This section describes five principal forms of local government regulation of conversions: conversion moratoria; tenant protection; buyer protection; protection of the rental stock; and preservation

## EXHIBIT XII-1

# LOCAL CONDOMINUM AND COOPERATIVE CONVERSION REGULATIONS IN THE NATION'S LARGEST METROPOLITAN AREAS

| Standard Metropolitan Statistical Areas | Conversion Moratorium (1970-1980) | | Conversion Ordinance or Policy | Standard Metropolitan Statistical Areas | Conversion Moratorium | | Conversion Ordinance or Policy |
|---|---|---|---|---|---|---|---|
| | Date | Length | | | Date | Length | |
| **Anaheim-Santa Ana-Garden Grove, CA** | | | | **New Orleans, LA** | | | |
| Anaheim City | | | ‡ | New Orleans City | | | |
| Santa Ana City | | | A B | **New York, NY-NJ** | | | |
| Garden Grove City | | | A B | New York City | | | § |
| Costa Mesa City | | | B C | Fort Lee City | 11/79-12/79⁴ | 2 mo | § |
| Newport Beach City | | | A B C D | **Newark, NJ** | | | |
| Orange County* | | | A B C D | Newark City | | | |
| **Atlanta, GA** | | | | Verona City | 8/79-12/79⁵ | 4 mo. | |
| Atlanta City | | | A B | **Philadelphia, PA** | | | |
| **Baltimore, MD** | | | | Philadelphia City | 9/79-3/81 | 18 mo | A B |
| Baltimore City | | | A  C¹ | Cheltenham Twp | | | A |
| **Boston, MA** | | | | Lower Merion Twp | | | A B |
| Boston City | | | A | **Phoenix, AZ** | | | |
| Brookline City | | | A | Phoenix City | | | |
| Cambridge City | | | C | Mesa City | | | B |
| **Buffalo, NY** | | | | **Pittsburgh, PA** | | | |
| Buffalo City | | | | Pittsburgh City | | | |
| **Chicago, IL** | | | | **Portland, OR-WA** | | | |
| Chicago City | 3/79-4/79² | | A B | Portland City | | | |
| Arlington Hts. | 6/78-8/78 | 2 mo | A B | **St. Louis, MO-IL** | | | |
| Evanston City | 7/78-3/79 | 9 mo | A B | St Louis City | | | |
| Skokie City* | 11/77-7/78 | 8 mo | A B | University City | | | A B |
| **Cincinnati OH-KY-IN** | | | | Webster Grove City | 8/79-2/80 | 6 mo | A B |
| Cincinnati City | | | . | **San Antonio, TX** | | | |
| **Cleveland, OH** | | | | San Antonio City | | | |
| Cleveland City | | | | **San Bernadino-Riverside-Ontario, CA** | | | |
| Beachwood City | 8/79-11/79 | 3 mo | A B C | San Bernardino City | | | C |
| Lakewood City | 2/79-5/79 | 3 mo | A B C | Riverside City | 2/79 | | ‡ |
| Lyndhurst City* | | | A B C | Ontario City | | | |
| **Columbus, OH** | | | | Montclair City | | | A B C |
| Columbus City | | | | Placentia City | 10/79-11/80 | 11 mo | ‡ |
| **Dallas-Ft. Worth, TX** | | | | Upland City* | 11/79 | | ‡ |
| Dallas City | | | | **San Diego, CA** | | | |
| Ft Worth City | | | | San Diego City | | | A  C |
| **Denver-Boulder, CO** | | | | Chula Vista City | | | A B |
| Denver City | | | A | La Mesa City | | | B C |
| Boulder City | | | A | Oceanside City* | 3/79-11/79 | 8 mo | A B C D |
| **Detroit, MI** | | | | **San Francisco-Oakland, CA** | | | |
| Detroit City | | | | San Francisco City | 4/74-5/75 | 13 mo | A B C D |
| **Hartford, CT** | | | | "        "        " | 5/79-8/79 | 3 mo | "  "  "  " |
| Hartford City | | | | Oakland City | 10/78-12/78 | 2 mo | A B C |
| Glastonbury | 12/79-11/80 | 1 mo | A  C | Concord City | | | A B C |
| **Houston, TX** | | | | Marin County | | | A B C |
| Houston City | | | | Walnut Creek* | | | A B C D |
| **Indianapolis, IN** | | | | **San Jose, CA** | | | |
| Indianapolis City | | | A B | San Jose City | 11/73-8/75 | | A B |
| **Kansas City, MO-KS** | | | | Cupertino City | | | A B C |
| Kansas City | | | | Mountain View | 3/74-9/75 | 18 mo | A B |
| **Los Angeles-Long Beach** | | | | "        " | 3/76-3/77 | 12 mo | "  "  " |
| Long Beach City | | | A B | "        " | 4/77-4/78 | 12 mo | "  "  " |
| Los Angeles City | | | A B C D | Palo Alto City* | 12/73-11/74 | 11 mo | A B C |
| Duarte City | 10/79-4/80 | 6 mo | A B C | **Seattle-Everett, WA** | | | |
| Gardena City | | | B C | Seattle City | 7/78-11/78 | | A B |
| Los Angeles County* | | | A  C D | Everett City | | | A B |
| **Miami, FL** | | | | Lynnwood City | 6/78-10/78 | | A B C |
| Miami City | | | | King County | | | A B |
| Miami Beach | 2/80-3/80³ | 1 mo | A | Mercer Island* | | | A B |
| **Milwaukee, WI** | | | | **Tampa-St. Petersburg, FL** | | | |
| Milwaukee City | | | | Tampa City | | | |
| **Minneapolis-St. Paul, MN-WI** | | | | St. Petersburg City | | | |
| Minneapolis City | | | A B | **Washington, DC-MD-VA** | | | |
| St Paul City | | | | Washington City | 2/76-2/80⁶ | 6 mo | A B C D |
| Little Canada | 12/79 | | ‡ | "        " | 2/80-8/80 | 6 mo | "  "  "  " |
| Wayzata | | | A B | Montgomery County | 7/79-11/79 | 4 mo | A B C D |
| **Nassau-Suffolk, NY** | | | | | | | |
| No Central City | | | | | | | |
| *§ | | | | | | | |

CODES

I   Ordinance Pending

*   Additional outside Central City jurisdictions in the
    SMSA having ordinances.

A.  Tenant Protection
B.  Buyer Protection
C.  Rental Stock Protection
D.  Preservation of Low- and Moderate-Income Housing

§   New York City has special state statutory authority
    covering elderly persons in conversions.

§   Local jurisdictions in Nassau, Rockland, and Westchester
    Counties may also be covered by state law protections for
    the elderly by passing a local option ordinance.  The
    following communities have opted to be covered by State
    law.

### Nassau County ( Nassau/Suffolk)

| | |
|---|---|
| Great Neck | Great Neck Plaza |
| Long Beach | North Hempstead |
| Thomaston | Rockville Centre |
| Russell Gardens | |

### Rockland County (New York SMSA)

| | |
|---|---|
| Clarkstown | Nyack |
| Haverstraw | Spring Valley |

### Westchester County (New York SMSA)

| | | |
|---|---|---|
| Eastchester | Greenborough | Pleasantville |
| Harrison | Hastings-on-Hudson | Port Chester |
| Larchmont | Irvington | Tarrytown |
| Mt. Vernon | Mamaroneck | White Plains |
| | New Rochelle | |

FOOTNOTES

1.  A Baltimore ordinance was struck down by a lower court;
    this decision was sustained on appeal.
2.  A Chicago moratorium ordinance was struck down in Federal Court.
3.  A Miami moratorium and conversion ordinance was struck down by a
    lower court and the case is on appeal.
4.  A Fort Lee,N.J. moratorium was struck down by a lower court.
5.  A Verona N.J. moratorium was struck down by a local court.
6.  A Washington, D.C. moratorium was struck down by a lower court.
    The lower court's ruling was sustained on appeal.

of low- and moderate-income housing. It relies primarily on the information collected from local ordinances in the 37 largest SMSAs. This information is summarized in exhibit XII-1.

Temporary Conversion Moratoria. As a threshold response to significant or impending conversion activity, a number of communities have imposed temporary moratoria on further activity. A moratorium is generally designed to preserve the status quo while the full ramifications of conversion activity on tenants, buyers, the rental stock, and low- and moderate-income housing is assessed and an appropriate local policy is developed.

Nationally, moratorium regulations have been passed by more than one-third of the local governments with conversion ordinances (6 percent of all local jurisdictions). These moratoria generally range from 30 days to one year, with more than one half running for one year. In a few cases, the moratorium has been for more than one year.

In Washington, D.C., for example, a series of moratoria on cooperative and condominium conversions has occurred since 1976. The use of a moratorium was complicated by the City Council's recurring use of its 90 day emergency legislative authority which does not require Congressional approval. While the 1976 Condominium Act regulated condominium conversions, cooperative conversions remained unregulated. Therefore, a 180 day moratorium on cooperative conversions was imposed in November 1976 to allow the city council time to pass permanent legislation on the subject. This moratorium was extended ten times over a period of three years. However, before the enactment of permanent cooperative legislation in September 1979, and because of rapidly increasing conversion activity, the city council  passed a new moratorium (Emergency Condominium and Cooperative Stabilization Act of 1979) for 90 days and created a study commission. The 90-day moratorium with certain "hardship" exemptions granted to converters was extended twice through emergency legislation. The operation of the latest 90-day moratorium was enjoined by a D.C. court but the injunction has been stayed pending an appeal. 4/ However, the city council passed a new 180 day moratorium in permanent legislation (reviewed by Congress and thus free from the legal issue raised in the above lawsuit) which became effective February 23, 1980. During the new moratorium period the District of Columbia City Council will consider new legislation on condominium and cooperative conversions.

---

4/  Washington Home Owner Council, Inc. v. District of Columbia, A.2d ___ (D.C. Court of Appeals, Case No. 79-1053, May 28, 1980.) The court held that the adoption of successive, interim moratoria on condominium and cooperative conversions was unauthorized by the District of Columbia Self-Government and Government Reorganization Act.

Nationally, moratoria are reported more frequently in the western and north central areas of the country, and least often in the northeast and south. Communities with populations of 50,000 to 250,000 more frequently employ moratoria. Eight of 21 central cities in the 37 largest metropolitan areas had passed a moratorium on conversion activity prior to the development of permanent legislation. 5/ Three central cities currently have moratoria on conversion activity pending the development of permanent legislation.

Several moratoria enacted by municipal governments have been struck down in state courts, principally on state preemption grounds, and one moratorium has been enjoined by a Federal court on constitutional grounds because it was judged vague and arbitrary.

Moratorium legislation, as defined here, consists of short-term and emergency measures pending the development of permanent conversion regulation under zoning, subdivision, planning or other areas of municipal law. However, many of the permanent ordinances passed by municipalities, either incidentally or by design, result in a partial or complete ban on future conversion activity. The uses of vacancy rate conditions, building or design standards, or broad approval criteria concerning the social impact of conversions, have often resulted in a virtual stoppage of conversion activity.

Tenant Protections. The most prevalent form of protection afforded tenants in a building undergoing conversion is a written notice of the proposed conversion or intent to convert. Three-fourths of local conversion ordinances require a minimum period of notice. (See table XII-3 Appendix ) Most of the notification periods run from 90 to 180 days, and many require that tenants be informed that their apartment must be vacated at end of the notice period. Many cities also require that tenants be given first option to purchase their own or another unit in the building. This "right of first refusal" often runs from 30 to 180 days and is tied to the notice of conversion or eviction arrangement. A number of cities prohibit the harassment of tenants before or during the conversion process and put limits on rent increases during the remainder of the tenants' residence in the building. Some localities require that the converter provide relocation information and services, moving expenses, or other benefits to tenants displaced by the conversion. About one-fourth of all communities with conversion ordinances require some form of relocation assistance. Only a few jurisdictions require tenant approval or consent to a conversion, or accord tenant groups a "right of first refusal" to purchase the building.

---

5/ See exhibit XII-1 for a detailed review of moratorium and other conversion legislation in the 37 largest metropolitan areas.

Special protections to the elderly, families with children, or the handicapped are provided by several localities. Nationally, one in five communities with conversion ordinances provide special protections for elderly renters, and only 15 percent provide special protection for low-income renters. Communities with heavy conversion activity are more likely than others to have passed ordinances giving protection to elderly tenants. These special protections generally include extended notification to vacate periods or rights to purchase, and relocation benefits. The few cities with regulations permitting lifetime tenancies to renters usually apply only to the elderly and handicapped.

The nature and extent of tenant protection measures is discussed in greater detail in the following pages. 6/

1. Notice of public hearing. Of the ordinances analyzed, only one local jurisdiction outside California requires notice of a public hearing prior to conversion. 7/ Hearing and notice provisions in California are often tied to the conversion approval procedure under California's unique Subdivision Map Act, and/or the Coastal Act of 1976, 8/ by which local governments regulate proposed development in accordance with local general plans. 9/

2. Notice of a proposed conversion and notice of eviction. The most frequent provision of local conversion ordinances is the requirement that the sponsor, declarant, or owner provide written notice to tenants of the intended conversion. The purpose is to provide

---

6/ The ordinances referred to in this chapter are cited in Appendix 2.

7/ Lynnwood, Washington requires five days notice of the city council's hearing on an application to convert rental housing to multiple ownership.

8/ Subdivision Map Act (Government Code Section 66424); Section 30620 of the Coastal Act of 1976.

9/ Local variations of hearing notice provisions in California include the following: Riverside requires both notice of a hearing and an appeal for an "aggrieved party" within ten days of a decision; San Francisco limits the notice requirement to conversion of building with five or more units; Walnut Creek, Duarte, Mountain View, and Oakland tie specific notice periods of five or ten days to Tentative Map approval; Concord, San Diego, and San Jose tie similar periods to Planning Commission approval of a conditional use permit; and Garden Grove to site plan approval. Montclair and Los Angeles require ten and fifteen days notice of any hearing.

**Additional Protections for Elderly and Handicapped Tenants**

| | Additional Notice of Conversion | Lease Extensions | Life Tenancies | Additional Decision Period to Extend Lease | Extended Right to First Refusal | Relocation Assistance |
|---|---|---|---|---|---|---|
| Beachwood, OH | X | | | | | |
| Boston, MA | X | | | | | |
| Cheltenham, PA | X | X | | | | |
| Chicago, IL | | X | | X | X | |
| Duarte, CA | | X | | | | |
| Indianapolis, IN | X | | | | | |
| Lakewood, OH | X | | | | | |
| Los Angeles, CA | X | X | | | | X |
| Lower Marion, PA | X | X | | X | X | |
| Lyndhurst, OH | X | | | X | X | |
| Minneapolis, MN | X | | | | | |
| Montgomery Co, MD | | | | | | X |
| New York, NY | | | X | | | |
| Newport Beach, CA | | X | | | | |
| Oakland, CA | | X | X | | | |
| Oceanside, CA | X | | | | | |
| San Diego, CA | | X | | | | |
| San Francisco, CA | | | X | | | |
| Skokie, IL | | | X | | | X |
| Walnut Creek, CA | | | | | | X |
| Wayzata, MN | X | | | | | |

tenants time to consider the conversion and either decide to buy a
unit or to seek alternative housing. The timing and length of notice
varies, but the most frequent approach is to mandate 120 days written
notice of conversion, after which the tenant may be evicted subject
to other eviction procedures. 10/ In some cases, the notice periods
range from 90 days to one year. 11/ Two-thirds of the local ordinances
analyzed use this approach, and in about one-fourth of these cases,
the statute specifies that the tenant may maintain occupancy for the
specified minimum period, or for the remainder of the existing lease,
whichever is longer. 12/ Usually the tenant must request in writing
that an expiring lease be extended to the end of the notice period.
About one-fourth of the localities which employ the notice of conver-
sion/eviction also provide additional time (usually 60 days) before
requiring elderly, handicapped or low income tenants to vacate. 13/

> Boston requires a one year notice period for tenants
> in rent-controlled or vacancy decontrolled units.
> This notice is extended to two years for tenants who
> are 62 years or older, disabled or who have incomes
> at or below established limits.

---

10/ The 120 days notice period is clearly the most common. However,
it should be noted that in some cases, particularly California,
state law mandates at least 120 days notice.

11/ Denver, Colorado and University City, Missouri require only 90
days; Montgomery County, Maryland, Webster Grove, Missouri, and San
Diego, California, 180 days; Philadelphia, Pennsylvania, Boston,
Massachusetts, Lower Merion, Pennsylvania and Mountain View, California,
one year.

12/ The municipalities include:  Indianapolis, Indiana; Arlington
Heights, and Chicago, Illinois; Lakewood, Lyndhurst, Ohio; Orange
County, California; Boston, Massachusetts; Philadelphia and Lower
Merion, Pennsylvania.  Under California State law, among others,
this may be assumed; a developer may not break an existing lease for
conversion purposes alone.

13/ Montgomery County, Maryland provides an additional 180 days for
the elderly.  Chicago, Indianapolis, Indiana; Minneapolis, Minnesota;
Wayzata, Minnesota; Oceanside, California; and Lakewood and Lyndhurst
provide an additional 60 days.  Beachwood, Ohio has a 90-day minimum, with at least four additional months based on length of
residence and a minimum of six months for the elderly.

Some of the ordinances specify a particular point in the conversion process at which notice must be given to tenants.  This is usually the filing date for the declaration or property report, 14/ or the approval of the conversion application, 15/ or at other points during the conversion process. 16/

In addition, most ordinances providing for tenant notification of a proposed conversion require that during such notice period any prospective tenants must be advised of the proposed conversion prior to signing a lease.

3.  Right to continued occupancy, lease extensions and lease renewals. While there is considerable overlap between the ordinances described in the previous section and those discussed here the provisions described here grant additional protection to tenants nearing the end of their leases.  Some conversion ordinances address the problem broadly, giving all tenants a right to continued occupancy for a specified period of time, while others grant a right to lease extensions or lease renewals.

One municipality has attempted to ban evictions for conversion purposes altogether.

> In Brookline, Massachusetts, the rent control bylaws
> state that no tenant who occupied a rental unit
> prior to the recording of the master deed for a condo-
> minium may be evicted by the landlord seeking to
> convert the building, or by the owner of a unit seeking
> to occupy the unit.

San Francisco's conversion ordinance is the only one that uses the term "lease renewal" in granting tenants an additional occupancy period.  Any tenant can renew a lease for one year following approval of the Final Subdivision Map.  The California cities of Cupertino, Garden Grove, and Palo Alto provide a 90-day lease extension if the lease expires before (or at the time) the Final Subdivision Report is issued or sales begin.

---

14/  Evanston, Illinois; Montgomery County, Maryland Everett, Seattle, King County, and Mercer Island, Washington; Lower Merion, Pennsylvania.

15/  District of Columbia and Lynnwood, Ohio.

16/  In some California cities, the notice is dated from a specified point in the Subdivision Map approval process; in Chula Vista, it begins with the establishment of a firm sale price; in Oceanside, 180 days notice can begin either with the notice of conversion or prior to commencement of sales.

Oakland, San Francisco, and Walnut Creek, California and New York
City are the only conversion ordinances analyzed that grant life-
tenancies to elderly tenants. 17/ Several local jurisdictions have
limited provisions for continued occupancy for protected classes of
tenants. 18/

4.  Right to quiet enjoyment.  A number of local jurisdictions have
ordinances designed to protect tenants from harassment during
the conversion process.  Several limit the timing and frequency
that a tenant's apartment can be shown to prospective purchasers. 19/
Others prohibit or limit any repairs or remodeling of the unit. 20/
Another type of protection is the prohibition or regulation of rent

---

17/  New York City, under state law, must offer life tenancies to
tenants (and spouses) 62 years of age or older on the date the
offering plan is declared effective.  This right is restricted to
tenants with a household income below $30,000, who maintain the
unit as their primary residence, and who have resided in the unit
for at least two years.  See exhibit XII-1 for the list of jurisdictions
in Nassau, Rockland, and Westchester Counties which have adopted the
"protection for the elderly" provisions.

18/  Skokie, Illinois grants elderly and handicapped tenants, as
well as families with children, a minimum lease extension of six
months, measured from the date the condominium declaration is filed.
Los Angeles and Los Angeles County both provide one year of continued
occupancy during relocation eforts; the city further states that
there is no limit on continued occupancy during relocation efforts
for the elderly, disabled, households with minor children, or
residents of low to moderate income housing.

19/  Chicago's ordinance provides that no occupied unit can be
shown to third parties for 30 days after the tenant receives notice
of the owner's intent to record the condominium documents.  Lakewood
and Lyndhurst state that the tenant shall not unreasonably withhold
consent from the developer to enter a unit to inspect or make
repairs, or to show it to third parties, but condition this provision
by defining entry by the landlord more than twice within a seven
day period as an "abuse of the right of access."

20/  Marin County and Oakland, California prohibit any remodeling
of an occupied unit for 30 days after the Final Subdivision Report
is issued.  Los Angeles County and Evanston, Illinois  have adopted
broadly worded measures stating that no remodeling or repairs may be
made until the tenant vacates or purchases the unit (Los Angeles
County), or while the unit is occupied (Evanston).

increases during the period the tenant is entitled to remain in the unit. 21/

While it is obvious that a tenant may not be evicted without good or just cause during any notice period contained in a particular conversion ordinance, some measures (King County and Seattle, Washington) contain an explicit statement to this effect. In addition, these ordinances forbid the sale of any unit if, in the preceding 150 day period, any tenant has been evicted without good cause.

5. Minimum tenant purchase or tenant approval. There are only a few ordinances in effect today which require that a certain percentage of tenants must either approve a conversion or agree to purchase units before the conversion can proceed. However, some ordinances have tenant approval provisions which exempt the conversion from other statutory requirements if the required tenant approval is obtained. This type of local law is discussed elsewhere in the study. 22/ The City of Newport Beach, California requires that at least 30 percent of the tenants express written interest in exercising their option to purchase their unit. San Francisco's conversion ordinance states that an application for conversion may not be filed unless 40 percent of the tenants have either signed intent to purchase forms, or indicate that they are eligible for, and interested in, lifetime leases. Those qualifying for lifetime leases are included in the 40 percent needed for conversion.

---

21/ Everett and King County, Washington forbid a rent increase during the 120 day notice period. Oakland forbids any increase after the date of notice conversion is given, for as long as 12 months after the date the Tentative Map is filed. San Francisco prohibits any increase between filing and relocation, up to a maximum of one year. Lower Merion's ordinance prevents any rent increase for one year after the condominium is approved. The longest ban on rent increases is found in the Walnut Creek ordinance, which prohibits rent increases for two years measured from the time of the application to convert until the unit is sold (or until the application is withdrawn) In Beachwood, Ohio the rent of existing tenants cannot be raised more than the average increase in the Consumer Price Index over the previous 12 months. The Mercer Island, Washington, conversion ordinance states that during the 120 day notice period, rent levels cannot exceed 110 percent of the average monthly rent collected in the 12 months prior to the notice of conversion.

22/ See the section below on the "Protection of the Rental Stock" for a discussion of tenant approval, exceptions to vacancy rate, or other prohibitions on conversion.

6. <u>Right of first refusal provisions.</u> The exclusive right of a tenant to purchase his or her unit is loosely referred to as a "right of first refusal." This is one of the most frequent tenant protections provided. This right generally lasts 30 to 180 days, with most ordinances specifying 60 or 90 days, measured from varying points in the conversion process. <u>23</u>/ Some ordinances provide secondary periods during which subtenants may exercise the right of first refusal if the tenant has not. <u>24</u>/ Several ordinances prohibit the developer from offering the unit on more favorable terms for a certain period after rejection by the tenant, and may grant the tenant an additional period to consider any new offer. <u>25</u>/

------------------------------------------------------------

<u>23</u>/ The shortest right of first refusal period (30 days from delivery of the Progress Report) can be found in the Skokie conversion ordinance and in Mercer Island's ordinance (30 days beginning at the end of the 120-day notice period). Indianapolis gives tenants 45 days after the notice of conversion. Washington, D.C.; Atlanta, Georgia; Montgomery County; Minneapolis; Wayzata; and Webster Grove require 60 days right of first refusal after notice of conversion. Under the Subdivision Map Act, all California jurisdictions must require the developer to provide at least 60 days. This is measured from the Final Subdivision Public Report in Long Beach, Marin County, Montclair, Mountain View, Oakland, San Diego, and Santa Ana. Duarte and Oceanside measure from the Final Report or start of sales, whichever is later. Some California jurisdictions grant 90 days, again either from the Final Report or commencement of sales: Concord, Cupertino, Garden Grove, La Mesa, Orange County, Palo Alto, San Jose. A 90 day right of first refusal measured from notice of conversion is provided in Beachwood, Lakewood, and Lyndhurst. Arlington Heights, Chicago, Evanston and Lynnwood require 120 days notice. Lower Merion requires 180 days from filing of condominium documents, and Philadelphia, 180 days from notice of conversion.

<u>24</u>/ The Washington, D.C. conversion ordinance provides that the tenant has a right of first refusal for the first 60 days. If the tenant does not exercise this right, any subtenant may exercise it during the succeeding 60 days. The D.C. ordinance contains the caveat that both the tenant and the subtenant must be in compliance with the lease, and the unit must be retained without substantial alteration. Everett, King County, and Seattle provide subtenants a right to first purchase.

<u>25</u>/ Atlanta prohibits better offers for 120 days; Minneapolis for 180 days, and King County for one year. Evanston prohibits better offers for 180 days, without offering those terms first to the tenant, who then has 15 days to accept the offer. Lakewood and Lyndhurst have a similar provision for 90 days and ten additional days to consider a new offer.

A few of the ordinances provide extended refusal periods for protected classes of tenants. 26/ Every ordinance with a right of first refusal provision also provides for notice to the tenant of such a right.

7. Tenant group right of first purchase. Three of the municipal conversion ordinances analyzed contain provisions which grant a right to purchase the building to a tenant organization. Each provision is markedly different and merits special attention.

> The Washington, D.C. ordinance mandates that the landlord may not sell a building containing more than four units unless the landlord first offers the building to a tenant organization at a bona fide price. Such an organization, in turn, has 90 days within which to contract with the landlord for the purchase of the building. If no tenant organization exists the tenants are given an additional 30 days to form an organization legally capable of owning real estate. No down payment over five percent may be required and settlement must take place within 120 days of contract. These two conditions also apply to the individual tenant's right of first refusal.

> In Montgomery County, Maryland, prior to the transfer of title to any rental facility, the contract purchaser must give written notice of the proposed acquisition to each tenant of the facility. The tenants, in turn, are given 30 days to form a tenant organization (which must represent either 25 percent of the units or five units, whichever is greater). At the end of the 30-day period, the tenant group then has 120 days to execute a contract with the owner to purchase the property and then must settle on the purchase within 180 days of the notice of proposed transfer.

> Minneapolis requires that the conversion notice state that the tenants may form an organization for the purpose of offering to buy the building. However, the ordinance goes on to specifically disclaim that this creates a right on the part of tenant organization to purchase such property, nor does it obligate anyone to negotiate with, finance, or sell such property to the tenants' association.

---

26/ Chicago extends the right of first refusal from 120 to 180 days for the elderly and handicapped; and Lakewood and Lyndhurst from 90 to 120 days.

8. <u>Relocation assistance.</u>  Some tenants will choose not to purchase their units.  About one-fourth of the local jurisdictions which have conversion ordinances mandate relocation assistance for nonpurchasing tenants, either in the form of moving or relocation expenses, or through a more comprehensive relocation assistance plan.  Those jurisdictions which require the developer to make assistance payments may specify that moving expenses are to be paid; either the actual moving costs subject to a maximum, or some set amount, usually in addition to other forms of assistance. 27/  Other ordinances may require the developer to make relocation assistance payments which are not directly tied to moving expenses.  This amount may be set by the ordinance, or derived from a formula based on monthly rent or other factors. 28/   Some of the ordinances analyzed limit relocation

---

27/ Evanston requires the developer to pay actual moving costs, or the higher of $300 or one month's rent.  The District of Columbia specifies $125 times the number of rooms in the unit, to be paid before the tenant vacates the unit (provided the tenant has given notice of intent to vacate.)  San Francisco requires payment up to $1,000 or an amount fixed by a Relocation Schedule; Los Angeles and Los Angeles County require $500 moving expenses in addition to relocation assistance; Santa Ana requires reimbursement of moving expenses up to $500 per unit.  It should be noted that California cities and counties which are under the jurisdiction of the California Coastal Commission must include provisions for relocation assistance.

28/ Seattle requires $350 per unit to be paid to any tenant or sub-tenant who vacates voluntarily or involuntarily.  King County requires $350 or two months rent, whichever is greater, to be paid to any tenant vacating after the 120-day notice period.  The landlord must also pay the depreciated value of any leasehold improvements made by the vacating tenant.  In Everett, an unusual provision limits assistance (of $350) to any tenant who moves in within 60 days prior to the notice of conversion and is not notified of such conversion.  Duarte provides a payment equal to one and one-half times the montly rent, while Walnut Creek stipulates two times the monthly rent.  Los Angeles County requires $1,000 be paid each household or, at the tenant's option, the monthly rent multiplied by the number of years the tenant occupied the unit.  Oceanside and San Diego mandate payment of one and two months current rent, respectively.

assistance to elderly or low- to moderate-income tenants, or provide additional benefits for these protected tenants. 29/ Two of the ordinances examined have additional provisions which resemble rental subsidies.

> In Washington, D.C., the measure stipulates that any-
> one displaced who has been a tenant for at least a
> year must be paid an amount equal to: (1) the
> difference between 25 percent of the monthly family
> income and the rent to be paid in the first month
> after relocation; or (2) the difference between the
> old rent and the new rent. The formula to be used
> would depend upon whether the old rent was more or
> less than 25 percent of the family income. Either
> amount must be multiplied by 24 to arrive at the
> figure which the converter must pay. For the suc-
> ceeding 36 months, the city makes the same payments.

> The City of Los Angeles requires that a rental sub-
> sidy, equal to the increase in rent necessitated by
> relocation, must be paid for one year, with a $100
> per month limit. An unconditional $500 payment
> must be made in addition to the rental subsidy.
> Specially protected classes (tenants over 62 years
> of age; handicapped or disabled tenants; families
> with one or more minor children; tenants occupying
> low- or moderate-income housing) are entitled to a
> $2,500 payment per household, in lieu of relocation
> expenses and rental subsidies.

Some municipalities require the developer to formulate relocation assistance plans, either in lieu of, or in addition to, any payment of moving expenses or other cash allowances. The relocation plans are often part of broader tenant assistance programs mandated by the particular ordinance. One frequent requirement is a list of comparable

---

29/ Montgomery County, Maryland provides $750 in moving expenses to those meeting or below income guidelines. The City of Los Angeles provides for a substantially greater payment ($2,500 per household) to special classes of protected tenants, including persons over 62, those who are handicapped or disabled, or households with minor children. In San Francisco, the relocation payments specified are only available to tenants during the 120-day period or the term of their lease. However, the elderly may receive this payment whenever they elect to move. Oceanside increases the payment from one to two months rent for low income tenants. Evanston and Skokie limit the provision of moving expenses to tenants eligible for or receiving (respectively) Section 8 housing subsidies.

rental housing available in the immediate area. 30/ A few communities require a developer to post security, usually a fixed amount per unit, to provide relocation costs. 31/ Several conversion ordinances not only require the developer to provide relocation services, but also mandate that a comprehensive plan be designed to minimize displacement in the first instance. 32/

A few cities offer tenants the services of their own relocation agencies in addition to developer efforts. In Washington, D.C., the city's Rental Accommodations Office furnishes information on comparable substitute housing and government housing program. The developer must also provide tenants with forms to apply for relocation expenses and housing assistance payments.

9. The right to cancel existing leases. Most of the conversion ordinances analyzed which provide for relocation assistance also contain a provision which enables tenants in a building about to be converted to terminate their leases upon notice, usually written, to the landlord. Thus, a tenant who has found new housing is not

---

30/ Walnut Creek (list of other rentals available in the area); Santa Ana (plan setting forth comparable replacement rental housing); and Oceanside (report listing comparable dwellings, but allows the developer to provide his own tenant-assistance plan, subject to approval by the City Council). Other ordinances that require relocation assistance programs include Mountain View (developer must provide temporary relocation of tenants during renovation); San Francisco (developer must provide temporary and permanent relocation service during the 120-day notice period or lease extension period); and Los Angeles (a covenant and agreement must be executed which outlines a relocation plan). Again, localities under the jurisdiction of the California Coastal Commission must provide relocation assistance.

31/ Santa Ana requires the developer to post security equal to $500 multiplied by the number of units being converted. Los Angeles County and San Diego specify that $500 per unit must be deposited for costs incurred in providing relocation assistance to special classes of tenants.

32/ Cupertino permits the developer to consider discounts, extended leases and moving allowances in order to mitigate the effect of lack of comparable housing accommodations. Oakland requires both a Preliminary and Final Assistance Program designed to minimize displacement as well as to assist tenants in relocating. In Orange County, an application to convert must include a Housing Program which contains a plan to provide affordable housing in the project as well as a relocation plan for displaced tenants.

bound to the lease and may move without delay. The typical lease-cancellation provision requires 30 days written notice to the landlord and allows the tenant to exercise the right of cancellation any time after notice of an impending conversion is given by the landlord. 33/ Notice periods in other ordinances range from 15 days to 120 days prior to vacating an apartment. 34/ The right to cancel a lease is sometimes linked to a special class of tenants, such as the elderly. 35/

10. Miscellaneous tenant protection measures. There are many miscellaneous or isolated tenant protection provisions found in particular conversion ordinances in addition to those discussed so far. Various tenant concerns, such as unit price, 36/ protection from landlord retaliation, 37/ and appeals from conversion approvals, 38/ are

---

33/ Cupertino, Garden Grove, Oakland, Palo Alto, Montgomery County, San Francisco, Skokie.

34/ Orange County only requires 15 days notice to the landlord by any tenant. Lakewood and Lyndhurst grant the right to cancel, with 45 days written notice, to anyone whose tenancy expires after 90 days from notice of conversion. Evanston and Webster Grove, Missouri require 60 days notice. In addition, Webster Grove stipulates that anyone who receives a notice of conversion within 30 days of signing a lease has 15 days to serve a 15-day notice of intent to vacate. Philadelphia requires 90 days notice to the landlord. Everett and Seattle require the most notice, 120 days, prior to vacating. The District of Columbia does not afford tenants any right to cancel existing leases, even though the District's ordinances contain extensive provisions dealing with relocation.

35/ San Francisco, while having a 30-day notice provision, only grants the right of cancellation to elderly tenants under life-tenancies.

36/ The City of Duarte's ordinance contains a unit price provision to the effect that the maximum price to be charged for a converted unit shall be the fair market value of the building, plus 20 percent of the fair market value and conversion costs, divided by the number of units.

37/ Mountain View and Oceanside both prohibit any kind of retaliation against tenants who oppose the conversion. Oceanside's ordinance also states that a tenant cannot waive any protection provision contained in the ordinance.

38/ The right of certain persons to appeal approval of a conversion application is contained in the ordinances of San Diego (any "affected tenant"), San Francisco (at least "20 percent of the tenants") and Riverside (any "aggrieved party").

typical of the areas covered. Finally, Montgomery County has a unique provision which grants any group that consists of 25 percent or more of the tenants the right to designate an engineer to do an independent study of the property being converted. The provision also obliges the owner to give the tenant's engineer access to the property to perform a complete inspection.

Buyer Protections. Most municipal ordinances seek to protect buyers through substantive standards concerning the physical condition of the building, and/or requiring full disclosure of the legal document-ation, financial status, and existing and future physical condition of the building. Many communities require condominium conversion to meet certain development standards, often those for new condominium construction, relating to parking, open space and recreational facili-ties, acoustics, separate utility metering, storage space and minimum unit size. Most ordinances mandate a city inspection for building code violations and require either their correction or disclosure to potential buyers. In some cases, the disclosure of code violations must be accompanied by an estimated cost to correct. Most cities require that any building code inspection results must be included in a property report prepared by an independent, registered engineer or architect.

Nationally, more than half of all communities with conversion ordi-nances attempt to protect unit purchasers by requiring that a property condition report be prepared on the building or complex. Besides presenting information on code compliance, the property report must assess the physical condition of the major structural and mechanical components of the building, their useful life and estimated cost to repair. A number of communities use the code inspection and property condition reports as key elements of a full disclosure package provided to prospective purchasers of a converted condominium. In addition, many communities require additional disclo-sures concerning the legal documentation, and past and projected operating budget of the building, as well as information on any warranties provided.

With regard to warranties, several cities mandate warranties on common areas and individual units for specific time periods, and, in a few cases, require an escrow fund to cover claims under warranties. Other consumer protections include the right to cancel or rescind contracts of purchase and the regulation of design and development standards.

The nature and extent of these provisions are discussed in detail in the following pages. Many communities with buyer protection ordinances are in states which also have condominium conversion protection measures. Thus, in some cases, municipal ordinances overlap with state buyer protec-tion measures in some respects, while in other respects local ordinances refine or substantially expand upon state condominium buyer protections.

1. <u>Building inspection, code compliance and disclosure</u>. Most ordinances mandate that all units to be converted must be inspected by
the appropriate local agency. Ordinarily, this is a department
concerned with building inspections and fire code violations. <u>39</u>/
Ordinances requiring a code inspection invariably require that any
violations thus discovered be corrected. <u>40</u>/ Many of the ordinances
that mandate inspection and code compliance also require disclosure
to prospective purchasers of a list of uncorrected violations and
the estimated cost of cure, or a statement of compliance with the
current codes. <u>41</u>/ A few ordinances provide for exceptions to code
compliance, usually if an escrow fund or bond has been created to
cover the uncured violations, <u>42</u>/ or if the items in question were
in compliance at the time of construction. <u>43</u>/

---

<u>39</u>/ Municipalities with a code inspection requirement include Chula
Vista, Concord, Costa Mesa, Cupertino, Gardena, La Mesa, Long Beach,
Los Angeles, Marin County, Mountain View, Oceanside, Palo Alto, San
Francisco, San Jose, Santa Ana, Walnut Creek, Skokie, University
City, Webster Grove, Beachwood, Lakewood, Lyndhurst, Everett, King
County, Mercer Island, and Seattle. Evanston and St. Louis require
a Condominium Code Assessment Report. In addition, the installation
of either fire or smoke detectors (or both) is specifically required
in Concord, La Mesa, Riverside, Walnut Creek, and University City.

<u>40</u>/ Chula Vista, and Costa Mesa, California, and University City,
Missouri, require that code compliance be indicated in the certifi-
cate of occupancy.

<u>41</u>/ Municipalities with statutes which contain this triad of
provisions include Concord, Marin County, San Jose, Washington,
D.C., Atlanta, Arlington Heights, Indianapolis, Everett, King County
and Seattle. In Beachwood, Ohio any variances which were originally
granted in connection with the property must be reapproved.

<u>42</u>/ In San Francisco and Walnut Creek, compliance with the building
code is not required prior to approval of a conversion proposal if
an escrow fund has been established to assure that violations will
be corrected and repair work in progress will be completed. In
Lakewood and Lyndhurst, Ohio, while the individual units must be in
compliance, the common area need not be, if this fact is disclosed
in the public offering statement and a bond equal to the amount of
estimated repairs to the common area is posted.

<u>43</u>/ The Skokie, Illinois ordinance states that compliance with
current codes may be waived with respect to the number of parking
spaces, the number and location of units, or other provisions of
the code, if these items were in compliance with the code in force
when the unit was built.

2. <u>Preparation and publication of a building, property or engineer's report</u>. Since conversion of rental dwellings involves existing rather than new structures, the physical condition of the premises is an area of vital concern to prospective buyers. The majority of ordinances analyzed require the converter to have a building or property report prepared, usually by a professional engineer. This report must be filed with the appropriate local agency having jurisdiction over conversions (such as the Planning Commission or Zoning Board) prior to the offering of units for sale. Usually, the ordinances require presentation of this report to tenants and other prospective purchasers. The report generally covers major structural and mechanical components, including the foundation, roof, electrical, and plumbing systems. Some ordinances require only the basic report, 44/ but others require an additional report on estimated repairs and the estimated useful life of the property. 45/ Some California local ordinances require additional reports in reference to state disclosure laws. 46/

3. <u>Full disclosure requirements</u>. Although some jurisdictions require only the disclosure of the property report described above 47/, or the property report and the project budget 48/, most of the

---

44/ Costa Mesa, Cupertino, Duarte, La Mesa, Los Angeles, Montclair, Mountain View, Orange County, Palo Alto, San Jose, Webster Grove, Riverside, and Walnut Creek require only a property condition report.

45/ Gardena (five-year projection of estimated repairs required), Oakland, Oceanside, District of Columbia, Atlanta, Arlington Heights, Chicago, Skokie, Montgomery County, Lakewood, Lyndhurst, Lower Merion, Philadelphia, Everett, King County, Mercer Island and Seattle.

46/ Pest reports are required in Concord, Costa Mesa, Cupertino, Duarte, Gardena, Los Angeles, Mountain View, Oakland, and Upland. A soil and geological report must be prepared in Cupertino, Duarte, Oceanside. Duarte also requires an appraisal report of the property that is about to undergo a conversion.

47/ Property reports alone are required in Gardena (20 days prior to closing), in Chicago (within 45 days of notice of intent to convert), and in Indianapolis, Montgomery County, Everett, and Mercer Island (within 15 days of notice of conversion).

48/ This is the case in Cupertino, Lower Merion (within 30 days of the filing of the condominium documents), Philadelphia (last three year's expenses and first year projected budget), and King County.

XII-23

ordinances analyzed mandate that the building report, projected
budget, and various legal documents must be part of a disclosure
package presented to purchasers.  Typically, any disclosure material
that must be given to an purchaser must also be submitted to the
local agency responsible for review and approval of conversions.
Disclosure packages 49/ may vary in the timing of presentation and
the specificaton if additional information is to be provided. 50/

4.  Warranties.  Some conversion ordinances mandate that the
converter give warranties covering the common elements (including
the structural, electrical, plumbing, heating and air conditioning
systems), as well as the roof and elevator(s).  These warranties
typically run for one or two years and are secured by an escrow

---

49/  The disclosure package is alternatively described in different
conversion ordinances by the term "Information Sheet" (Mountain
View), "Public Offering Statement" (District of Columbia, Lakewood
and Lyndhurst), "Property Report" (Skokie), or "Condominium Disclosure
Statement" (Webster Grove).

50/  In Duarte, Garden Grove, and Mountain View disclosure must be
presented to purchasers at the time the offer of a right of first
refusal is made.  Atlanta, Arlington Heights (45 days prior to
closing); Evanston, Skokie, (before binding contract); Webster
Grove, Lakewood, Lyndhurst (15 days prior to contract); the latter
two municipalities provide for 10 percent of the sales price to be
forfeited as liquidated damages in the event such disclosure is not
made), and Seattle (at least seven days prior to contract).  Certain
jurisdictions specify other documents to be included in disclosure
requirements:  Palo Alto includes a Primer on Community Housing;
San Jose includes the FHA regulatory agreement, if any; while in
Walnut Creek and the District of Columbia the declaration and bylaws
for the owners' association must be presented within ten days of
recordation.  In Los Angeles, Montclair, and University City, the
developer must provide the purchaser with a set of the legal documents which outlines the rights and duties of the unit owner in the
condominium or cooperative.  Cupertino requires that upon request
the disclosures be presented in Spanish; San Jose requires all disclo-
sures to be printed in English and in Spanish.

fund established by the developer. 51/ The units and the mechanical systems within them are sometimes the subject of developer warranties as well, but usually for a shorter time than the major systems. 52/

> Montgomery County, Maryland has a comprehensive warranty requirement, covering three years for the common elements, and one year for the unit, backed by a reserve fund established by the developer.

In some areas, such as Minneapolis and Wayzata, the representations and descriptions made by the sponsor-developer create express warranties. In addition, an implied warranty of good condition and suitability for uses attached to the individual units, and may be waived only for specific defects.

5. Purchasers' right to cancel or rescind contracts of purchase. Many municipalities include a right of cancellation provision among the buyer protection safeguards set forth in their conversion ordinances. Such a provision usually grants purchasers the right to rescind a signed purchase contract within a certain period of time, measured either from the date the contract was executed or the date disclosure material was received by the purchaser. Typically, all down payments are required to be returned to the purchaser, with any accrued interest thereon. The right to rescind a purchase contract

---

51/ A one-year warranty period for the common areas is contained in the local ordinances of Concord (only as to a pool and pool equipment), Mountain View, Skokie, (from date of purchase), King County, Seattle and Montclair. Two year warranties are provided for in the District of Columbia (from the data of completion of the common areas); Evanston, Lakewood and Lyndhurst (from the date of the first unit transfer), and Lower Merion. Escrow funds must be established in Duarte; the District of Columbia (10 percent of conversion costs); Skokie (3 percent of sales price of each unit); Montgomery County; Lakewood and Lyndhurst (1 percent of sales price of each unit); King County; and Seattle (10 percent of the projected cost of repairs).

52/ One year warranties on the unit are provided by Duarte, Montclair, Mountain View, the District of Columbia (from date of conveyance), Montgomery County, Skokie (from purchase), Lakewood, Lyndhurst, King County and Seattle. Lower Merion requires a two-year warranty on the units.

must be accomplished within the stipulated period ranging from three
to 15 days after its signing. 53/ The longest period is provided
for in the Evanston ordinance, which gives a purchaser the right to
rescind a contract within 30 days of receipt of the disclosure statement, if the disclosure statement is not given at least 30 days
prior to contract.

6. Design and development standards. Although University City,
Missouri requires separate utility metering and water control, all
of the other local ordinances analyzed which contain standards
of design were from jurisdictions in California. The high level of
conversion activity and strong state and local regulations have
led to relatively strict standards for parking, open space, and
sound and noise correction. 54/

7. Miscellaneous buyer protection provisions. Several ordinances
contain one or two buyer protection provisions in addition to those
discussed to this point. Mountain View prohibits discrimination
against households with children. The District of Columbia and
Evanston require that purchaser down payments be deposited in
an interest bearing escrow account. Management contracts are

---

53/ Purchasers may rescind their contract within 15 days of execution
thereof in Montclair; Mountain View; the District of Columbia (or
within 15 days of delivery of an Offering Plan, whichever is later);
Skokie; Montgomery County (or within 5 days of receiving the Final
Property Report, or at any time prior to closing if the developer
has not complied with the conversion ordinance); King County; and
Seattle. In Lakewood and Lyndhurst, if the Offering Statement is
not given at least 15 days in advance of contract, the purchaser has
15 days to rescind. The purchaser may rescind at any time up to
closing in Everett and King County, if the required notices and
diclosures are not given. Minneapolis and Wayzata allow a purchaser
5 days after contract within which to rescind. A tenant in Lakewood
or Lyndhurst is given 3 days.

54/ The number of parking spaces per unit, and the number which must
be enclosed are specified in Concord, Cupertino, Garden Grove, Gardena,
Mesa, Riverside, San Jose, Long Beach, and Los Angeles. Open space
areas are also required in most of these cities; in San Jose, reservation of open space could be a condition of conditional use permit
approval. Noise standards are required in most of the California
jurisdictions analyzed; many require a preliminary acoustical report.
Separate utility metering, particularly for water is usually required,
as is space for laundry facilities. Chula Vista, Duarte, La Mesa,
Riverside, and Walnut Creek's ordinances address landscaping as well.

specifically dealt with in Mountain View; no management contract
may run for more than 30 days after the unit owners assume majority
control of the condominium. Skokie requires that no exclusive
management contract may run for more than one year after the control
of the project is turned over to the unit owners. In Chula Vista,
purchasers must be informed that the property has been converted
from a rental apartment project. Garden Grove requires that any
appliance over three years old be replaced by the developer.
Lynnwood requires that all current assessments for public streets
and utilities be paid prior to closing of title to the first converted unit.

Other provisions are more closely related to the actual purchase
contracts for the units. Lakewood and Lyndhurst enumerate "specific
unlawful representations" such as falsely stating the number of back-
up sales contracts or making a false statement with respect to a
future rent increase. Montgomery County treats as void any waiver
of purchasers' rights.

Arlington Heights' ordinance contains an unusual provision that
oral representations are not binding on the developer and the
purchasers are directed to read the Full Disclosure Report provided
to them. In contrast, the ordinances in Everett and Seattle which
state that it is unlawful to make oral representations which differ
from statements made in the disclosure documents.

Even after tenant and buyer protection measures are adopted, the
issue of a decrease in the rental stock caused by conversions still
remains. The next section reviews several municipal ordinances
which place significant conditions on the possibility of conversion
or limit the amount of annual conversion activity allowed within the
locality.


Protection of Rental Stock

A few municipalities, mostly in California, have adopted ordinances
that condition the conversion of rental units on the status of the
jurisdiction's rental stock. One means adopted by communities to
protect the rental stock involves prohibiting conversions where the
vacancy rate falls below a level generally considered to reflect a
stable rental market. Nationally, less than one-fifth of the communities with conversion ordinances have rental vacancy rate conditions
to conversions. The vacancy rate threshold adopted by communities
ranges from three to six percent. Many vacancy rate ordinances
provide an exception if a majority of the buildings' tenants consents
to the conversion. The imposition of a vacancy rate condition in a
conversion ordinance often creates, in effect, a moratorium on any
further conversion activity. A few communities place a percentage
or a numerical based quota on the annual number of conversions allowed,

while others only allow conversions according to a formula tied to the production of new rental housing. Finally, a number of cities, again predominantly in California, use discretionary authority (in lieu of or in addition to the above conditions on conversion) in approving or disapproving specific conversion projects. The criterion used for approving a specific project application may include the conversion's effect on tenant displacement and the rental market; the need for low- and moderate-income housing; and the conversion's effect on the general health and welfare of the community.

Vacancy Rate Minimum. A number of municipalities, predominantly in California, have adopted vacancy rate conditions on conversion activity. The most commonly used vacancy rate thresholds are three, five, and six percent. 55/ The imposition of a vacancy rate condition often results in the immediate and perhaps permanent bar on conversion activity because of the tight rental housing markets and lack of any new rental construction in many communities. For example, the first ordinance of this kind was developed by the city of Palo Alto in 1974 and since that time, no conversion has occurred in that city. Palo Alto's original ordinance, and a number of other vacancy rate ordinances provide an exception to the prohibition if a majority or more tenants approve the conversion. In addition, the District of Columbia exempts luxury or high rent units from the vacancy rate bar.

Quota Approaches. A few municipalities have utilized a quota approach to ensure that conversions do not disrupt the rental market at any given time or seriously deplete the amount of rental stock. Conversion quota ordinances involve two kinds of formulae: an annual percentage of the rental stock limitation; and annual numerical limitation. Walnut Creek's ordinance is an example of a percentage quota that limits conversions to 5 percent of the city's potentially convertible rental stock in any one year. Palo Alto, Montclair, and other cities with vacancy rate conditions of conversion have adopted a quota approach when the vacancy rate threshold is exceeded. Palo Alto and Montclair define the number of vacant units in excess of three percent as a "vacancy surplus" and permit application for conversions which do not exceed the vacancy surplus plus 40 percent. San Francisco sets the maximum number of units which may be converted within the city (1,000 units).

---

55/ District of Columbia (3 percent or lower, unless a majority of tenants consent to conversion or the units are luxury or high rent units); Gardena (3 percent or lower, unless two-thirds of the tenants approve the conversion); Cupertino (below five percent); Marin County (below 5 percent, Planning Commission may deny approval); Newport Beach (5 percent or lower, unless two-thirds of tenants approve conversion, or project's effect is minimal); Orange County (5 percent or lower); and San Bernardino (below 6 percent).

New Construction Replacement. A third approach taken in tying
conversion regulations to the local rental supply involves new
construction. 56/ A few communities have developed formulae which
permit a certain number of conversions upon the addition of new
rental stock. La Mesa's ordinance, for example, states that the
maximum number of units which may be converted within a given year
shall be equal to 50 percent of the yearly average number of apartment units constructed in the previous two fiscal years. As one of
its criteria for reviewing a conversion, Marin County considers
whether the conversion will reduce the existing rental/homeowner
dwelling unit ratio without replacement housing being provided. The
Mountain View ordinance conditions approval upon the production of
new rental units, and limits annual conversion approvals (developer
and tenant consent to 5 percent of the total units. 57/

> The City of Oakland's conversion ordinance states
> that for conversions of five or more units, the
> developer must add a new rental unit to the housing
> stock for each unit converted. A developer can
> gain approval by showing proof that he has "conver-
> sion rights" through projects he has generated or
> through contracts from others. Conversion rights
> may be generated through new rental construction;
> by increasing the number of units in an existing
> residential rental building; by converting a non-
> residential building to residential rental units;
> or through major rehabilitation of a residential
> building that had been vacant for one year prior to
> the commencement of the rehabilitation. The Oakland
> ordinance also creates conversion rights through
> the construction of a new condominium or cooperative
> if the owner of the project agrees to offer the units
> to the public as conventional rentals for at least
> seven years. However, a developer may have to
> provide replacement housing in the same neighborhood
> as the conversion project if the city finds that it
> will create a shortage or have other negative impacts
> in a specific area of the city.

-------------------------

56/ The distinction between ordinances discussed in this section
and the following section on preservation of low- and moderate-
income housing is the target group the replacement housing must serve

57/ A conversion will only be approved in Mountain View if an equal
number of new rental units has been added to the rental stock, or a
majority of tenants agree to purchase their units. However, the
deduction of rental units occasioned by the tenant approved conversion constitutes a "deficit" in the base number of rental units. A
non-tenant approved conversion could only occur when this deficit
plus a number of units equal to the conversion has been made up by
new rental construction.

Montgomery County's ordinance has a unique provision which allows certain county agencies to exercise a right of first refusal within 120 days of notice of a proposed transfer of title to the property.

Discretionary Approval Criterion. Many localities, in lieu of (or in addition to) setting a vacancy rate minimum or quota, have given a local agency (e.g., Planning Commission) the discretionary authority to approve or disapprove conversions, based upon certain criteria. Uniformly recurring factors to be considered include the effect on tenant displacement, 58/ the effect on rental market, the need for low- and moderate-income housing, 59/ and the effect on the general health and welfare of the community.

The effect of apartment conversions on the stock of low- and moderate-income housing is a particular area of concern for many localities. Many of the municipal ordinances which set criteria for conversion approval (see preceding discussion of "Discretionary Authority") include the potential effect on low- and moderate-income housing as a factor in the decision to approve or disapprove a conversion application. The next section reviews

---

58/ The Marin County ordinance states that if the number of rental units would be reduced to less than 25 percent of the total dwelling units, approval may be denied. Concord, Duarte, and San Francisco consider evidence of "warehousing" (vacancies being held) within a particular project prior to conversion. In Glastonbury, a conversion permit for any unit will not be issued until (1) a tenant has purchased a unit; or (2) the tenant has relocated or waived the right to relocate; or (3) 12 months have expired since the permit was applied for (24 months in the case of tenants 60 years or older); or (4) the party seeking conversion approval has increased the rental stock by 50 units in the previous 3 months. The District of Columbia cooperative ordinance prohibits conversion of a rental building to a cooperative unless (1) fewer than 50 percent of the units in the building are occupied; (2) 50 percent or more of the units are occupied and the majority of the heads of these households consent in writing to conversion; or (3) the building is a high rent housing accommodation. Under a newly enacted, 6 month moratorium legislation effective in February 1980, only cooperative conversions under exception (2) above are possible in limited situations.

59/ In Walnut Creek, once the quota of converted units has been reached, approval will only be granted if the developer provides for low- to moderate-income households and senior citizens, or provides for the construction of new rental housing, or donates land or funds for new rental housing or senior citizen housing. See also discussion on preservation of low- and moderate-income housing.

ordinances which have specific provisions designed to protect the availability of low- and moderate-income housing, either by mandating rental and homeownership set-asides in a conversion project, or by requiring the developer to contribute funds for the construction of new low- and moderate-income housing.

## Preservation of Low- and Moderate-Income Housing

A very small number of communities have adopted provisions which seek to preserve or enhance the supply of low- and moderate-income housing. While benefiting individual low- and moderate-income households in conversions, the key focus of these measures is the future availability of low- and moderate-income housing opportunities. Under these ordinances, converters may be required to set aside a specific number of units for low- and moderate-income rental or homeownership, provide low- and moderate-income units in a new construction project, or contribute to a public fund which furthers low- and moderate-income housing opportunities.

Conversion ordinances which seek to preserve low- and moderate-income housing can be divided into the following two major categories: (1) set-aside provisions; and (2) replacement of low- and moderate-income housing.

Set-Aside Provisions. Set-aside provisions usually require that a certain percentage of the converted units be made available for persons of low or moderate income. The Marin County ordinance states that its Planning Commission may require a reasonable percentage of converted units to be reserved for persons of moderate income. Orange County stipulates that where "affordable" rental units are to be converted, and there are less than 25 percent of "affordable" rental units in the area, at least 25 percent of the units for sale in a particular project must be reserved as affordable units.

San Francisco has the oldest and most detailed set-aside arrangements. The San Francisco ordinance requires that in converting a building of five or more units, the converter must provide a 10 percent set-aside of units for rental or purchase by low- and moderate-income households (or retain the number of existing low- or moderate-income units, whichever is greater). 60/ If the units are to be retained as rentals, the rental rate should remain at the same level as at the time of the application for conversion, or the maximum rent within

---

60/ A converter in San Francisco has two alternatives (discussed in the next section on replacement housing) to the above percentage set-aside in a conversion project in meeting the city's desire to preserve low- and moderate-income housing.

low or moderate income levels, whichever is lower. 61/ Such rental
units must remain in the low- and moderate-income housing stock for
20 years, unless sold during that time under the following procedure.
If the units are to be sold, they must be offered at prices which
do not exceed two and one-half times the median income of low- or
moderate-income families in the area. In order to ensure the units
are maintained for low- and moderate-income households, the city has
a right of first refusal to buy the unit at a sum equal to the original purchase price plus adjustments. 62/ The city must then sell
the unit to other qualified low- and moderate-income households.

Replacement of Low- and Moderate-Income Housing. In addition to
(and in lieu of) set-aside approaches, a few communities have sought
to protect their rental stock by requiring converters to allocate a
portion of newly constructed units for low- and moderate-income
household use, pay a tax, or contribute to a public fund to be used
for furthering low- and moderate-income housing opportunities. As
an alternative to set-aside requirements, San Francisco allows a
converter to construct an equal number of units which will be available for low- and moderate-income rental or homeownership, or pay
into a City Housing Development Fund a sum of money equal to 10
percent of the difference between the total of proposed sales prices
for units in the building and the sales prices of the units for
moderate-income buyers. The Housing Development Fund can be used to
reduce the costs of construction of new low- and moderate-income
housing or expand homeownership opportunities through down payment
assistance, co-ownership and/or "equity partnership" programs.

Los Angeles requires that $500 per unit be paid to the city for the
development of low- and moderate-income rental housing. In Los Angeles
County one percent of the purchase price of each unit must be deposited
with the County Housing Authority to be used to develop lower-income
housing. Oceanside requires two percent of the purchase price of each
converted unit to be paid into a fund for the development of low income
housing.

Policy Preferences of Local Officials

The majority of local officials (75%) feel that the state and Federal
levels of government should remain neutral rather than encourage or
discourage condominium or cooperative conversions. While local

61/ Annual rent increases are generally limited to the residential
rent component of the Bay Area Cost of Living Index.

62/ Adjustments include the costs of any improvements by the owner,
plus a "market appreciation" based on the housing component of the
Bay Area Cost of Living Index.

officials are more likely to favor an active role for local, rather than state or Federal governments, with regard to conversions, the majority (61%) still favors a neutral role at the local level in this area. (See table XII-6 App.) Of those who favor action by the local level of government, slightly more prefer efforts which encourage rather than inhibit conversions (16% versus 11%), while another 12 percent indicate the need for some other type of local involvement, such as monitoring of conversion activity.

Since some local officials interviewed in the survey represented jurisdictions in which no conversion activity has occurred, their responses were separated from those officials in areas with conversion activity even if such activity was limited. The policy preferences of these two groups of officials differ to some extent but not very significantly. Local officials whose jurisdictions have not experienced conversions are more likely to feel that state and local governments should remain neutral, while representatives of areas with conversions are more likely to believe that state and especially local governments should become involved in some way. About one-fifth of those representatives in areas with conversions favor local actions to discourage conversions compared to only nine percent of officials in areas without conversions. (See table XII-7 App.) However, there is no difference between these two sub-groups of officials in terms of the Federal role they preferred: 75 percent of both groups believe that the Federal government should remain uninvolved in conversion activity. (See table XII-6 App.)

Since 77 percent of all conversions nationally have occurred in the 37 largest SMSAs, officials in these larger metropolitan areas have the most experience with this phenomenon; therefore, their policy preferences are of particular interest. The majority, (about three-fourths) once again, prefers that the Federal and state levels of government remain neutral with respect to conversions; however, substantially fewer (51%) feel the same way about local government, although the other 49 percent do not represent a consensus. Their policy preferences are divided almost equally among three alternatives: encourage conversions (15%); discourage conversions (17%); or be involved in some other way (17%). (See table XII-8 App.) However, within these SMSAs, the policy preferences of local officals in central cities differ from those outside central cities, with the former being more likely to favor involvement which would encourage rather than discourage conversion.

Most of the local officials who favor government intervention to discourage conversions appear to be concerned with protecting the rights of tenants and unit buyers. Most of the policy options suggested by this group of officials center on restrictive conversion regulations, promoting a healthy rental stock and protecting those renter households affected by conversions. Those who favor government encouragement of conversions often propose government assistance

# Policy Preferences of Local Officials for
# Government Intervention in Conversion Activity

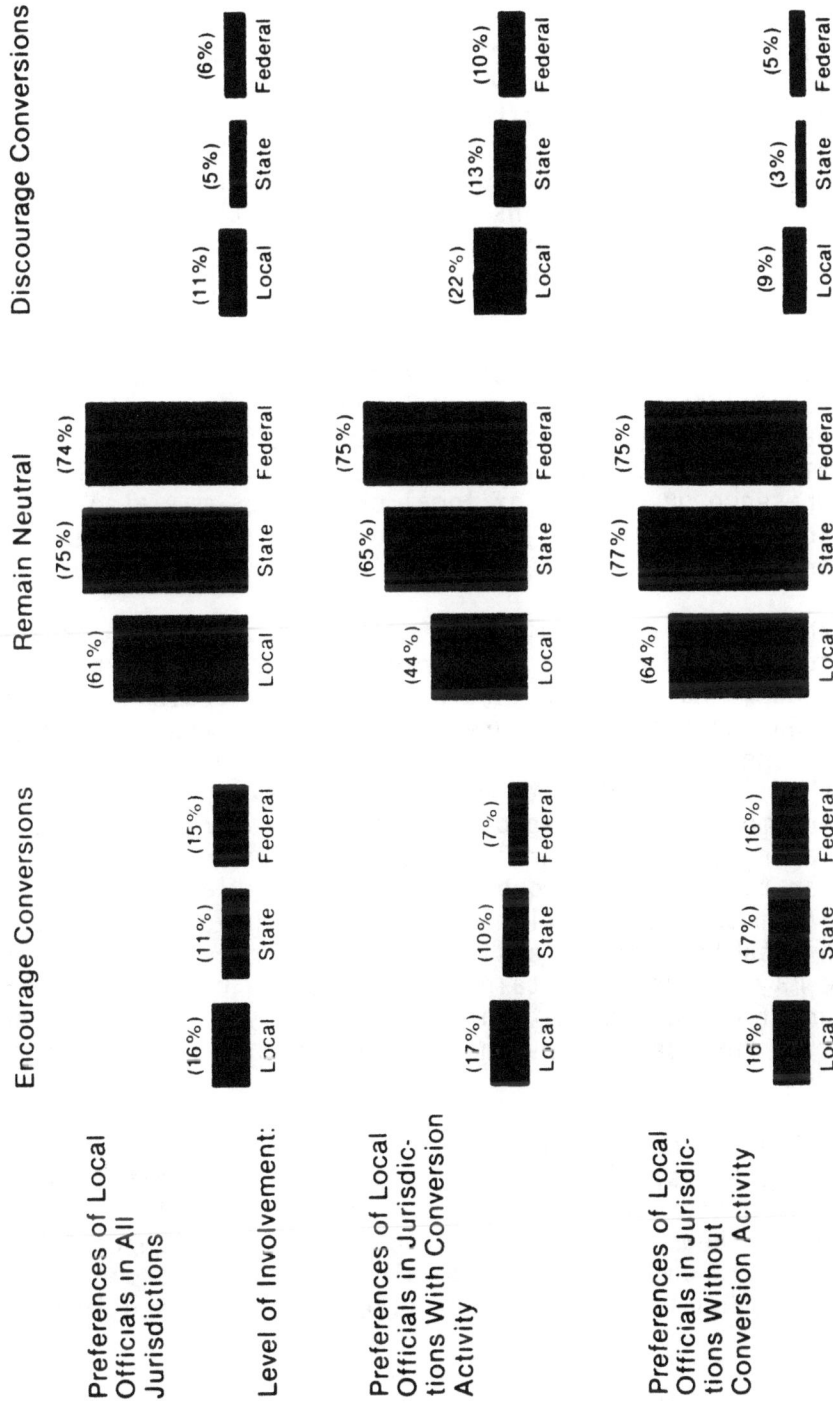

Encourage Conversions

Remain Neutral

Discourage Conversions

Preferences of Local Officials in All Jurisdictions

Level of Involvement:

(16%) Local
(11%) State
(15%) Federal

(61%) Local
(75%) State
(74%) Federal

(11%) Local
(5%) State
(6%) Federal

Preferences of Local Officials in Jurisdictions With Conversion Activity

(17%) Local
(10%) State
(7%) Federal

(44%) Local
(65%) State
(75%) Federal

(22%) Local
(13%) State
(10%) Federal

Preferences of Local Officials in Jurisdictions Without Conversion Activity

(16%) Local
(17%) State
(16%) Federal

(64%) Local
(77%) State
(75%) Federal

(9%) Local
(3%) State
(5%) Federal

Based on a National Telephone Survey of Local Officials

to low- and moderate-income households to purchase converted units. Apart from program proposals which unequivocally encourage or discourage conversion activity, some officials suggest that government action should depend on the impact of conversions on the community's rental stock and on renters. For example, some suggest that limiting conversions is important when vacancy rates are low, but that conversions should continue without impediment when there is an adequate supply of rental housing. Others suggest that conversions of buildings with predominantly low- and moderate-income tenants should be prevented, but conversions of buildings with upper income tenants should be allowed to proceed.

* * *

Although only a small percentage of localities across the nation have conversion activity and related ordinances, this proportion increases in large SMSAs, in those with high levels of conversion activity, and in communities in the west, particularly California. The presence or absence of local ordinances may also be related to the authority of local jursidictions to regulate condominiums and cooperatives.

One-third of the jurisdictions reporting conversion ordinances have imposed short-term moratoria prior to enacting a permanent conversion ordinance. Most of the jursidictions with ordinances have some form of tenant protection measures. Most often, these measures grant a tenant the right to a minimum tenancy period before eviction, and the right of first refusal to purchase a unit. Fewer jurisdictions require more extensive protections, such as relocation assistance. The majority of local ordinances also provide buyer protections similar to those granted by many state regulations. Only a few local communities, mostly in California, have adopted ordinances which establish conditions to be met before conversions are allowed; these may include a certain rental vacancy rate, a quota on the number of converted units allowed annually, or required set-asides of units for use as low- and moderate-income rentals or for homeownership.

Regulation of conversions by local governments is likely to grow in future years. Twenty percent of those communities with conversion activity indicate that an ordinance is likely to be passed in the next two years. In addition, 10 percent of officials in communities which already have an ordinance indicate that additional provisions are likely to be passed in the coming years.

On the other hand, the majority of local officials view the conversion process as a phenomenon which should neither be encouraged nor discouraged by any level of government. The minority who do favor some governmental role, however, prefer that it remain at the local level.

## Local Enactment of Conversion Ordinances

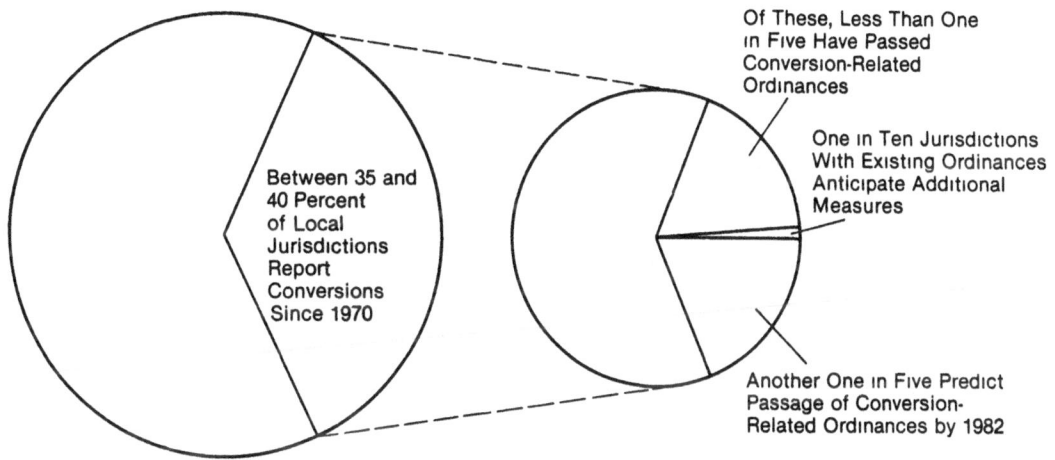

Between 35 and
40 Percent
of Local
Jurisdictions
Report
Conversions
Since 1970

Of These, Less Than One
in Five Have Passed
Conversion-Related
Ordinances

One in Ten Jurisdictions
With Existing Ordinances
Anticipate Additional
Measures

Another One in Five Predict
Passage of Conversion-
Related Ordinances by 1982

Based on a National Telephone Survey of Local Officials

## GLOSSARY OF TERMS

### Appreciation

An increase over time in a property's market value. Appreciation excludes income from rents that may have occurred or been generated by the property.

### "As Is" Conversion

Conversion to condominium or cooperative ownership accompanied by no or few renovations, such as painting of common areas and landscaping.

### Assessment, Tax Assessment

The value assigned to real property for purposes of levying a property tax. Since assessment practices vary, condominiums and cooperatives may be assessed in a different way and at different rates than other types of real property.

### Blanket Mortgage

A single mortgage covering the units and common areas of a multi-family building or complex. This is the type of mortgage held by a cooperative housing corporation.

### "Circuit Breaker"

A form of property tax abatement aimed at lessening the tax burden for a certain category of person (e.g., elderly) or property (e.g., owner-occupied residence).

### Common Areas, Common Elements, Common Estate

Those portions of a condominium or cooperative building, land, and amenities owned by the condominium association or cooperative corporation for use by all unit residents. Included are hallways, roofs, stairways, main walls, parking areas, and social and recreational space. The operation and maintenance of the elements is shared by all unit owner or shareholders.

### Community Development Block Grant ("CDBG")

A program under which HUD awards funds each year to eligible local governments to conduct a wide range of community development activities, such as neighborhood development and housing rehabilitation Spending priorities are determined at the local level, but the Housing and Community Development Act enumerates general objectives. Communities are required to estimate lower income housing needs and to show how these needs will be met in their CDBG grant application to HUD.

## Condominium

A multi-family building or complex or unit within such a property.
Units are owned by individuals who may either live in them or rent
them to others.  At the same time the unit is bought, the owner
acquires a proportionate interest in the common areas and voting
rights in the condominium owners association.

## Conversion

A change in the legal form of a multi-family rental property from
single to multiple ownership.  The change is made by filing a legal
declaration, master deed, or subdivision application to the appropriate government body.  After any necessary approval is received
units in the condominium or membership shares in the coopertive
may be sold.

## Conversion Moratorium

A threshold government response to significant or impending conversion activity, designed to preserve the status quo while the
impacts of conversion activity on the jurisidction can be assessed
and appropriate local policy developed.

## Cooperative

A housing corporation in which individual households own shares
entitling them to live in a particular unit in a multi-family
building or complex and to use the common areas of the building
or complex.

## Cooperative Mortgage

The long term loan made to the purchaser of a share in a cooperative
housing corporation.

## Cooperative Corporation

A legal entity that holds title to and controls a cooperative
building or complex.  Shareholders collectively govern the
cooperative and generally occupy units in the cooperative.

## Declaration of Condominium

A legal document filed with a state or locality containing conditions, covenants, and restrictions governing the sale, ownership,
use, and disposition of a property under the applicable state or
local condominium law.  In many instances, the filing of this
document is legally all that is required to convert a rental
property to the condominium form of ownership.  Also known as
"Master Deed."

## Depreciation

A presumed decline in the value of real property or other asset as determined by a legal formula. This loss of value may reduce the property owner's income tax liability. The rate at which a property's actual value increases (appreciates) or decreases (depreciates) may be quite different from the tax rate of depreciation.

## Disclosure

The provision of detailed information about the legal, financial, and physical condition of a converted property by the developer prior to the execution of a binding commitment for sale of a unit. Some condominium or cooperative regulations require disclosure in an effort to protect unit purchasers or shareholders.

## Discount

A reduction in the offering price for a condominium unit or cooperative share frequently offered tenants in a building or complex to be converted.

## "Empty Nesters"

People whose children no longer share a home with them.

## End Mortgage

The long-term loan made to the purchaser of an individual unit in a condominium.

## Equity

The difference between the current market value of a property and the value of any claims or liens against the property.

## Federal Home Loan Mortgage Corporation (FHLMC)

(Also referred to as "Freddie Mac" and "The Mortgage Corporation.") An organization chartered by Congress in 1970 to assist in the development and maintenance of a secondary market in conventional residential mortgage loans. FHLMC buys mortgages, primarily from savings and loan associations and resells them in the secondary market. A set of standards principally related to the condition of the converted condominium must be met before FHLMC will agree to purchase individual mortgages. FHLMC does not purchase cooperative mortgages, but the 1979 Amendments to the Housing and Community Development Act of 1974 authorize FHLMC to study the feasibility of purchasing such mortgages.

## Federal National Mortgage Association (FNMA)

(Also referred to as "Fannie Mae.") Originally created by the Federal government in 1938 to assist the Nation recovering from the Great

Depression, FNMA is now a privately-owned corporation operating in the public interest. FNMA's role in the secondary mortgage market is to borrow money from the capital markets when mortgage money is tight and use the funds to buy mortgages, primarily from mortgage banks. FNMA standards must be met before it will purchase mortgages for converted condominiums.

## Graduated Payment Mortgage

Under this type of mortgage, the mortgagor makes low monthly payments for the first few years of the mortgage term. The payments gradually increase for the next few years until they reach a level where they remain for the balance of the mortgage.

## Homestead Exemption

A form of tax relief aimed at reducing the property tax burden to a specific category of persons, usually to encourage homeownership. Functions somewhat like a direct grant of funds in that the same amount of money is offered as a tax relief.

## Interim Financing

A form of short term financing (usually ranging from one to three years) used by a developer to pay part of the cost of acquiring and renovating a building and retiring any existing mortgages. The loan is repaid as individual converted units are sold.

## Investor-Owners

Condominium or cooperative owners who buy units or shares for investment purposes rather than residences and usually expect future appreciation on the unit or share. An investor-owned unit is typically retained as a rental.

## Joint Venture

A partnership form of business in which each co-venturer contributes capital and/or expertise for a particular undertaking in return for a share of profits.

## Life Tenancy

Refers to a provision of law under which lifetime leases are offered to specific groups of tenants, usually the elderly or handicapped.

## "Limited Equity" or "Low Equity" Cooperative

A cooperative housing corporation whose bylaws regulate the resale value of membership shares. The resale price is determined by a formula which considers the original down payment plus increments for inflation, improvements to the building and unit, and a small percentage of the blanket mortgage covering the cooperative building.

## Limited Partnership

A partnership form of business composed of one or more general partners and one or more limited partners. The general partner(s) manages and controls partnership affairs, while the limited partner(s) is a passive investor with no control over the partnership.

## Loft Conversion

A change in a building's use from non-residential to residential purpose -- either as a rental, cooperative or condominium.

## Management Fee, Maintenance Fee

A charge usually paid each month by each condominium unit owner. The fee covers the cost of services provided by the firm which manages the property, the property's maintenance, and any utilities not individually metered. In a cooperative, the charge also includes a pro rata payment toward the blanket mortgage's monthly principal and interest.

## Master Deed

See "Declaration of Condominium"

## Mortgagee

The financial institution holding the interim, end, or blanket mortgages on a condominium or cooperative.

## Mortgagor

The individual or entity responsible for the repayment of an interim, end, or blanket mortgage.

## National Consumer Cooperative Bank

An independent bank established by the Federal government in 1978 to provide technical assistance and mortgage loans to consumer cooperatives, including housing cooperatives. Initially, the Treasury Department and borrowing cooperatives will own stock in the bank; eventually full ownership will be held by the cooperatives.

## Neighborhood Strategy Area

A neighborhood designated by a local government for intensive community development activities financing by Community Development Block Grant funds. The local government must present a comprehensive strategy to HUD for upgrading and stabilizing the neighborhood.

## Offering Plan

Information available to prospective purchasers which typically includes the declaration, bylaws, articles of incorporation of the association, management contracts, budget information, recreational leases, and any encumbrances, easements, liens or other matters affecting title. Designed to serve as a "disclosure package" and protection for prospective buyers.

## Owners Association

A group comprised of unit owners, and sometimes renters, which conducts the affairs of a condominium through an elected board of directors. State laws generally specify the manner in which control of the association is passed from the developer to the owners. Usually this occurs after all units are sold and a high proportion of the sales closed. Association bylaws specify items such as terms, power and authority of the board of directors as well as the rights and powers of tenants.

## "Pipeline" Conversions

Refers to any stage in the conversion process prior to the actual marketing of converted units. Estimates of conversion volume often include such "pipeline" projects which have not yet fully completed the conversion process.

## Proprietary Lease

An occupancy agreement under which a cooperative member has an exclusive right to occupy a particular unit; the lease also specifies the rules and regulations governing the occupancy and obligates the member to pay a proportionate share of the principal and interest on the blanket mortgage, operating and maintenance costs, and other expenses related to the operation of the cooperative.

## Real Estate Investment Trust (REIT)

A mutual fund which borrows funds in private capital markets. The proceeds are used to make construction and development loans, long-term mortgage loans, and loans for purchasing income-producing real estate.

## Revitalization

A substantial improvement in the condition of land and structures in a deteriorated area. The initiation of the process tends to stimulate further investment in the area and may result in increased market values of the land, housing, and other structures in the area.

## Right of First Refusal, First Right to Purchase

A provision in a law or real estate agreement giving a tenant an opportunity to buy a unit to be converted, or a tenant group the opportunity to buy a building to be converted, before the unit or building may be offered to other purchasers. Offers to buy from tenants or tenant groups must be made within a specified time period, usually 60 days.

## Secondary Mortgage Market

An informal network in which financial institutions making mortgage loans sell the mortgages to public and private institutions (such as FNMA or FHLMC) which either hold them or sell them to another participant in the capital market. The purposes are (1) to enable loan originators to liquidate the mortgages and use the proceeds to make further loans; and (2) to hold capital during times of loose money which can be released when money is less plentiful.

## Section 203(n)

A provision of the National Housing Act of 1934, which permits HUD to insure mortgages of households buying shares in cooperative housing corporations. To be eligible for the insurance the cooperative's blanket mortgage must also be insured by HUD.

## Section 213

A provision of the National Housing Act of 1934 which permits HUD to provide mortgage insurance for loans to finance the construction, acquisition, or rehabilitation of housing cooperatives and for loans to households purchasing shares in a housing cooperative.

## Section 213(i)

A provision of the National Housing Act of 1934 which permits HUD to provide mortgage insurance to finance housing cooperative conversions or to refinance an existing cooperative mortgage.

## Section 221(d)(3)

A provision of the National Housing Act of 1934 permitting HUD to provide mortgage insurance for loans to finance the construction or rehabilitation of cooperatives containing five or more units.

## Section 245

A provision of the National Housing Act of 1934 which permits HUD to insure mortgages to facilitate early homeownership for households that expect their incomes to rise substantially. This is known as the "graduated payment mortgage" program.

"SMSA" - Standard Metropolitan Statistical Area

A designation by the Federal Office of Management and Budget which applies to counties (or towns in New England) with at least one central city of 50,000 or more residents and any contiguous jurisdictions that are socially or economically integrated within the central city.

Special Assessment

A one-time surcharge levied on condominium unit owners or cooperative shareholders as approved by vote of the condominium association or the cooperative corporation. The proceeds finance any major unforeseen expenditure, for example, a new roof.

Stock Cooperatives

A cooperative housing corporation whose participants are stockholders whose shares entitled them to a proprietary lease of a specific dwelling unit located on the property owned by the corporation.

Substantial Rehabilitation

Improvements and repairs to a property that usually involve considerable cost. These may include major repairs to or replacement of mechanical systems (e.g., wiring or plumbing) or a structural feature (e.g., roof). Work may also include restructuring of the building's interior.

Tenure Status

A classification of housing units in relationship to their occupants, e.g., owner-occupied, renter-occupied.

"Third Party" Converter

A developer or converter who has no relationship to the converted property prior to the beginning of the conversion process, i.e., one who was not the landlord and did not assist a tenant organization in attempts to convert the building.

Time Shares/Time-Shared Ownership

The exclusive right to occupy a unit in a real estate develoment for a specified period of time each year. Time shared ownership is essentially a vacation or resort concept where the primary motivation for purchasing the right is personal use rather than investment.

### Turnover Rate

The proportion of rental housing units in a specific area changing
occupancy in a given time period. The rate is usually expressed
in annual terms.

### Uniform Condominium Act (UCA)

Developed by the National Conference of Commissioners on Uniform
Laws to unify and modernize the law of condominiums. Approved by the
American Bar Association in the winter of 1970; promulgated to
every state for its considertion.

### Vacancy Rate, Rental Vacancy Rate

Estimated percentage of the rental housing units in a locality
or region that are vacant and available for rent at a particular
time. The estimates are usually based on a sample survey.

RECENT REPORTS BY THE DIVISION OF POLICY STUDIES

Preliminary Findings from the Field Study:  Report of the Task Force on
Multifamily Property Utilization (August, 1977)

> Estimation of the types and frequency of problems facing financially
> troubled HUD-insured subsidized multifamily housing projects; assess-
> ments of the adequacy of project income, HUD management, and project
> management.

Problems Facing Financially Distressed Multifamily Housing:  A Field Study
of the HUD-Insured Unsubsidized Inventory (December, 1978)

> Estimation of the types and frequency of problems facing financially
> troubled HUD-insured unsubsidized multifamily housing projects;
> assessments of program and market factors, project development and
> management by developers, owners and managers, and HUD development
> and management practices.

Problems Affecting Low-Rent Public Housing Projects:  A Field Study (January,
1979)

> Estimation of the number and types of public housing projects believed
> to be in "troubled" condition; assessments of the financial, physical,
> managerial and social problems facing public housing.

Housing for the Elderly and Handicapped:  The Experience of the Section 202
Program from 1959 to 1977 (January, 1979)

> Evaluation of the design, administration, cost and performance of
> HUD's program of direct loans to nonprofit organizations for the
> purpose of developing and operating multifamily housing projects for
> elderly and handicapped persons.

A Survey of Citizens' Views and Concerns about Urban Life (February, 1978)

> Report on a national, cross-section survey of 7,074 Americans in
> cities, suburbs, towns and rural areas to record thir past
> experiences, their present attitudes, and their predictions about the
> future of the nation's cities and of their own communities.

The 1978 HUD Survey on the Quality of Community Life:  A Data Book (November,
1978)

> Compendium of responses to HUD's 1978 survey on how Americans view
> the conditions and problems of their communities, containing frequency
> tabulations of the answers to each survey question and breakdowns for
> region, location, occupation, marital status, age, education, income,
> tenure, race/ethnic group, sex and local census data.

Gautreaux Housing Demonstration:  An Evaluation of Its Impact on Participating
Households (December, 1979)

> Evaluation of a demonstration in the Chicago area designed to explore
> metropolitan-wide housing opportunities for low-income persons; des-
> cribe the characteristics of participating families; assess the
> extent of racial and economic dispersion resulting from the demon-
> stration; and compare participants with eligible non-participants and
> with participants in HUD's Section 8 Existing program.

www.ingramcontent.com/pod-product-compliance
Lightning Source LLC
Chambersburg PA
CBHW081457200326
41518CB00015B/2292